INTERNATIONAL TRADE

International
TRADE
New Patterns of Trade, Production and Investment

Nigel Grimwade

ROUTLEDGE
London and New York

First published 1989
by Routledge
11 New Fetter Lane, London EC4P 4EE

29 West 35th Street, New York NY 10001

© 1989 Nigel Grimwade

Typeset by J&L Composition Ltd, Filey, North Yorkshire
Printed in Great Britain by Mackays of Chatham PLC, Chatham, Kent

British Library Cataloguing in Publication Data

Grimwade, Nigel
  International trade: new patterns of trade,
  production and investment.
  1. Foreign trade
  I. Title
  382

  ISBN 0–415–00396–2
  ISBN 0–415–00397–0 Pbk

Library of Congress Cataloging in Publication Data is available

Contents

Abbreviations

ASEAN	Association of South-East Asian Nations
CACM	Central American Common Market
COMECON	Council for Mutual Economic Co-operation
CPEs	Centrally planned economies
DMES	Developed market economies
EBCs	Eastern bloc countries
EC	European Community
EEC	European Economic Community
EFTA	European Free Trade Association
EPZs	Export-processing zones
FDI	Foreign direct investment
GATT	General Agreement on Tariffs and Trade
GDP	Gross domestic product
GSP	Generalized System of Preferences
IMF	International Monetary Fund
LAFTA	Latin American Free Trade Association
LDCs	Least-developed countries
MFA	Multi-Fibre Agreement
MNCs	Multinational companies or corporations
MNEs	Multinational enterprises
NICs	Newly-industrializing countries
NIDL	New international division of labour
NTBs	Non-tariff barriers to trade
OAPs	Offshore assembly provisions
OECD	Organization for Economic Co-operation and Development
OMAs	Orderly marketing agreements
OPEC	Organization of Petroleum Exporting Countries
SITC	Standard International Trade Classification
TNC	Transnational corporation
UNCTAD	United Nations Conference on Trade and Development
VERs	Voluntary export-restraint agreements

Introduction

The original idea behind the writing of this book arose out of the need for a relevant, up-to-date text dealing with actual, real-world trends in world trade and world investment suitable for students doing courses in international business or international economics as part of an economics, business studies or international-studies degree. Courses in international business or international economics are increasingly being built into relevant degree courses in universities and polytechnics. Many business studies degrees now include an international business option or elective. Increasingly, too, the teaching of international economics on economics, international studies or modern-language degrees is assuming an international-business studies orientation reflecting the need to prepare students more practically for employment in the business world. In addition, international-business options or electives are often available on many MBA programmes and MA or MSc taught courses in economics or international studies.

Unfortunately, there is a dearth of suitable, applied economics texts dealing with new developments in world trade and production appropriate for use at this level. Many good theoretical texts suffer from being too weighty or too remote in their treatment of the real world. Such texts need to be supplemented by some suitable applied economics text which is informative and which enables the student to apply theory to the real world in which business is conducted. A further problem with many of the books currently available for use on such courses is that they are simply out-of-date. They fail to deal with the trends in the world economy which are the most important. This is especially true of many international-economics texts. The basic content of many of these books often seems to have changed little over the past quarter-century. Yet the world economy and the nature of world trade and production has changed radically over that period. The student who wants to be informed about recent issues which occupy conferences or seminars of economists has often to look up obscure and difficult articles in the various journals. These articles are written by economists for economists and are usually impossible for the uninitiated to understand fully.

One example of this is the literature concerned with the increasingly important phenomenon of intra-industry trade. A growing and dominant proportion of world trade now takes the form of intra-industry trade. Yet most economics texts continue to describe and explain a world in which trade is still of the inter-industry type. The student who wants to gain an understanding of the nature and causes of intra-industry trade has usually to seek out a variety of highly specialized sources which may leave him/her more confused at the end than beforehand! Yet the student of both international business and international economics must have an appreciation of the nature, extent, causes, and effects of intra-industry trade and specialization.

A further consideration which influenced the writing of this book was a dissatisfaction with the wholly artificial and misleading separation which exists between the subjects of international economics and international business. Although the sheer size of both these areas of subject-matter may necessitate their compartmentalization from a teaching point of view, the two areas are intellectually bound together. The understanding of international trade requires an appreciation of the importance and role of the multinational corporation. Multinational corporations now account for a major part of world trade. Overseas investment by multinational corporations may constitute an alternative to trade as a way of supplying an overseas market, or it may give rise to new trade flows as when a multinational reorganizes its production on a global level. At the same time, the study of international business requires a knowledge of the trading and monetary environment within which business operates.

There is a growing awareness by economists of the need to integrate these hitherto separate branches of economics. Unfortunately, however, much of the results of such attempts at integration remain inaccessible to the non-economics specialist. Even the student of economics has to search hard to find a volume which tackles issues of trade and international investment simultaneously. Lecturers who want to include both types of subject-matter within a single course typically have to recommend at least two different texts. This book attempts to bridge such a gap by treating both kinds of issue in a single volume.

It follows that this book will be of greatest benefit for students who are studying options or electives in international business or international economics as part of a degree course or postgraduate degree in economics, business studies, or international studies. It may be used as a main text or supplementary text to be used alongside a more theoretical volume. Lecturers teaching such courses should also find the book useful for structuring lecture or seminar programmes and as a source of suitable material. The book does assume a solid grounding in basic economic principles and is therefore not intended for first- or second-year undergraduates, although particular chapters may be of use for students studying at this level as well as for lecturers teaching on such courses. The reader should also be familiar with the basic theories of trade and trade policy, but a brief overview of these theories is included in Chapter 1 for the benefit of the student who is struggling in this area.

The reader may want to use this book sequentially or to dip into different chapters at different times. Although later chapters presuppose some understanding of issues covered in earlier chapters so that a sequential reading of the book is to be preferred, it is possible to read the book selectively. A glossary of terms has been included at the back of the book for the aid of the reader who uses the book for reference and has problems with recalling the meaning of various concepts.

A book dealing with new patterns of trade and investment has of necessity to be selective in the issues and themes to be included. This book has sought to bring together a number of themes which are considered to be central to an understanding of international business and the contemporary environment within which international business operates. The aim has been to examine a number of central related themes in the framework of a single volume such as is not otherwise available at the present time to students or lecturers involved in this field. Thus the book introduces the reader to a number of new types of trade which have become increasingly important in recent decades. The growth of intra-industry and intra-firm trade occupies a central place in the subject-matter of the early chapters. The growing importance of international barter or so-called countertrade is also discussed in Chapter 5.

Alongside a discussion of new patterns of world trade, the book examines important developments in international direct investment. The book discusses the increasingly two-way nature of foreign direct investment and the growth of what is being referred to as the new international division of labour. Chapter

5 also examines the growth of alternative forms of international business involvement, especially joint ventures, licensing agreements and buy-back agreements. A further theme is the change taking place in the geographical structure of both trade and investment. The last quarter-century has witnessed the rise of a number of new epicentres of world trade. The emergence of Japan as a front-rank exporting nation has been a development of monumental importance. In recent years, Japan has become the world's leading exporter of manufactures overtaking both West Germany and the United States. Japan's persistent trade surpluses have presented major adjustment problems for both Western Europe and the United States and has become a dominant issue in international trade policy.

The emergence of a number of developing countries as major exporters of manufactured goods has represented another important geographical shift in world trade. These countries are the so-called 'newly industrializing countries' (NICs). They include the fast-growing South-East Asian group of countries, namely South Korea, Hong Kong, Singapore, and Taiwan. Increasingly, too, these countries have begun to accumulate sizeable trade surpluses with the western industrialized countries which have posed major adjustment problems. The increased import competition posed by these countries has been a major source of protectionist pressure. The proliferation of restrictions on imports coming from such countries has been one of the most troubling developments in the world trading system in recent decades threatening the liberal trading order set after the Second World War. The latter was an important factor in making possible the trade-led growth enjoyed by the world in the quarter-century following the ending of the war.

A further theme examined in this book is the growth in importance of services both as a source of output and employment in the advanced industrialized economies and as a component of world trade. Many texts on international trade or international business fail to give sufficient weight to this element of world trade. However, in recent decades world trade in services has been rising as fast as world trade in goods. Services now account for a higher proportion of both output and employment than manufacturing in many industrialized economies. Foreign direct investment in service activities is now a major component of the outward investment of the major capital-exporting nations. The probability is that, in coming decades, the advanced industrialized countries will become dependent on the expansion of service activities for trade and growth. Moreover, if the forthcoming Uruguay Round of multilateral trade negotiations is successful, trade in services will become subject to similar freer trade rules to those applied to trade in goods.

The structure of this book is as follows. First, in Chapter 1 basic theories of trade and production are examined. As we have already said, this is designed to equip the reader who is weak in this area and does not want to spend valuable time bringing his/her theory up to scratch by wading into a major theoretical text. Next, Chapter 2 examines the changing structure of world output and world trade. The aim of this chapter is to set out the most important changes which have taken place in both the volume of trade and its composition. The growth of both world output and world trade over the last three or four decades is described. The accompanying changes in both the commodity and geographical composition of trade are similarly examined. Chapter 3 distinguishes between inter-industry and intra-industry trade and specialization. The growing importance of intra-industry trade is one of the major new developments in patterns of world trade of the last quarter-century. Well over two-thirds of trade in manufactured goods is now intra-industry in kind. Chapter 3 describes and explains the growth of this type of trade. It will be seen that the source of this type of trade lies in the increasingly imperfect nature of markets both nationally and internationally.

In Chapter 4 the growth of foreign direct investment and the rise of the multinational corporation is discussed. It will be seen that most explanations for the rise of the multinational corporation as a means of transmitting goods, capital, or technology between countries emphasise the imperfect character of markets. In other words, similar considerations underlie the growth of overseas direct investment in recent decades to those which have affected the nature of trade in manufactured goods. An attempt is made to explore the linkages between trade and investment. In particular, Chapter 4 discusses the growing importance of intra-firm or in-house trade as a component of world trade. One of the most important results of this has been its implications for the prices at which trade takes place. Where trade takes the form of trade between the parent company and one of its overseas affiliates, the prices used may diverge from the prices which prevail for so-called arm's-length trade. This phenomenon is known as transfer pricing and is discussed towards the end of Chapter 4.

Chapter 5 examines some of the new forms of international business involvement which have become of increasing importance in recent decades. It will be seen that much foreign direct investment (FDI) is now two-way investment between industrialized countries within the same industry. This phenomenon of intra-industry FDI has attracted growing interest among international economists. Another important recent development has been a tendency towards the vertical disintegration of the production process through direct investment abroad. This is increasingly giving rise to a new kind of international specialization widely referred to as the 'new international division of labour' (NIDL). Chapter 5 also discusses alternatives to direct investment abroad whereby companies can become involved in other countries. Joint ventures and licensing agreements are becoming of increasing importance. Finally, Chapter 5 discusses the increasingly important phenomena of countertrade or international barter. This is also attracting much interest among economists but sadly receives little treatment in basic texts available to students.

In Chapter 6 the growth of Japan and the emergence of the newly-industrializing countries is examined. Some explanations for both the rise of Japan and the 'take-off' of the NICs are reviewed. The causes of Japan's unbalanced trade and the problems which this has caused for her major trading partners are discussed. In the case of the NICs it will be seen that their overall trade with the advanced industrialized countries is balanced. The problems which have risen for the latter as a result of the rapid emergence of the NICs have been the nature of the competition which they have posed, the timing of their sudden rise, and the difficulties which the industrialized countries have faced in adjusting to the new competition. Chapter 7 examines the adjustment problem further. The growth of the New Protectionism is discussed. This is seen as being largely rooted in the increasing difficulty experienced by the industrialized countries in adjusting to the new competition posed by the NICs at a time of recession and rapid structural change in the former.

Finally, Chapter 8 examines the growing importance of trade

in services. The difficult conceptual problems involved in distinguishing trade in goods from services are examined. The causes of the growth of trade in services are also discussed alongside the expansion of the services sector in the mature industrialized economies. Finally, the problems involved in liberalizing trade in services are considered in the context of the current eighth Uruguay Round of multilateral trade negotiations.

1

Basic Theories of International Trade and Production

INTRODUCTION

In this chapter I shall examine some of the most important theories of international trade and production, which provide a necessary underpinning for an understanding of much of the rest of this book. The reader who has a solid grounding in basic economic theory may be able to skip this chapter. However, the reader whose grasp of basic theory is more tenuous must ensure that he fully understands the basic theories covered in this chapter before proceeding to Chapter 2. Much of the rest of this book assumes a familiarity with the basic theoretical ideas examined in this chapter.

I shall begin by discussing the principle of comparative advantage which underlies the economic case for trade and specialization. Introduced are some of the basic analytical tools frequently used to portray the gains accruing to countries from trade. Having introduced the principle of comparative advantage, I proceed to a consideration of the basis of comparative advantage. Why do countries possess a comparative advantage in the production of certain goods? I begin by discussing one of the earliest explanations for differences between countries in comparative costs of producing different goods – the Hecksher–Ohlin, or Factor Proportions, Theory of Trade. I shall discuss the usefulness of this explanation of comparative costs differences and seek to identify some of the weaknesses and limitations of this theory of trade.

Next I proceed to an examination of various demand-side theories of trade which provide a rather different explanation for the basis to trade. These theories emphasize differences in consumer preferences for different varieties of goods rather than differences in the costs of producing different goods. Such theories are especially useful for understanding some of the patterns of trade discussed in this book. At the same time, the conventional, neoclassical assumption of increasing costs or decreasing returns to scale can be dropped. I shall discuss some models of trade which incorporate the more realistic, real-world situation of decreasing returns to scale or falling average costs.

Next I move to a consideration of a variety of dynamic theories of trade which incorporate the reality of technological change. These theories seek to explain patterns of world trade in terms of the discovery of new products or new processes of production and the time-lags which exist in the diffusion of such knowledge around the world. These theories have the added attraction that they incorporate international investment alongside trade as alternative forms of servicing an overseas market. One of the themes of this book is the relationship between international trade and international investment. In recent years a variety of attempts have been made to bring both trade and investment together in a single framework to develop an integrated theory of international production. However, a survey of these theories must be postponed until later chapters. Such theories cannot be properly explained without first discussing some of the new forms of trade and the nature of multinational investment which constitute the themes of the first few chapters.

Finally, this chapter concludes with a brief outline of the basic theory of tariffs and a survey of post-war attempts to increase global economic welfare by reducing tariffs and other barriers to trade. This constitutes a necessary foundation for following the discussion in later chapters of this book relating to the New Protectionism and the liberalization of trade in services.

COMPARATIVE ADVANTAGE AND THE GAINS FROM TRADE

Why do countries engage in trade? Following the English classical economist, David Ricardo (1772–1823), economics has explained the basis for trade in terms of the principle of comparative advantage. Consider two countries – say, Britain and America. Suppose that each country produces just two types of products: steel and cloth. Suppose that Britain can produce cloth more cheaply than America and America can produce steel more cheaply than Britain. It is obvious that the two countries together will produce more steel and more cloth if they specialize, Britain in cloth and America in steel. Britain will export cloth to America and America will export steel to Britain. This is the case of where both countries are absolutely more efficient than the other country in at least one commodity. However, what if one of the two countries is absolutely more efficient in both commodities? Suppose America can produce both steel and cloth more efficiently than Britain. Specialization will still be beneficial if both countries possess a *comparative* advantage in just one commodity. Suppose that America's advantage is greatest in steel production and Britain's disadvantage least in cloth production. Then, according to the principle of comparative advantage, the two countries together will produce more steel and cloth if they specialize, America in steel and Britain in cloth. Once again, Britain will export cloth to America and America will export steel to Britain. Thus it is comparative and not absolute advantage which creates the basis for trade.

The principle of comparative advantage may be demonstrated by using the concept of opportunity costs. This expresses the cost of something in terms of the opportunity forgone in order to obtain that something. If I am considering whether to buy a theatre ticket or have a meal out, then the cost to me of either of these two options is the option which I thereby forgo. If I buy a theatre ticket, I forfeit the meal out. Similarly, the cost to a country of producing more of one commodity is the amount of another commodity which it thereby forgoes. For example, if a country chooses to devote more of its resources to armaments production, fewer resources will be available to produce consumer goods and services for satisfying various wants. If, of course, a country has large unutilized resources, it may be possible to produce more of a particular commodity without reducing the output of any other commodities. In this case, opportunity cost will be zero.

Let us assume that a certain country, say Britain, has all its resources fully employed in the production or two types of products: steel and cloth. In this case, in the short run, the production of one commodity, say steel, can only be increased by reducing the production of the other commodity, cloth. It follows that we can express the costs of producing one extra unit

3

of steel in terms of the number of units of cloth which must thereby be forgone. Conversely, the costs of producing one extra unit of cloth may be expressed in terms of the number of units of steel which must thereby be forgone. We can illustrate the nature of these choices with the aid of the production possibility or transformation curve. Britain's production possibility or transformation curve is shown in Figure 1.1. If Britain's resources are fully employed, she will produce somewhere along her transformation curve, such as points D or A. A point such as C would be inefficient since Britain would not be fully utilizing all her resources. A point such as B which lies beyond or outside her transformation curve is unobtainable with her existing resources. The exact point along her transformation curve where she will locate production will depend on the preferences of consumers. If consumers want more units of steel to be produced and fewer units of cloth, relative prices will change. Steel production will become more profitable and cloth production less profitable. Resources will shift out of cloth production and into steel production until profitability is the same in both activities.

The transformation curve could have been drawn as a straight line. This would have been the case if costs of production were constant. That is to say, the costs of producing cloth or steel do not vary with the scale of production. The fact that the transformation curve has been drawn as concave to the origin shows that the assumption has been made that costs are increasing. The marginal costs of producing cloth or steel rise with output. This seems more realistic, for as a point such as X or Y is reached, the resources which must be switched out of one activity and into the other are the resources which are most specific to just one activity and therefore the least suitable for being re-employed in another activity. For example, some resources will be highly specific to steel production and wholly unsuitable for being re-employed in cloth production. Some highly skilled steel-workers may possess skills quite inappropriate for cloth production. At the very least, it will be extremely costly to retrain such workers. It is, therefore, to be expected that the costs of producing cloth will rise as output increases and as point Y on the transformation curve is approached.

Now, the slope of the transformation curve at a particular point measures the marginal costs of production at that point.

Figure 1.1 Britain's transformation curve

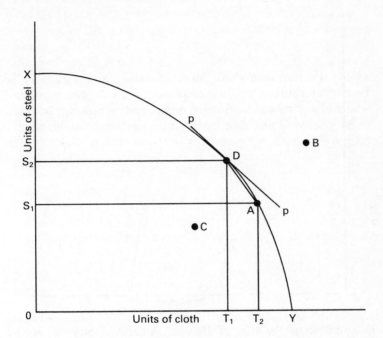

For example, the costs of increasing cloth output by T_1T_2 is S_1S_2 units of steel. That is shown by the gradient of the line DA. This measures the slope of the curve between the points D and A. The slope of a curve at a particular point such as D is given by the gradient of a line drawn tangent to the curve at point D. This is the tangent labelled pp; pp measures the marginal costs of producing cloth (or steel) at that point. The steeper the curve, the steeper the tangent and therefore the higher the marginal costs of producing cloth (the lower the marginal costs of producing steel). The flatter the curve, the flatter the tangent and therefore the lower the marginal costs of producing cloth (the higher the marginal costs of producing steel).

Next let us assume that America also employs all its resources fully in either the production of steel or cloth. However, let us further assume that America can produce both products more efficiently than Britain, but that America possesses a comparative advantage in steel production. America's transformation curve is shown in Figure 1.2. It can be seen that it has a

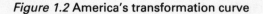

Figure 1.2 America's transformation curve

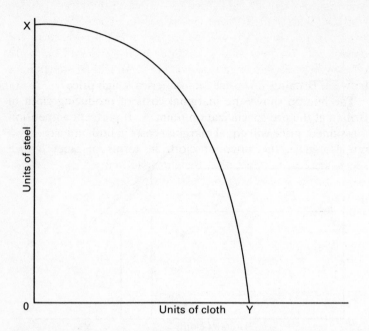

different shape to that of Britain. America's curve is much steeper indicating that marginal costs of producing steel expressed in terms of cloth output are lower in America. Similarly, the marginal costs of producing cloth expressed in terms of steel are lower in Britain. Note that it is not absolute costs which count but differences in comparative costs. The concept of opportunity costs enables us to express such differences while ignoring differences in absolute costs. So long as there exists a difference in comparative costs between any two countries, a basis exists for specialization and trade.

Now, let us see how each country gains from specialization. Figure 1.3 illustrates the case of Britain. Before specialization, Britain is assumed to have produced at point A. Output consisted of OS_1 steel and OT_2 cloth. After specialization, Britain increases production of cloth and reduces production of steel. Production shifts to point E. Britain now exports some of her cloth output in exchange for extra units of steel. The question is posed: how much steel does Britain obtain in exchange for cloth? This is what is commonly referred to as a country's 'terms of trade': the ratio of the price of her exports to the price of her imports. What is certain is that America will be willing to pay her a better price for her cloth than the price for which cloth sells in Britain. This is because costs are higher in America, so Americans will be willing to pay a good price for British cloth so long as it is cheaper than American cloth. In other words, the international price of cloth will lie somewhere between Britain's low price and America's high price.

The line pp shows the marginal costs of producing cloth in Britain at the pre-specialization point A. If perfect competition is assumed, price will equal marginal costs in both industries. So pp also gives the price of cloth in terms of steel before specialization. Suppose that the international price of cloth is given by the line p'p'. This is steeper than pp and therefore indicates a higher price of cloth expressed in terms of steel. Then Britain can exchange GE ($= T_4T_3$) units of cloth for GF ($= S_3S_4$) units of steel. Britain exports T_4T_3 units of cloth and imports S_3S_4 units of steel. This enables Britain to consume at point F. Britain is able to obtain OT_4 units of cloth (all

Figure 1.3 How Britain gains from trade

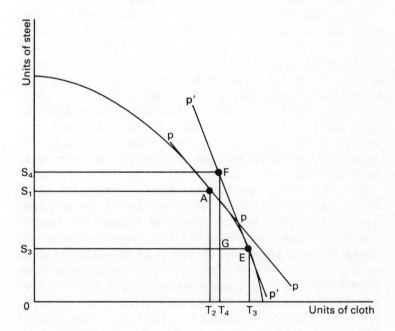

produced domestically) and OS_4 units of steel (OS_3 produced domestically and S_3S_4 imported from America). This is clearly superior to point A, where Britain was located before specialization. Point F lies beyond or outside Britain's transformation curve and was therefore unreachable without specialization. However, through specialization and trade, Britain is able to reach this point. As a result, she enjoys S_1S_4 more steel and T_2T_4 more cloth. This represents Britain's gain from trade.

Figure 1.4 illustrates how America also gains from trade. Before specialization, the marginal cost of producing steel expressed in terms of cloth was given by the gradient of the line pp. Assuming perfect competition, prices equal marginal costs in both activities. So pp also shows the price of steel expressed in units of cloth before specialization. However, British importers are willing to pay American steel producers a better price for steel providing the price is lower than the price of steel in Britain. The international price of steel is given by the line $p'p'$, which is the same as $p'p'$ in Figure 1.3. America specializes in steel production in which she has a comparative advantage. Resources shift out of cloth production and into steel production. America produces at point E, producing OT_1 cloth and OS_3 units of steel. With the terms of trade given by $p'p'$, America can exchange S_2S_3 units of steel for T_1T_3 units of cloth. This enables her to consume at point F, which is beyond her transformation curve and thus represents a superior position to point A, where her consumption was located before specialization. She exports S_2S_3 steel and imports T_1T_3 cloth. As a result, she is able to consume OS_2 steel (all produced domestically) and OT_3 cloth (OT_1 produced domestically and T_1T_3 imported). As a result she enjoys S_1S_2 more steel and T_2T_3 more cloth compared with before specialization. This represents America's gain from trade.

Thus it has been demonstrated that, given the existence of differences in comparative costs, both countries may gain from trade. In Figures 1.3 and 1.4 the volume of trade is given by the two trade triangles FGE in the two diagrams. These two triangles are the same and therefore equal in area. The gain to both countries is given by the movement from a consumption point located on their transformation curve (point A in both cases) to a point beyond their transformation curve (point F in both cases). In the long run, both countries could have reached this point through normal economic growth. Economic growth

Figure 1.4 How America gains from trade

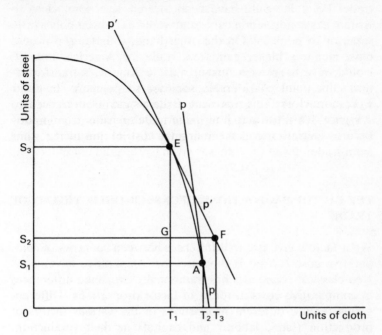

involves an outwards shift in countries' transformation curves. However, this may take some time to achieve. International specialization and trade enables countries to reach such a point much more quickly.

One final point must be made before leaving the principle of comparative advantage. The principle of comparative advantage states that countries will benefit from specialization whenever there exists a difference in comparative costs. A further requirement is that the international terms of trade must lie between the two countries pre-trade relative prices (pp in both diagrams). Clearly, unless Britain can get a better price for her cloth and America a better price for her steel than the price which they fetch on the home market, there will be no incentive to trade and no gain from trade. This tells us that the terms of trade are important in determining *how much* each will gain from trade. The nearer the terms of trade to a country's pre-trade relative price ratio, the smaller the potential gain to a country from trade. In this case, most of the gains from trade will accrue to the country's trading partner. In Figure 1.3, had p′p′ been of

9

a similar slope to pp, Britain would have gained little from trade. Point F would have been located at a point close to Britain's transformation curve and would have been only a little superior to point A. On the other hand, a flatter p'p' would have meant a bigger gain from trade for America. Point F would have been even further outside America's transformation curve and considerably superior to point A. In other words, most of the gains from trade would have accrued to America. Thus the actual terms of trade are of crucial importance to countries in determining the distribution of the gains from trade.

THE FACTOR PROPORTIONS, HECKSHER–OHLIN THEORY OF TRADE

What factors give rise to differences between countries in comparative costs? What is the basis for comparative advantage? Neo-classical economics has traditionally explained differences in comparative costs in terms of factor proportions. Different goods require different proportions of the various factors of production (land, labour, and capital) in their production. Some goods are land intensive, others labour intensive and others capital intensive. At the same time, God has endowed different countries with different amounts of these factors. Some countries are well endowed with land, others with labour and others with capital. This gives rise to differences between countries in relative factor prices. In countries well endowed with land, land is relatively cheap. Such countries will enjoy a comparative advantage in the production of land-intensive goods. Other countries are well endowed with labour, such that labour is relatively cheap. Such countries will possess a comparative advantage in labour-intensive goods. Finally, in some countries, capital is relatively abundant and hence cheap. Such countries will specialize in capital-intensive goods.

This theory of trade is sometimes referred to as the Hecksher–Ohlin theory after two economists – Eli Hecksher (1879–1952) and Bertil Ohlin (1899–1979) – who first expounded this theory. The theory is based upon a number of highly restrictive assumptions. Because of its importance for some of the issues discussed later in this book, we need to spell out the precise assumptions on which the theory is based:

1. There exist two goods, two factors of production and two countries (a so-called 2 × 2 × 2 model of trade).
2. Products are homogenous, that is there is no product differentiation.
3. Each country faces identical production functions, that is the proportions of the various factors required to produce a certain good are the same in all countries.
4. All countries enjoy equal access to the same body of technological knowledge; any new knowledge about how to produce a certain product is instantly diffused internationally.
5. Consumer preferences are assumed to be identical in all countries.
6. All factors of production are perfectly mobile within countries but immobile between countries.
7. Both product markets and factor markets are assumed to be perfectly competitive.
8. Transport costs are non-existent.
9. There exist no tariffs or other barriers to trade.

It is immediately apparent that many of these assumptions fail to hold in the real world. However, that does not constitute sufficient grounds for rejecting the theory. The important question is whether or not the predictions of the theory hold when the different assumptions are relaxed. For example, if we allow for the existence of transport costs, will the theory still correctly predict the pattern of international trade and specialization taking place between countries? Even if it does not, what may be required is a modification of the theory rather than a wholesale rejection of it.

One of the attractions of the theory is that it provides us with a set of fairly simple and readily testable predictions. The theory can be subjected to empirical testing to see how well it explains actual trade patterns. One of the first attempts made to test the theory was made by a Russian-born economist called Wassily Leontieff (b. 1906) in 1953. Using 1947 input–output tables for the United States, he sought to test the proposition that the United States had a comparative cost advantage in capital-intensive goods and therefore could be expected to export such goods and import labour-intensive goods. Leontieff measured the factor intensity of United States' exports and import replacements using the input–output tables. It was not possible to measure the factor intensity of US imports because input–output tables were not available for other countries exporting to the United States. This need not matter providing the same factor proportions were used in the United States to produce such import replacements as were used in other countries to produce exports to the United States.

In fact, Leontieff found that US imports were more capital-intensive than US exports. This apeared to refute the Hecksher–Ohlin theory. Leontieff's results provoked a great deal of interest among economists. Economists began a search to explain the 'Leontieff Paradox' as it came to be known. A variety of explantions were put forward of which the following were the most important:

1. The year chosen, 1947, was not very representative, being two years after the ending of the Second World War when trade patterns were still distorted by the dislocations of war. However, attempts to repeat the Leontieff test for more representative years have generally reproduced the same result.

2. The use of import replacements rather than imports may account for why US exports are more labour intensive than US imports. This is because of what economists call 'factor intensity reversal'. The same goods may be produced with differing factor intensities in different countries. Because labour is relatively expensive in the United States, American entrepreneurs will have an incentive to substitute capital for labour where technology permits. Thus goods which are labour intensive in the rest of the world are produced by capital-intensive methods in the United States. The use of import replacements rather than imports in the Leontieff study overestimates the capital–labour ratio for US imports. However, it is not proven that such factor-intensity reversals are as common in practice as is often supposed.

3. United States consumers have a stronger preference for capital-intensive goods than their trading partners. The Hecksher–Ohlin theory assumes identical tastes. However, tastes do differ between countries. If US consumers have a strong preference for capital-intensive goods, it is theoretically conceivable that capital-intensive goods could be relatively more expensive in the United States than in the rest of the world and that the rest of the world could possess a comparative advantage vis-à-vis the United States in capital-intensive goods. One explanation for this might be the higher level of US per capita incomes if the

demand for capital-intensive goods is income elastic. However, it remains questionable whether such differences in tastes between countries are strong enough to offset differences in comparative costs due to differing factor endowments.

4. United States workers are more efficient than their foreign counterparts so that with a given amount of capital an American worker produces more than the typical worker of any other country. Leontieff himself, in a search to explain his results, argued that the typical US worker was roughly three times as efficient as his/her foreign counterpart. If this is so, is it true to say that labour is the United States' scarce factor of production? Might it not be the United States' most abundant factor? However, greater empirical evidence is needed before this assertion can be accepted.

5. US exports are more capital intensive than they appear because they embody relatively large amounts of skilled labour, whereas US imports embody relatively large amounts of un-skilled labour. Skilled labour embodies large amounts of human capital. If account is taken of this, US exports will appear as being much more capital intensive than they seem. This illustrates a fundamental weakness of the simple version of the Hecksher–Ohlin theory adopted by Leontieff: it assumes only two factors of production – labour and capital. Yet labour is divisible into skilled and unskilled labour, and capital into physical and human capital.

6. The Leontieff study failed fully to take into account natural resources. The United States is both an exporter and importer of natural resources. It may well be that the kind of natural resources with which the United States is well-endowed are relatively more labour intensive than the natural resources which she is compelled to import. This further illustrates the need to use narrower categories of factors of production, in this case land.

7. US tariffs are biased against labour-intensive goods. High levels of protection existed in 1947, and the rate of protection may well have been higher on labour-intensive goods. If this were so, it could explain the low proportion of imports that consisted of labour-intensive goods and hence the high overall capital–labour ratio for imports.

It may well be that a variety of the above explanations can account for the Leontieff Paradox. Subsequent attempts to test the Hecksher–Ohlin theory taking account of some or all of these factors have yielded mixed results. Some have appeared to lend some support to the theory, others appear to refute it. Economics is unable to come to a conclusion on the validity of the theory. Perhaps, a reasonable conclusion would be to say that the theory may satisfactorily predict some real-world trade flows – for example between countries with vastly different factor endowments where different relative factor prices clearly do give rise to large differences in comparative costs – but that there remains a substantial, if not majority, component of world trade which fails to conform to the predictions of the theory.

Before we leave the Hecksher–Ohlin theory, mention should be made of an important subsequent extension to the theory. This is the so-called 'factor price equalization' theorem expounded first by Professor Paul Samuelson (Samuelson 1948). This states that, if all the assumptions of the Hecksher–Ohlin theory hold, then the opening up of trade between any two countries with different factor prices and therefore different comparative costs will lead to a tendency towards the equalization of factor prices in the two countries. It is important to emphasize 'a tendency towards' since the process is unlikely ever to be complete. To see this, consider two countries, one in which capital is relatively abundant and the other in which labour is relatively abundant. Capital will be cheap relative to labour in the former and labour will be cheap relative to capital in the latter. Put another way, the rate of profit will be higher in the latter than in the former and the average wage-rate will be higher in the former than in the latter. However, if the two countries specialize according to their comparative advantage, both the rate of profit and the wage-rate in the two countries will move closer together.

The logic behind this is as follows. In the capital-abundant country, specialization in capital-intensive goods will raise the demand for capital relative to the demand for labour. Hence, the rate of profit will rise relative to the wage-rate. In the labour-abundant country, specialization in labour-intensive goods will raise the demand for labour relative to the demand for capital. Hence the wage-rate will rise relative to the rate of profit. Factor prices in the two countries will thus tend towards equality. It follows that, if carried to the ultimate, the basis for trade between the two countries would disappear. Comparative costs would be the same in both countries and hence no basis for trade would exist. In reality, however, such a point would never be reached. The differences in factor prices between the two countries would narrow but never disappear altogether.

However, the factor price equalization theorem is interesting from another point of view. As the two economists Wolfgang Stolper and Paul Samuelson demonstrated in a pioneering article in 1941 (Stolper and Samuelson 1941) the possibility exists that the owners of a country's scarce factor of production may be worse off as a result of trade. For example, if labour is scarce in a particular country, trade will result in a fall in the wage-rate which may leave owners of labour worse off than before, even if the country as a whole gains from trade. The reason for being cautious in making such an assertion is that what counts is the real and not the money wage. If the opening up of trade brings a fall in the prices of consumer goods, real wages may still increase, providing that money wages do not fall by more than the fall in consumer goods prices. However, it is conceivable that workers as a whole could be worse off. Certainly, they will experience a deterioration in their position relative to other income groups. Specifically, their incomes will fall relative to the incomes of capitalists. In short, the opening up of trade will secure a redistribution of income from wages to profits. This fact may explain why some income groups resist the opening up of trade and clamour for protection even when protection reduces a country's total economic welfare.

ECONOMIES OF SCALE AND THE ROLE OF DEMAND-SIDE FACTORS IN TRADE

One of the weaknesses of the Hecksher–Ohlin theory of trade is that it ignores the part played by demand-side factors in international trade. Tastes are assumed to be identical in different countries. Hence demand-side factors have no influence on relative product prices in different countries. Differences in relative product prices are due entirely to differences in factor costs. Supply-side factors are the only determinant of trade. However, as we have seen, the theoretical possibility exists that relative prices could differ between any two countries even when factor endowments are identical. This would be the case if consumer preferences in the two countries diverged. In each country, the product for which demand was greatest would be relatively more expensive. Then a basis would exist for trade. The fact that a relatively large amount of world trade takes place between advanced industrialized countries with similar factor endowments would suggest that demand-side factors are quite important.

One of the first economists to incorporate the role of demand into a formal model of trade was the Swedish economist, Staffan Linder, writing in 1961 (Linder 1961). Linder argued that, while factor endowments played a dominant role in determining patterns of trade in primary commodities, the structure of demand was more important for trade in manufactured goods. Much trade in manufactured goods, he argued, took place between countries with similar factor endowments. The structure of demand for manufactured goods was primarily influenced by the level of per capita income of a country. Consumers in countries with high per capita incomes had demand patterns skewed towards high-quality goods. Consumers in countries with low per capita incomes had demand patterns skewed in favour of low-quality goods.

Linder further argued that firms initially produce goods to satisfy local demand. Eventually, however, once the domestic market becomes satiated, production for export commences. Producers seek out new markets for their product overseas. Linder argued that a country will initially export local varieties of a particular product to countries with a similar demand structure. Since the structure of demand is regarded as being mainly a function of per capita incomes, these will be countries with a similar per capita income. Thus Linder's 'theory of overlapping demand' leads to the prediction that countries with similar per capita incomes will do the most trade with one another. This is the opposite of the Hecksher–Ohlin theory, which predicts that countries with different factor endowments will do the most trade with one another. Differences in per capita income very often signify differences in the ratio of capital to labour. High per-capita-income countries generally have high ratios of capital to labour, low per-capita-income countries have low ratios of capital to labour. However, Linder's theory appears to come closer to predicting real world trade flows of manufactured goods, since, as we have seen, trade in manufactures has grown fastest between advanced industrialized countries. Linder also pointed to geographical proximity and cultural similarity as other factors which increase trade between countries. Products tailored to satisfy local tastes will sell better in countries with a similar culture and therefore greater similarity of tastes.

One prediction of the Linder theory of overlapping demand is that countries with a similar per capita income will exchange different varieties of the same product. Each country will export its own national variety of a certain product. Such trade in differentiated products is an important feature of much real-world trade in manufactured goods between advanced industrialized countries. For example, countries exchange different models of motor cars. Economists refer to such trade as 'intra-industry trade'. Chapter 3 considers the nature, importance and determinants of such intra-industry trade in some depth. At this stage we merely note the importance of intra-industry trade. One of the weaknesses of the Hecksher–Ohlin theory is that it cannot adequately explain this kind of trade because it assumes identical products. The products of different national producers are assumed to be homogeneous. Product differentiation has no place in a Hecksher–Ohlin model of trade.

Linder's model of trade can be improved by incorporating another important phenomenon of much real-world trade in manufactured goods, namely the existence of increasing returns to scale. The Hecksher–Ohlin model assumes that producers produce under conditions of decreasing returns to scale (increasing average costs). However, in many manufacturing industries, production takes place under conditions of increasing returns to scale (decreasing average costs). This is often the case with differentiated goods. In developing a new variety of a particular product, producers incur certain fixed costs. The importance of such fixed costs means that average costs fall with output. This can explain why only local firms produce varieties which cater for local tastes. It is unprofitable for all firms to seek to produce all varieties demanded by consumers. Thus producers in each country export varieties initially produced to satisfy local tastes. Other varieties are imported to enable consumers to enjoy the benefits of greater choice. This point is illustrated in Figure 1.5. A country is assumed to produce just two varieties of motor cars, Volvos and Fiats. The country's transformation curve is drawn as convex to the origin because of increasing returns to scale (decreasing average costs). Pre-trade domestic prices are represented by the price ray pp. Initially, a country produces at point A. The opening up of

Figure 1.5 Trade under conditions of increasing return

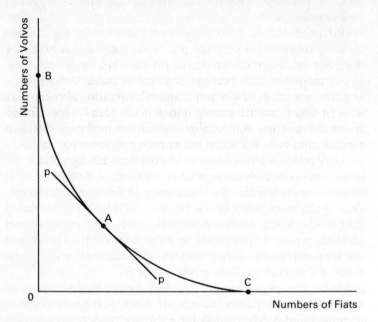

trade will however cause the country to move all the way to either point B or point C. If other countries can produce Volvos relatively more cheaply, the international terms of trade will be represented by a price ray steeper than pp. National producers will obtain a better price for their Fiats and so will be encouraged to increase their output of Fiats. However, because of the existence of increasing returns to scale, they will specialize completely in Fiats. Production of Volvos will be stopped, and resources will be redeployed in Fiat production.

TECHNOLOGICAL GAP THEORY AND THE PRODUCT LIFE-CYCLE

A weakness of both the Hecksher–Ohlin theory and Linder's demand-side theory of trade is that they are essentially static theories of trade. Neither theory incorporates the influence of technological change on patterns of trade and specialization. Yet there is plenty of superficial evidence for believing that technology and the process of its creation and diffusion internationally exerts a strong influence on the pattern of international specialization and trade. For example, for much of the post-war period the United States has enjoyed a comparative advantage in certain branches of manufacturing based entirely upon technological superiority. However, such superiority has often lasted for only a short period of time. Once the technology involved has become diffused around the world – whether as a result of US multinationals investing abroad or as firms in other countries have imitated US ideas – the United States has lost her comparative advantage in the products in question and even become a net importer of these products.

The Hecksher–Ohlin theory assumes that all countries have equal access to the same body of technological knowledge. It is possible to modify the theory to take account of technology. Thus technology could be treated as a factor of production alongside labour, land, and capital. This would lead to the prediction that countries well endowed with technology will specialize in the technology-intensive industries. However, such a theory is still unsatisfactory in several respects. In particular, it fails to explain adequately the process whereby comparative advantage in a particular product or industry changes over time as a specific technology is diffused internationally. In this process an important role is played by multinational corporations. In setting up new production facilities in other countries, multinational corporations transfer technology to other parts of the world. The Hecksher–Ohlin theory assumes that factors of production are internationally immobile.

One of the first economists to attempt to develop a model of trade which specifically incorporates technology was Michael Posner (Posner 1961). Posner proposed a model of trade in which an innovation is made in one country but the new technology is diffused internationally with a time-lag. The innovation may take the form of a new cost-saving method of production or a new product. Production is initially for the home market, but, at a later stage, exports commence. Posner suggested that there are two types of time-lag involved in the international diffusion of new technology. First, there is a 'reaction lag'. This is the interval between the moment when the innovation is introduced and the moment when producers in other countries recognize the need to respond to the change. Only when the innovating firm begins to export the product will firms in other countries feel the challenge of new competition and recognize the need to make appropriate adjustments. Second, there is an 'imitation lag'. A second interval follows during which competitors assimilate the new process or product. Eventually, they succeed in copying or imitating the idea developed by the original innovator. At this point, exports from the innovating country will begin to taper off. Domestic production will displace imports. Posner used the term 'technological-gap trade' to describe this kind of trade. The important point is that such trade flows are finite in time. They eventually come to an end as producers in other countries respond to the challenge posed by the new production method or product and imitate. Of course, the possibility exists that the first innovation may be followed by a second, in which case the first kind of trade flow will be followed by a second. In this case, one country, by virtue of its skill in innovation, may continue to enjoy a comparative advantage in a particular branch of manufacturing.

G.C. Hufbauer developed a similar model of trade to that of Posner to explain the influence of technological innovation on patterns of trade (Hufbauer 1966). As in Posner's model, exports resulting from the discovery of a new method of production or new product are considered to have a limited duration in time. Firms in the importing countries are assumed to respond successfully to the new challenge only after a time-lag. However, Hufbauer introduced another factor which might serve to increase the length of the imitation lag – the occurrence of long-run, dynamic economies of scale. In many industries, important cost savings result from 'learning by doing'. Because the use of new technology often involves such a learning process, average costs fall with the cumulative volume of output. This gives the most established producers of a product an important competitive advantage over producers setting up in production for the first time. For this reason, it may take some time before local producers who imitate the overseas innovator are able to match the latter's costs and prices. This will increase the length of time during which technological-gap trade lasts.

Hufbauer's model further assumed that high-wage economies would enjoy a comparative advantage in technological-gap exports. Such countries would have a greater incentive to invent labour-saving devices. Firms could be expected to devote considerable effort to introducing methods of production which economize on labour as well as to introduce new consumer goods which save on labour time (e.g. washing machines, hoovers, spin-dryers, washing-up machines, etc.). Hence technological-gap trade would tend to take the form of a flow of exports from high-wage to low-wage economies. Once, however, the new ideas have been successfully imitated, such exports will come to an end, and the comparative advantage in the production of such goods will shift to low-wage economies. High-wage economies will become net importers of the products which they originally discovered. The advantage of cheap labour enjoyed by low-wage economies will help to offset the disadvantage of being unable to capitalize on dynamic economies of scale. This will help to shorten the length of the imitation lag. Hufbauer's model leads to the testable prediction that high-wage countries will export the world's latest, most technologically advanced products and import the older, more traditional products. In so many words, they will exchange new for known products. Hufbauer provided empirical support for this hypothesis by examining trade in synthetic materials.

Raymond Vernon developed a similar model of trade to take account of the importance of product innovation (Vernon 1966). Vernon started from the premiss that, in many branches of manufacturing, products have limited lives. Account needs to be taken of the particular stage of development which a product has reached. Vernon distinguished between three such stages:

1. **The new-product stage** This is the first stage in the life of a new product. During this stage all production will be located in the innovating country. Several reasons for this may be given. First, most production will be for the home market. Exports will begin to take place but will initially be subordinate to domestic sales. The need to minimize transport costs will favour locating production as near to the consumer as possible. Second, in the early stages of the life of a new product, there will be a need to make constant adaptations and alterations to the product as the product is tried out and consumers respond. Producers need to be close to consumers to receive any feedback. Third, during the early years in the life of a new product, the innovator enjoys some immunity from competition. Almost certainly he will enjoy some form of patent protection. The demand for his product will be relatively price inelastic, which means that he can pass on higher costs in a higher price. Cost

considerations are therefore not paramount in determining location of production.

2. **The maturing-product stage** In this second stage in the life of a product there occurs a significant increase in overseas demand for the product. Initially, the innovator will seek to satisfy such demand through exports. Eventually, however, he will seek to do so by setting up a production facility in his major markets overseas. First, the increase in foreign demand for the product will be such as to justify the establishment of an overseas production subsidiary. Second, the innovating firm will face more severe competition as other firms begin to copy the innovation. The demand for the firm's product will become much more price elastic. He can no longer pass on higher costs in higher prices. Overseas production becomes important to reduce transport costs. If labour costs are also lower in overseas markets, this will make overseas production an even more attractive proposition. Finally, the innovator may face steep tariff walls or high non-tariff barriers which give local firms a competitive advantage. Overseas production enables the firm to jump such trade barriers. Thus, in the maturity stage, one can expect production of the product outside the original innovating country to grow. As a result, exports from the innovator country will taper off.

3. **The standardized-product stage** In this final stage in the product's life there is likely to take place fierce price competition. The product is now completely standardized such that price is the most important factor in ensuring that a firm maintains or enlarges its share of the market. Accordingly, all producers will seek out the lowest-cost locations for producing the product. Increasingly, they will shift production to new low-cost sites in developing countries where labour is relatively cheap. They will export the product from such sites to the major markets in developed countries. Thus, in the standardization stage, high-wage countries become net importers of the products in question. Low-wage countries become the most important exporters.

Figure 1.6 illustrates Vernon's product life-cycle. The United States is taken to be the innovating country. Like Hufbauer, Vernon predicted that high-wage economies will generate more innovations than low-wage economies. The high cost of labour is one reason for this. Another reason is the wider market from

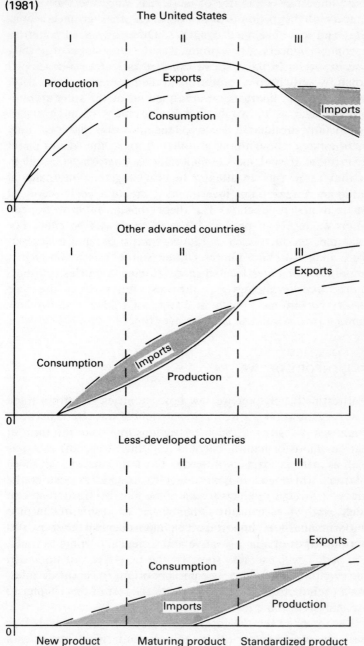

Figure 1.6 The product life-cycle model of trade. Source: Vernon (1981)

The United States

I   II   III

Production

Exports

Consumption

Imports

Other advanced countries

I   II   III

Exports

Consumption

Imports

Production

Less-developed countries

I   II   III

Exports

Consumption

Imports   Production

New product   Maturing product   Standardized product

which to launch a new product. The United States has been the most important generator of new ideas since the start of the century. A distinction is drawn between other advanced countries and less-developed countries. Other advanced countries become producers of new products in the later stages of novelty and exporters in the stage of standardization. Less-developed countries only become producers in the later years of maturity, becoming net exporters towards the end of the standardized-product stage.

Vernon's product life-cycle has the attraction that it not only incorporates innovation in a model of trade; the role of direct investment abroad and the multinational company is included. It thus represents an attempt to bring together international trade and international investment to create a single theory of international production. The theory has an intuitive appeal. Many examples of product life-cycle trade can be cited. For example, products such as radios, transistors, and televisions were all first produced in the United States but are now largely imported from sites located in developing countries. Furthermore, like technology-gap theories, the product life-cycle theory constitutes a dynamic theory of trade. It shows how comparative advantage changes over time.

THE THEORY OF TARIFFS

Earlier in this chapter we saw how countries gain from trade and specialization. However, in a variety of ways trade between countries is restricted. Such restrictions may take the form of various kinds of natural barriers (e.g. high transport costs) as well as artificial barriers to trade. The latter includes all those barriers which governments erect to exclude or restrict the entry of foreign products to the home market. Tariffs are one such kind of restriction. Other forms of restriction include import embargoes, import quotas, import deposit schemes, and various kinds of administrative and technical barriers to trade. Chapter 7 will examine some of the new types of non-tariff intervention which have become important in recent decades. As a prelude to this, we shall devote the rest of this chapter to an analysis of the effects of tariffs.

Tariffs may take the form of (1) a specific duty payable on each unit imported or (2) an *ad valorem* tariff expressed as a percentage of the value of the goods imported. Tariffs generally raise the price of goods imported, although the incidence of the tariff may be born by both the consumer in the importing country and the foreign supplier. In most cases the effect is to reduce the quantity imported. Tariffs are generally imposed either as revenue-raising devices or as a means of protecting home producers from foreign competition. In most cases, however, they reduce the level of economic welfare of the importing country.

Figure 1.7 illustrates the effects of a small nation imposing an import tariff. Because this country is a small trading nation, it faces a perfectly elastic world supply curve, P_w-S_w. It can buy all that it wants from the rest of the world at the world price P_w but is unable to influence the world price. In the absence of any tariff and disregarding any transport costs, consumers would pay the price P_w. Domestic consumption would equal OQ_4. Domestic production would equal OQ_1. Imports would equal Q_1Q_4. If a tariff equal to $P_wP_w^T$ were imposed, the price would rise to P_w^T. Domestic consumption would fall to OQ_3 and domestic production would rise to OQ_2. Imports would fall to Q_2Q_3. The fall in domestic consumption is called the 'consumption effect'. The rise in domestic production is called the 'protective effect'. In addition, the tariff generates revenue for the authorities. This is equal to area C and is known as the 'revenue effect'.

In addition, the tariff lowers the economic welfare of the importing country. This is given by the fall in consumer surplus consequent upon the rise in price. It is given by the areas $(A + B + C + D)$ which lie under the demand curve. Consumer welfare has been reduced by this amount due to the imposition of the tariff. However, not all of this loss of consumer welfare constitutes a loss to the importing country. Area C represents increased revenue to the government and thus a redistribution of income from consumers to government. Area A represents increased producers' surplus. Revenues to producers increase by areas $(A + B)$, but area B represents the increased cost required to produce Q_1Q_2. Thus, only area A represents higher profits to domestic producers. This constitutes a redistribution of income from domestic consumers to domestic producers and thus not a loss of income to the importing nation. If areas C and A are deducted from the total loss of consumer welfare, this leaves areas B and D, the two shaded triangles under the supply

Figure 1.7 The effects of a tariff: the small-country model

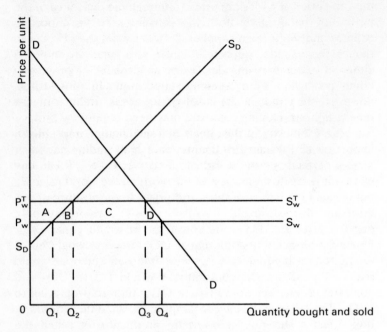

and demand curves respectively. This constitutes the *net* loss of welfare to the importing country due to the tariff or the 'deadweight loss' of a tariff. It follows that the removal of this tariff will raise the welfare of the importing country by this amount.

If tariffs lower economic welfare, it may be asked why do governments impose them? In many cases, the reasons are non-economic. Governments are responding to pressure from a particular sectional interest which stands to lose from free trade. It may be necessary for the political survival of a government to concede protection to this particular sectional interest. Alternatively, an industry might be considered of vital strategic importance to a country (e.g. aircraft production). Protection from foreign competition is deemed necessary for national security. In other cases, governments may simply be acting shortsightedly, unaware of the damage which tariffs cause. For example, it might be thought that a tariff boosts domestic employment in a particular industry or region by reducing imports and increasing domestic production. Although this may be true in the short term, the effect will be to shift unemployment to some other country and invite the latter to impose retaliatory tariffs. The first country will thus experience a fall in exports and thus domestic production and employment which cancels out the gain achieved by imposing a tariff. In addition, consumers suffer a welfare loss from the tariff.

However, there do exist some sound arguments for tariffs. One of these is the infant-industry argument. Infant or new industries in developing countries may need temporary protection before they have grown to a size large enough to be able to compete. This is because of the existence of dynamic economies of scale in many industries such that average costs fall with the growth of an industry. Only when that industry has reached a certain size will average costs match those of the established industries of other more industrialized countries. However, even in this case, it can be demonstrated that a tariff is a second-best policy. A domestic subsidy paid to the new industry would be economically more efficient because a subsidy, unlike a tariff, lowers price. On the other hand, a subsidy requires increased government expenditure which a developing country may be unable to finance.

A further economic argument for a tariff can be made out where a country is a large importer of a particular product and able to influence the terms of trade. Such a country may enjoy monopsony or buying power such that by imposing a tariff it can drive down the world price of the imported product. In this way it may be able to shift the terms of trade in its favour. Figure 1.8 illustrates the case of such a country. SS_{D+w} is the combined domestic and world supply curve which is flatter (i.e. more elastic) than the domestic supply curve, SS_D. P_O is the equilibrium price where demand equals (domestic plus foreign) supply. OQ_O is produced domestically and Q_OQ_3 is imported. Now a tariff equal to P_2P_1 (i.e. the vertical distance between SS_{D+w} and SS^T_{D+w}) is imposed. Price rises to P_1 and imports are reduced to Q_1Q_2. However, the rise in price is less than the amount of the tariff. This is because the world price now falls from OP_o to OP_2. Now, the country in question can obtain imports at a lower price than before. The terms of trade have moved in its favour. The welfare gain from the improved terms of trade is given by the rectangle, area E (which is the fall in the price of imports × the quantity imported). Against this must be set the net loss of consumer surplus due to the higher tariff. As in the small country case, this is given by the two triangles, B and D. However, if area E exceeds areas (B + D), the country will experience a net increase in economic welfare due to the imposition of a tariff.

Figure 1.8 The effects of a tariff: the large-country model

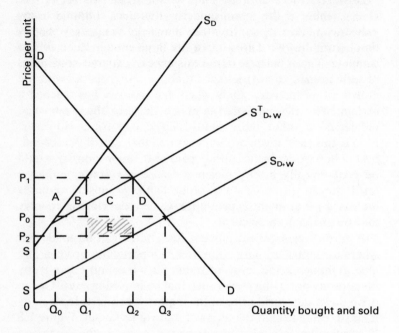

The practical usefulness of this model is doubtful. First, it is only applicable to a large importing nation which is able to exercise monopsony (buying) power. Second, even then it is difficult for such a country to measure in advance the different welfare effects of the tariff. It cannot be sure that the welfare loss from the tariff (areas B + D) will be more than offset by the welfare gain due to the improved terms of trade (area E). Third, the model ignores the likelihood of foreign retaliation. The improvement in the terms of trade of the importing nation means a deterioration in the terms of trade of other exporting nations. They may seek to counteract this deterioration in their terms of trade by imposing an equivalent tariff on the imports of the offending country. If they too possess monopsony power – attainable by agreeing to act collectively – they may be able to

28

bring about an offsetting fall in the latter country's terms c trade. In this case, it will have gained nothing at all.

A third sound argument for a tariff arises when an importing country faces 'unfair competition' from abroad. This is the case of so-called 'dumping' where an exporting country is subsidizing exports of goods such that the overseas price is below the price charged by the exporting country when the product is sold domestically. The intention may be to gain a foothold in the overseas market or to drive out domestic competitors before raising the price. The effects on domestic production and employment of such practices may be considered sufficiently harmful as to justify a tariff.

A number of other arguments for tariffs do exist, but a full discussion of the theory of protectionism lies outside the scope of this book. However, we can safely conclude that, these arguments aside, the effects of tariffs are generally economically harmful. As we have seen, they reduce the economic welfare of importing and exporting nations. This welfare loss is measurable, and attempts have been made to measure the welfare gain to countries from the elimination or reduction of tariffs. Areas B and D in Figure 1.7 can be measured for a particular country by (1) estimating the likely increase in imports resulting from a reduction or elimination of tariffs and (2) multiplying this amount by half the tariff reduction. This gives the area of the two triangles B and D. Attempts to estimate the cost of tariffs in this way have shown the welfare loss to be quite small. However, this is because such an exercise only counts the so-called 'static' loss from tariffs. Tariffs impose a variety of other costs on importing countries. By giving shelter to domestic producers, they encourage managerial slack or so-called 'X-inefficiency' in the import-substitution sector. The reduced level of exports prevents exporting countries from expanding their production of exports to the optimal (i.e. lowest cost) level of output. In short, they prevent the full exploitation of all available economies of scale. Finally, by raising the price of imports and by sheltering domestic firms from foreign competition, tariffs increase a country's rate of inflation and render the management of the macroeconomy more difficult. If all these longer-run or so-called 'dynamic' effects are included, the cost of tariffs is almost certainly quite high. It is this realization that has spurred countries to seek ways of reducing tariffs whether through international agreement or regional trading organizations. We shall now consider how this was brought about in the quarter-century which followed the ending of the Second World War.

INTERNATIONAL ECONOMIC INTEGRATION

The period since the ending of the Second World War has been a period of rapid expansion of world trade. In the next chapter we shall see how trade has regularly grown faster than output. One of the main causes of this rapid expansion of trade has been the willingness of countries to lower barriers on their trade with one another and to carry out trade according to an agreed set of rules. This liberalization of trade brought an increase in the degree of economic integration between countries. This contributed to the fast growth in output. In the last two decades there has occurred a reversion back to protectionism. Countries have increasingly resorted to a variety of new devices to restrict imports and protect domestic producers. Tariffs remain low but non-tariff barriers have become increasingly important. As a result, the volume of trade has grown more slowly. This has contributed to slower output growth. In Chapter 7 we shall examine some of the causes of this New Protectionism. Suffice it to say at this stage that countries have begun to forget the significance of the link between liberal trade and output growth. After the Second World War there was an awareness of the mutual benefits which accrue to countries from reciprocal tariff reductions and agreements not to raise tariffs except in an emergency. Freer trade leads to more trade. More trade means higher economic welfare for the countries involved, as we have seen earlier in this chapter. Tariffs reduce welfare by raising prices and distorting the allocation of resources within individual countries and on a global basis.

The most important vehicle of increased international economic integration after the Second World War was the General Agreement on Tariffs and Trade (GATT) set up in 1947. An important role was also played by certain regional trading organizations such as the European Community (EC) set up in 1958 and the European Free Trade Area (EFTA) set up in 1960. The GATT treaty was initially signed by some twenty-three countries but eventually gained the adherence of all the leading trading nations of the western industrialized world.

Today there are ninety signatory nations and a number of other countries which accept the provisions of GATT but are not full members. The GATT treaty consists of some thirty-eight articles the aims of which are (1) to provide a set of rules or code of conduct governing trading relationships between different countries and (2) to provide a framework within which trade can be progressively liberalized.

Three important principles underlie the GATT charter:

1. **The most-favoured-nation principle** GATT members agree to treat all other GATT members as 'most-favoured-nations'. This means that they agree not to discriminate against other GATT members, although they may discriminate against non-GATT members. This principle is embodied in article 1 of the Charter. It means that, if a tariff is imposed on imports from any one GATT member, the same tariff will be imposed on the same imports from all other GATT members. Equally, if a tariff is lowered on imports from one GATT member, the same cut will apply to the same imports from all other GATT members. One important exception to this principle is that of customs unions and free-trade areas. These involve the elimination of tariffs and other barriers on internal trade but not on imports from non-members. In the case of a customs union, the member countries apply a common customs tariff on extra-area imports, whereas, in a free-trade area, individual members are free to determine their own level of tariff on such imports. Thus customs unions and free-trade areas involve discrimination against countries which do not belong to the arrangement. Preference is given to imports from member states. The EC and EFTA are examples of a customs union and free-trade area respectively. Article 24 of the GATT permits such regional trading blocs providing that the external tariff after the formation of the customs union/free-trade area is no higher than the average tariff of the countries involved beforehand. Furthermore, where other GATT members are harmed by the setting up of such a customs union/free-trade area, they are entitled to compensation. Another exception to the non-discrimination principle was made in the 1970s when GATT members agreed to allow countries to introduce preferences on manufacturing imports from developing countries. This so-called 'generalized system of preferences' (GSPs) represented an attempt by GATT members to meet the demands of developing countries

31

for easier access to the markets of developed countries for their manufacturing exports. The argument was conceded that 'equal treatment of unequals' was unfair and that developing countries were entitled to positive discrimination in their favour.

2. **Protection should mainly take the form of tariffs** GATT is a charter for freer trade, not free trade. Tariffs are allowed although GATT seeks both to lower the level of tariffs and prescribe rules relating to the use of tariffs to protect domestic producers in an emergency. However, GATT rules outlaw quantitative restrictions on trade such as import quotas. This principle is contained in article 2 of the treaty. Import quotas were common in the inter-war period and during the Second World War. Countries which signed the GATT were expected gradually to dismantle all such restrictions. Quotas seek to restrict imports by requiring importers to obtain licences from the authorities before goods may be allowed into the country. Such quotas are generally considered to be more harmful than tariffs since they have a more detrimental effect on economic efficiency. An important exception to this rule concerns agricultural imports.

3. **Tariff rates should be negotiable** GATT signatories must be willing to make tariff cuts as concessions in international tariff negotiations in return for receiving equivalent concessions from other GATT members. They are not to regard their tariffs as purely domestic matters of no concern to other countries. One important aspect of this principle is that all members must be willing to make concessions in any round of tariff negotiations. No country is allowed to 'free-ride', receiving concessions from other GATT members but offering nothing in return. This is sometimes known as the principle of reciprocity. Each member is to reciprocate, offering some concession in return for receiving some concession from other members. In the 1960s one important exception was made to this principle: developing countries were allowed to free-ride. They were not required to make any concession at all while benefiting from concessions made by the developed countries. This was of less benefit to the developing countries than it may seem because tariff cuts made by the developed countries applied to goods of little interest to developing countries.

Few countries would have been prepared to sign the GATT agreement if the treaty had proscribed the use of tariffs to protect domestic producers from sudden, intense import competition. Thus the articles of the treaty provide various loopholes which enable members to impose tariffs under special circumstances. At the same time, rules are laid down about the manner in which such tariffs may be imposed and the duration of time allowed. One of the most important exceptions to freer trade is embodied in article 19 – the so-called Escape Clause, or Safeguard Clause. This states:

> If as a result of unforeseen developments and effects of obligations incurred by a member under GATT (including tariff concessions), a product is imported in such amounts as to cause or 'threaten' 'serious injury' to domestic producers, that country is free to suspend the obligation or modify the concession until the injury is remedied. But notice must be given in writing in advance to countries affected to provide opportunity for consultation. Prior consultation may be omitted if delay is likely to cause irreparable damage, in which case consultation must follow after action has been taken. If agreement cannot be reached among interested members, the country may proceed with the action. In that event not later than 90 days after such action is taken, the affected parties are free to suspend (after 30 days after prior written notice of the suspension) concessions or obligations under the Agreement, which the members do not disapprove of.

The requirement is that, in normal circumstances, consultation must precede Escape Clause action. If not, it must follow afterwards. Where necessary, affected parties must be compensated. The emphasis is on consultation and negotiation rather than unilateral action. Any tariff imposed must be non-discriminatory. As we shall see in Chapter 7 this requirement, alongside the need to consult and compensate every affected party, has made the Escape Clause excessively onerous for some countries. One result has been that it has been frequently bypassed. Members have found means other than tariffs for restricting imports. Finally, there is a requirement that any tariff imposed under Article 19 must be progressively lowered as the cause of the disturbance is removed. The Escape Clause is currently a source of contention. Some developed countries wanted the requirements of the clause (e.g. the non-discriminatory rule) to be changed to make it more acceptable to members. Other countries, mainly developing countries, want the rules tightened to make emergency action more difficult to use and to require countries progressively to lower any import barriers at a quicker rate than applies in practice.

Another important exception to the freer trade stance of the GATT concerns the case of 'dumping'. Article 6 defines this as:

When products of one country are introduced into the commerce of another country at less than the price of the same product when sold in the exporting country. If no such price exists, the relevant price is the highest price for the product sold in any third country. If no such price exists, then the relevant measure is the cost of production of the product in the exporting country plus a reasonable addition for selling costs and profit.

If dumping can be proved and the above criterion is satisfied, a country may impose a countervailing duty which must not be greater than 'the margin of dumping in respect of such products'.

A further important exception to freer trade is the case of a balance-of-payments disequilibrium. Article 12 permits a member state to introduce restrictions to safeguard its balance of payments but only: 'to forestall a serious decline in its monetary reserves or to achieve a reasonable rate of increase in reserves in the case of a low-reserve country'. Once again, countries imposing such restrictions must progressively relax them as conditions improve and eventually eliminate them when there is no further justification for continuing them.

GATT also provides a machinery for settling disputes between countries and supervises the rules. However, GATT has no power to enforce the rules of the agreement on member states. It depends for its effectiveness on the willingness of countries to abide by the agreement. If certain countries fail to adhere to the rules, it is left to other members to consider what action to take. Ultimately, member states may choose to withdraw concessions or even most-favoured-nation treatment from a country which persistently breaks the rules.

Since the inception of GATT in 1947, there have been some seven rounds of international trade negotiations carried out under the auspices of the GATT. An eighth round is currently in progress. These have brought about a substantial lowering of the level of tariffs applied to industrial goods. Progress in the area of agricultural trade has been much slower. The seven rounds of GATT were as follows:

1947, Geneva
1949, Annecy
1950–1, Torquay
1955–6, Geneva
1960–2, Geneva (the Dillon Round)
1964–7, the Kennedy Round
1973–9, the Tokyo Round

Of these seven rounds, the biggest tariff cuts were made in the first and sixth rounds. The first round involved cuts of roughly one-third on imports accounting for roughly one-half of world trade. The sixth round involved tariff cuts of over one-third on imports accounting for roughly three-quarters of world trade. The seventh Tokyo Round also involved substantial tariff cuts but covered a smaller proportion of trade, and the tariff cuts were staged over a period of ten years. The Tokyo Round was important in representing the first attempt by GATT members to tackle the perplexing problem of non-tariff barriers. This will be examined further in Chapter 7.

Each round of GATT since the war has tended to follow the US Congress granting the US president a new tariff-cutting authority. Without such an authority, the president cannot negotiate. The authority granted will also stipulate the maximum tariff cut which he is able to make. Given the importance of the United States in world trade, meaningful negotiations would be impossible without the involvement of the United States. Immediately after the war, the United States was keen to offer large tariff concessions to gain the adherence of the rest of the world to the GATT agreement. The early GATT rounds were largely concerned with this process. However, in the mid-1950s, congressional enthusiasm for further tariff reductions waned. There was a feeling that the United States had made enough concessions for the time being. However, the West European economies were keen to move further and faster towards freer trade. However, they could not do so without the involvement of the United States. The solution was to set up the European Community in 1958 and EFTA in 1960. These arrangements involved the European economies eventually eliminating all tariffs on trade between themselves. One of the effects of this was to put pressure on the United States to enter into a fresh round of tariff negotiations. The result was the passage of the 1962 Trade Expansion Act and the subsequent Kennedy Round of tariff negotiations. As we have seen, this resulted in both the United States and the West European countries making further substantial tariff cuts.

A similar fillip to the tariff-cutting process was given in 1973 with the enlargement of the European Community to admit the United Kingdom. This similarly posed a challenge to the United States. The result was the passage of the 1974 Trade Act, which empowered the president to begin a fresh round of negotiations, although his authority was more qualified than on any other occasion since the war. The Tokyo Round brought further tariff cuts – although, by then, industrial tariffs were lower than on previous occasions – and began an attempt to tackle the issue of non-tariff barriers. As a result of these GATT rounds tariffs on industrial goods are now very low. The major concern of the eighth round is unlikely to be a further lowering of tariffs. More important is the extension of the GATT process to tackle new areas of trade. Further progress in reducing non-tariff barriers to trade will be on the top of the agenda. Agricultural trade remains another important area of trade which has been largely untouched by the GATT process of liberalization. In recent years levels of protectionism in agriculture in all the western industrialized countries have been increasing. The issue of the reform of the Escape, or Safeguard, Clause is also likely to be important. Finally, the new GATT round will address itself to the issue of trade in services. In Chapter 8 we shall discuss the nature and importance of trade in services and consider some of the problems involved in extending the GATT to this kind of trade.

2

The Changing Structure of World Output and World Trade

INTRODUCTION

The forty years which have passed since the ending of the Second World War have been a period of extremely rapid economic growth. World output has grown at a faster rate than in any other period in history. It is true that, during the last one and a half decades, output growth has been much slower. Nevertheless, growth rates are still quite high in comparison with other equivalent periods in history. Over the past forty years, world trade has grown at an even faster rate than world output. This rapid growth in world trade has been one of the main causes of the growth in output. It has been the result of an increase in the degree of international specialization, especially in manufacturing industry and between industrialized economies. One of the reasons for the slowing down of economic growth in recent decades has been the slower growth of the manufacturing sector in the industrialized economies and slower growth of trade in manufactured goods.

The rapid growth of world trade relative to world output has meant an increase in the degree of international economic integration. The world has become much more of an interdependent whole. In all the industrialized countries the size of the trading sector as a proportion of national output has increased. Important changes have also taken place in the nature and pattern of world trade. It is with these new patterns of world trade that this book is primarily concerned. In this chapter I examine some of the broad changes which have taken place in the structure of world trade over the last quarter-century. This provides an essential framework for discussing some of the most important developments in international trade which have taken place and which constitute the main themes of this book.

In this chapter I shall first examine the growth of world output and the main changes which have taken place in the composition of output in different regions of the world in recent decades. Second, I shall examine the growth of world trade and the relationship between the growth in world trade and world output. Third, I shall discuss the major changes which have taken place in the commodity composition of world trade. The most important trends in both relative prices and the volume of trade of different commodities will be identified and explained. Fourth, I shall examine changes in the geographical composition of world trade. Changes in the share of world trade accounted for by different regions of the world will be examined. Changes in the importance of different trading flows will also be analysed. Finally, future prospects for world output and world trade will be considered in the light of the experience of the last four decades. Some suggestions will be made as to how former growth rates might be restored. Many of the themes of this chapter will be considered more fully in subsequent chapters.

THE GROWTH OF WORLD OUTPUT

The rates of economic growth for different regions of the world are shown in Tables 2.1 and 2.2. Table 2.1 shows the average annual rate of growth of real gross domestic product (GDP) and Table 2.2 of real gross domestic product per capita (per head of the population). Real GDP differs from money GDP in being adjusted for inflation. GDP per capita differs from GDP in allowing for growth of population. It can be seen that the developed market economies enjoyed fast growth in the 1960s with GDP rising by 4.8 per cent a year and GDP per capita by 3.8 per cent a year. Of the major developed market economies (DMEs), Japan had a very high rate of growth; her GDP rose by 12.4 per cent a year and her GDP per capita by 11.3 per cent a year. France had the second highest growth rate followed by West Germany and the United States. The United Kingdom had the lowest rate of growth.

In the 1970s the rate of growth fell in all the *developed countries*. GDP grew at a rate of 3.3 per cent a year and GDP

Table 2.1: Annual average rates of growth of real gross domestic product at market prices by region, 1960 to 1983, percentages

Countries Territories	1960–70	1970–80	1970–5	1975–6	1976–7	1977–8	1978–9	1979–80	1980–1	1981–2	1982–3	1982 GDP $ millions
DEVELOPED MARKET ECONOMIES,	4.8	3.3	3.5	4.9	3.9	4.0	3.4	1.4	1.7	−0.2	2.3	7,691,135
of which:												
United States	4.5	3.2	2.9	5.4	5.5	5.0	2.8	−0.3	2.5	−2.1	3.7	3,052,087
West Germany	4.4	2.7	2.5	5.4	3.1	3.1	4.1	1.9	0.1	−0.9	0.9	658,879
United Kingdom	2.9	2.1	2.5	3.9	0.9	3.8	2.1	−2.1	−1.2	1.9	3.3	478,588
Japan	12.4	4.6	5.0	5.3	5.3	5.0	5.1	4.9	4.2	3.0	3.4	1,062,867
France	5.7	3.6	4.2	5.2	3.1	3.8	3.3	1.0	0.2	2.0	0.7	540,124
DEVELOPING COUNTRIES,	5.9	5.1	5.7	7.2	5.4	2.8	5.4	1.8	−0.2	0.5	−0.1	2,077,124
of which:												
Oil exporters	7.5	4.8	6.1	9.2	4.0	0.4	7.1	−2.1	−3.6	−0.4	−4.1	845,964
Major exporters of manufactures	5.6	6.4	7.3	7.2	6.9	3.6	7.0	4.4	−0.7	0.3	1.4	492,096
Least developed	3.5	3.9	3.5	6.3	3.2	4.8	2.2	1.9	3.6	0.6	2.4	59,138
SOCIALIST COUNTRIES (Eastern Europe)	6.7	5.3	6.2	5.8	4.9	4.6	2.4	3.1	2.4	3.0	4.2	1,001,229

Source: UNCTAD Handbook of International Trade and Development, 1985.

Table 2.2: Annual average rates of growth of real per capita GDP at market prices by region, 1960–81 (%)

Countries Territories	1960–70	1970–80	1970–5	1975–6	1976–7	1977–8	1978–9	1979–80	1980–1	1981–2	1982–3	1982 GDP per capita $
DEVELOPED MARKET ECONOMIES, of which:	3.6	2.4	2.5	4.1	3.1	3.2	2.6	0.6	0.9	-0.9	1.7	9,583
United States	3.2	2.1	1.9	4.4	4.5	3.9	1.7	-1.4	1.6	-3.0	2.7	13,157
West Germany	3.5	2.7	2.1	5.9	3.3	3.2	4.0	1.6	0.0	-0.9	1.3	10,689
United Kingdom	2.3	2.0	2.3	4.0	1.0	3.9	2.1	-2.2	-1.2	1.8	3.2	8,501
Japan	11.3	3.5	3.6	4.1	4.2	4.1	4.2	4.1	3.5	2.3	2.7	8,974
France	4.6	3.0	3.5	4.8	2.7	3.4	2.9	0.6	-0.2	1.5	0.3	9,962
DEVELOPING COUNTRIES, of which:	3.2	2.6	3.1	4.6	3.0	0.4	3.0	-0.6	-2.5	-1.9	-2.5	893
Oil exporters	4.4	2.0	3.2	6.2	1.3	-2.3	4.3	-4.7	-6.2	-3.0	-6.7	1,889
Major exporters of manufactures	2.8	4.1	5.0	4.9	4.7	1.5	4.8	2.2	-2.7	-1.7	-0.6	2,218
Least developed	1.2	1.3	1.1	3.6	0.5	2.0	-0.6	-0.9	0.8	-2.1	-0.4	198
SOCIALIST COUNTRIES (Eastern Europe)	5.5	4.4	5.3	5.0	4.1	3.8	1.6	2.4	1.7	2.3	3.4	2,612

Source: UNCTAD Handbook of International Trade and Development, 1985.

per capita at a rate of 2.4 per cent a year. Japan was still the fastest-growing developed country and the United Kingdom the slowest growing. Although there were signs that growth in the DMEs was weakening as early as the late 1960s, the immediate cause of the slowdown was the oil crisis of 1973 to 1974. It began with an oil embargo imposed by the Middle East states on countries supporting Israel in the Yom Kippur War. The resultant shortage of oil enabled the oil-producing countries who belonged to the Organization of Petroleum Exporting Countries (OPEC) to enforce a quadrupling of the world price of oil. This drastically cut real incomes in the western industrialized countries dependent on the Middle East for imported oil. The fall in real incomes caused a fall in aggregate demand for domestically produced goods and services and a slump in output.

The oil crisis is sometimes explained as being the result of the formation of OPEC. However, OPEC was only able to impose a higher oil price on the rest of the world because of an imbalance in the world oil market. Over the course of the 1950s and 1960s oil consumption had expanded rapidly. This had been encouraged by the fall in the real price of oil. Oil had become cheaper than other sources of energy. As a result, many western industrialized economies had become heavily dependent on oil imported from the Middle East. The low price of oil discouraged investment by oil companies in the exploration and development of higher-cost oil-fields in other parts of the world. Production failed to keep pace with oil consumption. In addition, the United States, who consumed about one-third of the world's supply of oil, moved from a position of self-sufficiency to dependence on imports to meet her fuel requirements. By the early 1970s, conditions on the world oil market were favourable towards an enforced rise in oil prices. The fact that a large proportion of world output was accounted for by a relatively small group of politically aligned Middle East states meant that production could be controlled. At the same time, the low short-run price elasticity of demand for oil meant that demand for oil did not fall in proportion to the rise in price. In the long-run, however, the rise in price could be expected to lead to a fall in oil consumption as oil consumers substituted other sources of energy for oil.

41

The effect of the rise in oil prices in 1974 was not only to squeeze real incomes in the western industrialized countries. It also resulted in a sharp rise in the rate of inflation coinciding as it did with a general rise in world commodity prices. As workers and firms sought to resist a cut in their real incomes by forcing up the price of labour and of goods, the rate of inflation increased. Governments in the western industrialized countries sought to combat the rise in inflation by tightening their monetary and fiscal policies. This further reduced aggregate demand and hence output. Higher oil prices also caused a worsening in the balance of payments of the western industrialized economies. The attempts of these countries to reduce these deficits by deflating their economies added to the contractionary effects on incomes and output of the rise in oil prices. In particular, deflation in the 'stronger' OECD countries (e.g. West Germany and Japan), who enjoyed relatively healthy non-oil payments balances, made adjustment more difficult for the 'weaker' OECD countries (e.g. the United States and United Kingdom).

Neither Table 2.1 nor Table 2.2 fully illustrates the extent of the slowdown in world output which occurred between 1974 to 1975. For the first time since the war a number of developed market economies experienced an actual fall in their real GDP. However, in 1975–6, growth was resumed. From 1975 to 1979, the DMEs continued to grow albeit at a somewhat slower rate than in the previous decade. One reason was a rise in output in the oil-exporting countries. The rise in the price of oil redistributed income from oil-importing to oil-exporting countries. However, the rise in real incomes in the oil-exporting countries did not result in a rise in aggregate demand in these countries sufficient to match the drop in aggregate demand in the oil-importing countries. A number of the major oil-exporting states used their increased revenues to finance the purchase of more physical and financial assets in the western industrialized countries. Although this did serve to bring about a recycling of oil revenues, thus enabling the western industrialized countries to finance their current account deficits, it did not directly add to the world demand for goods and services.

However, the recycling of oil revenues did enable developed and developing countries alike to maintain aggregate demand to a greater extent than might otherwise have been possible. In particular, output in the US economy grew quickly over the period up to 1978. Between 1975 and 1978 the US economy was expanding faster than in earlier decades. This was an important factor in the world's relatively quick recovery from the effects of the first oil crisis. Because of the size of the US market, rising incomes in the United States created additional demand for the exports of other industrialized and industrializing countries. However, growth rates in the other DMEs, notably the West European economies, were disappointing, being well below the rates of the 1960s.

Over the period from 1975 to 1978 the real price of oil stabilized. First, slower growth in the western industrialized countries caused a slower growth in the demand for oil. Second, the rise in the oil price caused countries to substitute other sources of energy for oil. Third, the economies of the oil-importing countries began to adjust to higher oil prices. Resources shifted out of the less profitable, energy-intensive industries and into the more profitable, less energy-intensive industries. All of these factors caused a fall in the world's demand for oil. Between 1976 and 1981, while the GDP of the OECD countries rose by 14 per cent, oil consumption fell by 9 per cent (Stewart 1983). Japan, who was more dependent on imported oil to meet her domestic energy requirements than other industrialized countries, was the most successful in achieving this adjustment. Oil consumption in Japan fell by 10 per cent over the same period. Finally, the higher price of oil acted as an incentive for oil companies to invest in exploring and opening up new, higher-cost, marginal oil-fields in other parts of the world. One result of this was a decrease in the proportion of world production controlled by OPEC.

However, in 1979 the OPEC countries were enabled to bring about a second large rise in world oil prices. The revolution in Iran threatened an interruption in world oil supplies. Fear of another shortage of oil caused oil consumers to increase their stocks of oil. This stockpiling of oil supplies combined with some drop in supply enabled the OPEC countries to enforce a new higher price. The effects were similar to the oil price rise of 1973–4. Real incomes were reduced in the oil-importing countries. Aggregate demand and hence output fell. Between 1979 and 1981, real GDP grew at a rate of only 1.5 per cent a year. In 1981–2 it fell. The United Kingdom experienced an especially large fall in GDP between 1979 and 1981. Japan was the only leading DME to maintain a reasonable growth rate during this period. As we shall see in Chapter 6, this was achieved through export expansion. Fast export growth offset the effect on the domestic economy of higher oil prices.

Recovery from the second oil-induced recession was slower. One reason was the adoption of tight monetary policies in a number of OECD countries, including the United States and the United Kingdom. These were a direct response to high and rising rates of inflation. They resulted in extremely high levels of real interest rates. These had a dampening effect on aggregate demand not only in the United States but the entire western industrialized world. A second reason was the inability of balance-of-payments-constrained countries to finance their oil-induced deficits by borrowing. A number of countries, mainly developing and East European ones, had borrowed so extensively in the wake of the first oil crisis that they were unable to repay or service their foreign debts. The rise in world interest rates enormously added to their difficulties. At the same time, western banks were reluctant to increase their exposure by lending more to countries with large outstanding debts.

However, the pursuit of tight monetary policies in the OECD countries did prove successful in reducing inflation. A large drop in world commodity prices played a central role in bringing this about. In addition, there occurred a big fall in world oil prices. This began in 1982 and continued through into 1986. By 1987 the price of a barrel of oil had fallen to $18, or one half the price of 1981. The drop in the real price of oil was even greater. Once again, slower economic growth in the western industrialized countries caused oil consumption to moderate. Destocking by oil consumers also played an important role. The attempts of OPEC to hold prices up by cutting production were unsuccessful. One reason was the growth of non-OPEC sources of oil production. If the OPEC countries cut their output, non-OPEC countries merely increased their share of the world market. This made some OPEC members reluctant to agree to production limits.

All of these factors have led to faster growth in the western industrialized countries in recent years. However, rates of growth remain disappointingly low. Only in the United States, spurred by a large budget deficit, has growth been sufficient to permit a significant fall in the rate of unemployment. Falling oil prices have failed to work in the same way in reverse as did rising oil prices in the 1970s. First, falling oil prices have caused a very large fall in aggregate demand in some oil-exporting countries. Second, falling oil prices have not been fully passed on to the consumers of the oil-importing countries in the form of lower prices. Hence, there has been little extra aggregate demand generated within the western industrialized economies. In addition, consumers in the western industrialized countries have chosen to save rather than spend any extra income received. Finally, the drop in world oil prices has hit certain parts of the economy of western industrialized countries, such as the oil-producing states of the United States. It remains to be seen whether in the coming years the developed countries will be able to return to the growth rates of the earlier post-war decades.

Tables 2.1 and 2.2 (pp. 39–40) show that during the 1960s the *developing countries* achieved a faster rate of GDP growth than the developed countries. They grew at a rate of 5.9 per cent a year compared with 4.8 per cent a year for the DMEs. However, because they also experienced rapid population growth, GDP per capita increased by only 3.2 per cent a year compared with 3.6 per cent a year for the DMEs. This was disappointing given that the GDP and GDP per head of developing countries (shown in the last columns of Tables 2.1 and 2.2) were well below that of the developed countries. The GDP per capita of developing countries in 1982 was barely one-tenth of that of DMEs. Thus developing countries need to grow at a faster rate than developed countries merely to prevent a widening in the gap in per capita incomes. Moreover, developing countries group together a large number of diverse countries. At one end of the spectrum are the very poor, least developed countries. As can be seen from Table 2.2, these countries managed a growth in per capita GDP of just over 1 per cent a year. Thus the gap between these countries and other developing countries was widening.

The rise in world oil prices plus the rise in other primary commodity prices had a beneficial effect on economic growth in certain developing countries in the mid-1970s. On the other hand, the non-oil producing developing countries were damaged by the rise in oil prices. A number of developing countries were able to ride out the first oil crisis by borrowing from western banks awash with funds deposited by the oil exporters. This explains why the developing countries were able to maintain reasonably fast growth in the early 1970s at a time when the developed countries were experiencing a slowdown. In particular, the major exporters of manufactures among the developing countries grew at a faster rate than in the 1960s. As we shall see in Chapter 6, they did so by specializing in the export of relatively cheap, labour-intensive manufactures to the advanced industrialized countries. These countries have come to be known as the 'newly-industrializing countries', or NICs. In the period between 1970 to 1975 these countries grew at a rate of 7.3 per cent per annum faster than any other group of developing countries and more than twice the rate of the DMEs.

However, the developing countries were more severely hit by the second oil crisis. As we have already seen, these countries were unable to increase their borrowing from western banks to finance their balance-of-payments deficits. Western banks became increasingly unwilling to lend additional funds to countries unable to repay their existing debts. At the same time, the sharp rise in world interest rates made it increasingly difficult for many of these countries to meet the interest charges on their outstanding debt. The only way which they could meet their debt repayments and debt service charges was by sacrificing domestic growth. Finally, the dramatic fall in primary commodity prices since the mid-1970s hit the export earnings of a number of developing countries and reduced economic growth.

Finally, Tables 2.1 and 2.2 show the growth of output in the *Socialist countries* of Eastern Europe. In the decade from 1960 to 1970, GDP grew at a rate of 6.7 per cent per annum, which was good in comparison with the developing countries of the non-socialist world. The growth in GDP per capita of 5.5 per cent a year was equally impressive. Along with the rest of the world, these countries experienced slower growth in the 1970s. They were also affected by the second oil crisis of the 1980s. It is noticeable that growth was beginning to fade as early as the mid-1970s.

THE COMMODITY COMPOSITION OF WORLD OUTPUT

Table 2.3 shows the main changes which have taken place in the sectoral composition of GDP over the post-war period. In the developed market economies, the most important change has

Table 2.3: Sectoral composition of GDP, selected years (%)

Grouping[a]	Agriculture			Mining			Manufacturing			Services[b]			Others[c]		
	1960	1970	1978	1960	1970	1978	1960	1970	1978	1960	1970	1978	1960	1970	1978
Developing countries by income group:[d]															
Low (28)	51.5	43.3	39.6	2.6	3.0	3.4	5.7	8.6	9.9	35.5	39.2	40.9	4.7	5.9	6.2
Lower middle (23)	39.2	32.9	31.5	5.0	6.7	5.4	9.9	11.9	12.9	39.9	42.8	43.7	6.0	5.8	6.5
Intermediate (20)	30.2	25.0	22.0	3.5	4.4	6.6	13.4	16.0	16.6	46.7	48.1	47.4	6.2	6.5	7.4
Upper middle (10)	17.3	12.5	10.0	7.8	7.5	10.5	15.6	17.9	18.5	51.5	54.1	52.6	7.8	7.9	8.4
High (8)	13.4	7.5	5.5	7.6	15.5	18.6	14.2	15.5	16.4	56.7	52.5	49.7	8.0	9.0	9.8
All countries by size and resource endowment[e]															
Large countries (27)	28.2	22.8	20.0	3.5	3.7	4.7	19.4	20.8	20.6	43.0	45.5	47.0	5.8	7.2	7.8
Small countries with modest resources (52)	41.4	34.2	31.3	2.1	2.8	3.6	8.9	11.4	12.4	41.8	45.0	45.8	5.7	6.6	6.9
Small countries with ample resources (32)	18.6	13.6	12.6	7.6	10.0	10.7	17.4	19.0	18.0	47.7	48.5	49.2	8.7	8.9	9.5
OPEC countries (9)	29.7	22.1	12.7	12.2	21.4	30.4	8.8	10.2	9.6	42.5	39.8	36.6	6.8	6.5	10.6
Developing countries Total (89)	36.3	29.8	27.2	4.4	5.9	6.8	10.3	12.8	13.7	42.9	45.0	45.2	6.0	6.5	7.1
Developed market economies, total (22)	12.3	7.7	6.5	2.3	1.7	2.3	28.6	28.8	25.8	47.8	51.5	55.3	9.1	10.2	10.2

Source: UNIDO (1982)

[a] The figure in parentheses is the number of countries in the grouping.
[b] Including wholesale and retail trade, transport and communication, financing, insurance and real estate, community, social and personal services.
[c] Including construction, electricity, gas and water.
[d] Developing countries were grouped according to the following levels of per capita GNP in 1975: <$265; $265–$520: $521–$1075; $1076–$2000; >$2000. Where GNP was not available, GDP was used.
[e] The demarcation between large and small countries was a population of 20 million in 1970.

been the growth of the services sector. The share of services in GDP rose from 47.8 per cent in 1960 to 55.3 per cent in 1978. The growth of services took place at the expense of agriculture and manufacturing. The agricultural sector shrank from 12.3 per cent of GDP in 1960 to 6.5 per cent in 1978. The share of the manufacturing sector was roughly constant up to 1970 but declined from 1970 to 1978. It is this decline of manufacturing in the developed countries which has led to talk about 'de-industrialization' and the growth of the 'service economy'.

In the developing countries also, the services sector has increased in importance, but not as dramatically as in the developed countries. The services sector is smaller than in developed countries, which is consistent with the view that the demand for services is income-elastic and so increases with per capita income. However, there is not a perfect relationship between the share of services in GDP and the level of a country's per capita income. Thus the share of services in GDP is lower in high-income developing countries than in upper-middle-income developing countries. The growth in the services sector in developing countries has been largely at the expense of agriculture. This fell from 36.3 per cent of GDP in 1960 to 27.2 per cent in 1978. At the same time, the manufacturing sector increased in importance from 10.3 per cent in 1960 to 13.7 per cent in 1978. The growth in manufacturing was a trend which was common to all developing countries. In the OPEC countries, however, manufacturing declined in importance after 1970. This was entirely due to the increased importance of mining, including oil production. Finally, we note that country size appears to have no influence on the relative importance of agriculture in GDP. On the other hand, it does appear to affect the size of the manufacturing sector. Degree of resource endowment is clearly a major factor affecting the size of the mining sector in GDP.

The growth of the manufacturing sector in developing countries has enabled developing countries to increase their share of world manufacturing production. This is illustrated in Figure 2.1. In 1960 developed market economies accounted for 78 per cent of world manufacturing value-added, developing countries for 14 per cent and centrally planned economies for 8 per cent. By 1981 the share of the DMEs had fallen to 64.7 per cent and that of the developing countries and centrally planned economies had risen to, respectively, 24.9 per cent and 10.3 per

Figure 2.1 Share of economic groupings in world manufacturing value added at constant prices, 1960–81

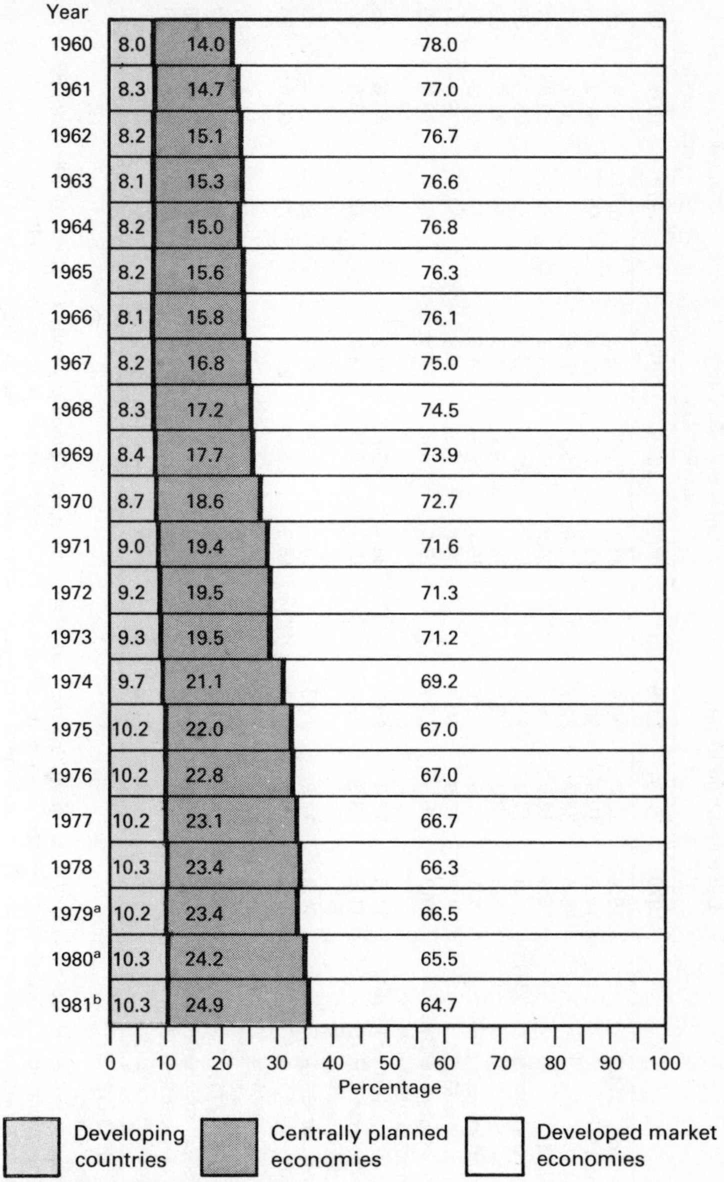

Year	Developing countries	Centrally planned economies	Developed market economies
1960	8.0	14.0	78.0
1961	8.3	14.7	77.0
1962	8.2	15.1	76.7
1963	8.1	15.3	76.6
1964	8.2	15.0	76.8
1965	8.2	15.6	76.3
1966	8.1	15.8	76.1
1967	8.2	16.8	75.0
1968	8.3	17.2	74.5
1969	8.4	17.7	73.9
1970	8.7	18.6	72.7
1971	9.0	19.4	71.6
1972	9.2	19.5	71.3
1973	9.3	19.5	71.2
1974	9.7	21.1	69.2
1975	10.2	22.0	67.0
1976	10.2	22.8	67.0
1977	10.2	23.1	66.7
1978	10.3	23.4	66.3
1979[a]	10.2	23.4	66.5
1980[a]	10.3	24.2	65.5
1981[b]	10.3	24.9	64.7

Percentage: 0 10 20 30 40 50 60 70 80 90 100

Source: UNIDO (1982).
Note: Percentages may not add exactly to 100 because of rounding.
[a] Preliminary figures.   [b] Estimates.

Table 2.4: Distribution of value added at constant prices, by economic grouping,[a] selected industrial branches, selected years (%)

Branch[b,c]	Developing countries			Centrally planned economies			Developed market economies		
	1970	1975	1979	1970	1975	1979	1970	1975	1979
Food products (311/2)	15.2	15.2	15.8	23.7	25.9	25.3	61.1	58.9	58.9
Beverages (313)	14.2	15.8	19.2	20.3	22.0	21.4	65.5	62.2	59.3
Tobacco (314)	28.8	30.7	32.7	13.8	15.2	15.5	57.4	54.1	51.9
Textiles (321)	16.8	18.5	18.6	24.8	29.0	29.6	58.5	52.6	51.8
Wood and cork products (331)	9.8	10.8	11.5	17.5	21.1	19.6	72.7	68.1	68.9
Paper (341)	6.6	8.0	8.5	6.9	9.1	8.0	86.5	82.9	83.5
Industrial chemicals (351)	6.1	7.6	7.6	20.7	26.5	24.8	73.2	65.8	67.6
Other chemicals (352)	14.3	17.6	18.4	5.8	7.4	6.8	80.0	75.0	74.8
Petroleum refineries (353)	37.3	35.8	34.7	10.6	15.3	16.3	52.1	49.0	49.0
Miscellaneous products of petroleum and coal (354)	11.3	13.9	16.0	38.1	40.5	40.2	50.6	45.6	43.8
Rubber products (355)	11.5	13.3	13.6	15.7	20.2	19.9	72.8	66.5	66.5
Pottery, china and earthenware (361)	11.8	12.9	12.8	26.6	34.7	37.3	61.6	52.4	49.8
Glass (362)	8.1	10.2	10.1	18.2	24.2	25.3	73.8	65.6	64.6
Other non-metallic mineral products (369)	8.2	10.2	11.7	28.6	33.7	31.1	63.3	56.1	57.2
Iron and steel (371)	6.2	8.2	9.4	18.9	23.2	22.8	74.8	68.5	67.7
Non-electrical machinery (382)	2.7	4.6	4.7	16.4	22.5	24.7	80.9	72.9	70.6
Transport equipment (384)	5.2	7.2	7.0	16.1	22.0	24.2	78.8	70.7	68.8
Total manufacturing (300)	8.7	10.2	10.2	18.6	22.8	23.4	72.7	67.0	66.5

Source UNIDO (1982)

[a] Excluding China.

[b] As defined in *International Standard Industrial Classification of All Economic Activities* (United Nations publication, Sales No. 68 XVII.8). The descriptive titles are abbreviated to save space and the ISIC Code number is given in parentheses.

[c] Country coverage of the baic data was not sufficient in some manufacturing industries to allow share of net output to be shown for all 28 industrial branches.

cent. Thus at the same time as the developed countries have been experiencing a shift of resources towards services, developing countries have succeeded in increasing their share of world manufacturing output. It seems probable that some of the increase in manufacturing output of the developing countries has been at the expense of the developed countries.

Table 2.4 shows the industries in which this geographical shift of manufacturing production has been taking place. In all the industrial branches shown, the DMEs experienced a drop in their share of manufacturing value-added. The developing countries and centrally planned economies increased their shares. Over the period in question, the biggest falls in DMEs' shares occurred in pottery, china and earthenware, non-electrical machinery, and transport equipment. Glass, iron and steel, beverages, miscellaneous products of petroleum and coal, textiles, and rubber all experienced quite large reductions in the DMEs' share. These products tend to consist of relatively simple, quite labour-intensive, light manufactures. These are the kind of manufactures in which developing countries enjoy a comparative advantage. In Chapter 6 we shall examine in greater depth the rise of the newly-industrializing countries which account for the bulk of the increase in manufacturing output in the developing world.

Finally, in Figure 2.2 the course of world commodity output over the period since 1950 is set out. It can be seen that the fastest growth in world commodity output occurred in manufacturing. Growth was exceptionally rapid between 1958 and 1974. Downturns in manufacturing occurred in 1954, 1958, 1975, and 1982 with the last two recessions being more severe than the previous ones. Over the course of the 1950s and 1960s, mining output grew faster than agricultural output but slower than manufacturing. However, since 1970, mining output has grown more slowly than agriculture. Output fell sharply in 1975 and again in 1980. Indeed, since 1980, mining output has been in a depressed state, falling back to the level of 1976.

THE GROWTH OF WORLD TRADE

Figure 2.3 depicts the growth in world trade since 1950. The chart shows the growth of world merchandise exports in volume terms. Over the period since 1950, world merchandise exports

51

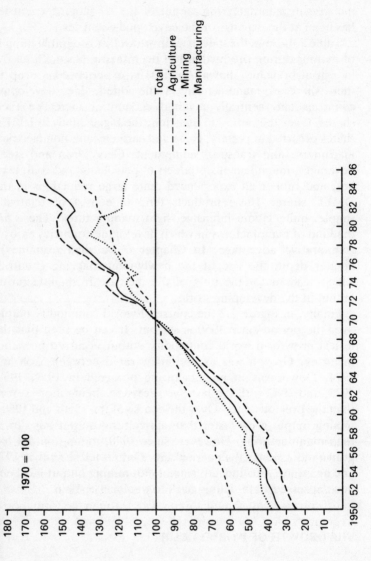

Figure 2.2 Growth in the volume of world commodity output, 1950–85. Source: GATT (1987)

have increased roughly ninefold in volume terms. This compares with an increase in the volume of world commodity output of roughly fivefold. Thus world trade has grown nearly twice as fast as world output. However, since 1970, world trade has grown only slightly faster than world output. This slowing down of the growth of world trade relative to the growth of world output may have been one of the factors contributing to the world economic slowdown of the last two decades.

Figure 2.3 shows that world trade grew consistently over the post-war period with a fall in the volume of world trade occurring in only three years — 1958, 1975, and 1982. The most dynamic element in world trade has been trade in manufactures. Over the period since 1950, trade in manufactures has risen more than sixteenfold. This compares with a growth in world manufacturing output of roughly sevenfold. Thus trade in manufactures has increased by well over twice as fast as manufacturing output. It follows that the increase of world trade in manufactured goods has been the primary cause of the fast growth of world trade as a whole. The growth in trade has, in turn, played a major role in stimulating world output. The kind of economic growth enjoyed by the developed market economies after 1945 may be described as having been trade-led growth. In this process, trade in manufactures has played the leading role.

This growth of trade in manufactures was made possible by the gradual lowering of tariffs on trade in manufactured goods and the removal of other quantitative restrictions in the quarter-century since the ending of the war. This was achieved through the establishment of the GATT in 1947 and the various GATT tariff-cutting 'rounds' in subsequent years. The gradual admission of most of the world's leading trading nations to GATT meant that these countries agreed to refrain from certain kinds of trading practices. This gave an increased certainty to companies involved in international trade and investment and further served to stimulate trade. Even greater progress was made in eliminating tariffs on trade in manufactured goods through the formation of regional trading blocs such as the EC (1958) and EFTA (1960). Both of the latter gave a considerable boost to intra-European trade in manufactured goods without leading to trade-diversion. Although they did involve granting preference to other West European suppliers, they also resulted in a lowering of the tariff applied by Western Europe to imports from outside Europe.

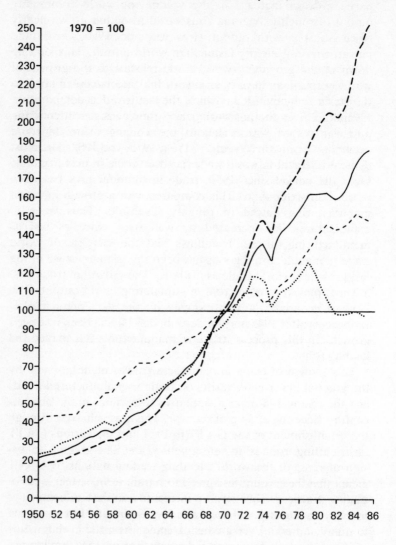

Figure 2.3 Growth of world merchandise exports, 1950–86

1970 = 100

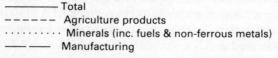

——————— Total
– – – – – Agriculture products
· · · · · · · · · · Minerals (inc. fuels & non-ferrous metals)
—— —— Manufacturing

Source: GATT (1987).

This liberalization of world trade helped encourage more international specialization in manufacturing. Much of this took place between the western industrialized countries. Trade in manufactured goods between western industrialized countries proved to be the fastest growing element in world trade. It involved a much narrower kind of specialization than in the past. Whereas in the past, countries had specialized in specific industries or activities in which they enjoyed a comparative advantage, over the post-war period there was a tendency for countries to specialize in narrow product ranges within specific industries. The former is referred to as inter-industry specialization and the latter as intra-industry specialization. At the beginning of the post-war period the scope for more inter-industry specialization, at least between the western industrialized countries, was probably quite limited. On the other hand, in many of the new, fast-growing, technologically more-advanced sectors of manufacturing, there was still considerable scope for intra-industry specialization. Such increased intra-industry specialization played the main role in the growth of trade in manufactured goods.

Trade in other commodities grew at a slower rate than trade in manufactures. Since 1950 world exports of minerals have increased by 4.3 times and of agricultural products by 3.6 times. Over the same period, the growth in world output was fivefold. Thus trade in minerals has grown at roughly the same rate as world output. Until 1973 trade in minerals grew at roughly the same rate as world manufacturing output. However, since 1973 various factors have worked to depress trade in minerals. In particular, the western industrialized countries have sought to reduce the amount of energy consumed per unit of manufacturing output in response to the rise in fuel prices. In addition, there has occurred a fall in the quantity of metals used in manufacturing production in the industrialized world. New manufactured materials have tended to displace natural materials in many industries. As a result trade in minerals has been falling. However, for most of the post-war period, the volume of trade in minerals was determined by the volume of manufacturing output. The latter was governed by the level of output of the industrialized countries.

Trade in agricultural products grew more slowly than world output. This is consistent with the fact that the demand for food is income-inelastic. The demand for food has not grown as fast as the increase in world per capita incomes. In fact, trade in agricultural products has grown only slightly faster than world agricultural output. Thus there has been little increase in the degree of specialization in agriculture over the post-war period. Trade in agricultural products was largely exempt from the process of trade liberalization conducted through GATT. Many of the GATT rules enshrined in the GATT Charter were not applied to trade in agricultural goods. Instead, most of the advanced industrialized countries have adopted policies which have increased the degree of protection afforded to agriculture. Such policies have been designed to increase the self-sufficiency of industrialized countries in food production.

Thus the single, most dynamic factor in the growth of world trade over the post-war period has been increased specialization in manufacturing products. Trade in primary commodities (food and raw materials) has tended to follow output, whereas trade in manufactured goods has led output. In recent decades, however, trade in manufactures has not grown as fast. This is illustrated by Table 2.5. In the 1960s, exports of manufactured products grew at a rate of 10.5 per cent a year. In the next decade, growth dropped to only 7.5 per cent a year. From 1980 to 1983, manufactures grew at a mere 2 per cent a year. In 1984 there took place an upturn and manufacturing exports grew by 12 per cent. However, in the following year, growth fell back to a disappointing 6 per cent. This loss of vitality in what has been the major growth factor of the post-war era has undoubtedly been a major cause of the slower growth of world output.

Table 2.5: Growth of world merchandise trade and production, 1960 to 1985
Average annual percentage change in volume

	1960–9	1970–9	1980–3	1984	1985
PRODUCTION					
All merchandise	6.0	4.0	0.0	5.5	2.0
Agriculture	2.5	2.5	2.0	5.0	2.0
Mining	5.0	3.5	−3.5	0.0	−2.0
Manufacturing	7.5	4.5	1.0	7.0	4.0
EXPORTS					
All merchandise	8.5	5.5	0.5	9.0	3.0
Agriculture	4.0	3.0	1.5	4.0	−1.0
Mining	6.5	2.5	−5.5	2.0	−2.5
Manufacturing	10.5	7.5	2.0	12.0	6.0

Source: GATT (1986)

Trade in agricultural and mineral products also grew at a slower rate after 1970, with trade in mining products actually falling in the 1980s. However, as we have seen, trade in primary commodities has tended to follow world output. Thus the fall in the rate of growth of trade in these goods largely reflects the slower growth of world output. In the case of mining, other factors were at work causing trade to fall at a time when world output was stagnant. Of course, some of the drop in the rate of growth for manufactures reflected the slower growth of world output. However, the dominant feature of the post-war period has been that trade in manufactures has led rather than followed output. It follows that the future course of world output is heavily dependent upon a revival of trade in the manufacturing sector if the pattern of trade-led growth of the post-war period is to be maintained.

CHANGES IN THE COMMODITY COMPOSITION OF WORLD TRADE

The growth of world trade over the period since 1945 has brought major changes in the commodity composition of world trade. The latter refers to the share of world trade accounted for by different groups of products. Table 2.6 shows the main changes which have taken place. Changes in the share of world trade accounted for by any particular group of products may be due to either:

1. A faster (or slower) growth in the volume of trade taking place in the products in question relative to other products.
2. A faster (or slower) rise in the unit values (i.e. the prices) of the products in question relative to other products.
3. Both.

Thus the share of a particular product group may increase merely because the unit values (or prices) of the products within that group have risen relative to other products. It may be the case that the quantity of trade in this particular product group has risen more slowly than other product groups or even fallen, yet the share of the product group in world trade has risen entirely on account of a much faster rise in unit values. This is the case with fuels in Table 2.4. The rise in the share of fuels in world trade is entirely due to the increase in the world oil price in the 1970s and 1980s.

Table 2.6: The commodity composition of world trade, 1955 to 1985

	1955		1978		1985	
	$bn	%	$bn	%	$bn	%
PRIMARY PRODUCTS						
Food	20.42	21.9	162.60	12.5	199.20	10.4
Raw materials	12.13	13.0	52.05	4.0	65.70	3.4
Ores and minerals	3.44	3.7	24.50	1.9	33.80	1.8
Fuels	10.26	11.0	223.60	17.2	356.40	18.5
Non-ferrous metals	3.62	3.9	27.80	2.1	36.80	1.9
Total	49.87	53.5	490.60	37.7	691.90	36.0
MANUFACTURES						
Iron and steel	4.25	4.6	57.15	4.4	69.30	3.6
Chemicals	4.91	5.3	100.60	7.7	163.40	8.5
Other semi-manufactures	4.47	4.8	65.20	5.0	86.40	4.5
Engineering products:	19.59	21.0	439.05	33.7	682.00	35.5
Machinery specialized	6.43	6.9	117.45	9.0	150.60	7.8
Office and tele-communications	5.82	0.9	38.80	3.0	97.90	5.1
Road and motor vehicles	3.32	3.5	99.45	6.9	158.30	8.2
Other machinery and transport equipment	7.72	8.3	147.90	11.4	216.30	11.3
Household appliances	1.30	1.4	35.40	2.7	58.90	3.1
Textiles	4.72	5.1	40.70	3.1	55.40	2.9
Clothing	0.80	0.9	28.35	2.2	49.20	2.6
Other consumer goods	3.00	3.2	57.50	4.4	91.60	4.8
Total	41.73	44.7	788.50	60.5	1197.30	62.3
TOTAL EXPORTS	93.30	100.0	1303.00	100.0	1921.50	100.0

Source: GATT (1986)

Therefore, in analysing the main changes which have taken place in the composition of world trade, it is necessary to establish the main trends which have taken place in product prices over the post-war period. Figure 2.4 illustrates the course of primary commodity prices relative to manufactured goods prices over the period from 1948 to 1982. The price indices used were estimated by the World Bank using a sample of primary commodities which accounted for approximately 75 per cent of developing country exports. The values of developing country exports over the period from 1977 to 1979 were used as weights. It can be seen that over the period from 1948 to 1970 the price of petroleum was falling in relation to the prices of manufactured goods. In 1974, however, there occurred a dramatic rise in world oil prices. Prices slipped back somewhat from 1974 to 1978, before increasing sharply for a second time between 1979 and 1981.

The prices of other primary commodities have behaved somewhat more erratically, but the general trend has been for prices to fall relative to the prices of manufactured goods. There occurred a sharp rise in primary commodity prices from 1950 to 1952. Further minor upturns took place in 1954–6, 1959–60, 1964–6 (for metals and minerals) and 1968–9. Another large rise in prices occurred between 1973–4. Since 1974, prices have fallen fairly consistently, rallying slightly in 1979–80. By 1982, primary commodity prices had fallen to their lowest level relative to manufactured goods prices since 1948.

These trends in the prices of primary commodities relative to manufactured goods prices provide part of the explanation for the share changes shown in Table 2.6. In particular, they constitute one explanation for the overall fall in the share of primary commodities in world trade (although the share of fuels rose) and the rise in the share of manufactured goods. However, other factors were also at work. These are different for each product group. In order to discuss these factors, it is convenient to divide products into five broad categories: food, raw materials, fuels, ores and minerals and non-ferrous metals, and manufactures.

Food

The share of food in world trade fell from 21.9 per cent in 1955 to 12.5 per cent in 1978 and to 10.4 per cent in 1985. This was due to both a declining trend in food prices relative to the prices of manufactured goods and a slower growth in the volume of trade in food products than for trade as a whole. The fall in food prices relative to the prices of manufactures is less pronounced than for other primary commodities. Nevertheless, a secular trend is discernible. The explanation lies in long-run world

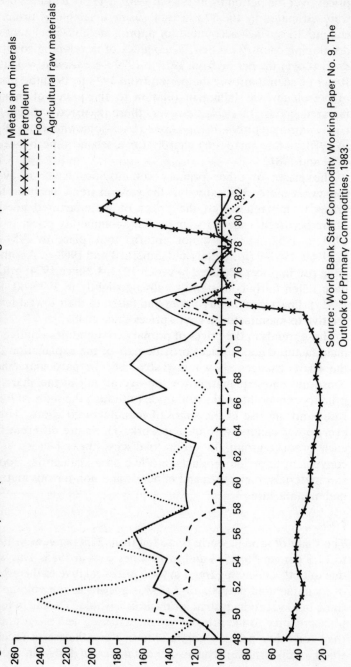

Figure 2.4 The prices of primary commodities relative to manufactured goods prices (1977–9 = 100)

——— Metals and minerals
×–×–×–× Petroleum
– – – Food
·········· Agricultural raw materials

Source: World Bank Staff Commodity Working Paper No. 9, The Outlook for Primary Commodities, 1983.

demand and supply trends. On the demand side, the demand for food is income-inelastic. This means that the demand for food does not rise proportionately with world per capita income. In the poorest countries of the world, people still spend large proportions of their income on food. However, in the richer countries, the proportion of income spent falls as per capita incomes rise. On the supply side, technological change has brought large increases in agricultural output over the post-war period. New farming methods, the application of scientific knowledge to farming, and larger, more efficient farm structures have all served to boost output. In addition, all the advanced industrialized countries have adopted policies to boost domestic food production and to increase their self-sufficiency in food. These policies have increased agricultural production within the developed market economies of the world and reduced these countries' demand for food from other parts of the world. These policies have involved both the subsidization of farming and the imposition of different kinds of restrictions on food imports. Prices of agricultural products have often been fixed at levels well above world prices and maintained by government support-buying. High artificial prices have encouraged over-production. The resultant surpluses have then been dumped on world markets exerting a depressing effect on world prices.

By 1985 the developed countries as a whole exported nearly as much food as they imported. On the other hand, food production has not been keeping up with food consumption in the developing countries taken as a whole. Although the developing countries are net exporters of food, over recent decades their food imports have been growing faster than their food exports. In addition, the eastern-bloc countries are unable to produce sufficient food to meet their requirements and are dependent on the rest of the world for imports. The failure of food production to grow fast enough to match consumption in both the developing countries taken as a whole and the eastern-bloc countries has acted as a counteracting factor to over-production of food in the developed countries. It has helped maintain food prices at a higher level than would otherwise be the case. On the other hand, it has not been a sufficiently powerful factor to prevent world food prices from falling relative to the prices of manufactured goods.

The share of food in world trade would have held up had the falling price been compensated for by a rapid growth in the volume of trade in food products. However, as was observed earlier, world exports of agricultural products have grown at a slower rate than world trade as a whole. Between 1950 and 1985, world exports of agricultural products increased by 3.6 times in volume terms. During the same period, world merchandise exports of all commodities increased roughly ninefold in volume terms. This contributed to the declining share of food products in world trade. As we have seen, the reasons for this trend lie largely in the low-income elasticity of demand for food. Rising world per capita income leads to a less-than-proportionate increase in the demand for food. In addition, the western industrialized countries have been unwilling to allow free trade in agricultural products. Instead, they have adopted highly protectionist policies towards agriculture. As we observed earlier, agricultural trade was largely exempt from the process of trade liberalization brought about through the GATT over the post-war period. As a result, there did not occur the same increase in the degree of international specialization in agriculture as took place in manufactured goods.

It remains to be seen whether or not the coming decades will bring any change in these policies. At the time of writing, agricultural trade is being discussed as part of the eighth Uruguay Round of GATT tariff negotiations. The possibility exists that some agreement will be reached to moderate the scale of subsidies granted by governments in the industrialized countries to agriculture. If this leads to less surplus production and less 'dumping' of food surpluses, food prices could harden to the benefit of agricultural exporting countries. On the other hand, it seems unlikely that the industrialized countries will dismantle the complex machinery of protection which they have erected to protect their farming industries. For these reasons, it seems likely that agricultural prices will remain depressed. This, combined with slow growth in the volume of trade in agricultural products, is likely to lead to a continuation of the decline in the share of food in world trade. The only likely factors that could prevent such an outcome would be an increased food deficit in the eastern-bloc countries and the failure of food production to grow fast enough in the developing countries to match population growth. Both of these two factors depend heavily on the kind of policies adopted by governments in these countries towards their agricultural sectors.

Raw Materials

Raw materials include a wide variety of products extracted from the earth before being subjected to the manufacturing process for conversion into finished products. They include products such as rubber, natural fibres, hides and skins, wood, lumber and cork, and pulp and paper. Some of these products may be regarded as part of the output of the agricultural sector but it is often convenient to treat them separately from food. Ores and metals might also be included in this category. However, in Table 2.6 they are listed separately and so we shall examine them apart. The share of raw materials in world trade has fallen from 13 per cent in 1955 to 4 per cent in 1978 and 3.4 per cent in 1985. As with food products, this trend is the result of both a downward trend in raw material prices relative to manufactured goods prices and slow growth in the volume of trade in raw materials. Figure 2.4 shows that agricultural raw material prices have fallen more decisively in relation to manufactured goods prices than other primary commodity prices. However, it is apparent that the prices of raw materials are much more volatile than food prices. Sharp upward and downward movements are apparent. Thus prices peaked in 1950–1, 1954–5, 1959–60, 1968–69, 1973, 1976 and 1979–80. Each of these peaks coincided with an upturn in the level of economic activity in the industrialized countries. The troughs which followed coincided with recessions or periods of slacker activity in the industrialized countries.

Raw material prices are highly sensitive to fluctuations in the demand for raw materials. This is because the supply of raw materials is highly inelastic in the short run. The output of most raw materials cannot be instantly increased in response to a rise in demand. For example, the supply of rubber can only be increased at some time in the future as rubber producers in Malaysia plant more rubber trees. With the supply of such raw materials being relatively inelastic, the effect of a rise in demand is to force up the price. Supply responds with a time-lag to changes in price such that, in later years, an increase in supply has the effect of forcing down the price. In other words, raw material prices would appear to be subject to a cobweb cycle with price fluctuating a great deal from one period to the next.

Large fluctuations in raw material prices mean that the share of raw materials in world trade is highly variable. Nevertheless, the clear long-run trend has been for raw material prices to fall and hence for the share of raw materials in world trade to decline. At the same time, as we saw earlier, the volume of trade in raw materials has grown at a rate no faster than the growth of world trade as a whole. Although trade in raw materials is relatively free, trade in raw materials cannot grow faster than the output of the industrialized countries. Moreover, the post-war period has witnessed a tendency for manufacturing industry to substitute synthetic products for natural materials, which has had a dampening effect on the demand for raw materials. For example, synthetic fibres (rayon, nylon, etc.) have been substituted for natural fibres (cotton, wool, etc.), and synthetic rubber has replaced natural rubber. This has meant that the demand for raw materials has tended to grow at a slower rate than industrial output. Although a revival in economic activity in the industrialized countries will lead to some rise in raw material prices in the future, the share of raw materials in world trade looks certain to remain quite small. Only a sudden, very large scarcity of raw materials leading to an equally sharp rise in prices seems likely to alter this situation.

Ores and Minerals and Non-ferrous Metals

The share of ores and minerals in world trade fell from 3.7 per cent in 1955 to 1.9 per cent in 1978 and 1.8 per cent in 1985. The share of non-ferrous metals also fell from 3.9 per cent in 1955 to 2.1 per cent in 1978 and 1.9 per cent in 1985. As with raw materials, this is due both to a fall in the relative prices of these products and slow growth in the volume of trade in such products. However, the prices of metals and minerals have not fallen by as much as agricultural raw material prices. Indeed, until 1970 some tendency for metal and mineral prices to rise in relation to the prices of manufactured goods could be discerned. It is really only in the decade since 1970 that the prices of these products have fallen noticeably.

As with agricultural raw materials, metal and mineral prices are highly volatile. Prices peaked in roughly the same years as did agricultural raw material prices. The early 1960s were one exception. Metal and mineral prices remained relatively flat between 1959 and 1960, when agricultural raw material prices rose. Between 1964 and 1966 metal and mineral prices rose sharply while agricultural raw material prices fell. In general, however, metal and mineral prices are affected by similar considerations to those affecting agricultural raw material prices. Supply is relatively inelastic in the short run so that fluctuations in demand cause relatively large fluctuations in price.

As with agricultural raw materials, the volume of trade in such products is governed by the level of economic activity in the industrialized countries. Trade follows output. However, in recent decades, the industrialized countries have reduced the amount of metal consumed per unit of manufacturing output. New technology has made it possible to produce the same output with less metal. In particular, there has been a tendency to substitute other materials for metals. One example of this is the substitution of fibre optics for copper wires in the tele-communications industry. Increasingly, new composite materials, which are often cheaper than mined metals, have taken the place of traditional metals. Thus the demand for metals has been depressed. This has caused a slump in the volume of trade in such products. As is shown in Table 2.5, trade in mining products fell by 5.5 per cent between 1980 and 1983. Metal prices have also taken a hammering. Since 1974, the prices of metals and minerals have fallen by more than one-third relative to the prices of manufactured goods. A contributory factor has been overinvestment in mining. The rise in metal prices between 1973 and 1974 encouraged mining companies to invest in new capacity. However, declining demand for metals in the decade since resulted in much of this capacity being unused. As a result, metal prices have tumbled. It is possible that the next decade will see some hardening of metal prices as industrial output in the world economy picks up. On the other hand, technological trends are such that the demand for metals is likely to remain modest. It follows that the share of these products in world trade is likely to remain low.

Fuels

Fuels are the only category of primary commodities whose share in world trade increased over the post-war period. It rose from 11 per cent in 1955 to 17.2 per cent in 1978 and 18.5 per cent in 1985. As we have already stated, this is due entirely to the rise in world oil prices which took place after 1973. Although 'fuels' consists of a variety of different products (gas, electricity, coal, as well as oil), oil has been the most important element in world trade over the post-war period. In the two and a half decades before the oil crisis, the real price of oil was relatively stable, falling somewhat relative to the prices of manufactured goods. It was these low prices which encouraged the western industrialized countries to increase their dependence on oil to meet their energy requirements. As far as Western Europe and Japan were concerned, most of this oil had to be imported from the Middle East. The low prices of the 1950s and 1960s ensured that it was economic to do so. By way of contrast, the United States was a major oil producer in her own right, although the costs of extracting oil were higher in the United States than in the Middle East.

As we know, the situation changed dramatically in the early 1970s. The background to the oil crisis includes the formation of OPEC in 1960. The original purpose of OPEC was to enable the oil-producing countries to get a better price for their oil and to reduce the share of the price taken by the western, multinational oil companies. In fact, OPEC developed into a fully fledged oil-producers' cartel. Controlling as they did well over one-half of the world output of petroleum, the OPEC countries were able to impose a higher price on the oil-consuming industrialized countries by restricting supply. However, as was stated earlier, they were only able to do this because of changed conditions in the world oil market. Specifically, oil consumption had risen at a faster rate than oil production encouraged by an artificially low oil price. World demand for oil had been further boosted by the transformation of the United States into a net importer of oil. The United States was no longer able to meet all her energy requirement from domestically produced oil. In 1973 the posted price of a barrel of Saudi Arabian crude oil rose from $3.30 to $11.59, or roughly fourfold (Moore 1985).

As we have already seen, the higher oil price was much more than was needed to restore balance between world demand and supply and set in motion adjustments within the industrialized countries which a decade later brought about a large fall in oil prices. The industrialized countries cut their dependence on oil. In the ensuing decades the oil consumption of the industrialized countries fell. Slower growth of industrial output in the developed countries further acted to reduce the world demand for oil. The OPEC countries sought to counteract this tendency by further raising their prices. For a short while, between 1979 and 1982, they were able to do so. The outbreak of the revolution in Iran created fears of another world oil shortage and prompted large-scale stockpiling of oil. The posted price of a barrel of Saudi Arabian crude oil rose further to $34.41 in 1981. This was roughly seven times the 1970 price measured in real terms (Moore 1985).

However, the ability of the OPEC countries to enforce such a price was limited because of a decline in the proportion of world oil production which they were able to control. The higher price had made it profitable for the oil companies to invest in the exploration and development of higher-cost oil-fields in other parts of the world. The United Kingdom and Norway had both emerged as major producers of oil following the discovery of North Sea oil. At the same time, large-scale destocking of oil further depressed the demand for oil. Divisions opened up within OPEC. Some of the poorer OPEC countries became increasingly less willing to accept production limits. Beginning in 1985, the price of oil began to tumble.

It remains to be seen whether or not oil prices will harden once again. It would seem, however, that a permanent change has taken place within the world oil market. The oil crisis of the 1970s has encouraged the industrialized countries to reduce their dependence on imported oil. At the same time, the OPEC countries now account for a much smaller share of world production than was once the case. This means that they are much less able to enforce a higher price by restricting supply. The industrialized countries have also invested in much larger oil reserves and are therefore better able to cope with any interruption of oil supplies caused by developments outside their control. Accordingly, it would seem unlikely that the share of world trade accounted for by fuels in 1985 will prevail in the long run. Certainly, the volume of trade in fuels can be expected to grow no faster than world output and therefore more slowly than world trade as a whole. Only another sharp rise in oil prices relative to the prices of other goods could cause an increase in the share of world trade taken by fuels.

Manufactures

The share of manufactures in world trade has increased from 44.7 per cent in 1955 to 60.5 per cent in 1978 and to 62.3 per cent in 1985. This is principally due to the much faster growth of manufacturing trade than trade in other products. At the same time, manufacturing goods prices have risen slightly in terms of non-fuel primary commodities. As we have already seen, this growth of trade in manufactures was the result of a growth of specialization in manufacturing industry between the advanced industrialized economies. This has taken the form of intra-industry as opposed to inter-industry specialization and has represented both a narrower and more advanced level of specialization than in the past. This rapid growth of trade in manufactures has been the main dynamic behind the post-war growth of world trade. Faster growth of world trade has in turn made possible a rapid growth of world output. In recent decades, however, trade in manufactures has grown at a slower rate. This has contributed to the slowdown in the rate of economic growth in the industrialized countries.

Table 2.6 reveals that the share of both iron and steel manufactures and textiles fell, while that of all other manu-factures increased. Over much of the post-war period, trade in both these sectors has been more restricted. The western industrialized countries have been much less willing to allow freer trade in these products. Accordingly, scope for increased international specialization has been limited. However, as we shall see in Chapter 3, scope for intra-industry specialization may be more limited in these traditional branches of manu-facturing. Consequently, trade in such products could not grow as fast as trade in other kinds of manufactures. It is also noteworthy that these industries were slower-growing industries within the industrialized economies. The output of these in-dustries grew at a slower rate than that of other manufacturing industries. The main reason for this has been the low income elasticity of demand for such products. The demand for these products grows more slowly than average industrial output once countries have reached the stage of maturity in their industrial development.

Intra-industry specialization has been more prevalent in the other branches of manufactures leading to a fast rate of growth of trade in these products. As we shall see in the next chapter, intra-industry specialization has been highest in the chemicals and engineering industries. In these industries world trade has grown fastest. These industries have experienced big increases in their share of world trade. Thus the share of chemicals in total trade rose from 5.3 per cent in 1955 to 8.5 per cent in 1985, and the share of engineering products rose from 21 per cent in 1955 to 35.5 per cent. Within the engineering industry the growth in the share of office and telecommunications and road and motor vehicles is especially noteworthy. Another distinguishing feature of these branches of manufacturing has been the pace of technological innovation. Both product innovation and process innovation has been faster in these sectors than in other branches of manufacturing. The rapid rate at which new products have come on to the market has stimulated trade. Much of this trade has taken the form of intra-industry trade in which industrialized countries exchange similar products. Process innovation has resulted in lower costs of production leading through into lower prices. Firms introducing such new methods have been able to enlarge their markets at home and abroad.

CHANGES IN THE GEOGRAPHICAL COMPOSITION OF WORLD TRADE

The geographical composition of trade refers to the proportion of world trade which is accounted for by different regions or countries of the world. It is instructive to examine how this has changed over the post-war period. Table 2.7 shows the main changes which have taken place in the geographical composition of trade over the period since 1963. Over two-thirds of world trade is accounted for by the developed countries. Between 1963 and 1973, the share of world trade accounted for by developed countries rose from 67.3 per cent to 70.8 per cent. However, in the next decade, the share of the developed countries fell to 64 per cent. The main reason for this decline was the rise in the share of world trade accounted for by the developing countries and, to a lesser extent, the eastern trading area. In particular, there occurred a big increase in the shares of the Middle Eastern countries and the South-East Asian countries. Part of the explanation for this was the rise in world oil prices, which increased the value of exports from Middle Eastern countries. The other part of the explanation was the

Table 2.7: The geographical composition of world trade, 1963–85

Region	1963		1973		1983		1985	
	$bn	%	$bn	%	$bn	%	$bn	%
North America	29.6	19.1	95.5	16.6	267.0	14.8	290.8	15.1
Japan	5.3	3.4	36.9	6.4	146.8	8.1	176.0	9.2
W. Europe, of which:	66.1	42.8	258.9	45.1	709.6	39.2	771.2	40.1
EC	52.6	34.0	211.8	36.9	570.3	31.5	613.8	31.9
EFTA	9.7	6.2	37.5	6.5	103.9	5.7	114.4	6.0
Australia, New Zealand and S. Africa	5.1	3.3	15.4	2.7	34.0	1.9	37.0	1.9
Developed countries	104.1	67.3	406.7	70.8	1157.4	64.0	1275.0	66.4
Latin America	11.3	7.3	29.5	5.1	104.5	5.8	103.0	5.4
South and East Asia	8.4	5.4	31.6	5.5	159.0	8.8	176.0	9.2
Middle East	5.3	3.4	27.5	4.8	123.0	6.8	98.0	5.1
Africa	6.6	4.3	20.9	3.6	59.0	3.3	61.0	3.2
Developing countries	31.9	20.6	110.4	19.2	447.1	24.7	440.0	22.9
Eastern trading area	18.7	12.1	57.2	10.0	204.0	11.3	206.5	10.7
World total	154.7	100.0	574.3	100.0	1808.5	100.0	1921.5	100.0

Source: GATT, 1986.

rapid growth of exports from newly-industrializing countries (NICs), especially the South-East Asian countries (Hong Kong, Singapore, Taiwan, and South Korea). After 1983, the share of the South and East Asian developing countries continued to rise. However, the share of the Middle Eastern countries fell. This was due to a fall in the value of their oil revenues as the industrialized countries reduced the level of their oil imports from the Middle East, and the world price of oil began to fall. This caused a drop in the developing countries' share of world trade and a recovery in the share of the developed countries. The share of the eastern trading areas also fell back to the level of 1973.

It can be seen that the bulk of the trade of the developed countries is accounted for by North America (the United States and Canada), Japan, and Western Europe (the EC and EFTA).

Before 1973 the tendency was for the share of the North American countries to fall, while that of Japan and Western Europe rose. In the following decade, both the North American and the West European share fell. However, Japan managed to increase her share still further. Since 1983, North America's share has continued to fall while that of Western Europe has recovered slightly, although it is still below the level of a decade earlier. Japan's share has risen further reaching 9.2 per cent compared with only 3.4 per cent in 1963.

As with commodities, changes in a particular region or country's share of world trade may be due to either:

1. A faster (or slower) growth in the volume of the exports of the country in question than in the volume of total world exports.
2. A faster (or slower) rise in the average price of a country's exports relative to the average price of total world exports.
3. Both.

We need to examine world trends in both of these sets of factors.

Figure 2.5 shows the growth in the volume of exports of different geographical regions over the period between 1960 and 1982. Over the course of the 1960s, world trade grew in volume terms in all regions. The fastest growth of exports was apparent in the developed market economies. The exports of the oil-exporting developing countries grew almost as quickly. However, the exports of the least-developed countries grew at a much slower rate. Many of the latter group of countries were to be found in the continents of Latin America and Africa. Accordingly, their share of world trade fell. The exports of the Middle Eastern oil-exporting countries and the NICs of South-East Asia rose. All regions experienced a fall in the volume of their exports between 1973 to 1975. From 1975 onwards, the exports of the NICs grew at an explosive rate, as they had been doing in the early 1970s before the recession. The exports of the developed market economies also recovered but grew at a much slower rate than in the previous decade. Between 1980 and 1982 the exports of the DMEs were virtually static. Much the same was true of the exports of the least-developed countries. After a brief recovery in 1976, they fell in 1977. Growth was resumed between 1978 and 1980 but disappeared thereafter. Finally,

Figure 2.5 Volume of world exports by regions, 1960–82

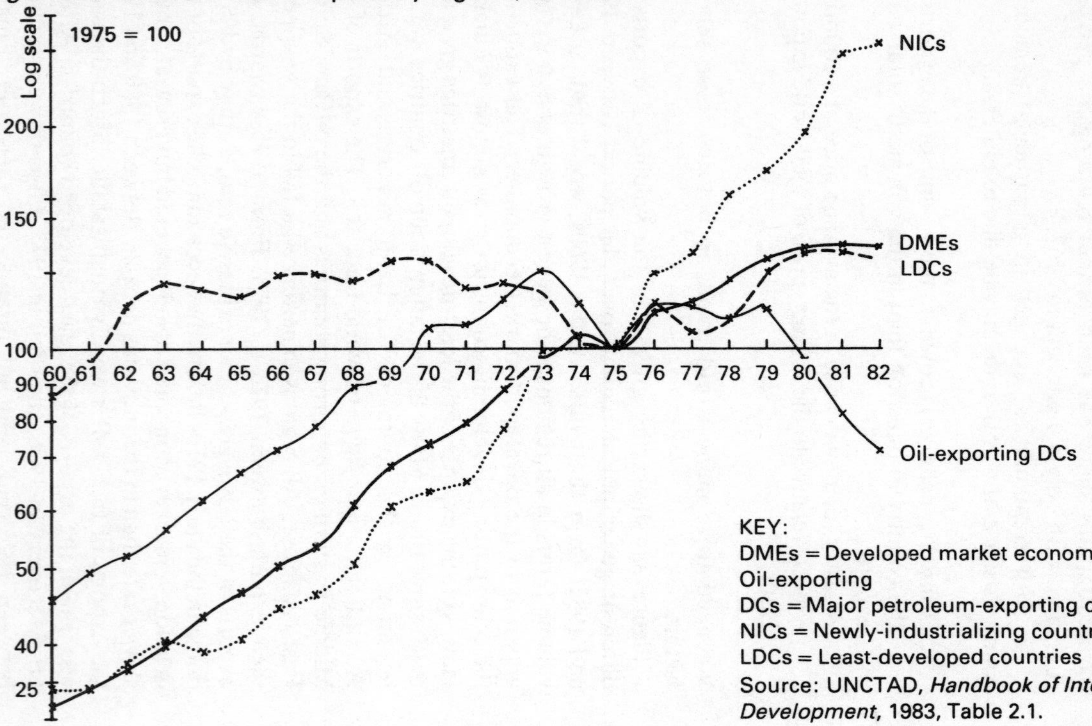

1975 = 100

Log scale

NICs

DMEs
LDCs

Oil-exporting DCs

KEY:
DMEs = Developed market economies
Oil-exporting
DCs = Major petroleum-exporting developing countries
NICs = Newly-industrializing countries
LDCs = Least-developed countries

Source: UNCTAD, *Handbook of International Trade and Development*, 1983, Table 2.1.

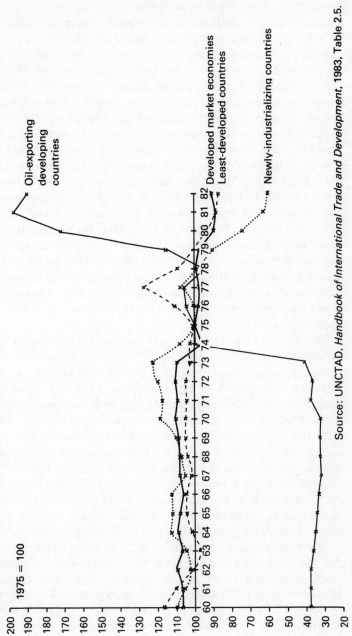

Figure 2.6 Terms-of-trade index numbers, 1960–82

1975 = 100

Oil-exporting developing countries

Developed market economies

Least-developed countries

Newly-industrializing countries

Source: UNCTAD, *Handbook of International Trade and Development*, 1983, Table 2.5.

after a brief recovery in 1976, the exports of the oil-exporting developing countries fell substantially. This was because of declining oil consumption in the western industrialized countries following the quadrupling of world oil prices.

Figure 2.6 shows changes in the terms of trade of different geographical regions over the period from 1960 to 1982. A country's terms of trade measure changes in a country's average export prices divided by changes in a country's average import prices. A rise in a country's terms-of-trade index means that her export prices have been rising faster than her import prices. Her terms of trade are said to have improved. Conversely, a fall in a country's terms-of-trade index means that her import prices have been rising faster than her export prices. Her terms of trade are said to have deteriorated. Thus the large and sudden rise in world oil prices between 1973 and 1974 and, again, between 1979 and 1981 brought a very large improvement in the terms of trade of the oil-exporting countries. This accounts for the rise in the share of world trade up until 1983 accounted for by the Middle East countries. As we have seen, the favourable movement in the export prices of these countries was partially offset by slower growth and eventually a fall in the volume of their exports.

The terms of trade of the developed market economies were broadly constant from 1960 to 1973, so the increase of their share of world trade over this period was entirely due to relatively fast growth in export volume. However, after 1973 their terms of trade deteriorated. This helps explain the fall of their share of world trade over the period up to 1982. After 1982 the share of the developed market economies increased largely on account of falling oil and other commodity prices. The terms of trade of the NICs also deteriorated after 1973 (except for a small improvement in 1977). However, this was more than offset by the rapid growth in the volume of exports of these countries, so that they increased their share of world trade. After falling sharply in the early 1960s, the terms of trade of the least-developed countries were roughly stable up until the mid-1970s. Between 1975 and 1977 rising primary commodity prices brought a major improvement in their terms of trade. However, after 1977, primary commodity prices fell sharply and the terms of trade of these countries deteriorated. This has contributed to the fall in the share of world trade experienced by the poorest developing countries.

Table 2.8: World's leading exporters of manufactures, 1973, 1979, 1983–5
Percentage shares of total world trade of manufactures.

	1973	1979	1983	1984	1985
Japan	10.0	10.4	13.3	14.3	14.1
West Germany	17.0	15.5	13.5	12.7	13.2
United States	12.6	12.1	12.4	12.4	12.0
France	7.3	7.8	6.3	6.0	6.0
Italy	5.3	6.3	5.8	5.4	5.6
United Kingdom	7.0	7.2	5.5	5.3	5.5
Canada	3.5	3.0	3.8	4.3	4.3
Belgium-Luxembourg	4.9	4.3	3.4	3.1	3.2
Netherlands	3.9	3.5	2.0	2.9	2.9
Taiwan	1.1	1.5	2.1	2.4	2.3
South Korea	0.8	1.4	2.1	2.3	2.3
Hong Kong[a]	1.3	1.5	1.9	2.3	2.3
Switzerland	2.4	2.5	2.2	2.1	2.1
Sweden	2.6	2.3	2.0	2.0	2.0
Soviet Union	2.4	1.9	1.7	1.5	..
East Germany	1.7	1.3	1.6	1.5	..
Spain	0.9	1.4	1.3	1.4	1.4
Czechoslovakia	1.5	1.2	1.4	1.3	..
Austria	1.2	1.4	1.2	1.2	1.2
Singapore	0.5	0.7	1.0	1.1	1.0
Total	87.8	87.1	85.5	85.4	85.8
Total (value)	$305.0 bn	$822.7 bn	$903.4 bn	$976.5 bn	$1028.0 bn
Total world trade in manufactures	$347.5 bn	$945.0 bn	$1057.0 bn	$1143.5 bn	$1197.5 bn

Source: GATT, 1986.
[a] Includes significant transhipments.

Earlier we saw that the largest and most dynamic component of world trade over the post-war period has been manufactured goods. It is, therefore, important to examine the geographical composition of trade in manufactures as a separate component of trade. Table 2.8 shows the world's leading exporters of manufactures over the period from 1973 to 1985. In 1973 the twenty countries listed in the table accounted for almost 88 per cent of all manufacturing exports. Three countries (West Germany, the United States, and Japan) accounted for nearly 40 per cent of manufacturing exports. Nine countries accounted for 71.5 per cent of manufacturing exports. The degree of concentration fell somewhat during the next twelve years. All the top ten manufacturing exporters, except for Japan, saw their share of world manufacturing exports fall. Japan, however, significantly increased her share and overtook both the United States and West Germany to become the world's leading exporter of manufactured goods. The most noticeable change of the period from 1973 to 1985 was the increased share of world manufacturing exports accounted for by the NICs. Taiwan, South Korea, Hong Kong, and Singapore all achieved a big increase in their shares of world manufacturing trade. Thus it is apparent that the increase in the NICs share of world trade was entirely due a rapid rise in the volume of their manufacturing exports. The increase in their share of world manufacturing trade was achieved at the expense of all the western industrialized countries except for Japan.

CHANGES IN THE DIRECTIONAL FLOW OF WORLD TRADE

In addition to changes in the geographical origins of exports, it is also useful to examine changes in the directional flow of trade. This refers to the flow of trade between different geographical regions of the world. It is concerned with both the origin and the destination of trade. It is useful to know which trade flows have been the most important in recent decades and how the relative importance of different types of trade flows has changed. Table 2.9 shows the geographical network of world trade and how it has changed over the period since 1963.

As we saw earlier, the developed countries' share of world trade rose from 67.1 per cent to 70.9 per cent from 1963 to 1973. It then fell back to 62.9 per cent in 1981 before rising to 66.3 per cent in 1985. It is striking that in 1963 nearly three-quarters of the trade of the developed countries was with other developed countries. Trade between developed countries has been the fastest-growing component of world trade. In 1985 trade with other developed countries still accounted for roughly three-quarters of the exports of the developed countries. The only significant change in the directional flow of developed-country exports was an increase in the importance of the eastern-bloc countries.

The developing countries remain extremely dependent on the developed countries for a market for their exports. Over the period from 1963 to 1973, the proportion of their exports going to developed countries rose. By 1973 almost three-quarters of developing-country exports went to the developed countries. However, since 1973 the importance of the developed countries as a market for developing-country exports has diminished. The importance of other developing countries, on the other hand, has increased. Thus more developing-country exports go to other developing countries now than was true twenty-five years ago. Developing countries would appear to be doing more trade with each other. However, the importance of such trade should not be exaggerated. Only one-quarter of developing-country exports went to other developing countries in 1985 compared with two-thirds going to the developed countries.

The share of the eastern-bloc countries in world trade fell from 12.3 per cent in 1963 to 9.9 per cent in 1973 before recovering to 11.3 per cent in 1983. By 1985 it had fallen back to 10.8 per cent. In 1963 nearly two-thirds of the exports of the eastern-bloc countries went to other eastern-bloc countries. However, since 1963 this share has been falling. By 1983 only one-half of the exports of these countries went to other eastern-bloc countries. In particular, the importance of the developed countries as a market rose from 21 per cent in 1963 to 26 per cent in 1973 and 30 per cent in 1983. Exports of developed countries to eastern-bloc countries have also risen quickly but remain relatively less important to the developed countries. In 1963 they accounted for less than 4 per cent of developed countries' exports. By 1985 this had risen to just over 5 per cent. However, east–west trade has clearly been one of the fastest-growing flows of trade over the past twenty-five years.

Table 2.10 shows the geographical network of world trade in manufactured goods only and how this has changed over the period since 1963. Given the dominant part which manufactures have played in the growth of world trade over the post-war period, it is interesting to examine the network of this type of trade in isolation. The share of developed countries in world exports of manufactures has been falling steadily since 1963 as we observed in the last section of this chapter. The counterpart to this declining share has been the rising share of the developing countries. The eastern-bloc countries have also lost ground to the developing countries. It is noticeable that a significantly larger share of developed-country manufactures are exported to developing countries than for total trade. This is to be expected

Table 2.9: World merchandise exports by major areas, 1963, 1973, 1979, 1980–5

Origin	Destination	Developed countries $bn	Developed countries %	Developing areas $bn	Developing areas %	Eastern trading area $bn	Eastern trading area %	World $bn	World %
Developed countries	1963	77	49.7	23	14.8	4	2.6	104	67.1
	1973	316	55.1	72	12.5	19	3.3	407	70.9
	1979	783	47.9	334	14.3	52	3.2	1069	65.4
	1980	900	45.2	294	14.8	62	3.1	1256	63.1
	1981	855	43.6	320	16.3	59	3.0	1234	62.9
	1982	821	44.5	296	16.1	54	2.9	1171	63.5
	1983	833	46.1	272	15.0	52	2.9	1157	64.0
	1984	908	47.6	268	14.1	56	2.9	1232	64.6
	1985	957	49.8	253	13.1	65	3.4	1275	66.3
Developing areas	1963	23	14.8	7	4.5	2	1.3	32	20.6
	1973	83	14.5	22	3.8	5	0.9	110	19.2
	1979	299	18.3	99	6.0	16	1.0	414	25.3
	1980	396	19.9	138	6.9	21	1.1	555	27.9
	1981	373	19.0	150	7.6	22	1.1	545	27.7
	1982	318	17.2	140	7.6	22	1.2	480	26.0
	1983	295	16.3	129	7.1	23	1.3	447	24.7
	1984	314	16.5	126	6.6	25	1.3	465	24.4
	1985	295	15.3	117	6.1	28	1.5	440	22.9

Eastern trading area	1963	4	2.6	3	2.0	12	7.7	19	12.3
	1973	15	2.6	9	1.6	33	5.7	57	9.9
	1979	47	2.9	26	1.6	79	4.8	152	9.3
	1980	58	2.9	31	1.6	89	4.5	178	8.9
	1981	57	2.9	37	1.9	90	4.6	184	9.4
	1982	58	3.2	40	2.1	95	5.2	193	10.5
	1983	59	3.3	41	2.3	104	5.7	204	11.3
	1984	62	3.3	41	2.1	107	5.6	210	11.0
	1985	59	3.1	38	2.0	109	5.7	207	10.8
World	1963	104	67.1	33	21.3	18	11.6	155	100.0
	1973	414	72.2	103	17.9	57	9.9	574	100.0
	1979	1129	69.1	359	21.9	147	9.0	1635	100.0
	1980	1354	68.0	463	23.3	172	8.7	1989	100.0
	1981	1285	65.5	507	25.8	171	8.7	1963	100.0
	1982	1197	64.9	476	25.8	171	9.3	1844	100.0
	1983	1187	65.6	442	24.4	180	10.0	1808	100.0
	1984	1284	67.3	436	22.9	187	9.8	1907	100.0
	1985	1312	68.2	408	21.2	202	10.5	1922	100.0

Source: GATT, *International Trade, 85–86* (Geneva, 1986)

Table 2.10: World exports of manufactures by major areas, 1963, 1973, 1979, 1980–5

Origin	Destination	Developed countries		Developing areas		Eastern trading area		World	
		$bn	%	$bn	%	$bn	%	$bn	%
Developed countries	1963	48	59.0	17	20.6	2	2.7	67	82.3
	1973	222	63.8	54	15.7	13	3.6	289	83.1
	1979	552	58.4	187	19.8	38	4.0	777	82.2
	1980	624	57.0	230	21.0	42	3.8	896	81.8
	1981	592	54.3	251	23.0	38	3.6	881	80.9
	1982	572	54.3	235	22.3	36	3.5	843	80.1
	1983	585	55.3	211	20.0	37	3.5	833	78.8
	1984	648	56.7	206	18.0	39	3.4	893	78.1
	1985	696	58.1	197	16.5	50	4.2	943	78.8
Developing areas	1963	2	2.4	1	1.8	0	0.1	3	4.3
	1973	16	4.7	7	2.0	1	0.2	24	6.9
	1979	53	5.7	31	3.2	2	0.2	86	9.1
	1980	63	5.7	40	3.7	3	0.3	106	9.7
	1981	67	6.1	45	4.2	4	0.3	116	10.7
	1982	67	6.4	43	4.1	4	0.3	114	10.8
	1983	77	7.3	42	4.0	4	0.4	124	11.7
	1984	96	8.4	45	3.9	6	0.5	147	12.8
	1985	97	8.1	43	3.6	9	0.7	149	12.4

	Year								
Eastern trading area	1963	1	1.4	2	2.0	8	10.0	11	13.4
	1973	6	1.6	5	1.3	24	7.1	35	10.0
	1979	16	1.6	14	1.5	53	5.6	83	8.7
	1980	18	1.6	17	1.5	59	5.4	93	8.5
	1981	17	1.6	20	1.8	55	5.1	92	8.4
	1982	17	1.6	21	2.0	58	5.5	96	9.1
	1983	17	1.6	21	2.0	62	5.9	100	9.5
	1984	18	1.6	21	1.8	65	5.7	104	9.1
	1985	19	1.6	19	1.6	67	5.6	105	8.8
World	1963	51	62.8	20	24.4	10	12.8	81	100.0
	1973	244	70.1	66	19.0	38	10.9	348	100.0
	1979	621	65.7	231	24.5	93	9.8	945	100.0
	1980	705	64.3	287	26.2	104	9.5	1095	100.0
	1981	676	62.0	316	29.0	97	9.0	1089	100.0
	1982	656	62.3	299	28.4	98	9.3	1053	100.0
	1983	679	64.2	274	26.0	104	9.8	1057	100.0
	1984	763	66.7	272	23.7	109	9.6	1144	100.0
	1985	812	67.8	260	21.7	125	10.5	1197	100.0

Source: GATT, International Trade, 85–86 (Geneva 1986).

given the developed countries' relative specialization in manufactures. However, over the period from 1963 to 1973 the developing countries appeared to become less important as a market for developed countries' manufactures. Since 1973 the importance of developing countries has once again increased despite some slippage in the last few years. In addition, the eastern-bloc countries have become an increasingly important market for developed-country manufactures.

It is also apparent that a rising proportion of developing-country exports of manufactures have gone to developed countries. In 1963 roughly 56 per cent of developing country manufacturing exports went to developed countries. By 1985 this share had risen to 65 per cent. Thus developing-country exports of manufactures to developed countries has been the fastest-growing element of developing countries' trade. The developed countries still represent the most important and fastest-growing market for the manufactures of developing countries. Other developing countries accounted for only 30 per cent of developing-country exports of manufactures in 1985 compared with 42 per cent in 1963. Clearly, if developing countries are seeking export-led growth, developed country markets look more promising than the markets of other developing countries. Only if the developed countries should seek to close their markets to developing-country manufactures through the erection of new trade barriers would developing countries do well to concentrate their efforts on increasing their exports to the rest of the developing world.

In a similar way, the fastest-growing market for the eastern-bloc countries' manufactures has been that of the developed countries. A rising proportion of these countries' manufacturing exports has gone to the developed countries of the west. The proportion going to other eastern-bloc countries fell from nearly three-quarters in 1963 to two-thirds in 1985. In 1963 roughly 10 per cent of eastern-bloc manufacturing exports went to the developed countries of the west. By 1985 this had risen to 18 per cent. This represents a proportionately greater increase than for east–west trade as a whole.

FUTURE PROSPECTS FOR WORLD OUTPUT AND WORLD TRADE

In this chapter we have seen how post-war economic growth was essentially export-led growth. The developed market economies enjoyed rapid economic growth based upon the expansion of trade. Trade grew faster than output and helped to bring about rapid economic growth. The basis for this expansion of trade was essentially an increase in the degree of specialization within manufacturing industry. The western industrialized economies increased the degree of specialization existing between them in manufacturing products. Much of this took the form of intra-industry specialization. Countries specialized in narrow ranges of products within given industries. This led to the industrialized countries carrying out more trade in products belonging to the same industry. This is known as intra-industry trade and will be discussed further in the next chapter. All of this was made possible by lowering of trade barriers achieved through organizations such as the GATT, the EC, and EFTA and the certainty created by applying the GATT Charter to a growing proportion of trade. The dismantling of exchange controls, restoration of currency convertibility and stable exchange rates played an important supporting role. Increased specialization and trade between the developed countries enabled these countries to enjoy fast growth. This, in turn, led to increased demand for primary commodities which benefited the developing countries. However, because trade in primary commodities could grow no faster than industrial output in the developed countries, growth was generally slower in the developing world. Only the NICs and oil-exporting developing countries were enabled to achieve fast economic growth.

What implication does this process of trade-led growth have for the future? Does the world economic slowdown of the last fifteen years mean that trade-led growth has come to an end? If so, what are the prospects and possibilities for its resumption? It is a fool who would seek to predict the future. However, an understanding of what has been happening in the world economic system over the last forty years is a prerequisite for making any forecasts concerning the future. Many different views exist as to why fast growth disappeared in the 1970s. Certainly, the oil crisis which broke out between 1973 and 1974 was an immediate cause of the recession which ensued. However, as we have argued earlier in this chapter, the oil crisis was only a contributory, albeit important, cause of the slowdown. Even before the rise in world oil prices, there were signs that growth was slackening in the western industrialized economies.

Earlier in this chapter it was suggested that one cause of slower output growth was the slower rate of growth in the volume of world trade, especially that of manufactures. Exports of manufactures were growing more slowly in volume terms. As a result, the rate of growth of output moderated. Slower growth in the advanced industrialized economies meant a more modest increase in the exports of the developing countries. As we have seen, exports of primary commodities can grow no faster than the industrial output of the developed countries. The developing countries remain dependent on the developed countries for markets for both their manufactures and non-manufactures. Only the NICs were able to make their exports grow faster by achieving greater penetration of the markets for manufactures in the developed countries.

Professor Arthur Lewis has drawn attention to the central importance of the manufacturing import–consumption ratio of the advanced industrialized economies in promoting rapid growth in world trade (Lewis 1981). Throughout the post-war period, the ratio of imports of manufactures to consumption rose in all the western industrialized economies. This was most noticeable in the member states of the European Community, where trade barriers were lowered at a faster rate than elsewhere. This is a reflection of the increased degree of specialization in manufacturing taking place between the western industrialized economies. However, should this ratio stabilize, slower growth of world trade will result. Trade in manufactures will only be able to grow at the same rate as output. Trade-led growth will disappear. Instead, trade will follow output. This will result in a slower growth of output in the industrialized countries unless some other source of growth can be created. Slower output growth in the industrialized countries will reduce the rate of growth of developing country exports given the dependence of developing countries on the markets of the industrialized countries. Developing countries will accordingly experience less growth.

It is not apparent that the manufacturing import-consumption ratio has yet stabilized in the industrialized countries. Earlier in this chapter, we confronted evidence that the ratio of export growth to output growth had been falling since 1970. This would suggest that the degree of specialization in manufactured goods between the industrialized economies has slowed down. One reason for this may be a spread of new forms of protectionism. The GATT was successful in lowering tariff barriers on trade in manufactures, and in Western Europe tariffs on industrial products have been largely eliminated. However, non-tariff barriers have proliferated. In Chapter 7 I shall discuss the nature and causes of this so-called New Protectionism. I will show that much of this protectionism has been aimed at imports of manufactures coming from Japan and the NICs. It follows that it is critical to the future growth of world trade that agreement is reached on the need to contain and reverse this spread of protectionism.

Later in this book it will be argued that a continuation of the trend towards intra-industry specialization which typified the early decades of the post-war era, holds out the best prospects for world economic growth in the future. I will show that intra-industry specialization generally poses fewer adjustment problems and encounters less domestic resistance than inter-industry specialization. It also permits trade to grow faster than output. The degree of inter-industry specialization between countries is inevitably limited. On the other hand, the process of technological change and competition between firms opens up almost limitless opportunities for more intra-industry specialization. Scope for intra-industry specialization is greatest between industrialized countries. However, as many developing countries industrialize and accumulate capital, the scope for intra-industry specialization between industrialized and developing countries will also increase. A willingness to maintain open markets and an environment of stable exchange rates are important for such specialization to flourish.

In the next chapter it will be seen that intra-industry specialization is generally greatest in the most technologically advanced, science-based manufacturing industries. The high levels of research-and-development (R&D) expenditure and the rapid rates of product innovation which typify such industries mean that conditions of classical price competition rarely prevail. Firms compete by methods other than price. Considerable scope exists for intra-industry specialization. It seems likely that the importance of these industries within manufacturing will increase in coming decades in both industrialized and newly-industrializing countries. This can be expected to lead to an increase in the level of intra-industry specialization. If this is so, the prospects for faster growth of trade in manufactured products are good. However, this is conditional upon the industrialized countries being willing to lower or remove those barriers which currently impede such trade.

On the other hand, the growth of manufacturing export industries in the developing countries and eastern-bloc countries may be expected to make for increased tension in international trading relations. Earlier in this chapter I noted the relative decline of manufacturing industry in the developed market economies and the increasing importance of manufacturing industry in the developing countries. Also I showed how the share of manufacturing exports accounted for by the developed countries has been falling and that of the developing countries rising. We saw that had it not been for the rapid growth in manufacturing exports coming from the NICs, the volume of world trade in manufactures would have grown at an even slower rate in recent decades. It is apparent that there has occurred some shift of manufacturing from the western industrialized countries to certain newly-industrialising developing countries. I shall discuss this trend in greater depth in Chapter 6. While the extent of this shift is often exaggerated, it clearly represents one of the most important changes in the world trading system in recent decades. If this trend were to continue in future decades, might it not be expected to exert a dampening effect on economic growth in the advanced industrialized countries?

Before I consider the answer to this question, it should be noted that that this shift of manufacturing from industrialized to developing countries conforms with the predictions of the product life-cycle theory discussed in Chapter 1. Many of the new industries and products of the post-war era have reached maturity. Many have even passed through to the phase of standardization. The developed countries have lost their former comparative advantage in such products. Developing countries are able to offer superior sites for producing such products because of their much lower labour costs. Increasingly, products such as radios, televisions, washing-machines, fridges, pocket calculators, and so on which were first produced in the advanced industrialized countries are produced abroad and imported by the latter. As I will show in Chapter 5, in many cases what has happened has been a splitting up of the production process and hiving-off of the most labour-intensive stages or processes to developing countries. This has been made possible by the application of new technologies to production, product design, and methods of transport.

This has meant the disappearance or contraction of some older manufacturing activities with a consequent shedding of labour in the advanced industrialized countries. However, the real problem has been the failure of sufficient new industries or activities to emerge to take their place. All too often the advanced industrialized countries have been preoccupied with protecting the older activities in the face of more competition from abroad. This has been at the expense of the newer industries which hold the key to future economic growth. The latter depend on innovation. Those industrialized countries which have adopted policies which encourage the creation of new enterprises and activities and invention and innovation have generally been the most successful in meeting the new challenge. Countries which have sought to protect their older, declining activities have fallen behind. Indeed, the attempts of the advanced industrialized countries to protect and prop up their old industries has resulted in global overcapacity. This has exerted a depressing effect on prices and profit margins in the industries concerned leading to the introduction of yet more protectionism. Instead of resources being released into new industries and activities, they have been shut into the old, slow-growing lines in which the developed countries find it increasingly difficult to compete. As a result, growth has suffered. In Chapter 7 I shall examine some of the problems of adjustment to the expansion of trade which confront many industrialized economies and the kind of policies which can be pursued to bring about faster and smoother adjustment.

Thus an important key to achieving fast growth in the future lies with the willingness of the industrialized countries to adopt policies which encourage adjustment and the development of new activities to replace the old ones, which are increasingly being shifted to the developing world. Such new activities may include service activities as well as manufacturing activities. Earlier we saw how the decline of the manufacturing sector in the advanced industrialized economies has been balanced by the expansion of the services sector. In Chapter 8 I shall discuss the nature and importance of the services sector in the industrialized countries. Although many services are by their very nature non-tradable, trade in services has grown at least as rapidly as trade in manufactures in recent decades. Might not increased trade and specialization in services enable the advanced industrialized countries to maintain fast trade growth at a time when trade in manufactures is growing more slowly than in the past? As we shall see, there are many grounds for believing that the advanced industrialized countries enjoy a comparative advantage in services. If this is so, the next quarter-century could witness a new stage in the growth of international specialization, as developed countries increasingly trade services for manufactures and trade in services takes up the slack created by slower growth of trade in manufactures. I shall consider this possibility in greater depth in Chapter 8.

3

Intra-industry Trade and Specialization

INTRODUCTION

One of the most important trends in post-war trade, especially trade in manufactured goods, has been the growth of intra-industry trade. This has been defined as the simultaneous export and import of products belonging to the same industry. For example, a country may simultaneously export and import automobiles. Britain may export Austin Maestros to France, while France exports Renaults to Britain. This is different from inter-industry trade, which involves countries exchanging the products of different industries. For example, Britain may export automobiles to Portugal and Portugal export wine to Britain.

Much of what is written in international economics textbooks is still couched in terms of inter-industry specialization. Models are constructed in which each country specializes in a particular industry or activity in which it enjoys a comparative advantage. In such models, the opening up of trade between any two countries or the removal of barriers to trade leads to each country concentrating on particular activities. This implies a contraction of certain other industries as resources shift into the expanding industry. Such inter-industry specialization results in a relocation of economic activity. In effect, certain activities move geographically to the country where comparative costs are lowest. One result of such specialization is a growing dissimilarity between the products which a country exports and those which it imports. By implication, industry trade balances — the difference between exports and imports of individual industries — widen.

Although inter-industry specialization does still take place, this has not been the form which specialization between advanced industrialized countries has largely taken over the post-war period. Individual countries have not concentrated on whole industries or activities. Rather, they have undertaken a much narrower type of specialization. This has involved specialization in the production of particular products or groups of products within a given industry. Such specialization is known as intra-industry specialization. With this type of specialization there is no wholesale contraction or disappearance of certain industries from particular countries following the opening up of trade. This can be seen from an examination of the economies of the original six members of the European Community following its establishment in 1958. There were very few cases of industries disappearing from any single country. Industries stayed where they were, but the range of products manufactured and sold by each country changed. By implication, industry trade balances narrowed as each country exchanged different products yet products which belonged to the same industry.

What was true for the European Community has also been true (although to a slightly lesser extent) for all the advanced industrialized economies. Although much trade in primary commodities still takes the form of inter-industry specialization, a growing proportion of trade in manufactured goods has involved intra-industry specialization. As we shall see in later chapters of this book, this may have important implications for trade policy. Where intra-industry specialization follows the lowering of trade barriers, international specialization may give rise to fewer adjustment problems. There need be no wholesale disappearance of single industries from particular countries. Hence there will be less of a need to redeploy resources (especially labour) in other industries. One can expect less resistance to trade barriers. On the other hand, the gains from such specialization will not be the same as those which result from conventional inter-industry specialization.

In this chapter, I shall be discussing the nature, extent, and causes of intra-industry trade and specialization. First, intra-industry trade is defined. Second, I examine various alternative formulae proposed for measuring intra-industry trade and discuss some of the problems involved in measurement. Third, I discuss the so-called 'aggregation problem', which plagues all attempts to measure intra-industry trade accurately and which has cast doubt on the significance of the distinction between inter- and intra-industry trade. Fourth, I discuss some factors which give rise to intra-industry trade and which may account for the increased importance of this type of trade since the war. Fifth, I examine the actual extent of intra-industry trade and differences between countries and across industries in the level of intra-industry trade. Finally, I conclude with a comment on possible reasons why the distinction between inter- and intra-industry specialization is important.

DEFINITION AND MEASUREMENT

I have defined intra-industry trade as the simultaneous export and import of products belonging to the same industry. Inter-industry trade is the exchange of products which belong to different industries. I have also defined intra-industry specialization as the specialization of a country in a narrow range of products within a given industry. Inter-industry specialization involves a country specializing in a whole industry or activity. Inter-industry specialization leads to inter-industry trade and intra-industry specialization will lead to intra-industry trade. However, it is possible for intra-industry trade to take place between any two countries without either country undergoing intra-industry specialization. Therefore not all the increase in intra-industry trade of recent decades need be caused by intra-industry specialization. However, as we shall see later on in this chapter, most intra-industry trade results from intra-industry specialization. Hence, throughout much of this book, the terms are used interchangeably.

If intra-industry trade is the export and import of products belonging to the same industry, the question arises as to what constitutes an industry. Does the term 'industry' have any economic meaning. If it does not, the distinction between inter-industry and intra-industry trade is meaningless. Clearly, economists do mean something specific when they use the term 'industry', although the term is generally used rather loosely by non-economists. However, there does not exist any universally agreed, exact, and fully satisfactory definition of an industry. Three criteria are generally used in grouping products together and defining them as constituting the output of an industry:

1. Substitution in production, which means that each product produced by the industry has roughly similar input requirements or factor intensities (e.g. automobiles and tractors).
2. Identical technology intensity, which means that each product is manufactured by a roughly similar method or process of production.
3. Substitution in consumption, which means that each product has broadly similar uses such that consumers can in some measure substitute one for the other in use (e.g. plastic containers and metal containers).

It is apparent that there exists a potential conflict between certain of these criteria. Products which have a high substitution in consumption (e.g. leather- and rubber-soled shoes) may have a low or non-existent substitution in production. This may make it difficult to apply all three criteria to a group of products in justifying categorizing them together. One may have to make a choice between one of the three criteria depending on the purpose for which the data are required. Thus, if our concern is to test the predictive powers of the Hecksher–Ohlin model of trade, substitution in production is the most appropriate criteria to use. On the other hand, there is some evidence that technology is the most important factor determining real-world trade flows, in which case technology intensity may be the more appropriate criteria. If, however, we are keen to test the predictive power of differences in tastes in explaining trade flows, substitution in consumption may be the preferred criteria.

It is apparent that, because of the difficulty in agreeing on a precise definition of an industry, the concept of intra-industry trade suffers from a degree of ambivalence. It may prove difficult in practice to decide how to classify different products and, therefore, how to distinguish between inter- and intra-industry trade. Some kinds of trade may assume the form of a hybrid of inter- and intra-industry trade (Dunning and Norman 1985). Moreover, as we shall see later, even when we can agree to group together a collection of products, which possess in common all or some of the above criteria, trade statistics may employ a different method of classification. Indeed, systems of international trade classification are often based more on statistical convenience than any set of economic criteria. For these reasons it is generally not possible to accurately measure the extent of intra-industry trade.

Leaving aside the problems of definition and product classification, how can we measure intra-industry trade? Various alternative formulae have been proposed by different economists. The following are four alternative approaches to the measurement problem.

Grubel and Lloyd

Grubel and Lloyd were among the first economists to seek to measure the importance of intra-industry trade (Grubel and Lloyd 1975). They measured intra-industry trade as the percentage of a country's total trade (exports plus imports) in the products of a given industry which was matched or balanced, that is exports equal imports. For an individual product group or industry i, the formula is:

$$B_i = \frac{(X_i + M_i) - |X_i - M_i|}{(X_i + M_i)} \times 100 \tag{1}$$

Where X_i and M_i stand, respectively, for the exports and imports of product group i. The straight brackets around $X_i - M_i$ denote that the sign of the trade balance is ignored. If all trade was balanced, B_i would equal 100. If all trade was one-way, B_i would equal zero. Thus the closer is B_i to 100, the greater the importance of intra-industry trade. The closer is B_i to zero, the greater the importance of inter-industry trade.

For convenience, the simple Grubel–Lloyd formula above may be rewritten as follows:

$$B_i = \left[1 - \frac{|X_i - M_i|}{(X_i + M_i)} \right] \times 100 \tag{2}$$

This may be an easier form to use in calculating the level of intra-industry trade and is frequently confronted in the literature.

To obtain the average level of intra-industry trade for a country, Grubel and Lloyd proposed calculating a weighted mean, using the relative size of exports and imports of a particular product group as weights. The formula is as follows:

$$B_j = \frac{\sum\limits_{i}^{n} B_i \, (X_i + M_i)}{\sum\limits_{i}^{n} (X_i + M_i)} \times 100 \qquad (3)$$

The $\sum$ sign is the Greek capital letter 'sigma' and is used to denote 'the sum of'. It means that we must add together all the terms like the one following, that is all the B_is weighted by total trade (exports and imports) of that product group. The j means that the formula is for the jth country and the i means the ith of n industries.

For convenience the Grubel and Lloyd summary measure may be rewritten in one of two ways:

$$B_j = \frac{\sum\limits_{i}^{n} (X_i + M_i) - \sum\limits_{i}^{n} |X_i - M_i|}{\sum\limits_{i}^{n} (X_i + M_i)} \times 100 \qquad (4)$$

or

$$B_j = \left[1 - \frac{\sum\limits_{i}^{n} |X_i - M_i|}{\sum\limits_{i}^{n} (X_i + M_i)} \right] \times 100 \qquad (5)$$

for n set of industries.

Table 3.1 sets out a simple example of how the Grubel and Lloyd summary formula may be used to obtain a measure of a country's average level of intra-industry trade. There are assumed to be just five industries — A, B, C, D, and E. B_i is calculated for each. The average level of intra-industry trade, B_j, is obtained using the above formula and comes to 64 per cent. To have taken the average of all the B_is would have given a misleading average because the importance of some product groups is greater than the others. The Grubel and Lloyd formula is a weighted mean.

One problem with B_j is that it makes no allowance for any imbalance in a country's total trade. Where a country has a large trade imbalance (surplus or deficit), B_j will be biased downwards and the true extent of intra-industry trade will accordingly be underestimated. To tackle this problem, Grubel and Lloyd proposed an alternative formula which adjusts for any trade imbalance:

$$C_j = \frac{\sum_i^n (X_i + M_i) - \sum_i^n |X_i - M_i|}{\sum_i^n (X_i + M_i) - |\sum_i^n X_i - \sum_i^n M_i|} \times 100 \qquad (6)$$

Compare (6) with (4). It can be seen that the denominator in (4) has been reduced by the amount of country j's overall trade imbalance. Accordingly, the greater a country's trade imbalance, the greater the difference between C_j and B_j. Clearly, whenever a country's total trade is unbalanced, C_j is the preferred formula. This can be seen from Table 3.1. The C_j formula gives a mean level of intra-industry trade of 81 per cent compared with 64 per cent for the B_j formula.

Table 3.1: An example of how to calculate intra-industry trade using the Grubel and Lloyd indices

Product groups	X_i	M_i	$|X_i - M_i|$	B_i
A	40	30	10	86
B	80	40	40	67
C	10	60	50	29
D	70	70	0	100
E	200	60	140	46
$\sum$	400	260	240	

$$B_j = \frac{(660 - 240)}{660} \times 100 = \frac{420}{660} \times 100 = 64$$

$$C_j = \frac{(660 - 240)}{(660 - 140)} \times 100 = \frac{420}{520} \times 100 = 81$$

Balassa

In estimating the extent of intra-industry specialization in the European Community, Bela Balassa adopted an alternative formula (Balassa 1974). He measured intra-industry trade by taking the sum of the ratios of trade balance (exports less imports) to total trade (exports plus imports) for each product group and then dividing by the number of product groups:

$$E_j = \frac{1}{n} \sum_{i}^{n} \frac{|X_i - M_i|}{(X_i + M_i)} \qquad (7)$$

where j stands for country j and i for product group i out of n industries. In the Balassa formula, E_j tends towards zero when all trade is intra-industry trade and towards one when all trade is inter-industry trade. Thus Balassa took a fall in E_j as evidence for intra-industry specialization.

Aquino

Aquino has criticized the Grubel and Lloyd formula for failing to correct fully for an imbalance in a country's overall trade (Aquino 1978). He has argued that, as a result, Grubel and Lloyd underestimated the true extent of intra-industry trade. His argument is that C_j above is itself a weighted average of the individual product group ratios, B_i. However, these are downwardly biased also whenever a country's total trade is unbalanced. Therefore it is not enough to correct the summary formula B_j by the overall trade imbalance to obtain C_j. Each B_i needs to be adjusted for the trade imbalance, not just the summary formula, B_j.

The easiest way of understanding Aquino's argument is by means of an example. Consider Table 3.2. Two hypothetical cases are shown. In both cases, the country's overall trade surplus is the same. The unadjusted Grubel and Lloyd formula, B_j, gives an average level of 66.7 per cent in both cases. However, because of the imbalance in total trade, B_j gives a downwardly-biased estimate of the true level of intra-industry trade. If, however, we apply the adjustment proposed by Grubel and Lloyd to obtain C_j, we obtain a level of 100 per cent in both cases. However, while this is correct in the first case, Aquino has argued that it is incorrect in the second case. In the first case, all trade is clearly intra-industry trade as the ratio of exports to imports is the same for all product groups. Therefore it is appropriate to adjust the average level of intra-industry trade by the size of the overall trade balance. However, in the second case, this is clearly not so. Not all trade is intra-industry trade. Rather, there is a clear tendency towards specialization in textiles relative to chemicals and machinery. Yet C_j is the same in the second case as in the first case.

Table 3.2: An example of the trade-imbalance distortion effect of using the Grubel and Lloyd summary intra-industry trade index

Product group	Case 1			Case 2		
	X_i	M_i	$\|X_i - M_i\|$	X_i	M_i	$\|X_i - M_i\|$
Chemicals	20	10	10	10	10	0
Textiles	10	5	5	40	5	35
Machinery	40	20	20	20	20	0
$\sum$	70	35	35	70	35	35

$$B_j = \frac{105 - 35}{105} = 66.7 \qquad B_j = \frac{105 - 35}{105} = 66.7$$

$$C_j = \frac{105 - 35}{105 - 35} = 100 \qquad C_j = \frac{105 - 35}{105 - 35} = 100$$

Table 3.3: An example of the Aquino trade-imbalance adjusted method of measurement of intra-industry trade

Product group	Case 1			Case 2		
	X_i^e	M_i^e	$X_i^e - M_i^e$	X_i^e	M_i^e	$X_i^e - M_i^e$
Chemicals	15.0	15.0	0	7.5	15.0	7.5
Textiles	7.5	7.5	0	30.0	7.5	22.5
Machinery	30.0	30.0	0	15.0	30.0	15.0
$\sum$			0			45.0

$$Q = \frac{105 - 0}{105} = 100 \qquad Q = \frac{105 - 45}{105} = 57.1$$

Accordingly, Aquino has proposed adjusting each B_i whenever a country's total trade is unbalanced and then estimating the overall average for the country using the adjusted B_i ratios. He proposed estimating hypothetical export and import values for each product group i on the assumption that total trade is balanced. The formulae for calculating these hypothetical export and import values are:

$$X_i^e = \frac{X_i \cdot \frac{1}{2} \sum_i^n (X_i + M_i)}{\sum_i^n X_i} \qquad (8)$$

$$M_i^e = \frac{M_i \cdot \frac{1}{2} \sum_i^n (X_i + M_i)}{\sum_i^n M_i} \qquad (9)$$

These hypothetical values may then be inserted into formula (4) to obtain a trade-imbalance-adjusted summary measure of intra-industry trade:

$$Q = \frac{\sum_i^n (X_i + M_i) - \sum_i^n |X_i^e - M_i^e|}{(X_i + M_i)} \times 100 \qquad (10)$$

Table 3.3 gives an example of the Aquino method for adjusting for trade imbalance. The data used are those contained in Table 3.2. Q_j equals 100 per cent in the first case and 57 per cent in the second case. In this particular example, the Aquino formula gives a lower estimate of intra-industry trade than the Grubel–Lloyd formula. However, where a country's total trade is unbalanced, the Grubel and Lloyd formula may also underestimate the true extent of intra-industry trade.

Aquino's approach has been criticized for a number of reasons. First, it implicitly assumes that any trade imbalance is equiproportionately spread across all industries. Thus, in Tables 3.2 and 3.3 it is assumed that the imbalance of $70/35 = 2/1$ is evenly spread across chemicals, machinery, and textiles. The validity of this assumption is questionable. Thus a country may have moved strongly into surplus on account of a uniquely good performance in just one of the three sectors (say, textiles in the second case). Is it then appropriate to apply accordingly an adjustment to the B_i ratios for the other sectors (chemicals and machinery)? Does this not create a new kind of distortion to the measurement of intra-industry trade? Second, it fails to allow for cyclical or other exceptional influences on a country's overall trade balance. The basis for the adjustment is the country's trade balance for the year in question, but this might not be a normal year. The trade balance is subject to cyclical fluctuations in the level of economic activity. Periods of economic upswing tend to correspond with a deterioration in a country's external balance of trade. If the year in question is one such year, overadjustment will result. However, it is not clear how this problem can be overcome. Ideally, we would need some estimate of a country's trade balance adjusted for cyclical influences, but this would be difficult to obtain.

Bergstrand

A criticism of all the above methods of measuring the level of intra-industry trade has been made by Bergstrand (Bergstrand 1983). He has argued that they wrongly measure intra-industry trade as a proportion of a country's total trade with all other countries, i.e. the country's multilateral trade. Instead, intra-industry trade should be measured as a proportion of a country's bilateral trade, that is the country's trade with each trading partner. For example, in measuring for intra-industry specialization in the European Community, intra-industry trade should be estimated in relation to each bilateral trade flow between each pair of member states. There exist strong theoretical grounds for doing so. If our concern is with the validity of the Hecksher–Ohlin theory as a model of trade and its ability to predict the direction and magnitude of trade flows, the appropriate level at which to evaluate the theory is that of bilateral trade between any pair of countries. It can be demonstrated that it is only at that level that the Hecksher–Ohlin theory can hold. Berstrand argues as follows:

> in a multicountry, multicommodity, two factor, factor-price nonequalised world, the commodity version of the H–O theorem need not hold for a country's multilateral trade, but will hold for any pair of countries. The inability of this generalised commodity version of the H–O theorem to hold for multilateral trade suggests that the existence of multilateral IIT (intra-industry trade) is not unexpected; hence, the prominence of multilateral IIT is uninteresting. The holding of this H–O theorem's commodity version for bilateral trade suggests that the presence of bilateral IIT is interesting (because this version of the theorem precludes it). (Bergstrand 1983)

This consideration had led Bergstrand to propose a bilateral intra-industry trade index. However, the question arises as to how this should be corrected for a trade imbalance in a country's overall trade. Should we take the imbalance in a country's overall, multilateral trade or the imbalance in the country's trade with the partner in question? Bergstrand favoured the first of these alternatives: bilateral trade flows should be adjusted for a country's multilateral trade imbalance. He proposed the following *bilateral* intra-industry trade index adjusted for each country's *multilateral* trade imbalance:

$$G_{ij}^{k*} = 1 - \left[\frac{|X_{ij}^{k*} - X_{ji}^{k*}|}{X_{ij}^{k*} + X_{ji}^{k*}} \right] \tag{11}$$

where

$$X_{ij}^{k*} = \tfrac{1}{2} \left[\frac{(X_{i.} + M_{.i})}{2X_{i.}} + \frac{(X_{j.} + M_{.j})}{2M_{.j}} \right] \times X_{ij}^{k} \tag{12}$$

$$X_{ji}^{k*} = \tfrac{1}{2} \left[\frac{X_{j.} + M_{.j})}{2X_{j.}} + \frac{(X_{i.} + M_{.i})}{2M_{.i}} \right] \times X_{ji}^{k} \tag{13}$$

In this formula, X_{ij} refers to the value of bilateral exports from country i to country j (or bilateral imports of country j from country i) in industry k. Conversely, X_{ji} refers to the value of bilateral exports from country j to country i (or bilateral imports of country i from country j) in industry k. If country i's overall trade is balanced and $X_{ij}^{k} = X_{ji}^{k}$, all trade between country i and country j in industry k will be intra-industry trade and the intra-industry trade index for industry k, G_{ij}^{k}, will be equal to one. However, when country i's total (i.e. multilateral) trade is unbalanced, adjustment must be made. Equations (12) and (13) involve the calculation of hypothetical export and import values, X_{ij}^{k*} and M_{ji}^{k*} respectively, for each flow of bilateral trade in industry k between each pair of countries involved, utilizing the adjustment formula proposed by Aquino. However, Bergstrand's method is subject to similar criticisms to Aquino. In particular, is it appropriate to distribute the multilateral balancing proportionately between individual industries? Can the multilateral trade imbalance for any one particular year be used as a measure of long-term disequilibrium? Might it not be influenced by the level of economic activity in that particular year and other cyclical influences?

THE AGGREGATION PROBLEM

One of the greatest problems involved in accurately measuring the extent and importance of intra-industry trade is the aggregation problem. It has been argued that intra-industry trade is largely a statistical and not a real phenomenon because it is due to a large number of different products being treated as belonging to the same industry. At least, it is argued, the true extent of intra-industry trade has been exaggerated. Even if we reject this argument, it has to be conceded that accurate measurement of intra-industry trade is, in practice, quite difficult.

Trade data are published according to a specified form of classification. The most commonly used is the Standard International Trade Classification (SITC). Products are grouped together at several different levels of aggregation. The level of aggregation is shown by the number of digits in the number used in the product classification. The highest level of aggregation is the one-digit level. The second-, third-, fourth-, and fifth-digit levels involve an increasing degree of disaggregation. Take 'Chemicals' (SITC Group 5) as an example. Some of the subdivisions for this product group are listed in Table 3.4. Chemicals is made up of nine two-digit product groups. Each two-digit group can be further subdivided into various three-digit product groups. The case of 'Chemical elements and compounds' (SITC Group 51) is listed in the table. It subdivides into four three-digit product groups. Each of these can be further subdivided into a number of four-digit groups. Thus 'Organic chemicals' (SITC Group 512) subdivides into nine four-digit product groups.

Thus it is possible to choose the level of aggregation which is considered most appropriate. Usually, intra-industry trade is measured at the three-digit level of the SITC as product groups defined at this level of aggregation are generally thought to accord as closely as possible to an economic definition of an

Table 3.4: An example of the method of classifying trade statistics used by the SITC Group 5, Chemicals

- 51 Chemical elements & compounds
  - 512 Organic chemicals
    - 5121 Hydrocarbons & derivs.
    - 5122 Alcohols, phenols, etc.
    - 5123 Ethers, epoxides, etc.
    - 5124 Aldehyde, ketone, etc.
    - 5125 Acids & derivs.
    - 5126 Inorganic esters
    - 5127 Nitrogen function comps.
    - 5128 Organo-inorganic comps.
    - 5129 Other organic chems.
  - 513 Inorganic chemicals
  - 514 Other inorganic chemicals
  - 515 Radioactive & associated materials
- 52 Mineral Tar & crude chemicals from coal, petroleum & natural gas
- 53 Dyeing, tanning & colouring materials
- 54 Medicinal & pharmaceutical products
- 55 Essential oils & perfume materials; Polishing & cleansing preparations
- 56 Fertilizers manufactured
- 57 Explosives & pyrotechnic products
- 58 Plastic materials, regenerated cellulose & artificial resins
- 59 Chemical materials & products

industry. However, it is sometimes argued that, even at this level of aggregation, intra-industry trade is overestimated. Products are often grouped together which fail to meet the criteria generally used in the definition of an industry. Economists may disagree about how serious is such aggregation bias, but none would deny that some element of aggregation bias exists. The product groups used by the statisticians are often based more on considerations of statistical convenience than economic meaningfulness. The important question concerns whether the existence of aggregation bias is such as to account for all or most of the measured intra-industry trade. In other words, is all intra-industry trade due simply to aggregation bias or does it have some real non-statistical basis?

Before we proceed to answer this question, it is important to be clear about the nature of aggregation bias. As we have seen, it arises when products are grouped together which are essentially different products and, therefore, cannot be regarded as being part of the output of the same industry. This will be the case where the input requirements or factor intensities are different. Where this is so, aggregation bias will have two elements: (1) an 'opposite-sign' effect and (2) a 'weighting' effect (Gray 1979). Suppose that a product group, X, has two sub-groups, X_1 and X_2, both of which have different input requirements or factor intensities and which, therefore, are outputs of different industries. Aggregation bias will result when these two subgroups have opposite signs, a trade surplus in one and a trade deficit in another. Indeed, at the extreme, where the trade surplus in one product (say X_1) exactly equals the trade deficit in the other (say X_2), there will exist a zero trade balance in X and all trade in X will appear to be intra-industry trade. All trade will be balanced and a conventional measure of the level of intra-industry trade will record a level of 100 per cent as the amount of intra-industry trade. This is the 'opposite-sign' effect.

On the other hand, if the two products, X_1 and X_2, both have the same signs—whether a trade surplus or trade deficit—there will be no opposite-sign effect and intra-industry trade will not be overestimated. Indeed, the use of a conventional Grubel–Lloyd formula will have the highly desirable quality that it will give a weighted average measure of the level of intra-industry trade in the two subgroups, X_1 and X_2. The amount of trade in each subgroup will act as the weights. Thus it is only when the two subgroups have opposite signs and the products in question have different factor intensities that aggregation bias distorts the measurement of intra-industry trade.

There are a number of ways of testing for the degree of aggregation bias. One obvious approach is to calculate intra-industry trade at a higher level of disaggregation, for example to use four- or even five-digit product groups. It is extremely time-consuming to carry out a comprehensive study of a country's level of intra-industry trade using highly disaggregated data of this kind. The number of product groups involved will be very large and the amount of calculation very great. Moreover, product groups defined at the fourth- or fifth-digit level of the SITC may not be economically meaningful. Products with the same factor intensities may appear in different product groups. In this case, some intra-industry trade will show up as inter-industry trade. However, it may be possible to regroup data into a variety of three-digit and four-digit product groups to achieve more meaningful product groups, while excluding some of the least meaningful groups (e.g. the miscellaneous categories). Again, however, the amount of work involved is likely to be quite considerable. It would be difficult to carry out a comprehensive exercise covering all the industries of one or more countries using such an approach.

With reference to the chemical industries of the European Community, I attempted to carry out such an exercise. Some fourteen product groups were identified covering most but not all chemical products. These involved a mixture of three- and four-digit levels of aggregation. A high average level of intra-industry trade was found to exist for all nine member states. The average for all countries rose from 57 per cent in 1973 to 61 per cent in 1980. Other studies covering the effects of disaggregation on the level of intra-industry trade strongly suggest that the extent of aggregation bias is not such as to question the real significance of intra-industry trade. Thus Greenaway and Milner calculated the average level of intra-industry trade for the United Kingdom at the third-, fourth-, and fifth-digit levels of the SITC. The average level of intra-industry trade was found to fall from 56 per cent to 47 per cent to 46.5 per cent as the level of aggregation fell from the third- to the fourth- to the fifth-digit level (Greenaway and Milner 1983). The fact that, at the fifth level of aggregation, 46.5 per cent of trade was found to be intra-industry, would seem to refute the argument that intra-industry trade is largely a statistical phenomenon.

A further way of testing for the degree of aggregation bias has been proposed by Greenaway and Milner (Greenaway and Milner 1983). Consider the case of a three-digit product group, j, which is made up of four four-digit product subgroups, A, B, C, and D. The levels of exports and imports for each product are shown in Table 3.5. A conventional Grubel–Lloyd formula for measuring intra-industry trade, B_j, gives the level of intra-industry trade for industry j to be 86.7 per cent. It is apparent that some aggregation bias exists because product D has a different trade balance sign to products A, B, and C. If the factor intensities of all four products are different, the level of intra-industry trade will be overestimated. The extent of aggregation bias may be calculated by using the following formula to measure intra-industry trade:

$$C_j = 1 - \frac{\sum |X_{ij} - M_{ij}|}{\sum (X_{ij} + M_{ij})} \times 100 \qquad (14)$$

where j is the jth set of n industries and i is the component subgroup categories for the jth industry. This differs from B_j in that the numerator uses the sum of the trade balances regardless of the sign. It can be seen from Table 3.5 that the use of this formula yields a measure of intra-industry trade of 66.7 per cent, somewhat lower than B_j. This is a measure of the degree of aggregation bias. If all four products had the same trade balance sign, then B_j would equal C_j. Thus the greater the divergence of B_j from C_j, the stronger the opposite sign effect and the greater the degree of aggregation bias.

Table 3.5: An example of how to test for categorical aggregation in the measurement of intra-industry trade: the Greenaway–Milner method

Product Sub-groups	The jth of n industries			Trade balance sign
	X_i	M_i	$X_i–M_i$	
A	20	20	0	0
B	60	40	20	+
C	40	30	10	+
D	10	80	70	−
$\sum$	130	170	100	−

105

$$B_j = \frac{300 - 40}{300} = 86.7$$

$$C_j = \frac{300 - 100}{300} = 66.7$$

Therefore, $C_j < B_j$ due to the opposite sign effect.

Greenaway and Milner applied this test to United Kingdom and Switzerland trade statistics for the year 1977 (Greenaway and Milner 1983). They found that, as was to be expected, values for C_j were typically less than those for B_j. Clearly, aggregation bias was present. However, the differences were quite small. This would seem to give support to the view that aggregation bias accounts for only a small proportion of observed intra-industry trade. One interesting finding was that aggregation bias was greater in foodstuffs and raw materials (SITC 0–4) and less in semi- and finished-manufactures (SITC 5–8).

Thus the available evidence is against the view that intra-industry trade is merely a statistical phenomenon. High levels of intra-industry trade appear to exist even when the data is disaggregated. Moreover, as we shall see in a later section of this chapter, the level of intra-industry trade appears to be increasing over time. While aggregation bias may lead to the overestimation of intra-industry trade in any given year, it cannot satisfactorily explain why the level of observed intra-industry trade is increasing over time. Although this could be due to a proliferation of products with different factor intensities within a given statistical classification, it seems unlikely that this can explain the tendency for the level of intra-industry trade to rise.

THE LEVEL OF INTRA-INDUSTRY TRADE

A large number of studies have been carried out to measure the level of intra-industry trade in different countries. This section refers to just a few such studies in order to demonstrate the growing importance of intra-industry trade. One of the first comprehensive studies of intra-industry trade was H. G. Grubel and P. J. Lloyd's 'Intra-Industry Trade' (Grubel and Lloyd 1975). This measured the average level of intra-industry trade in ten OECD countries covering some 160 product groups at the three-digit level of the SITC. The formulae used were those given earlier in the chapter. They found that the average level of intra-industry trade rose from 36 per cent in 1959 to 48 per cent in 1967. The highest levels of intra-industry trade were obtained for trade in manufactured goods. The average level of intra-industry trade for manufactured goods rose from 54 per cent in 1964 to 57 per cent in 1967. Lassudrie-Duchêne and Muchieli updated Grubel and Lloyd's figure for manufactures and found that, by 1974, the ratio had risen to over 60 per cent (Lassudrie-Duchêne and Muchieli 1979).

Tables 3.6 and 3.7 summarize these results. They show that the West European countries—notably, France, the United Kingdom, Belgium–Luxembourg, and the Netherlands—had the highest levels of intra-industry trade. The United States, Canada, Japan, and Australia all had much lower intra-industry trade ratios. Nevertheless, the level of intra-industry trade increased as a share of total trade in all ten countries except the Netherlands. The biggest increases were recorded for Belgium–Luxembourg and the United Kingdom. Table 3.7 shows that the highest levels of intra-industry trade were to be found in chemicals and machinery products. The average levels of intra-industry trade in primary commodities (SITC 0–4) were lower. Intra-industry trade as a proportion of total trade increased most quickly in manufacturing goods.

Table 3.6: Intra-industry trade ratios for trade in manufactures among OECD countries, 1964, 1967, 1974

Country	Change 1964–74	1964	1967	1974
France	+ 7	74	77	81
Netherlands	− 1	73	72	72
United Kingdom	+ 9	68	71	77
Belgium–Luxembourg	+11	68	71	79
Italy	+ 3	58	58	61
West Germany	+ 6	52	55	58
United States	+ 8	46	49	54
Canada	+ 8	40	41	48
Japan	+ 8	46	49	54
Australia	+ 3	26	26	29
All countries	+ 6.7	53.7	56.5	60.4

Table 3.7: Intra-industry trade ratios and growth in total trade for OECD countries, 1959–67

SITC Section Code	Intra-industry trade ratios				Increase in total trade 1959–67 (%)
	1959	1964	1967	1974	
(0) Food and live animals	22	25	30	–	72
(1) Beverages and tobacco	40	42	40	–	68
(2) Crude materials	26	28	30	–	49
(3) Mineral fuels	30	29	30	–	80
(4) Oils and fats	41	39	37	–	23
(5) Chemicals	56	60	66	63	122
(6) Manufactures	43	49	49	58	325
(7) Machinery	43	53	59	62	202
(8) Misc. manufacturing	45	53	52	58	149
(9) Commodities, n.e.s.	34	45	55	–	180

Source: Grubel and Lloyd (1975); Lassudrie-Duchêne and Muchieli (1979); UNCTAD Secretariat (1980).

As we saw earlier in the chapter, Grubel and Lloyd's formula was criticized by Aquino for failing to adjust fully for an imbalance in a country's overall trade (Aquino 1978). Aquino argued that, for this reason, Grubel and Lloyd underestimated the true extent of intra-industry trade. Using a different formula, Aquino measured the level of intra-industry trade in some twenty-six countries covering some twenty-five product groups. Thus the product coverage was considerably more limited than that of Grubel and Lloyd. In addition, it was confined to manufactures only. However, Aquino used a mixture of three- and four-digit product groups to reduce the extent of aggregation bias. Aquino's results are shown in Table 3.8. The average level of intra-industry trade in France and the United Kingdom was over 80 per cent. In most other West European countries, it was over 70 per cent. However, a much lower level of intra-industry trade existed for Australia, the United States, and Japan. The ratios are generally higher than those obtained by Grubel and Lloyd due to the adjustment which Aquino made for imbalance in a country's overall trade. The fact that Japan's intra-industry trade ratio was still lower than that of other western industrialized economies would suggest that her trade surplus was not the cause. Alternative explanations must be sought. Finally, it should be noted that quite high levels of intra-industry trade were found for certain newly-industrializing countries (NICs), although intra-industry trade was generally less important in developing countries. The high ratio obtained for Singapore must have been due in part to the level of her entrepôt trade.

Table 3.8: Levels of intra-Industry trade as a proportion of total trade in manufactured goods by country, 1972

Country	IT Ratio (%)	Country	IT Ratio (%)
France	87.4	Australia	58.5
United Kingdom	81.9	United States	57.3
Netherlands	78.7	Yugoslavia	55.3
Sweden	76.3	Japan	54.8
West Germany	76.0	Mexico	54.8
Austria	75.0	Brazil	49.8
Canada	73.5	Spain	49.1
Norway	72.5	Portugal	40.9
Italy	72.3	Korea Republic	39.2
Singapore	71.4	Hong Kong	39.2
Denmark	70.3	Greece	35.7
Belgium	70.1	India	22.9
Ireland	64.5		
Switzerland	60.9		

Source: A. Aquino, Intra-Industry Trade and Inter-Industry Specialisation as Concurrent Sources of International Trade in Manufactures, *Weltwirtshaftliches Archiv*, vol. 114, no. 2, 1978, pp. 275–96, Table 1.

A more recent attempt to measure the level of intra-industry trade in different countries was a study by Claudy Culem and Lars Lundberg. This covered trade in manufactured goods calculated at the four-digit level of the SITC for eleven industrialized countries. The formula preferred was the adjusted summary measure proposed by Grubel and Lloyd (Culem and Lundberg 1986). Their results are summarized in Tables 3.9 and 3.10. The average level of intra-industry trade ranged from 29 per cent in Japan to 80 per cent in France. Once again it can be seen that the highest levels of intra-industry trade are to be found in the West European industrialized countries. France, the United Kingdom, Belgium, and the Netherlands have the highest levels of intra-industry trade of all countries. For all countries except Australia, intra-industry trade is more important as a share of trade with developed countries (DCs) than with less-developed countries (LDCs). Trade with centrally planned economies (CPEs) is also characterized by relatively low levels of intra-industry trade. Certain regional patterns are apparent. Thus high levels of intra-industry trade exist for Japan's trade with the Asian NICs. Western Europe's trade with South Europe also involved much intra-industry trade, as did the United States trade with Latin America. This would suggest that intra-industry trade is greatest between countries in close geographical proximity to each other.

Table 3.9: Shares of intra-Industry trade in total trade and in trade with certain groups of countries in 1980

| Country | World | Trade with | | | | | | CPEs |
		South Europe	Asian NICs	Latin America	Other LDCs	All LDCs	All DCs	
Australia	35.8	16.3	26.9	19.4	22.9	29.2	22.7	5.5
Belgium	79.7	54.1	29.8	11.4	33.4	40.1	77.6	29.0
Canada	58.5	30.6	15.7	25.0	11.0	33.0	56.7	18.1
France	80.4	64.4	29.7	16.3	31.4	44.2	79.2	40.0
West Germany	65.4	42.3	24.4	13.0	28.9	34.6	74.1	31.6
Italy	65.4	55.1	36.0	19.8	28.1	44.3	59.8	40.2
Japan	28.8	14.8	27.2	10.6	10.1	17.6	33.6	11.8
Netherlands	74.2	43.0	24.8	17.7	35.5	45.5	70.3	22.6
Sweden	66.5	29.2	15.1	7.6	8.8	17.4	72.5	30.7
United Kingdom	79.1	50.7	27.4	24.0	38.6	44.2	77.5	30.9
United States	60.7	33.8	26.5	29.6	25.8	35.0	66.7	37.9

Definitions: *South Europe*: Greece, Portugal, Spain, Cyprus, Gibraltar, Israel, Malta, Turkey, Yugoslavia. *Asian NICs*; Hong Kong, Macao, Singapore, Taiwan, South Korea. *CPEs*: European centrally planned economies.

Table 3.10: Change in the share of intra-industry trade between 1970 and 1980 (percentage units)

| Country | World | Trade with | | | | | | CPEs |
		South Europe	Asian NICs	Latin America	Other LDCs	All LDCs	All DCs	
Australia	5.4	−0.7	−8.3	2.8	3.8	0.1	4.2	−10.6
Belgium	4.1	15.3	10.7	−1.1	17.1	16.3	5.2	−17.7
Canada	−3.4	19.6	7.9	13.0	−8.4	11.6	−5.4	−6.5
France	3.6	29.4	9.2	1.5	11.0	19.0	6.4	4.0
West Germany	6.6	14.5	7.5	4.9	14.1	15.1	7.4	−4.2
Italy	6.6	26.8	1.1	9.3	7.5	20.5	0.3	8.7
Japan	−7.3	7.3	10.3	2.9	−2.5	1.9	−4.6	−21.5
Netherlands	5.5	7.8	11.3	−9.1	−1.2	7.0	5.7	−18.8
Sweden	4.1	9.3	9.0	2.7	−1.2	4.8	5.8	−0.6
United Kingdom	18.3	21.1	−0.8	7.3	12.7	12.8	12.3	−3.4
United States	1.4	8.1	2.4	6.3	1.1	4.3	5.8	6.9

Source: Culem and Lundberg (1986).

Table 3.10 shows that the level of intra-industry trade increased in all eleven countries except Japan and Canada between 1970 and 1980. One wonders whether the fall in Japan's index was due to the rise in her trade surplus as the formula adopted was that of Grubel and Lloyd which may fail to make a sufficient adjustment for trade imbalance. However, the fact that the ratio continued rising in all other countries is significant. The rise in the United Kingdom's ratio is particularly noteworthy. Another striking feature of Table 3.10 is the increase in intra-industry trade between developed and developing countries. Except for Australia, Sweden, and the United States, intra-industry trade grew faster between DCs and LDCs than between DCs and other DCs. More of the trade taking place in manufactured goods between developed and developing countries (mainly NICs) is of the intra-industry type. Especially large increases in intra-industry trade were also apparent for trade between some West European countries and South Europe.

THEORETICAL EXPLANATIONS FOR INTRA-INDUSTRY TRADE

One of the reasons why economists have been interested in the growth of intra-industry trade is that, on the whole, it contradicts the predictions of conventional trade theory. According to the latter, each country will specialize in those products in which it enjoys a comparative advantage. It will exchange those products for others in which other countries possess a comparative advantage. Conventional trade theory stresses (1) differences in factor endowments between countries and (2) differences in the factor proportions required for producing different goods as the basis for comparative advantage. Countries are differently endowed by nature with the various factors of production (land, labour, and capital) required for production. This means that, in the absence of trade, the relative prices of these factors will differ between countries. Land will be relatively cheap in countries well endowed with land, labour will be relatively cheap in countries well endowed with labour, and capital relatively cheap in countries well endowed with capital. By implication, this assumes that factor markets are perfectly competitive.

At the same time, different factor proportions are required

for the production of different goods. Some productive processes are highly labour intensive, others capital intensive, others land intensive. For example, steel production is quite capital intensive. Capital costs account for a high proportion of total costs. By way of contrast, most forms of cloth making are labour intensive. Labour costs account for a high proportion of total costs. It follows that countries which are well endowed with unskilled labour will tend to have a comparative advantage in labour-intensive activities such as clothing manufacture. Other countries well endowed with capital will have a comparative advantage in capital-intensive activities like steel manufacture. Accordingly, countries will specialize in these activities, exporting the products of those industries in exchange for imports of products of other industries. This is well known as the Hecksher–Ohlin or Factor Proportions Theory of Trade.

The Hecksher–Ohlin theory, may be modified to make it more realistic. For example, instead of just three factors of production—land, labour, and capital—these categories may be subdivided into narrower groups, for example skilled and unskilled labour, physical and human capital, agricultural and non-agricultural land, and so on. Technology may be incorporated as another factor of production to ensure that another important determinant of trade is included. Thus some countries well endowed with scientists and engineers may enjoy a comparative advantage in knowledge-intensive, science-based industries. However, even with these modifications, the Hecksher–Ohlin theory leaves a lot of actual trade unexplained. Some patterns of trade fail to accord with the predictions of the Hecksher–Ohlin theory. As discussed in Chapter 2, the fastest-growing area of trade in the post-war period has been trade between the advanced industrialized economies. Many of these countries possess broadly similar factor endowments. Moreover, most of this trade has taken the form of intra-industry trade. Yet the Hecksher–Ohlin theory largely (but not wholly) predicts inter-industry trade.

To see this, we need to recall the criteria usually adopted for defining an industry. Although economists differ in the criteria which they adopt, substitution in production is normally included. That is to say, products which are grouped together as belonging to the same industry must have broadly similar factor intensities or input requirements. If this is so, it follows that a country which possesses a comparative advantage in just one product belonging to an industry will possess a comparative advantage in all the products of that industry. It will not merely specialize in one or just some of the products of that industry. Rather, it will, all other things being equal, specialize in the full range of products. Certainly, it will not export some of the products of that industry, yet import others. In short, intra-industry trade is largely incompatible with the Hecksher–Ohlin theory. There are certain exceptions to this as we shall see. On the whole, however, the theory predicts inter-industry trade and inter-industry specialization.

Thus the existence of intra-industry trade and intra-industry specialization rather suggests that the Hecksher–Ohlin theory has only a limited usefulness as a theory seeking to predict patterns of trade and specialization in the world. In particular, it fails rather badly to explain the most important type of trade over the last quarter century, namely, trade between industrialized countries in manufactured goods. If conventional trade theory is unhelpful, how can we explain intra-industry trade? What causes intra-industry trade? Why has it increased in importance in recent decades? In seeking to give reasons for intra-industry trade, it is helpful to distinguish between (1) trade in functionally-identical commodities and (2) trade in differentiated commodities. As will be seen, most intra-industry trade occurs in the second category. In fact, some writers have chosen to define intra-industry trade as trade in differentiated commodities. However, intra-industry trade can occur in commodities which are identical, although it is generally not statistically very important.

Trade in Functionally-Identical Commodities

Functionally-identical commodities are commodities which have perfect substitutability in use. They are perfect substitutes for each other. Another way of putting this is to say that they have a high positive cross elasticity of demand. Consumers have no reason to prefer one to the other. Conventional trade theories, such as the Hecksher–Ohlin theory, generally make such assumptions about commodities. Although normally trade in such products will take the form of inter-industry trade, intra-industry trade can take place. Listed below are seven possible causes of intra-industry trade in functionally-identical commodities:

1. **Aggregation bias** We have already discussed this problem earlier in this chapter. It is possible that products may be grouped together which are not close substitutes in production, that is they are not produced using the same factor proportions or input requirements. As such, they belong to different industries. Hence, what appears to be intra-industry trade is in fact inter-industry trade. It may well be caused by differing factor intensities and relative factor prices in accordance with the Hecksher–Ohlin theory.

2. **Cross-border trade** This can occur in products which are 'weight-gaining'. This means products whose weight (in relation to the unit value of the product) increases with the degree of manufacturing. Examples might be bricks, cement, glass bottles, and so on. This necessitates locating production as near as possible to the market. Because of the costs of transporting such products, it will not be profitable for producers to transport the product long distances. Hence, each producer will confront a potential market area determined by transport costs. In Figure 3.1, producer A in country X confronts a potential market given by the circle around the point of his production. Likewise, producer B in country Y confronts a potential market given by the circle around his point of production. Trade will flow in different directions at different points along the border. Producer A in country X will export some of his output to consumers in country Y. Producer B in country Y will export some of his output to consumers in country X. Both countries will simultaneously export and import the product in question. The existence of tariffs and other trade barriers may serve to reduce such trade. In this case, the removal of such restrictions will lead to a flourishing of such trade. It is believed that some of the intra-industry trade in iron and steel products following the establishment of the European Coal and Steel Community (ECSC) in 1952 may have been of this type (Adler 1970).

3. **Differentiation in time** Some goods are only available at certain times of the year. Fresh fruit and vegetables come into this category. It may be that during these times of the year such products are imported from abroad, while, at other times of the year, some of what is grown locally is exported. In this event, intra-industry trade results. The same happens in the case of other commodities, the demand for which fluctuates. Take electricity as an example. Because of the heavy fixed costs in the electricity supply industry, it is important to keep power

Figure 3.1 An example of intra-industry trade occurring in weight-gaining products across borders

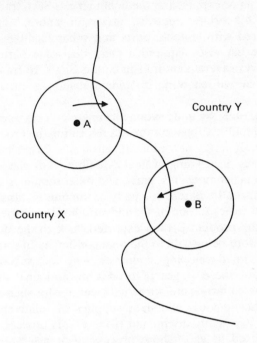

stations operating at near full capacity. This may mean that it is more efficient to supplement domestically generated power with imported electricity at peak times, while exporting electricity at off-peak times when domestic demand is inadequate to ensure full utilization of capacity. Again, intra-industry trade is the result.

4. **Joint production and joint consumption** Some products are produced jointly. In some cases the proportions in which they are produced cannot be varied. Apparently, this is quite common in the chemical industries. Unless local demand combines these products in the same proportions, the result will be excess supply of some products and excess demand for others. The result may be that the country in question will both export certain products and import other products. The result will be intra-industry trade. The same situation may result where products are consumed jointly. Unless they are available in the right proportions domestically, home production may have to be supplemented by imports. Yet some of the output may, at other times, be exported.

5. **Entrepôt trade** This refers to the importation of a finished product for packaging, labelling, warehousing, and so on, before being re-exported to the final market. Such trade is very important for certain countries, such as Singapore. Singapore is well situated with suitable ports and other facilities for such trade. She has also acquired a great deal of experience and acumen over several centuries in conducting such trade. Much of this trade will show up in trade statistics as intra-industry trade.

6. **Cross hauling by multinational companies** This refers to the practice of multinational companies relocating the processing or final assembly stages of manufacturing at sites based in developing countries. Processing or final assembly takes place at these factories using components, parts, and other semi-finished goods imported from the parent company of the multinational or one of its subsidiaries in one of the industrialized countries. When finished, the product is then exported back to the developed country before being sold to the final consumer. In some cases, producers in developing countries may be subcontracted to carry out these stages of processing and final assembly. Developing countries are attractive locations for such activities because they possess abundant supplies of relatively cheap, unskilled, but highly disciplined labour. This process is sometimes referred to as offshore processing or assembly. It has become increasingly important in recent decades, especially in the electronics and textile/clothing industries. In some cases it has been encouraged by special tariff provisions in the industrialized countries, which treat imports of such products more leniently than other equivalent imports. Chapter 6 will examine the growth of this type of activity in greater depth. This chapter merely notes its importance as a source of intra-industry trade affecting mich trade in manufactures between industrialized and developing countries. In fact, however, such trade more closely resembles the inter-industry trade of the Hecksher–Ohlin theory. It is based on relative factor intensities, specifically the comparative advantage which developing countries possess in labour-intensive activities. Therefore, we ought to regard such trade as inter-industry rather than intra-industry, although it may appear as intra-industry. This is because trade statistics often group together components, parts, semi-finished goods, and finished goods, For some purposes, this is appropriate. Since, however, such trade conforms more closely with

conventional Hecksher–Ohlin predictions, it might be preferable to treat it as inter-industry. However, the practices of different economists differ, and some choose to treat this as a special type of intra-industry trade. Sometimes, the term 'vertical intra-industry trade' is used to distinguish this from the more common horizontal intra-industry trade.

7. **Reciprocal dumping** One other more complex case of intra-industry trade in functionally-identical commodities has been suggested by Brander and Krugman (1983). The model involved is complicated and will not be examined in this book. The interested reader should either consult the original article or a specialist text on the subject (e.g. Greenaway and Milner 1986). In fact, its practical usefulness is quite limited. It is based on the special case of where two monopoly producers of an identical commodity, each located in a different country, confront each other in trade. It is possible to show that, on the basis of certain assumptions about their behaviour (so-called Cournot behaviour), intra-industry trade will result. Each producer will sell one-half of his output in the market of his rival. If transport costs are incorporated into the model, the situation changes slightly. The marginal costs of exporting increase in relation to the marginal costs of selling at home. Hence each producer reduces the amount which he produces for exporting and charges a higher price. However, the higher price is not enough to pay for the costs of transport, so that the ex-factory price charged on exports is lower than that charged on sales to the home market. This is why the situation is described as one of reciprocal dumping. ('Dumping' is the term used by economists to refer to a situation where a producer charges a lower price on sales to the foreign market than sales to the home market.)

Thus, intra-industry trade is possible in functionally-identical commodities. It follows that the Hecksher–Ohlin theory is not wholly incompatible with intra-industry trade. However, none of the above cases could properly be described as examples of intra-industry specialization. They illustrate how it is possible to have intra-industry trade (or what shows up as intra-industry trade) without intra-industry specialization. Statistically, there is no way of saying how important are such types of intra-industry trade. However, it seems unlikely that they can explain much more than a small proportion of intra-industry trade.

Trade in Differentiated Commodities

Most intra-industry trade takes place in commodities which are differentiated. It is this which leads to intra-industry specialization. Differentiated commodities are like commodities which are close, but not perfect, substitutes for each other. They have high, but not perfect, cross elasticity of demand. Where products are differentiated, a basis exists for intra-industry trade, although the existence of product differentiation does not amount to a sufficient condition for intra-industry trade. Alongside the existence of product differentiation, there must exist some element of increasing returns in production (or decreasing average costs) which causes producers to specialize. If average cost were constant or rose as production increased, producers would seek to supply consumers with all available varieties of a given commodity. They do not do so because the production of each variety involves incurring substantial fixed production costs. A large output is needed over which to spread these costs. Yet no one producer can achieve this output if all producers seek to produce the full range of varieties. So each producer specializes.

Product differentiation can take a number of different forms and it is helpful to draw a distinction between each of these. One useful approach is to identify three broad types of differentiation:

1. **Horizontal differentiation** This occurs where commodities share certain 'core' attributes but combine these in different proportions. Consumers have diverse preferences for the different varieties available. Such differentiation is very common in industries such as the tobacco industry (different brands of cigarettes) or the detergents industry (different brands of soap powder) or clothing (different styles of men's suits) or the footwear industry (different styles of ladies' shoes). Indeed, to varying degrees, horizontal differentiation is present in most industries. Nevertheless, in certain industries it is the predominant type of differentiation. Such differentiation partly reflects consumer demand for more variety and choice with rising per capita incomes. It may also be the result of competition with each producer seeking to increase their market share by differentiating their product from that of their rivals. (This is the case of monopolistic competition.) Equally, product

differentiation may be the result of attempts by producers to erect barriers to deter potential new entrants to the industry.

2. **Vertical differentiation** This occurs where products differ in quality from one another. For example, a Rolls Royce is known to be a superior quality car to an Austin Metro. Such quality differentiation is extremely common in the motor car industry. Firms compete by making quality improvements to their various model ranges. It is common in many other consumer goods industries — for example watches, musical equipment, personal computers, typewriters, and so on. The essence of vertical differentiation is that consumers are able to rank the different varieties in some kind of order according to the quality of the product.

3. **Technological differentiation** This refers to the kind of differentiation which results from technological change, specifically, the development of new products. Product innovation is very common in certain industries. One example is the pharmaceuticals industry. New drugs to treat particular illnesses or conditions are constantly being brought onto the market by drugs producers. The electronics industry is another example of an industry where the rate of product innovation has been extremely rapid in recent years.

Although intra-industry specialization may occur with all three kinds of product differentiation, each case may be slightly different. It has been suggested that technological differentiation is more likely to lead to inter-industry specialization consistent with the Hecksher–Ohlin model of trade. As we have seen, the Hecksher–Ohlin model may be adapted to incorporate technological change. Technology may be treated as an additional factor of production. This would lead to the prediction that countries well endowed with technological knowledge (i.e. those with large numbers of scientists and engineers) will produce the greatest number of new products. Therefore they will enjoy a comparative advantage in the 'newest', most technologically advanced, science-based industries. This is inter-industry and not intra-industry specialization. Chapter 1 discussed the product life-cycle model of trade applicable to industries characterized by product innovation. Where 'new' and 'old' products are classified as belonging to the same industry, the product life-cycle may give rise to intra-industry trade. Advanced industrialized countries will import 'old' products and export 'new' ones. Conversely, developing countries may import 'new' products while exporting 'old' ones. Equally, an industrialized country may export certain new products, while importing other new products which have been discovered in another industrialized country. For example, a country may export personal computers while importing video cassette recorders.

Thus technological differentiation may give rise to intra-industry specialization, where a country develops an innovative capability in a certain range or type of product. The existence of increasing returns to scale in science-based industries would appear to be another factor leading to intra-industry specialization. Such industries are typified by high levels of research-and-development (R & D) expenditure relative to turnover. These expenditures have to be incurred before a product is actually produced and sold. They are recuperated in later years to the extent that the new product is a success and sells well. However, even a successful new product is likely to have quite a short life. For example, in the pharmaceuticals industry, new patented products normally have market lives of only six to ten years. This is a comparatively short time in which to recuperate the amounts spent on R & D and earn a decent return on these expenditures. An innovating firm must therefore sell as much as possible as quickly as possible and for the highest price that the market will bear. These considerations lead to the expectation that, in many science-based industries, intra-industry specialization will in fact be quite great. By specializing on a small range of products, producers can spread their fixed R & D costs over a large output and recuperate these costs more quickly.

At the other end of the spectrum is the case of horizontal differentiation. One of the causes of such differentiation is the existence of diversity of consumer tastes. Different consumers have different preferences for products. They differ in their preference for the actual type of 'attribute mix'. It has been suggested that tastes differ between countries. The result is the emergence of what may be called 'national varieties' of a particular product. However, where there exists a strong local demand for a particular variety, exports may follow. The existence of diversity of preferences even within individual countries means that a potential demand always exists for the exporter of a 'national variety'. The result is intra-industry trade. At the same time the existence of increasing returns means that it is not possible for each producer to produce all the varieties demanded by the consumer. Intra-industry specialization results.

Industries characterized by such horizontal differentiation are not, in general, research intensive. There is little product innovation or product improvement. Rather, the emphasis is upon altering the appearance, packaging, style, etc of the product to cater for diversity of consumer preference and to increase market share. Advertising costs and sales promotion expenditures will constitute high fixed costs such that a large output may be needed to recuperate these costs. This would favour intra-industry specialization. On the other hand, as we shall see in later chapters of this book, foreign direct investment is often quite important in such industries. Firms may initially seek to tap an overseas market through exports. Once, however, sales have reached a certain level, the firm may prefer to produce abroad. In this case he will have the advantage of being close to the consumer and better able to adapt his product to the particular preferences of consumers in the foreign market. Foreign production also enables him to minimize transport costs and get round any tariff or non-tariff barriers to imports. The relatively simple nature of the product in question may also mean that fixed production costs are low. Therefore economies of scale in production are small. Geographically dispersed production will therefore not be too unprofitable. In this case intra-industry trade may be quite low.

Finally, there is the case of vertical differentiation. In this case consumers rank different varieties by quality. Each country exports products of a certain quality while importing products of a different quality. For example, a country may export large automobiles with heavy fuel consumption while importing small economy-type models. Once again the existence of increasing returns to scale can explain intra-industry specialization. As with technological differentiation, levels of R & D expenditure are likely to be quite large relative to turnover, but not as large as in industries where product innovation is more common. Since the emphasis is on quality improvements rather than product innovation, the 'development' aspect of R & D is likely to be more important than the 'research' aspect. However, the occurrence of high levels of R & D expenditure means that unit costs will fall with output. Intra-industry specialization will therefore be beneficial.

However, the question is posed: why do countries specialize in particular quality ranges? Why do some countries export the high-quality substitutes, while others export the lower-quality substitutes? One possibility is that demand patterns differ between countries. Demand for high-quality alternatives is likely to be greater in countries with a high per capita income. In this case, the lower per capita income countries will export the lower quality ranges. Another possibility is that demand patterns vary with the distribution of income. Demand for higher-quality alternatives will be greater in countries with a more uneven or skewed distribution of income. In both cases the existence of strong local demand for high-quality substitutes may lead a country to specialize in these goods. However, the existence of economies of scale means that it is not profitable for all producers in the country concerned to produce all the quality ranges. To satisfy demand at the lower end of the income scale, lower-quality manufactures are imported.

It has been suggested that the case of trade in vertically differentiated goods fits in with a Hecksher–Ohlin theory of trade (Falvey 1981). The argument is that the production of higher-quality goods is more capital intensive than the production of lower-quality goods. Then capital-abundant countries will export the higher quality ranges and labour-abundant countries the lower-quality ranges. This conforms with the predictions of the Hecksher–Ohlin theory. Alternatively, one could say that higher quality goods require larger inputs of skilled labour and lower-quality goods larger inputs of unskilled labour. This also conforms with a modified version of the Hecksher–Ohlin theory. If this is true, it is the case that the Hecksher–Ohlin theory can explain more kinds of intra-industry trade than it may first seem. On the other hand, it ignores the influence of the demand-side determinants of trade discussed above. Moreover, it is not clear that all higher-quality goods are more capital intensive, although they probably do require more inputs of skilled labour.

One factor which can be expected to lead to intra-industry specialization in products which are vertically differentiated, is the existence of increasing returns to scale. Although these may not be as important as in technologically differentiated goods, they are probably more important than in horizontally differentiated goods. Making quality improvements to products requires large expenditures. If these fixed costs are spread over a large output, unit costs will fall sharply. This favours geographically concentrated production. For this reason, firms are less likely to service foreign markets through foreign production and more likely to do so through exports. At the same time, it may be less important to be near to the consumer than in the case of horizontally differentiated goods since diversity of consumer preference is not of overriding importance. Intra-industry trade may therefore tend to be proportionately greater in such industries.

Some of the literature on intra-industry trade has attached more importance to market structure than product differentiation. Specifically, the growth of oligopolistic markets in the industrialized countries is seen as the primary cause of increased intra-industry trade. We have already referred to one model which leads to intra-industry trade in identical commodities. Other models involving oligopolistic markets have also been constructed. We do not intend to discuss all of these in this book. Some of these models are mathematically quite complex. The interested student should consult a specialist text on the subject (see Greenaway and Milner 1986). However, it is important to see the linkage between market structure and trade involved. The essence of oligopoly is that the market is concentrated in the hands of a few firms each of which controls a significant share of the market. It involves extreme uncertainty for each producer because, in determining his price–output policy, he has to take account of the likely reaction of his rivals. Because of this uncertainty, firms may avoid overt price competition which reduces the joint profits of all producers. Instead, firms may seek to increase their market share by methods other than price competition. This will include product differentiation.

At the same time, the oligopolistic nature of markets may force firms to seek expansion overseas. Individual firms may be reluctant to upset the equilibrium existing in the domestic market. Yet the only way of increasing domestic sales further may be by entering into more fierce competition with rivals. The international expansion of the firm may be a means of overcoming this dilemma. The firm seeks to increase sales by extending its influence to foreign markets. Tamir Agmon has suggested that intra-industry trade is one stage in this process of international expansion. Firms first seek to expand internationally through exports. Later, this gives rise to overseas production (Agmon 1979). Consider Figure 3.2, which illustrates the case of a firm which faces oligopolistic competition in the home market and free competition in the world market. Hence its domestic demand curve, D_d, is downward-sloping, while the demand curve which it faces in the world market is perfectly elastic, D_w. MR is his marginal revenue curve for domestic sales and MC his marginal cost curve. Profits are maximized where marginal costs equal marginal revenues, that is output OB. However, marginal revenue in the domestic market is given by MR. With marginal costs equal to OP_w, the profitable output for selling on the home market is OA. This will be sold at the price OP_d. The remainder of output, AB, is sold on the world market at the world price, OP_w. Thus the firm divides its output between the domestic and the world market, unloading on the world market what it cannot sell profitably at home. Since the price charged on sales abroad is below that charged on domestic sales, dumping has resulted. This conforms with reality when frequent allegations of dumping are common.

Figure 3.2 Intra-industry trade under oligopoly

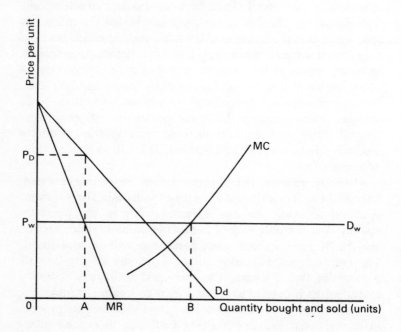

Now, if there exists another producer in another country producing a similar yet differentiated product and who also faces an oligopolistic situation at home, intra-industry trade can result. Each producer seeks to export his differentiated product to each other's market. However, the argument is that the main source of this kind of intra-industry trade lies in the oligopolistic structure of markets rather than product differentiation. The oligopolistic nature of markets forces firms to seek outlets abroad for surplus output. Product differentiation is a tactic for achieving this, but not the cause of intra-industry trade. Eventually, however, exports may give way to overseas production. One result of this will be increasing foreign investment by firms in each other's home markets. Since this will take place within the same industry, it is sometimes referred to as intra-industry foreign direct investment (FDI). The next chapter will examine the nature of intra-industry FDI. However, at this stage it is noted that it may tend to follow on from intra-industry trade. Firms seeking to expand overseas achieve initial market penetration through exports. This is especially appropriate where there exists uncertainty about the foreign market. Exporting is less risky than foreign investment. It is a way of 'buying' information about conditions in the foreign market as a prelude to overseas production. Once uncertainty has been overcome, foreign investment follows. Intra-industry trade gives way to intra-industry FDI.

One of the attractions of this view of intra-industry trade is that it also explains the growth of foreign direct investment. The next chapter examines the growth of FDI. Intra-industry trade and foreign direct investment may be regarded as different methods whereby firms expand internationally. Both are a response to the oligopolistic character of markets in the advanced industrialized countries. As we shall see in the next chapter, much the most important type of FDI has been between the industrialized countries. In this respect, it resembles intra-industry trade, which has also grown fastest between the industrialized countries.

THE DETERMINANTS OF INTRA-INDUSTRY TRADE

A considerable amount of empirical work has been carried out to test the various possible explanations for inter-country and inter-industry differences in levels of intra-industry trade. In the light of such research, what can be said about the determinants of intra-industry trade? It is necessary to distinguish between country differences and industry differences in the level of intra-industry trade.

Country Differences in the Level of Intra-industry Trade

A number of factors can be expected to affect the level of intra-industry trade of a country:

1. **The level of a country's per capita income** The higher the level of a country's per capita income, the greater the demand for variety. As per capita income rises, so consumers demand more variety. The demand for variety leads to an increase in the degree of product differentiation. This promotes intra-industry trade and reduces inter-industry trade as a component of total trade. The fact that intra-industry trade has increased with the rise in per capita incomes in the western industrialized countries would lend support to this view. On the other hand, other factors may have been at work increasing intra-industry trade— for example, the liberalization of world trade and the establishment of the EC and EFTA in Western Europe.

2. **The degree of income equality between any pair of countries** The more equal the level of per capita income of any two countries, the greater the amount of intra-industry trade that will take place between them. Level of per capita income is known to exert a strong influence on the pattern of demand. It follows that the pattern of demand will be similar in countries with a similar level of per capita income. Therefore it is likely that products initially developed to meet local tastes will sell best in other countries with a similar per capita income. Cultural similarity and close geographical proximity will further enhance such trade. Much of this trade will take the form of intra-industry trade (Linder 1961). Strong empirical support exists for this hypothesis. Thus Balassa found that inequality of per capita income had a significant negative effect on the United States' level of intra-industry trade with different trading partners (Balassa 1986). Culem and Lundberg also found that differences in per capita GNP had a significant negative effect on bilateral intra-industry trade between countries (Culem and Lundberg 1986).

Table 3.11: Intra-industry trade indices for developing and industrialized countries, 1978 (%)

Non-NIC developing countries				Newly industrial-izing countries		Industrial countries	
Algeria	1.5	Kenya	13.9	Argentina	42.3	Australia	25.3
Cameroon	6.1	Malawi	6.6	Brazil	37.8	Austria	74.1
Central African Republic	0.7	Malaysia	32.4	Greece	21.1	Belgium–Lux.	79.2
Chile	10.1	Morocco	10.9	Hong Kong	40.8	Canada	66.9
Colombia	20.0	Nigeria	0.2	India	37.4	Denmark	67.0
Costa Rica	32.4	Pakistan	14.8	Israel	61.9	Finland	45.4
Dominican Rep.	6.9	Peru	10.3	South Korean	34.9	France	80.3
Egypt	6.8	Phillipines	15.0	Mexico	31.9	West Germany	62.7
El Salvador	33.0	Senegal	18.7	Portugal	32.8	Ireland	61.3
Ghana	4.3	Sri Lanka	4.8	Singapore	66.9	Italy	59.0
Guatemala	32.7	Sudan	0.8	Spain	52.1	Japan	26.0
Guyana	19.6	Thailand	17.3	Taiwan	34.7	Netherlands	74.2
Haiti	46.3	Trinidad	14.3	Yugoslavia	50.7	New Zealand	25.9
Ivory Coast	13.4	Tunisia	17.3			Norway	44.4
Jamaica	14.4	Turkey	7.9			Sweden	68.3
Jordan	14.9					Switzerland	59.5
						United Kingdom	81.0
						United States	59.4
Average	14.5			Average	41.9	Average	58.9

Source: O. Havrylyshyn and E. Civan, Intra-Industry Trade and the Stage of Development, in Tharakan (1983), p. 118, Table 1.

3. **The stage of economic development of a country** The higher the stage of development of a country, the greater the importance of manufacturing industry in national output. Since intra-industry trade is higher in manufacturing products, the country's level of intra-industry trade will be higher. Obviously there is a close relationship between a country's stage of economic development and its level of per capita income, so these two factors will work together to influence the level of a country's intra-industry trade. However, it is possible for a country to have a high per capita income yet be at quite a low stage of development. If so, the level of its intra-industry trade will also be quite low despite having a high per capita income. Empirically, it is impossible to measure separately the influence of per capita income and stage of development on the level of a country's per capita income. Table 3.11 illustrates the influence of stage of development.

4. **The difference in the level of economic development of any two countries** When any two countries are at different stages of economic development, inter-industry trade is likely to be relatively more important than intra-industry trade. This is because the stage of development affects the ratio of capital to labour in a country. The more economically advanced a country, the greater the ratio of capital to labour. Differences in factor endowments promote inter-industry not intra-industry specialization. As we have seen, the level of intra-industry trade is lower for trade between developed and developing countries than between developed and other developed countries. However, one can expect that, as developing countries industrialize and accumulate more capital, more of their trade with developed countries will assume the form of intra-industry trade. As we saw in an earlier section of this chapter, there is evidence that this has been taking place in recent decades.

5. **The size of a country** There are grounds for believing that the level of intra-industry trade will be higher in larger countries. What is important is not the geographical size of a country but the size of its gross domestic product. Countries with a large GDP offer producers a wide market within which to sell. This is important for differentiated goods produced under conditions of increasing returns to scale. It is less important for standardized goods where unit costs rise with output. Thus, large countries will tend to be relatively more competitive in differentiated goods, small countries in standardized goods. However, it does

not follow that all small countries will have low intra-industry trade ratios and all large countries high intra-industry trade ratios. Other factors (e.g. per capita income) may exert a counteracting influence. Thus a fairly small country like Belgium has quite a high intra-industry trade ratio, while a large country like the United States has quite a low intra-industry trade ratio. On the other hand, the smallness of Norway may contribute towards her low intra-industry trade ratio and the largeness of France to her high intra-industry trade ratio. It is difficult to separate the influence of the size factor from other influences at work. One interesting study which lends some support to this hypothesis was carried out by Dermot McAleese for the Republic of Ireland. He found support for the view that Ireland's specialization in more standardized goods was due to the smallness of the country. The share of differentiated goods in Ireland's total exports was found to be quite small (McAleese 1979). For this reason, Ireland's intra-industry trade ratio is quite low. Following entry to the EC in 1973, Ireland appears to have undergone inter-industry and not intra-industry specialization (Glejser 1983). If the smallness of the domestic market has given Ireland a comparative advantage in standardized goods, it is to be expected that membership of a trading bloc such as the EC will lead to inter-industry and not intra-industry specialization. One offsetting factor to the large country hypothesis concerns the role played by primary commodities. Large countries are likely to be better endowed with natural resources. Hence it seems likely that a significant proportion of their exports will take the form of primary commodities. Since intra-industry trade is less in primary commodities, this will tend to reduce the size of their intra-industry trade ratio. This may explain why a country as large as Australia has a low intra-industry trade ratio.

6. **The degree of integration existing between countries** High levels of intra-industry trade exist between countries which are part of a regional trading zone, such as a free-trade area, customs union, or common market. Thus high levels of intra-industry trade have been found to exist for trade between the member states of the EC. Grubel and Lloyd calculated that the average level of intra-industry trade for trade between the member states of the EC was 54 per cent in 1959 and 67 per cent in 1967. This compares with 36 per cent and 48 per cent for the same two years for the trade of the OECD countries (Grubel

Table 3.12: Representative ratios of trade balances for intra-European trade

Country	(1) Intra-EEC trade in manufactures			(2) Intra-Europe OECD in manufactures		(3) Intra-OECD trade in all commodities	
	1958	1963	1970	1970	1976	1970	1976
Belgium	0.46	0.40	0.34	0.35	0.32	0.39	0.36
Netherlands	0.49	0.43	0.36	0.36	0.33	0.41	0.40
France	0.39	0.32	0.27	0.25	0.25	0.36	0.34
Italy	0.58	0.52	0.41	0.40	0.40	0.50	0.50
West Germany	0.53	0.43	0.33	0.32	0.32	0.42	0.37
United Kingdom				0.32	0.27	0.42	0.38
Sweden				0.34	0.35	0.46	0.45
Switzerland				0.49	0.41	0.54	0.51
Denmark				0.47	0.44	0.51	0.47
Austria				0.43	0.41	0.52	0.50
Finland				0.60	0.56	0.63	0.60
Norway				0.62	0.59	0.63	0.63
Portugal				0.77	0.70	0.75	0.72

Source: Kreinin (1979).

and Lloyd 1975). Bela Balassa has shown that the establishment of the EC led to intra-industry and not inter-industry specialization. He calculated 'representative ratios of trade balances' see pp. 95–6 for each of the Six, a fall in the ratio indicating increased intra-industry specialization. Column 1 of Table 3.12 shows Balassa's results. The level of intra-industry specialization increased in all six countries. Morchedai Kreinin has extended Balassa's calculations to cover the second phase of integration which took place after 1973 (Kreinin 1979). Column 2 shows representative trade ratios for trade between all European OECD countries, not just EC member states. It is apparent that there was no reversal of the trend towards intra-industry specialization in any of the original six member states while both the United Kingdom and Denmark experienced increased intra-industry specialization. It is significant too that the level of intra-industry specialization increased in all other West European economies except Sweden. Column 3 shows the trend for all commodities not just manufactures. Ratios fell in all countries. However, there is some evidence that recent decades have seen some weakening of the trend towards intra-industry specialization in the EC (Glejser 1983). As we have already noted, Ireland appears to have experienced more inter-industry than intra-industry specialization since joining the EC.

It is not only among the member states of the EC that regional integration has led to intra-industry specialization. The same has been true of regional integration involving developing countries. Thus Balassa found that the level of intra-industry trade taking place between the members of the Latin American Free Trade Area (LAFTA) and between the members of the Central American Common Market (CACM) was higher than trade between these countries and the rest of the world. Balassa's results are shown in Table 3.13 (Balassa 1979). Another study by Ezran and Laird examined intra-industry trade as a component of trade between ASEAN member states. Table 3.14 summarizes their findings. In 1980 nearly 50 per cent of trade between ASEAN countries was intra-industry trade. This compares with 43 per cent for trade with other developing countries, 36 per cent with principal developing country exporters of manufactures (PEMs), 29 per cent with developed countries, and 12 per cent with the socialist countries (Ezran and Laird 1984). Thus regional economic integration between countries appears to be one factor promoting intra-industry trade. This will be the case whenever the countries in question have similar per capita incomes, are at a similar stage of development, are situated close to each other, and share a similar culture. If, however, these factors are missing, it is equally possible that regional integration may lead to inter-industry specialization.

Table 3.13: Intra-industry trade ratios for trade in manufactures for six LAFTA and three CACM countries, 1975

Country	World	Other LAFTA	Other CACM
LAFTA:			
Argentina	33	43	–
Brazil	31	40	–
Chile	14	19	–
Colombia	22	53	–
Mexico	39	45	–
Venezuela	3	17	–
CACM:			
Costa Rica	38	–	60
Honduras	16	–	35
Nicaragua	27	–	44

Source: B. Balassa, Intra-Industry Trade and the Integration of Developing Countries in the World Economy, in Giersch (1979), p. 250, Table 1.

Table 3.14: ASEAN intra-industry trade with partner groups and the world

ASEAN's trade with:	1965	1975	1980
Other ASEAN	39.6	40.1	49.7
PEMs	29.3	35.9	35.8
Other developing countries	58.3	55.0	43.3
Developed market economies	13.3	23.5	29.3
Socialist countries	5.4	11.4	11.9
World	35.7	39.8	44.2

Source: Ezran and Laird (1984).

7. **Geographical closeness** The greater the geographical distance separating any two countries, the smaller will be the level of intra-industry trade taking place between them. Intra-industry trade is greatest between countries which either share a common border or are in close geographical proximity. Of course, large geographical distances and hence high transport costs reduce trade in general, whether it be inter-industry or intra-industry trade. However, intra-industry trade is especially increased by geographical closeness.

8. **The existence of large trade imbalances between countries** Some methods of measuring intra-industry trade fail to adjust fully for imbalances in a country's overall trade. In this case, countries with very unbalanced trade will have low intra-industry trade ratios. As was observed earlier in this chapter, this partly, but not wholly, accounts for Japan's low intra-industry trade ratio.

Industry Differences in the Level of Intra-industry Trade

Earlier in this chapter it was noted that higher levels of intra-industry trade exist for manufactured goods than for primary commodities. Intra-industry trade has also increased fastest in manufactures. Within manufacturing there exist differences in the importance of intra-industry trade. Levels of intra-industry trade appear to be especially high in chemical products and machinery. Table 3.15 illustrates these differences for UK trade. The highest intra-industry trade ratios are apparent for machinery and transport equipment and chemical products. The low coefficient of variation means that these product groups are less affected by extreme values. Intra-industry is consistently higher in these industries. The main factors giving rise to high levels of intra-industry trade in a particular group of products are listed below.

Table 3.15: Average levels of intra-industry trade in the United Kingdom by product group, 1964 and 1977

SITC Division[a]	1964	1977	Coefficient of variation
(0) Food and live animals	21.6	35.0	0.73
(1) Beverages and tobacco	27.5	35.0	0.63
(2) Crude materials (inedible except fuel)	18.5	40.0	0.83
(3) Mineral fuels, lubricants and related materials	34.4	58.0	0.63
(4) Animal and vegetable oils	29.3	50.3	0.75
(5) Chemicals and related products	56.4	68.3	0.32
(6) Manufactured goods	52.7	68.9	0.34
(7) Machinery and transport equipment	50.7	69.4	0.30
(8) Miscellaneous manufactured articles	75.0	79.6	0.20

Source: Greenaway (1983).
[a] At the three-digit level of the SITC.

1. **The degree of product differentiation** The greater the degree of product differentiation, the higher the level of intra-industry trade. The more standardized the product, the greater the likelihood of inter-industry specialization. Econometric research lends qualified support to this hypothesis. A number of different variables have been used as proxies for product differentiation. These have included the following:

(i) The number of subgroups within a single three-digit product group (which is a measure of the degree of product heterogeneity).

(ii) The variation of the unit values of exports within the product group (the so-called Hufbauer index).

(iii) The ratio of selling costs (advertising, sales promotion, market research) to total costs.

(iv) The ratio of research and development (R & D) expenditures to sales (as a measure of the degree of product innovation).

Although results differ according to the particular study undertaken, most of these variables have been found to have a positive influence on the level of intra-industry trade. However, there is some ambiguity concerning the influence of advertising intensity (as measured by selling costs) on the level of intra-industry trade. Caves has claimed support for the view that advertising expenditures exert a negative influence on the level of intra-industry trade. He has drawn a distinction between two prototypes of differentiation: 'complexity' and 'information'. The first type of differentiation arises from the structure of production. Such products are technologically complex combinations of different attributes, for example automobiles. Such products are typically produced under conditions of increasing returns (decreasing average costs). This means that producers cannot produce all the varieties which consumers want. Hence, to the extent that consumer preferences are diverse, intra-industry trade results.

On the other hand, some products are physically much alike but are differentiated by small differences in appearance or image in the eyes of the consumer. This kind of differentiation is highly subjective. It arises from the fact that consumers lack sufficient useful 'objective' information to guide them in choosing between alternative products. Such differentiation is common in many consumer non-durable goods industries, for example cigarettes, soaps, soap detergents, perfumes, paints, and so on. Such industries tend to be characterized by high levels of promotional expenditure. Caves has argued that high levels of advertising create a bias against trade. This is because most advertising tends to be specific to the culture of the country where the product is sold. The producer needs to be close to the consumer. This favours local production rather than exports. Therefore this kind of differentiation will be positively related to direct investment abroad but negatively related to intra-industry trade. Caves claimed empirical support for this hypothesis (Caves 1981). However, other studies have obtained a different result. For example, Balassa found that marketing expenditures as a percentage of total costs had a positive effect on the level of intra-industry trade (Balassa 1986).

2. **The extent of economies of scale** There is a theoretical expectation that the level of intra-industry trade will increase with the importance of economies of scale. As we have seen, it is not product differentiation *per se* which gives rise to intra-industry specialization. Rather, it is the existence of a high degree of product differentiation and a tendency for average costs to fall with output (increasing returns) that leads to intra-industry specialization. If average costs rose with output, it would pay producers themselves to produce the full range of

products demanded by consumers. It is the fact that average costs typically fall with output which makes it unprofitable for each producer to produce all the varieties consumers want. Somewhat surprisingly, econometric research appears to refute such a hypothesis. Most studies show a negative relationship between economies of scale and the level of intra-industry trade. For example, Caves found strong support for the opposite relationship, namely that the level of intra-industry trade falls with the extensiveness of scale economies (Caves 1981). Balassa also found that intra-industry trade was negatively correlated with economies of scale (Balassa 1986).

However, this is because most studies have tested the relationship between the level of intra-industry trade and the economies of large plant size. The minimum efficient scale (MES) is one variable frequently used in such studies as a proxy for scale economies. Industries in which such economies of scale are important are often characterized by high levels of standardization and a low degree of product differentiation, for example petrochemicals, steel manufacture, and so on. Hence the level of intra-industry trade is quite low. The type of economies of scale which lead to intra-industry specialization are those associated with long production runs. Long production runs can be achieved in quite small but highly specialized plants. In industries where substantial cost savings result from such long production runs, high levels of intra-industry trade are to be expected. On the other hand, economies of large plant size are likely to have a negative effect on the level of intra-industry trade.

3. **The type of market structure** The relationship between market structure and intra-industry trade is ambiguous. As has been seen, some models predict that high levels of intra-industry trade will be found in highly concentrated, oligopolistic industries. Intra-industry trade is a stage in the international expansion of rivalrous oligopolies. On the other hand, a monopolistically competitive market structure, in which a large number of firms sell a differentiated product, may equally well lead to intra-industry trade. Econometric research provides little evidence for a positive relationship between intra-industry trade and conventional measures of oligopoly. For example, the degree of oligopoly may be measured by the level of industrial concentration. The share of total sales accounted for by the top five firms, the so-called five-firm concentration-ratio, is one

measure frequently used for industrial concentration. The level of entry barriers may be further taken as a measure of the degree of oligopoly. However, measures such as these often fail to capture the degree of international oligopoly prevalent in a particular industry. Yet it is the extent to which an industry is dominated by a few large firms at the world level which is important for intra-industry trade. One solution is to adjust the domestic concentration ratio for the share of imports in the output of an industry so as to allow for competition from abroad. However, even after such an adjustment there is no clear-cut evidence for a positive relationship between intra-industry trade and the degree of concentration. In fact, Balassa obtained a negative relationship between the level of intra-industry trade and the internationally adjusted degree of concentration (Balassa 1986). One possible explanation for this is that a falling internationally adjusted concentration ratio measures the level of oligopolistic rivalry prevalent in a particular industry. It is evidence for the interpenetration of each other's markets by rivalrous firms. This is consistent with theoretical expectations concerning the relationship between oligopoly and intra-industry trade.

4. **The importance of foreign direct investment** The relationship between intra-industry trade and the level of foreign investment in a particular industry is similarly ambiguous. Direct investment abroad may be a substitute for and complement to trade. Caves has argued that where the 'information' aspect in product differentiation predominates, foreign investment will tend to displace trade. This is because of the importance of advertising and marketing in competition. Producers need to be as close as possible to the consumer to adapt the product to local tastes and to tailor advertising to the specific features of the national market. On the other hand, where the 'complexity' aspect is predominant, it is better to concentrate the production of a given product in single plants located in a few countries so as to reap all available economies of scale. This will make for high levels of intra-industry trade (Caves 1981). Caves has claimed econometric support for such a hypothesis. He found that advertising expenditures and the level of foreign direct investment in a particular industry were strongly correlated. At the same time, advertising expenditures had a negative effect on the level of intra-industry trade. In other words, where the degree of advertising intensity was high, foreign investment

exerted a negative influence on the level of intra-industry trade. Balassa similarly found that high levels of direct investment abroad were negatively correlated with the level of intra-industry trade (Balassa 1986).

However, some foreign investment clearly is complementary to trade. In such industries, the level of intra-industry trade will be positively related to the level of foreign investment. This will be the case for industries in which considerable offshore processing takes place. As has been seen, much of this takes the form of companies based in developed countries setting up affiliates in developing countries to carry out final assembly or processing stages using parts and components supplied by the parent company. The finished product is then re-exported back to the home country for sale on local markets. To the extent that the finished product is classified as belonging to the same industry as the various components and parts used in its manufacture, this will show up as intra-industry trade. Several studies have found evidence for a positive linkage between the level of intra-industry trade and such offshore processing (Caves 1981).

5. **The degree of product innovation** There are grounds for believing that the level of intra-industry trade will be high in industries characterized by a high degree of product innovation. The latter could be measured by the ratio of research and development expenditures (R & D) to total turnover in a particular industry. Where such R & D costs are high relative to turnover, average costs will fall with output. This will favour intra-industry specialization. Greenaway found weak support in econometric tests for such a relationship between intra-industry trade and technological innovation (Greenaway 1986).

6. **The importance of trade barriers** There exists no evidence for the view that intra-industry trade is higher in industries where trade barriers are lower. This is not surprising since lower trade barriers are as likely to increase inter-industry as intra-industry trade. There is no reason why lower trade barriers should increase the ratio of intra-industry to total trade. However, the variability of tariff rates may influence the level of intra-industry trade. The lower the variance of tariff rates, the higher the level of intra-industry trade. Caves obtained some weak support for this hypothesis (Caves 1981). In addition, the inclusion of offshore assembly provision within tariff schedules will further enhance intra-industry trade. These allow imports

137

of finished products to enter a country at a reduced rate of tariff to the extent that they embody parts and components supplied by the importing country. Such offshore assembly provisions have encouraged vertical specialization in the production of certain products based upon the different factor proportions required at each stage of production. Balassa found that such offshore procurement served to increase the level of intra-industry trade (Balassa 1986).

7. **Transport costs** Intra-industry trade will be greater in products which are costly to transport. The products of weight-gaining industries are generally subject to considerable amounts of border trade. This will show up statistically as intra-industry trade. Thus a negative association is expected between transport costs and the level of intra-industry trade. Econometric studies lend some weak support to this hypothesis.

CONCLUSION

In this chapter, we have seen that an increasing proportion of world trade, especially trade in manufactured goods, has taken the form of intra-industry trade. This is the result of increased intra-industry specialization in manufacturing products between countries. In what respects does the intra-industry specialization of the last quarter-century differ from the inter-industry specialization of previous eras? Is intra-industry specialization qualitatively different from inter-industry specialization or is it just a deeper form of specialization? In one sense, intra-industry specialization is just an extension of inter-industry specialization. It represents a finer degree of specialization than in the past with each country specializing in narrow product ranges within individual industries as opposed to specialization in single industries. However, there are also certain qualitative differences between inter-industry and intra-industry specialization.

First, as we have already explained, the basis for most inter-industry specialization is the difference in comparative costs between countries arising from different factor endowments. By way of contrast, the basis for intra-industry specialization is the existence of product differentiation and increasing returns to scale. Countries which are differently endowed with the various factors of production will tend to engage in inter-industry trade and specialization. This is true of much trade between developed and developing countries. Countries which are similarly endowed with different factors of production will tend to engage in intra-industry trade and specialization. This will be especially true of countries with similar per capita incomes, similar cultures, and in close geographical proximity. Thus, much trade between industrialized countries has been of the intra-industry type. Increased economic integration between such countries such as has been achieved through the GATT, the EC, and EFTA can be expected to enhance the degree of intra-industry specialization.

Second, intra-industry specialization is likely to give rise to fewer adjustment problems than inter-industry specialization. This is because it necessitates a movement of resources within rather than between industries. Inter-industry specialization necessitates a movement of resources from import-competing to export-expanding industries. Adjustment problems can arise where resources, especially labour, are geographically and occupationally immobile in the short run. Large-scale structural unemployment might result. To a large extent, intra-industry specialization is achieved without the necessity for workers to leave a particular industry or region. The risk of structural unemployment is reduced. As was seen in Chapter 1, there is the possibility that the owners of a country's scarce factor of production will suffer from increased inter-industry specialization. In the absence of compensation, they will definitely experience a relative loss due to a fall in the relative price of their factor. They might also experience a decline in their real income if the price of consumer goods falls by less than their money incomes. Intra-industry specialization is not based on different factor proportions. Hence it is not accompanied by changes in factor prices. Therefore no income group is likely to experience a welfare loss. These considerations may help to explain the relative ease with which industrial tariffs were lowered on trade between industrialized countries after 1947. Since much of this trade took the form of intra-industry specialization, there were no vested interest groups within the industrialized countries who stood to lose from the lowering of tariffs. Where there was resistance to trade liberalization, it tended to occur in those industries where inter-industry specialization was the outcome. These were the older, more traditional branches of manufacturing in which decreasing returns (increasing unit costs) were common, for example iron and steel production, clothing, and textiles (Meyer 1979).

We have seen how exceptionally high levels of intra-industry trade exist for the West European countries. This reflects the advanced level of intra-industry specialization achieved by these countries. It follows that the main result of increased economic integration in Western Europe has been intra-industry specialization. It is not surprising that the elimination of tariff barriers in Western Europe through the establishment of the EC and EFTA met with such little internal resistance. Had it taken the form of inter-industry specialization, adjustment problems would have been greater and distributional effects more important. Greater resistance to tariff disarmament would have resulted. In addition, it may have been the case that the gains from integration were also greater. This is because intra-industry specialization is likely to open up greater opportunities for the exploitation of economies of scale. As we have seen in earlier parts of this chapter, the gains from intra-industry specialization take the form of cost savings due to long production runs. Consumers also enjoy benefits from increased variety and choice. On the other hand, the conventional welfare gains resulting from lower prices and an improved use of resources which are associated with inter-industry specialization will not result from intra-industry specialization. However, these gains are known to be statistically quite small. On the other hand, the potential gains from intra-industry specialization are quite great. Chapter 7 will discuss these differences between inter-industry and intra-industry specialization in greater depth. At this stage it is merely noted that the effects of intra-industry and inter-industry specializations are quite different.

The greater adjustment problems and distributional effects of inter-industry specialization, combined with the likelihood that the potential gains from inter-industry specialization are less, can help explain some of the tensions apparent in trade between developed and developing countries. Such trade is less balanced. It gives rise to greater adjustment problems for industrialized countries. Owners of scarce factors stand to lose from a liberalization of such trade. Adequate compensation is not always guaranteed. At the same time, the welfare gain from increased specialization may be smaller and highly dispersed. The emergence of the newly-industrializing countries as major exporters of manufactures in recent decades has been one source of such tension. Much of the New Protectionism of recent years has been aimed at the exports of NICs. Japan has been another target of such protectionism. As we have seen in earlier sections of this chapter, Japan has a much lower index of intra-industry trade than other advanced industrialized countries. This largely reflects a lower level of intra-industry specialization. Because much of her specialization has taken the form of inter-industry specialization, it has created more friction between herself and her trading partners. We shall examine these issues further in Chapter 6.

4

The Rise of the Multinational Corporation and Intra-firm Trade

INTRODUCTION

Accompanying the rapid growth in world trade over the period since the Second World War, there has taken place an equally rapid growth of foreign investment. The most dynamic element within this total has been private long-term investment by companies. This has involved companies, mainly based in the advanced industrialized countries, setting up overseas subsidiaries to produce goods and services in countries other than their home country. One of the results of this process has been the emergence of multi-plant, multinational corporations, who plan and co-ordinate production on a global basis. Although multinational corporations were heard of before the Second World War, their importance has grown enormously since. Big improvements in methods of international travel and communications played the major role in bringing this about. Only with such technological advances did it become possible truly to manage a company on a global scale.

The growth of the multinational corporation has had many implications for both individual countries and the world economic system as a whole. For the purposes of this book, the focal point of interest is the effect which such enterprises have had on the world trading and production system. Multinational corporations now account for a large proportion of trade, especially in the western industrialized world. In 1970 about 68 per cent of the manufacturing exports of the United States were carried out by multinational corporations. The ability of such companies to switch production of a certain good from one country to another can have a major effect both on individual countries' pattern of trade and balance of trade. It follows that, increasingly, we cannot examine changes in the structure of world trade without reference to the production decisions of multinational companies.

Furthermore, a substantial amount of trade now takes place within multinational companies. This may take the form of a parent company selling goods to an overseas affiliate, or an overseas affiliate exporting goods back to the parent company, or one overseas affiliate exporting goods to a related affiliate. This is what is commonly referred to as intra-firm trade. Possibly as much as one-third of the trade between industrialized countries may be of this kind. For some countries (e.g. the United States) it is higher. It is by no means clear that such trade is affected by the same considerations as arm's-length trade between nominally independent buyers and sellers. Rather, it seems likely that developments within the multinational company have a major bearing on the amount and direction of such trade. In particular, the pricing of goods traded in this way may be governed by rather different considerations to those relating to arm's-length trading between independent partners.

For these reasons, any book concerned with new patterns of trade needs to give a primary place to a discussion of the role of the multinational corporation and its influence on world trade. This chapter will examine the growth of foreign investment carried out by multinational companies since the Second World War. It will try to set this in the context of the growth of world trade and world output discussed in Chapter 2. Second, it will trace the rise of the multinational corporation brought about by direct investment abroad. Third, it will discuss the major determinants of such direct investment abroad and seek to account for the three main types of multinational company in existence — the horizontally integrated, the vertically integrated, and the conglomerate multinational company. Fourth, it will consider the nature and extent of intra-firm trade as a component of world trade. Finally, I will discuss the nature of pricing policy for intra-firm trade. As we have already noted, prices charged on such intra-group sales may diverge significantly from prices charged on arm's-length trade. This is what is commonly known as transfer price manipulation. Chapter 5 will discuss certain other aspects of multinational activity with major implications for world trade.

143

THE GROWTH OF FOREIGN DIRECT INVESTMENT SINCE THE SECOND WORLD WAR

Private long-term foreign investment may take one of two forms. First, there is portfolio investment, which is the purchase by an individual, company, or financial institution of interest-bearing overseas securities. It involves a transfer of mere money capital. The aim is to acquire a financial asset which will yield an annual flow of income and/or which can be sold at a future date for a higher price than that at which it was bought, thus realizing a financial gain for the investor. Much pre-war foreign investment was of this type. Indeed, in the half-century before the First World War, it was the most common type of private long-term overseas investment. Although such investment has continued to grow rapidly over the last quarter-century, it has been eclipsed by the growth of direct investment. This is the establishment by a company of an overseas subsidiary or the acquisition by such a company of a controlling interest in an overseas company. Although definitions vary between countries, a controlling interest is usually taken to be a minimum of 10 per cent of equity capital. In contrast to portfolio investment, direct investment involves more than a transfer of mere money capital. Money capital is just one element in a package of resources, which includes ownership, control, management, technology, and other resources. Although one motive may be to earn a return on capital, it is generally not the sole motive. Direct investment is more risky than portfolio investment, so that a company seeking a mere financial return would do better to undertake portfolio investment. It follows that there must exist motives other than a financial return which account for direct investment overseas.

Later, this chapter will discuss some determinants of different types of direct investment overseas. However, at this point, it is noted that direct investment is one method whereby firms expand their operations overseas. Exporting is one method for tapping an overseas market for a particular product. In some cases it constitutes the best, most profitable, and least risky approach. However, this is not always so. In certain circumstances a firm may do better to set up a subsidiary in the overseas market to produce its product wholly or partly abroad. Alternatively, it may wish to set up a subsidiary in another country to produce an important raw material which it is costly or risky to purchase from abroad. Still another motive for investing overseas may be to acquire a company producing an entirely different product or range of products. The motive may be to achieve a diversification of his international operations. Whatever the case, direct investment always involves an extension of the operations of a company on a global scale. As such, it may be seen as an advanced stage in the growth of the firm. Motives other than securing a higher return on capital are likely to be involved.

Our concern in this book is principally with direct investment. That is not to say that portfolio investment is unimportant. On the contrary, it remains of major importance, having grown rapidly over the post-war period. Markets for long-term capital have become increasingly internationalized. A major part of the portfolios of banks, insurance companies, pension funds, investment trusts, and so on, now consists of overseas securities. However, space prevents full consideration being given to this particular type of international economic activity. This book is principally concerned with international trade and production and so we have chosen to focus attention on direct investment. It is this type of overseas investment which probably has the closest relationship with trade.

It has been estimated that over the period from 1951 to 1964, foreign direct investment (FDI) accounted for as much as four-fifths of gross, private long-term investment (Dunning 1974a). Although there has been some slackening in recent decades, the growth of FDI has continued apace. Thus FDI is now the most important type of private, long-term investment overseas. This contrasts with the half-century before the First World War — also a period of intense overseas investment activity — during which the bulk of foreign investment assumed the form of portfolio investment. Much of the latter took place between the rich, capital-abundant colonial powers and their poor, capital-scarce colonies. It involved a flow of capital from developed countries relatively well endowed with capital to underdeveloped countries faced with a relative scarcity of capital. By way of contrast, most of the direct investment of the past fifty years has taken place between industrialized, capital-abundant countries. FDI in developing countries has been less important than FDI between developed countries.

The growth of FDI over the period since the Second World War can be portrayed in one of two ways: the flow of direct investment abroad or the stock of direct investment abroad. It is important to examine the trends in both of these.

The Flow of Direct Investment Abroad

This shows the amount of new direct investment activity taking place each year. This is usually shown as part of the balance-of-payments statistics of the capital-exporting country. Although practices vary between countries, it usually includes the unremitted profits of overseas affiliates. If an overseas affiliate reinvests profits, this is treated as direct investment by the parent company, since the company is effectively adding to its stock of investment abroad. However, such unremitted profits are not always included. Moreover, other ways in which a multinational company may expand its overseas operations are likely to go unrecorded. Thus, if the company expands its overseas operations by borrowing on the capital markets of the host country or some third country, this will not be included in any measure of the flow of investment abroad. Indeed, it seems likely that the more established a company overseas, the less will be the dependence of overseas affiliates on the parent company for additional funds. Thus figures showing the flow of direct investment abroad are likely to underestimate the extent of actual FDI taking place. This will be all the more the case for countries having companies with well-established overseas operations.

In addition, data for both the flow and stock of direct investment abroad take no account of other forms of international business involvement. It should not be thought that foreign investment is the only way in which a company may expand its operations overseas. The next chapter of this book will discuss some of the alternative forms of business involvement which companies undertake. These include joint ventures (whereby two companies combine equity capital to create a new concern), licensing agreements, management contracts, international subcontracting, and others. Indeed, there is some evidence that, in recent years, these alternative methods of international business involvement have increased.

Table 4.1 shows the gross flow of FDI for developed and developing countries for the two decades from 1960 to 1970 and 1970 to 1980 respectively. The gross inflow and outflow of FDI may be compared with the growth of world trade, GNP, and domestic capital formation. These figures are in current US dollar terms. Because of rising inflation in the 1970s and changes in exchange rates, this means that the real growth of FDI in the 1970s is overstated. Since the bulk of the outflow of FDI is accounted for by the developed market economies, we can say that the growth in the gross outflow of direct investment abroad, measured in current US dollar terms, averaged 11.5 per cent in the 1960s and about 15.5 per cent in the 1970s. In the 1960s the outflow of direct investment abroad was growing at a slightly faster rate than world trade and a significantly faster rate than domestic fixed investment and the GNP of the developed market economies. However, in the 1970s the out-flow of FDI from the developed market economies grew at a slower rate than world trade and barely much faster than the growth of domestic fixed investment and the GNP of the developed countries. Thus it would seem that, after growing extremely rapidly in the 1960s, the outflow of direct investment abroad slowed down in the 1970s.

Table 4.1: Rates of growth of GNP, trade, and investment at current prices in the world's market economies, 1960–80 (%)

	Developed market economies		Developing market economies		Total market economies	
	1960–70	1970–80	1960–70	1970–80	1960–70	1970–80
Gross national product	8.9	14.0	7.6	18.8	8.4	15.2
Gross capital formation	9.7	14.0	8.9	22.1	9.6	15.3
Imports	10.9	19.6	8.3	24.0	10.4	20.5
Exports	10.9	18.7	8.6	24.7	10.4	19.9
Inflow of foreign direct investment	11.7	14.6	7.5	16.7	10.2	15.0
Outflow of foreign direct investment	11.5	15.6	–	41.3	–	15.6

Source: UNCTC (1985), Table 11.1, p.14.

The rapid growth in FDI from developing countries in the 1970s is not significant because the developing countries account for such a small proportion of FDI in comparison with the developed countries. It is noticeable, however, that the flow of FDI from developed countries to developing countries increased more quickly in the 1970s than from developed to developed countries. In the 1960s, the reverse had been true: FDI between developed countries grew more quickly than from developed to developing countries. However, a further glance at the table shows that the economies of the developing countries also grew much more quickly. In relation to the GNP of developing countries, the inflow of FDI to developing countries was actually somewhat slower in the 1970s than in the 1960s. It would appear that direct investment in developing countries in relation to GNP played a somewhat reduced role in the 1980s.

Table 4.2 shows the geographical distribution of the flow of direct investment abroad both by home country and host country. From this table, it can be seen that the developed market economies account for over 98 per cent of the gross outflow of FDI, although their share is declining. The share of developing countries in the gross outflow of FDI rose from 0.3 per cent in 1970–2 to 1.6 per cent in 1978–80. Of the developed countries, the United States has the largest share, but its share has fallen from over 72 per cent in 1960 to 46 per cent in 1978–80. Similarly, the shares of the United Kingdom and France have fallen, although both countries increased their share of the total during the 1970s. The fall in the shares of these countries has been matched by the rise in the shares of West Germany, Japan, and Canada. The Netherlands has also increased her share by a smaller amount. Thus, whereas in 1960 nearly three-quarters of all direct investment abroad was undertaken by the United States, now a much larger number of industrialized countries are major overseas direct investors.

Table 4.2 also shows that the great bulk of direct investment still goes to developed market economies. In 1978–80 this share stood at 76.5 per cent, little down on 1970–2. The developing countries only attracted 23.5 per cent of all direct investment in 1978–80. What is also noticeable is the rise in the share of the inflow of FDI accounted for by the United States. Even in 1970–2, the United States attracted only 8 per cent of all direct investment abroad. By 1978–80 her share had risen to 30 per cent. Thus the United States has increasingly become an importer as well as exporter of direct investment abroad. The same is also true of other developed countries. Increasingly, FDI is taking the form of a two-way flow of investment between developed countries. This is illustrated by Table 4.3, which shows net flows of direct investment abroad. As recently as 1970 the United States was alone in having a large net outflow

Table 4.2: Foreign direct investment for certain developed market economies and developing countries, 1970–2 and 1978–80($m)

Country	Outflow of foreign direct investment reported by home country		Inflow of foreign direct investment reported by host country	
	1970–2	1978–80	1970–2	1978–80
Developed market economies:	13,203 (99.7)	41,563 (98.4)	8,724 (78.2)	25,905 (76.5)
United States	7,649 (57.8)	19,547 (46.3)	929 (8.3)	10,205 (30.1)
United Kingdom	1,597 (12.1)	5,756 (13.6)	982 (8.8)	3,756 (11.1)
West Germany	1,161 (8.8)	4,262 (10.1)	1,220 (10.9)	1,257 (3.7)
Japan	481 (3.6)	2,552 (6.0)	155 (1.4)	173 (0.5)
Netherlands	564 (4.3)	2,210 (5.2)	575 (5.2)	1,038 (3.1)
France	455 (3.4)	2,359 (5.6)	612 (5.5)	2,902 (8.6)
Canada	316 (2.4)	2,617 (6.2)	807 (7.2)	1,138 (3.4)
Developing countries	43 (0.3)	682 (1.6)	2,428 (21.8)	7,973 (23.5)
Total	13,245 (100.0)	42,245 (100.0)	11,151 (100.0)	33,878 (100.0)

Source: UNCTC (1985), Table 11.2, p.15.
Note: Figures in parentheses show percentages of total foreign direct investment

of FDI. US net exports of FDI amounted to 81 per cent of her gross outflows in 1970. By 1980 the share had fallen to 42 per cent. At the same time, a number of other countries emerged as major net exporters of FDI on a par with the United States.

The Stock of Direct Investment Abroad

An alternative measure of the growth of direct investment abroad focuses on the stock of assets held abroad by companies with investments abroad. The growth in the stock of direct investments abroad by a country may be taken as a better measure of the country's overseas investment activity because of any expansion of overseas operations achieved by tapping sources of finance other than the parent company. On the other hand, there is the problem of how to value such assets. In particular, the overseas assets of companies are often valued at historical cost, which fails to take account of inflation and the cost of replacement.

Table 4.4 shows the stock of direct investment abroad of various countries as a percentage of their exports valued respectively at current and constant prices. It can be seen that, if current prices are used, the stock of direct investment activity

149

Table 4.3: Net flows of foreign direct investment by country, 1970–80 ($m)

Year	United States	United Kingdom	West Germany	Netherlands	France	Japan	Canada	Total for developed countries
1970	−6,125	−460	−278	18	249	−261	566	−4,188
1971	−7,251	−568	86	145	128	−151	688	−4,877
1972	−6,786	−817	369	−128	92	−565	220	−4,372
1973	−8,595	−2,175	356	−55	192	−1,931	61	−10,833
1974	−4,317	−1,689	217	−760	1,072	−1,672	33	−37,501
1975	−11,607	−1,235	−1,323	−670	−23	−1,530	−187	−14,505
1976	−7,585	−2,417	−1,385	−769	−587	−1,870	−1,061	−14,328
1977	−8,184	−978	−1,389	−1,157	907	−1,611	−475	−10,111
1978	−8,163	−2,744	−2,078	−1,088	895	−2,354	−1,301	−13,154
1979	−12,106	−2,034	−3,527	−981	508	−2,662	−764	−19,477
1980	−7,757	−1,221	−3,410	−1,447	226	−2,122	−2,373	−14,345

Source: UNCTC (1983).

Table 4.4: The stock of foreign direct investment of selected countries expressed as a percentage of exports, 1967–80

Country of origin	1967 At current values	1967 At 1975 constant prices	1971 At current values	1971 At 1975 constant prices	1975 At current values	1975 At 1975 constant prices	1980 At current values	1980 At 1975 constant prices
United States	181	96	190	116	117	117	100	144
Canada	35	19	37	22	32	32	30	49
United Kingdom	126	56	106	60	69	69	64	122
West Germany	14	10	19	14	18	18	20	23
France	53	32	35	26	21	21	18	28
Italy	24	12	20	11	10	10	9	19
Netherlands	151	96	97	68	54	54	54	71
Belgium–Luxembourg	28	18	19	13	13	13	11	14
Switzerland	143	100	164	129	136	136	111	118
Sweden	38	19	32	20	25	25	23	36
Japan	14	9	18	12	29	29	29	30
Australia	12	6	10	6	7	7	9	15
All 12 countries	83	47	72	47	49	49	43	60

Source: Stopford and Dunning (1983).

fell between 1967 and 1980. However, since the stock of FDI does not fully adjust for inflation, constant prices are more appropriate. On this score, the stock of direct investment has grown as a percentage of exports, although the ratio was constant from 1967 to 1971. In four countries — France, Italy, the Netherlands, and Benelux — the ratio did fall over the period as a whole but rose over the period from 1975 to 1980. Thus figures for the stock of direct investment abroad appear to suggest that the level of direct investment abroad has not tapered off in the 1970s. This is a somewhat different conclusion from that which is apparent from examining direct investment flows. However, as has been seen, the latter probably under-estimates the true extent of FDI activity.

Table 4.4 shows some interesting differences between countries in the importance of direct investment abroad. The United States, United Kingdom, and Switzerland stand out as the three countries with the highest levels of direct investment abroad as a proportion of exports. At the other extreme, Belgium–Luxembourg, Italy, and Australia all have quite low ratios of direct investment abroad to total exports. The country which experienced the fastest increase in the ratio of direct investment abroad to exports over the period in question was the United Kingdom.

Table 4.5 shows the geographical distribution of the stock of direct investments abroad. This shows that 97 per cent of the stock of direct investment abroad was owned by the developed countries, although the share of the developing countries has increased since 1960. The United States owned the largest share, but her share fell from 49 per cent in 1960 to 42 per cent in 1980. Over the same period, the United Kingdom share also fell, although since 1975 her share has increased significantly. France and the Netherlands also experienced some fall in their share of direct investment abroad. On the other hand, Japan and West Germany have both experienced a big increase in their shares. In 1960 both of these two countries had hardly any stake in overseas direct investments. Finally, Switzerland's share also increased over the period in question.

Thus the period since the Second World War has witnessed a rapid growth in foreign direct investment. Accurate measurement of the full extent of such investment abroad is difficult. Data showing the gross flow of direct investment abroad show that in the 1960s FDI was growing at least as fast, if not faster,

Table 4.5: Stock of direct investment abroad by major country of origin, 1960–80

Country of origin	% distribution, end of:					
	1960	1967	1971	1975	1978	1980
Developed countries:	99.0	97.4	97.7	97.0	96.8	97.3
United States	49.2	48.3	48.1	45.8	41.4	42.2
United Kingdom	16.2	14.9	13.8	11.2	12.9	14.5
Netherlands	10.5	9.4	8.0	7.0	7.2	7.8
West Germany	1.2	2.6	4.2	5.9	7.3	7.4
Japan	0.7	1.3	2.6	5.9	6.8	7.3
Switzerland	3.0	4.3	5.5	6.5	7.1	6.5
France	6.1	5.1	4.2	4.1	3.8	3.9
Canada	3.7	3.2	3.8	3.8	3.5	3.7
Sweden	0.6	1.5	1.4	1.6	1.5	1.4
Belgium–Luxembourg	1.9	1.7	1.4	1.3	1.4	1.3
Italy	1.6	1.8	1.7	1.2	1.4	1.3
Australia	0.3	0.3	0.3	0.3	0.3	0.4
Other developed countries	3.7	3.1	2.6	2.4	2.3	2.1
Developing countries	1.0	2.6	2.3	3.0	3.2	2.7
Total	100.0	100.0	100.0	100.0	100.0	100.0

Source: Stopford and Dunning (1983).

than world trade. However, these figures probably understate the actual level of FDI activity. There is some evidence in support of the view that FDI activity, when measured by the gross outflow of FDI, fell in the 1970s. However, this is not supported by data for the stock of direct investment abroad. In the period since 1967 this appears to have grown faster than world trade measured at constant prices. Moreover, as we shall see in Chapter 5, other non-equity forms of international business involvement may have been increasing during this period.

THE RISE OF THE MULTINATIONAL CORPORATION

The growth of foreign direct investment has led to the growth of the multinational corporation (MNC) or multinational enterprise (MNE). The MNC (or MNE) is defined differently by different sources. However, the simplest approach is to define a MNC as 'an enterprise that controls and manages production establishments in at least two countries' (Caves 1982). Another source defines a MNC as 'a corporation which owns (in whole or in part), controls and manages income-generating assets in more than one country' (Hood and Young 1979). The essential point about both definitions is that (1) the company operates in more than one country and (2) the parent company exercises control over the affiliate company. Some sources have stipulated that the overseas activities of a company must be at least as great as the domestic activities for the company to be truly multinational, but this is unnecessary and too restrictive. Control of the overseas affiliate infers that the parent holds a substantial share of the equity capital of the affiliate. Ten per cent is often taken as the required minimum, but in some companies, control may be exercised with a smaller stake. The exact percentage is not important.

It should not be thought that the MNC is a post-Second World War phenomenon. MNCs did exist before 1939. Indeed, the Dutch and English trading companies of the sixteenth and seventeenth centuries may be regarded as the first examples of such companies. Substantial amounts of direct investment overseas took place in the late nineteenth and early twentieth centuries, although, as we have seen, such investment was less important than portfolio investment. Much of this tended to assume the form of investment in primary commodity production by companies in the colonial countries. Further substantial direct investment took place in the inter-war period, although foreign investment in general was hit by the world economic crisis of that period. However, during this period, a number of important MNCs came into existence. US companies such as Ford and General Motors and the big oil companies constitute early examples of MNCs. Phillips and I.G. Farben are two examples of pre-war European MNCs.

However, none of these companies were fully integrated on a global basis in the manner of present-day MNCs or indeed domestic multi-plant firms of that time. It was much more difficult for management to travel between parent company and overseas affiliate on a regular basis. Information took much longer to communicate across the world. Hence global planning of production was very difficult to implement. However, after the Second World War, conditions changed rapidly. Major revolutionary improvements in methods of transport and communication (the jet aeroplane, modern telecommunications) dramatically altered the situation. Global planning of production became feasible. The activities of several different plants each based in a different country long distances apart could now be co-ordinated with increased ease.

At the same time, the economic and political conditions of the post-war period proved highly conducive towards the international expansion of the firm. First, Europe was successful in achieving a rapid recovery from the devastation of the war. There was no rélance back to the depressed conditions of the inter-war years as was feared. The developed countries of the world managed to achieve faster rates of economic growth than at any other time in the past. Governments adopted expansionary domestic economic policies in an attempt to ensure full employment. Next, on the international front, trade was given a boost by the success which was achieved in liberalizing trade, especially in manufactured goods. A large number of countries signed the GATT agreement, thus agreeing to negotiate lower tariffs and refrain from certain kinds of bad-neighbourly trading practices. In Western Europe even more rapid progress was made in liberalizing intra-European trade with the establishment of the European Community (EC) in 1958 and the European Free Trade Association (EFTA) in 1960. This eventually led to the elimination of all tariffs on trade in manufactured goods between the countries of Western Europe. In addition, the international movement of capital was similarly encouraged by the gradual dismantlement of many of the worst types of exchange controls operated before and during the war. Finally, political conditions, especially in Western Europe, became generally more stable than they had been for a long time.

In the post-war upsurge of multinational activity, United States companies led the way. The US economy emerged from the war in a much stronger position than any other country. The dollar shortage of the post-war period meant that many European countries were keen to attract US investment, while the US administration saw such investment as one means of alleviating the dollar shortage. On the supply side, US firms needed larger markets for their manufactures to ensure adequate expansion. Scope for further expansion at home was limited. The tough anti-trust laws operating in the United States prevented companies from achieving faster growth through enlarging their market share in industries where they already enjoyed considerable dominance. In addition, the oligopolistic character of many product markets meant that expansion through

155

increasing market share risked upsetting market equilibrium and provoking rivals into retaliatory action. US companies enjoyed a strong technological leadership in a number of manufacturing sectors, such as electronics, telecommunications, automobiles, aerospace, and synthetic materials. They were keen to exploit this lead. Although they could have done so through increased exports, they were better able to do so through setting up new plants abroad.

According to Vaupel and Curhan, US companies established new overseas subsidiaries at a rate of roughly fifty-five per annum between 1946 to 1952, a rate which was roughly twice that of the inter-war period. This rate nearly doubled to ninety-four per annum from 1953 to 1955, rose further to 146 per annum from 1956 to 1958 and doubled again to 300 per annum from 1959 to 1961 and 319 per annum from 1962 to 1964 (Vaupel and Curhan 1974). Thereafter the rate of expansion stabilized. Thus the early 1960s appear to have been the period of fastest growth of US MNCs. The most important region in which US companies set up affiliates was Western Europe. Approximately one-third of the new subsidiaries set up in the early 1960s were established in Western Europe. Before 1959 Europe had been somewhat less important. However, Western Europe was the logical market for US companies to exploit their leadership in sophisticated consumer and capital goods. The European market was large and per capita incomes were relatively high and rising fast. Because the distances involved were large and thus transport costs high, European production was preferable to exporting. Europe also offered the advantage of somewhat lower labour costs (although lower productivity cancelled out some of the benefits from lower wages). Finally, the establishment of the EC and EFTA in the late 1950s gave an extra stimulus to US investment. The removal of barriers to trade between member states plus the EC's common external tariff placed at a disadvantage US companies which continued to rely upon exports to service the European market. Setting up plant in Europe through direct investment was a way of jumping European trade barriers.

In the late 1960s and early 1970s the rate of new investment by US companies in Western Europe began to taper off. US MNCs began to seek out new locations in other parts of the world. Latin America and the Middle and Far East became important new locations for US direct investment overseas.

One reason was that Europe was losing its advantage as a location for manufacturing production. Wages were beginning to catch up with US levels. Trade-union power brought US managements into increasing conflict with their workforces. New social security legislation, minimum-wage laws, and employment protection measures all raised the costs of employing labour. The fall in the value of the dollar in relation to the European currencies may also have reduced the attractiveness of acquiring productive assets in Europe. It may also have been the case that many US products were coming of age. This would favour locating their production where labour was cheapest. These considerations favoured seeking out new sites in developing countries which could, in turn, be used as a base for exporting back to the US and European market.

Nevertheless, the effect of the large-scale export of US capital to Europe in the late 1950s and early 1960s was to give US companies a dominant position in many European markets. In a number of key sectors of manufacturing, US MNCs were successful in achieving a substantial degree of concentration. These have tended to be the technologically most advanced industries, such as electronics (especially computers, microchips, etc.), telecommunications, synthetic materials, and so on. However, beginning in the 1960s a number of European companies began to challenge the US dominance. European companies also began to expand overseas. A number of European companies already had substantial overseas investments. British companies, in particular, had quite a high profile abroad. However, in the mid-1960s, there occurred a marked acceleration in the number of new overseas subsidiaries established by European-based MNCs. Whereas in the period from 1959 to 1964, the average number of new subsidiaries set up by continental, European-based MNCs was about seventy-three per annum, by the late 1960s this rate had risen to some 343 new subsidiaries per annum. The average number of new subsidiaries set up by UK-based MNCs also rose sharply from 111 per annum in 1959–61 to 243 per annum from 1968 to 1970. (Vaupel and Curhan 1974). The most popular location for setting up an overseas subsidiary was another European country. Thus a large amount of the direct investment carried out by European MNCs took the form of cross-European investment with European companies investing in each other's home market. However, some European direct investment was also aimed at the North American market, as European companies began to challenge their US rivals in the latter's own back garden.

In the 1970s the example set by the European companies was followed by Japanese companies, although direct investment by Japanese companies has remained more modest. The rising yen and the increasing difficulty which Japanese companies have faced in expanding their exports to the US and European markets are causing them increasingly to set up production overseas. Until recently, much direct investment overseas by Japanese companies has been directed to South and East Asia. Relatively little has gone to the developed countries of North America and Western Europe. Already this situation is changing as Japanese companies face growing trade restrictions when selling to these markets. Recent years have also witnessed the emergence of a number of MNCs in certain newly-industrializing countries (e.g. South Korea).

It is evident that the United States no longer dominates multinational activity. The MNC is no longer a largely US phenomenon if ever it was. By 1980, only 34 per cent of the affiliates of transnational corporations were owned by US-based companies. The United Kingdom accounted for a further 25 per cent of such affiliates, West Germany for 7.5 per cent, France and the Netherlands for a further 4.5 per cent each, Switzerland for 4 per cent, and Japan for 3 per cent. Thus Japanese companies continue to lag behind American and European companies in the degree of their multinational activity. However, mere numbers of affiliates fail to measure accurately the true extent of multinational activity, since this ignores the size of each investment.

Thus the period since the beginning of the 1970s has seen the rapid emergence of the MNC in a large number of countries. At the same time, the nature of the MNC is changing. The activities of MNCs are now spread over a wider area. No longer are they confined to the United States and Western Europe. Increasingly, US companies have sought out locations outside Europe, especially Latin America and the Far East. European companies have begun to extend their activities, while Japanese companies have set up plants in Europe and North America. At the same time, there has been a tendency for the individual plants of each MNC to become more specialized. Instead of each plant producing broadly the same product for sale locally or in the surrounding region, the tendency is for each plant to specialize in a particular link within the chain of production. Different parts and components are produced in different subsidiaries before being assembled in one or more specially designed plants. This increased degree of specialization on the part of the various subsidiaries necessitates much greater global co-ordination and planning. This tends to mean more centralized control and management. Increasingly, the parent company of the typical MNC is becoming a non-producing, decision-making centre. Increasingly, they are coming to resemble holding companies or even large banks concerned with providing finance in the context of a global, company plan.

Before we discuss these trends further, it is necessary to examine two other aspects of post-war multinational activity: (1) the regional distribution of multinational investment activity and (2) the sectoral distribution of multinational investment activity.

The Regional Distribution of Multinational Investment Activity

Table 4.6 shows the main differences in terms of regional distribution of foreign affiliates of MNCs of different countries. It is apparent that for all five countries shown, except Japan, the large majority of overseas affiliates of nationally based MNCs were located in developed market economies. US MNCs tended most towards Europe and Latin America. British MNCs had a strong orientation towards Europe and the Commonwealth countries such as Australia and New Zealand. German MNCs located their affiliates predominantly in other regions of Europe. Canadian MNCs had a strong bias towards North America (i.e. the United States) and Europe.

Japanese MNCs had a strikingly different regional profile from that of other countries. Only 42 per cent of the affiliates of Japanese MNCs in 1980 were located in other developed market economies. Some 58 per cent were located in developing countries, with most of these being found in the countries of South and East Asia. We saw earlier that Japanese companies have demonstrated a much lower propensity to set up production overseas than their rivals in Europe and North America. They have preferred to sell their goods to other developed countries by means of exports rather than foreign production.

Table 4.6: Regional distribution of foreign affiliates of
multinational companies of selected home countries, 1980(%)

Host region	United States	United Kingdom	Germany	Japan	Canada
DEVELOPED MARKET ECONOMIES					
North America	12.9	14.1	9.0	17.1	34.9
Europe	42.6	35.2	68.2	19.5	39.7
Other*	9.7	26.5	5.2	5.2	8.1
Subtotal	65.3	75.8	82.4	41.8	82.7
DEVELOPING COUNTRIES					
Latin America	21.4	4.7	9.2	13.4	12.6
Africa	2.3	7.7	3.0	2.2	1.3
West Asia	0.9	0.9	0.8	0.8	0.4
South and East Asia	10.0	10.4	4.4	41.7	2.8
Europe	0.1	0.5	0.2	–	0.2
Subtotal	34.7	24.2	17.6	58.2	17.3
TOTAL	100.0	100.0	100.0	100.0	100.0

Source: UNCTC (1983), Table 11.8, p.34.
*Australia, Japan, and New Zealand

Such direct investment as they have undertaken has tended to
be of a rather different kind to that from western companies.
Three sets of motives would appear to have underlay the
decision to invest: (1) the need to ensure access to vital natural
resources, (2) the need to take advantage of low labour costs
in the production of mass consumer goods, and (3) the need
to relocate pollution-creating activities overseas to contain
the environmental problem. Such investment as has taken place
in other developed market economies has been more geared to
the marketing of Japanese goods (distribution, transport,
maintenance services). However, in recent years, as we
noted earlier, the situation has begun to change. The rise
in the external value of the yen and the proliferation of
restrictions on Japanese exports by other developed countries
are causing many Japanese companies to set up manufacturing
plants in developed countries.

The Sectoral Distribution of Multinational Investment Activity

Table 4.7 shows the sectoral distribution of overseas direct investment for five leading industrialized countries. For all five countries except Japan, manufacturing attracted the largest share of FDI. In the case of West Germany, roughly 70 per cent of FDI was concentrated in manufacturing, although this represented a fall from 80 per cent in 1971. In Japan, the UK, and the United States, a somewhat higher proportion of FDI was to be found in the extractive industries (which includes oil exploration). Japan also had a much higher proportion of FDI in the services sector. The United States had a relatively high percentage of FDI in banking and insurance.

Thus the most important sphere of multinational investment activity over the post-war period has been the manufacturing sector. This contrasts with earlier periods of direct investment overseas, such as the quarter-century before the First World War, where the concentration was on investment in the extractive industries. Since the Second World War, the extractive industries have become relatively less important, although the need to secure adequate supplies of raw materials and energy resources has been an important motive for certain kinds of direct investment abroad. FDI has expanded faster in the manufacturing sector. However, in recent decades a noticeably larger share of FDI has been going into the services industries. Multinational investment activity has become increasingly important in banking, insurance and other areas of finance, advertising, management consultancy, hotel and catering, and other service industries. In Table 4.7 the share of services in the regional distribution of FDI increased in all five countries.

Table 4.8 illustrates the spread of multinational investment activity within the manufacturing sector, drawing a distinction between high-, medium- and low-technology industries. The degree of multinationality within a particular industry is measured by the overseas production (OP) ratio. This shows the average ratio of overseas affiliate sales to total world-wide sales of the largest firms within a given industry. The table reveals that the degree of multinationality was generally highest in the most research-intensive industries, although it was generally higher in low research-intensive industries than medium research-intensive industries. Japan was an important exception. Japanese companies in the most research-intensive

Table 4.7: The sectoral distribution of foreign direct investment abroad of selected developed market economies, 1971 and 1978

Country of origin and economic sector	1971		1978	
	$m	%	$m	%
CANADA				
Total industry	6,524	100.0	11,355	100.0
Extractive	938	14.4	2,588	—
Manufacturing	3,437	52.7	5,519	—
Services	2,149	32.9	3,248	28.6
Banking & insurance	405	6.2	965	8.5
GERMANY				
Total industry	7,277	100.0	31,834	100.0
Extractive	350	4.8	2,272	7.1
Manufacturing	5,796	79.8	22,132	69.5
Services	1,131	15.6	7,430	23.4
Banking & insurance	494	6.8	3,491	11.0
JAPAN				
Total industry	10,270	100.0	26,809	100.0
Extractive	3,290	32.1	6,330	23.6
Manufacturing	3,260	31.7	9,177	34.2
Services	3,720	36.2	11,302	42.2
Commerce, banking & insurance	2,149	20.9	5,626	21.0
UNITED KINGDOM				
Total industry	23,717	100.0	31,277	100.0
Extractive	8,051	33.9	8,747	28.0
Manufacturing	10,043	42.3	14,131	45.2
Services	5,633	23.8	8,399	26.8
Banking & insurance	1,212	5.1	1,410	4.5
UNITED STATES				
Total industry	101,313	100.0	168,081	100.0
Extractive	30,989	30.6	40,322	24.0
Manufacturing	44,370	43.8	74,207	44.1
Services	25,954	25.6	53,553	31.9
Banking & insurance	9,726	9.6	24,065	14.3

Source: UNCTC (1983), Table 14, pp.46–7.

industries had a low degree of multinationality. Indeed, Japanese companies had a low degree of multinationality in comparison with western companies in all industries. However, the difference was specially great in the high research-intensive industries. This is consistent with what has already been said about the nature of post-war Japanese FDI: it has been mainly concentrated in low-technology manufactures and resource-based industries.

Table 4.8 also shows a high level of multinational activity in the resource-based petroleum industry. US companies also have high OP ratios in office equipment, measurement, scientific and photographic equipment, rubber, tobacco, and chemicals and pharmaceuticals. They have relatively low ratios in the more traditional labour-intensive industries, such as shipbuilding, textiles and clothing, and leather goods. European-based companies have high OP ratios in tobacco, food, office equipment, chemicals and pharmaceuticals, and building materials. In particular, European MNCs appear to have a high OP ratio in chemicals and pharmaceuticals when compared with their US counterparts. One reason for this may be the shortage of raw materials in Europe, which has necessitated much higher levels of direct investment abroad. They also have higher OP ratios than US companies in certain low-technology industries such as textiles, clothing, and leather goods. This probably reflects greater 'export-platform' investments by European companies in low-wage countries in these industries. This has involved relocating labour-intensive finishing stages of manufacture in such countries to take advantage of abundant supplies of relatively cheap and well-disciplined labour. The offshore assembly provisions built into tariff schedules have further encouraged this type of investment.

UK-based MNCs had a broadly similar OP ratio profile to that of other European companies. The highest degree of multinationality was in evidence in tobacco, paper and wood products, textiles, clothing and leather goods, and industrial and farm equipment. In particular, UK companies tended to have higher OP ratios than US companies in the low-technology industries. For Japanese companies, the highest OP ratios were to be found in textiles, clothing and leather goods, rubber, motor vehicles and shipbuilding, railway and transportation equipment. In industries such as motor vehicles, much of the FDI which has taken place has assumed the form of investment in marketing. Japanese affiliates have been concerned with distribution and maintenance rather than manufacturing. In the lower-technology industries, Japanese affiliates have been concerned with labour-intensive production of mass-consumer goods. As wage costs rose, production of these goods was

Table 4.8: Average overseas production ratios of sample firms by industry and by area, 1977 (%)

Industry	United States	Europe	United Kingdom	Japan
HIGH RESEARCH INTENSITY				
Aerospace	7.8	10.2	NAS	
Office equipment (incl. computers)	42.2	42.5	NAS	
Petroleum	49.1	66.8	70.2	1.6
Measurement, scientific & photog. equipment	35.2	5.6		
Electronics & electrical appliances	21.2	27.9	31.8	4.3
Chemicals & pharmaceuticals	26.6	40.5	39.9	4.4
Subtotal	37.3	47.1	51.7	3.7
MEDIUM RESEARCH INTENSITY				
Industrial & farm equipment	23.1	30.8	40.6	2.8
Shipbuilding, railway & transport equipment	5.0	0.1	–	7.1
Rubber	31.6	–	–	7.0
Motor Vehicles (incl. components)	21.4	21.3	23.2	18.2
Metal manufacturing & products	11.4	17.0	33.6	3.4
Subtotal	20.1	20.2	32.9	8.6
LOW RESEARCH INTENSITY				
Building materials	21.1	39.5	30.4	3.0
Tobacco	29.0	58.7	61.0	
Beverages	23.8	14.3	14.3	NAS
Food	20.7	56.4	36.9	2.1
Paper & wood products	13.7	33.8	50.7	
Textiles, apparel & leather goods	10.8	38.1	41.7	12.4
Publishing & printing	6.3	20.8	22.9	
Subtotal	18.8	48.5	70.9	5.9
Other manufacturing	16.9	0.8	NAS	
TOTAL	29.2	37.5	41.8	6.7

Source: Dunning and Pearce (1981), Table 6.1A, p.119.
Notes:
1. The overseas production ratio shows the ratio of the sales of overseas affiliates and associate companies (excluding goods imported from parent for resale) to world-wide sales of the group expressed as a percentage.
2. The sample was a sample of 523 large firms in the world.
3. NAS means that results are not available for reasons of confidentiality and disclosure, although the information is included in the aggregates.

increasingly shifted to low-wage-cost locations in South-East Asia, enabling Japanese companies to retain a presence in these industries.

One interesting difference between Japanese FDI and that of the United States concerns the effects that overseas investment has had on trade. Kojima has argued that much Japanese FDI has been 'trade-oriented'. That is to say, it complements the comparative advantage both of the country in which the investment takes place and Japan. As we have seen, much Japanese FDI has been resource-based, designed to ensure access to vital natural resources which Japan lacks. In addition, much Japanese FDI has been designed to take advantage of the low labour costs enjoyed by developing countries. Both of these two types of investment exploit the comparative advantage of the country concerned. At the same time, they are beneficial to the Japanese economy, enabling Japanese firms to obtain adequate supplies of vital natural resources and enabling Japanese firms to cut costs of production by locating labour-intensive stages or processes where labour costs are lowest. By way of contrast, Kojima has argued that much United States FDI has been 'anti-trade-oriented'. That is to say, it is undertaken by export-competing firms either in order to jump trade barriers or as a defensive measure to prevent rivals from eroding the firm's market share. US exports are thereby reduced. In so far as the United States enjoys a comparative advantage in such products, such direct investment abroad runs counter to her pattern of comparative advantage (Kojima 1978).

THE DETERMINANTS OF FOREIGN DIRECT INVESTMENT

It is sometimes helpful to distinguish between three different types of foreign direct investment and, correspondingly, three types of multinational company:

1. **Horizontal FDI and the horizontally integrated MNC** Horizontal FDI occurs when a company locates the manufacture of the same product or group of related products at more than one plant located in different countries. This may take place through the setting up of a new overseas subsidiary (a so-called greenfield venture) or through acquiring a controlling interest in an overseas company producing the same product (or related

group of products) or through a merger with such a company.

2. **Vertical FDI and the vertically integrated MNC** Vertical FDI takes place when a company locates different stages in the production and marketing of a single product or group of related products in different countries. Again, this may take place through a greenfield venture establishing a new subsidiary abroad or through the acquisition of or merger with another company producing at a different stage of production/marketing. Where the newly established or newly acquired subsidiary is producing at an earlier stage of production, this is referred to as backwards vertical FDI. For example, a rubber manufacturer invests in a rubber plantation in Malaysia. Where the newly established or newly acquired subsidiary is producing at a later stage of production or involved in the marketing of the finished product, this is referred to as forwards vertical FDI. For example, an oil company involved in oil drilling and extraction invests in a plant involved in oil-refining or petrochemicals. The oil companies provide a very good example of vertically integrated MNCs since they often have investments in every stage of oil production – extraction, transportation, refining, and distribution. Some oil companies also hold investments further downstream in the production of petrochemicals widely used as intermediate products by other branches of manufacturing.

3. **Conglomerate FDI and the diversified or conglomerate MNC** Conglomerate FDI takes place when a company acquires a controlling interest or amalgamates with another company located in a different country and which is involved in the production of an unrelated product or group of products. In this way, a MNC is enabled to achieve increased product diversification. ITT is a well-known example of an internationally diversified MNC having investments in a wide range of industries including electronics, telecommunications, pharmaceuticals, cosmetics, insurance, and hotels. Conglomerate FDI rarely happens through a greenfield venture since a company rarely possesses the necessary expertise or knowledge to break into a new, unrelated type of activity on its own. Usually, it will do so by buying up another company already involved in a particular line of production using the latter's accumulated skill and experience.

The determinants of each of these types of FDI are likely to differ. Therefore we shall consider the determinants of each type separately.

Horizontal Foreign Direct Investment

Much post-war FDI has been of the horizontal type. A variety of different theories have been proposed to explain this type of direct investment. One of the most useful approaches is that proposed by Caves (Caves 1982), which emphasizes the so-called 'transactional advantages' of the horizontally-integrated MNC. There are certain advantages which accrue from placing under single ownership and control a number of plants each producing the same product but located in different countries. The argument is based on the following propositions:

1. Firms possess a variety of unique, firm-specific and intangible assets from which they seek to obtain the highest possible rent. Caves has stressed (i) technological knowledge about how to produce a product or how to produce it more cheaply, possibly but not necessarily embodied in a patent, and (ii) special marketing skills which enable a firm to differentiate its product from that of its rivals, possibly but not necessarily embodied in a particular brand name or trademark.
2. The existence of imperfections in the market for such assets which creates an incentive to internalize transactions involving such assets. Caves has identified two types of market imperfections:

   (i) The public good nature of intangible assets of the kind listed above. This means that once a piece of knowledge has been produced (e.g. about how to produce a particular product more cheaply), it costs next to nothing to put that knowledge to use in another place (e.g. another country). Since the marginal costs of supplying such knowledge to another producer are zero, the price that such knowledge would fetch in a perfect market would be zero. If, however, the firm possessing such knowledge can internalize the use of such knowledge (i.e. sell it to another subsidiary based in the country in question), it can ensure a greater return.
   (ii) The problem of information impactedness and uncertainty. A seller of a certain body of knowledge cannot reveal all the details of the knowledge which he is selling to the potential buyer or else the buyer will be free to use the knowledge without paying for it. However, this

167

results in the buyer being willing to pay a price for the knowledge which does not adequately reflect its value. The problem is compounded by the fact that there is often great uncertainty about the usefulness and hence value of a given body of knowledge. This makes it extremely difficult to price knowledge. Because most people are risk-averse, they will tend to offer a price which is less than the potential worth of the knowledge in question. Once again, the firm which possesses knowledge of this kind will have an incentive to internalize the sale of such knowledge (i.e. to bypass the market) in order to maximize the rent from such knowledge.

3. The MNC constitutes the means whereby transactions in such intangible, firm-specific assets can be internalized and the firm can achieve the highest possible rent from owning such assets. For example, if a firm posesses unique knowledge about how to produce a particular product more cheaply than other producers, he can exploit that knowledge in one of three ways: (i) by exporting the product to other countries, (ii) by selling the information to other producers in return for a share in the future profits, or (iii) setting up a plant to produce the product in another country. Exporting may be a possibility but will necessitate incurring transport costs. In addition, the product in question may face tariff or non-tariff barriers when entering the importing country. Licensing the information is unlikely to ensure an adequate rent from the information because of the market imperfections discussed above. The market fails to ensure adequate appropriability. Hence, the firm will exercise a preference for internal markets over arm's-length transactions. This it can achieve by establishing a plant in the country in question which will utilize the information possessed.

This theoretical explanation for the existence of the horizontally integrated MNC leads to the conclusion that such MNCs will be most common in industries where firms are in possession of a large number of intangible, firm-specific assets of the kind described above. These will tend to be industries characterized by high levels of R & D expenditure and advertising and sales promotion outlays. There exists substantial statistical support for this relationship. Earlier in this chapter, we saw that the highest degrees of multinationality tended to occur in the most research-intensive industries (i.e. the high-technology branches of manufacturing).

The pharmaceutical industry provides a good example of such an industry. Rugman has argued that there are good reasons for expecting high levels of FDI in such an industry (Rugman 1985). Such an industry is highly research intensive. The rate of product innovation is extremely rapid. Knowledge about a product will often be held in the form of a patent. The innovator firm will be keen to maximize the return from such knowledge. Since patents are not always respected in all countries, the firm will be reluctant to sell such knowledge to another producer. Full appropriability can best be ensured by making an internal market.

Caves has pointed to three other possible extensions of the above argument which can help explain horizontal FDI (Caves 1982):

1. Excess managerial capacity. Many intangible assets are 'discontinuous' or lumpy such that, at any given time, they may be underutilized. Such may be the case with the managerial capacity of a firm. FDI becomes a way of ensuring fuller utilization of such capacity.
2. Excess capacity in internally generated funds. A firm may be unable to use all its retained earnings profitably through expansion of its existing activities. Such funds may command a low opportunity cost in comparison with externally secured funds. Hence they could more readily be invested in a marginal activity which would be unprofitable if the funds had to be raised externally. Horizontal FDI becomes a means of ensuring fuller utilization of such funds.
3. The fact that many intangible assets possessed by firms cannot be separated from the firm which owns them. Hence they cannot be marketed in the normal way. FDI becomes the only way in which such assets can be transferred internationally. For example, information possessed by the managers and employees of a firm may be bound up with the expertise of the company's managers and employees such that the information cannot be sold to another firm. If it were sold, its value would be substantially reduced. Much firm-specific knowledge may be of this kind.

Finally, horizontal FDI may give rise to certain economies of scale arising from operating a number of plants in several different countries. For example, the firm may be able to acquire raw materials more cheaply. Economies of transportation may also result. The multi-plant firm is less affected by localized fluctuations in demand. If demand in one country is depressed, more of the output of the plant located in the country concerned can be exported to plants based in other countries where demand is buoyant. Finally, the multi-plant firm may be able to achieve cost saving from product specialization. Each plant may be able to specialize in the production of a particular good leading to longer production runs.

Caves has rejected the criticism that his transactional approach to explaining the horizontally integrated MNC has only a static application. It can be adapted to explain how a firm grows over time. Firms grow initially through domestic expansion. Firms which come to possess some firm-specific advantage will initially seek to utilize that advantage domestically. This is because the information costs associated with domestic expansion are less than those associated with expansion abroad. However, eventually a point will be reached where the profitability of further domestic expansion becomes quite low. The firm can increase its market share only by reducing the market share of competitors. At this point it may become more profitable to expand abroad. Initially, the firm will tend to set up plant in other countries with a similar language and culture. Information costs will thereby be lower. At the same time, the possession of some unique, firm-specific intangible asset will, to some degree, help offset the extra costs which face a foreign firm producing in any country.

Caves's transactional approach to the explanation of horizontal FDI has close similarities with the theory of international production expounded by Dunning and Norman (Dunning and Norman 1985). The latter have stressed the existence of three sets of factors in the determination of horizontal FDI:

1. Ownership-specific advantages: advantages or assets which are exclusive or proprietary to the firm and which give the firm a comparative advantage over the firms of other countries.
2. Location-specific advantages: advantages or assets possessed by a particular country which make that country attractive

as a location for international production, for example low labour costs, generous tax and other government incentives, large and fast-growing market, and so on.

3. Internalization advantages: the advantages of administering certain transactions internally rather than through using external markets.

It is the simultaneous existence of these three sets of advantages — ownership-specific (O), location-specific (L), and internalization (I) — which help explain FDI. Dunning and Norman have called this the OLI paradigm, or theory of international production.

It is apparent that it closely resembles Caves's approach. The ownership-specific advantages in the OLI framework are much the same as Caves's firm-specific advantages or intangible assets. The OLI paradigm equally stresses the existence of imperfections in the markets for such intangible assets and the advantages to the firm from creating internal markets for such assets in order to ensure full appropriability. The location-specific advantages in the Dunning paradigm have no direct counterpart in Caves's theory of transactional advantages. However, they can readily be incorporated.

Vertical Foreign Direct Investment

As with horizontal FDI, vertical FDI involves a conscious decision on the part of the firm to replace arm's-length trade with internalized markets. However, the markets in question are the markets for intermediate goods (semi-processed goods, components, raw materials). It involves the co-ordination of several different stages of production, with each stage being located in a different country. Such vertical integration brings advantages and disadvantages to the firm. Where the benefits exceed the costs, firms will have an incentive to engage in vertical FDI.

Professor Mark Casson has attempted to list the various kinds of benefits and costs which confront the vertically integrated MNC (Casson 1986). He has identified the following as factors which have a positive effect on the level of vertical integration:

1. **The inability of arm's-length contracts to cope with rigidities and irreversibilities in the production process** Casson lists the following examples of such rigidities:

(i) High fixed costs confront an upstream producer, such that the competitive price for the intermediate product distributes inadequate rent to the upstream producer to enable him to cover his fixed costs. On the other hand, the downstream producer makes more than sufficient profits to be able to compensate the former for his losses and earn a satisfactory rent for himself. However, in the absence of vertical integration, there exists no mechanism for bringing this about, such that the upstream producer has no alternative but to withdraw from production altogether. Vertical integration, leading to an internalization of the market for the intermediate good, may provide a solution.

(ii) Large non-recoverable costs are incurred by the producer of an intermediate product, such as the costs of investment in highly-specific equipment which has no alternative uses and no scrap value. Having committed himself to such an investment, such a producer is vulnerable to threats by major customers not to buy the output derived from such equipment unless more favourable contract terms are renegotiated. Such uncertainty may deter upstream producers from committing themselves to such non-recoverable costs. One solution may be for such a firm to merge with customer firms.

(iii) The use of continuous flow technology by a downstream producer places a premium on ensuring adequate supplies of essential inputs. An interruption in the supply of inputs will disrupt production with 'spill-over' effects for all stages of the production run. Holding large stocks is one solution but is likely to be very costly. Forward purchases of inputs is another solution, but such contracts may be difficult to enforce. Therefore the downstream producer may choose to integrate with an upstream supplier of such inputs to avoid such disruptions.

(iv) Where the intermediate products involved are perishable, storage of inputs is not possible. If no forward market exists, vertical integration may be the natural solution.

(v) The buyer of an intermediate product is confronted with uncertainty about the quality of the product. Sellers know more about the quality of the product than buyers such that buyers are suspicious about the quality of a product. Internalization of the market for the intermediate product through vertical integration overcomes this problem by giving the buyer access to the seller's information.

2. **The tendency for arm's-length pricing to distort decisions regarding substitution in production over time and space** First let us consider substitution over time. Casson gives the example of a sudden increase in demand for downstream output, which requires that resources be switched away from upstream and into downstream production so as to increase the speed at which the intermediate product is transformed into a finished product. Where each stage of production is carried out by independent producers, it may be difficult to bring this about. Vertical integration will bring about greater flexibility of working capital. As regards substitution over space, where production at one stage is distributed over space and fluctuations occur in the supply or demand for the intermediate product, large stocks may need to be held. Vertical integration may permit economies in the holding of such stocks since it will be easier to redirect supplies of the intermediate product to locations faced with a shortage and to do so at quite short notice.

3. **The distortion of intermediate product prices brought about by the exercise of monopoly power** First, Casson cites the case of a monopolist who is an upstream producer and who charges a monopoly price for his intermediate product. As a result, he faces substitution against his product by downstream producers. If the downstream producer is also a monopolist, there will occur a second mark-up on costs when the final product is sold to the consumer. The effect will be to cause a very substantial reduction in the derived demand for the intermediate product. On the other hand, if the monopolist integrates forward with the downstream producer, the price charged for the intermediate product is a mere 'shadow' price equal to the marginal cost of upstream production, so avoiding any substitution against the intermediate product. Since upstream and downstream production are under common ownership, the distribution

173

of profits between the two stages is a matter of indifference. The only concern is to maximize the joint profits of the two producers.

Second, vertical FDI may be a means whereby a dominant firm can create a barrier to entry for potential rivals at different stages of production. Thus, by refusing to supply a rival with an intermediate product or refusing to buy an intermediate input from him, he forces the rival firm to make costly new investments either at the upstream or downstream stages. Effectively, a barrier to entry has been erected.

4. **The introduction of a new division of labour may create an incentive for vertical integration** Much innovation involving both the development of new processes of production and new products gives rise to a new, higher division of labour. Casson has drawn attention to the way in which technological advances since the Second World War have led to the splitting up of many production processes into a larger number of separate activities. This gives rise to a new set of intermediate products. However, at the early stages of introducing new technology of this kind, there are advantages for firms in relying on internalized markets rather than letting each separate activity be performed by independent producers with trade taking place on an arm's-length basis. Specifically, there is the need for producers to synchronize their investments so as to get all the plants on stream at the same time. Centralized planning based on common ownership of all the separate stages of production is preferable.

5. **Government interventions in markets giving rise to incentives to transfer pricing** Transfer pricing will be discussed as a separate topic later in this chapter. It refers to the prices which MNCs charge on their intra-group sales, whether sales of intermediate goods from parent to affiliate or from one affiliate to another. Such prices may diverge markedly from arm's-length prices. As we shall see later, manipulation of such transfer prices may bring certain advantages to the vertically integrated MNC. One cause of such transfer-price manipulation is difference in levels of taxation between countries. For example, where taxes are higher in the home country than the host country where the MNC's affiliate is based, global tax liability can be minimized by underinvoicing parent company sales of intermediate products to the affiliate company. In this way, recorded profits are shifted from the home country where

taxes are high, to the host country where taxes are low. Other incentives for transfer pricing arise from other forms of government intervention such as tariff barriers, price controls, restrictions on profits repatriation, and exchange controls. Each of these will be discussed in a later section of this chapter. At this stage we merely note that such transfer pricing may be one incentive for companies to engage in vertical FDI.

Against these possible benefits from vertical integration must be set various costs. First, there are the managerial diseconomies involved in co-ordinating the activities of each of the various stages of production, especially where these are separated by long distances. Second, there are the technical diseconomies which arise where each of the different stages of production operate more efficiently at different scales of output. This requires that the scale of operation of the enterprise as a whole be set at the level of the lowest common multiple of the minimum efficient scale of output of each stage. This may exceed the potential market for the final product. The outcome is that some of the stages of production will have to operate at less than their most efficient level. One way of resolving this problem is by means of partial internalization. Thus, where the actual output of a particular stage is below the minimum efficient scale of output, excess output could be sold on the external market. Finally, vertical FDI may create problems where subsidiaries are located in politically unstable countries or countries which discriminate against foreign firms. In such countries there exists the risk of expropriation or other discriminatory controls being introduced. In these circumstances the firm may prefer to buy its intermediate goods on an arm's-length basis from an independent source.

Conglomerate Foreign Direct Investment

Conglomerate or internationally diversified MNCs appear to be less common than the horizontally and vertically integrated types. Nevertheless, they are not unimportant. The reason usually given for FDI of this type is the desire on the part of investors to minimize risk through diversification. It is argued that investors are risk averse. For this reason they seek a portfolio of investments which minimizes the variance of the return on an investment. They can achieve this by spreading

175

their investments over a number of holdings rather than concentrating their investments in one basket. The only requirement is that the return on each holding should be imperfectly correlated.

However, it is argued that imperfections in the capital market make it costly for an individual shareholder to achieve such an 'efficient' portfolio. Hence an alternative is for an investor to invest in an investment trust which will achieve the necessary portfolio diversification for the individual investor. However, investment trusts may find it difficult to achieve optimum diversification because of the costs involved in acquiring information about the prospective return on different types of investment. Investment trusts may, accordingly, spread their investments over a relatively small number of fairly large shareholdings. It may prove easier for the investor to achieve optimum diversification through purchasing shares in an internationally diversified MNC. The latter is able to achieve risk minimization for shareholders because it holds investments in a number of other companies which (1) produce unrelated products and (2) are located in different countries. Thus a slump in the demand for one product may be offset by buoyant demand for another, or a slump in one geographical market may be offset by booming sales in another.

Thus the conglomerate or internationally diversified MNC may be viewed as 'a potential surrogate vehicle for financial asset diversification' (Rugman 1985). In addition, it could be argued that such MNCs reflect the desire not only of investors but also, perhaps more so, of salaried management for risk-minimization. Salaried management may attach great importance to stability of salaries and job security in welfare maximization. Such goals are often thought to be more important than profit maximization in the objectives of managers as opposed to shareholders. It is often argued that, in the modern large corporation, effective control has passed from shareholders to management. Hence the desire of managers for risk reduction may provide a further explanation for the internationally diversified MNC.

A further explanation for conglomerate FDI has been suggested by Aliber (Aliber 1970). He regards the internationally diversified MNC as largely a currency-area phenomenon. Investors who place their investments in assets denominated in different currencies face an added risk — namely, the risk that the currency in which the assets are denominated will depreciate. One way of protecting themselves against such an eventuality is to take out forward cover on the foreign-exchange market. However, such forward cover is not free. Consequently, investors will require some interest premium to compensate for the risks of currency depreciation. Specifically, investors will want some premium on assets denominated in currencies which look likely to depreciate. If interest rates fail to offer a sufficient premium, investors will be disinclined to hold assets denominated in such currencies. They may also require a premium to offset any other risks, such as political risks (e.g. the sudden imposition of exchange controls preventing the withdrawal of capital from a country) which they associate with a particular currency.

Aliber has suggested that investors who buy shares in nationally based MNCs are myopic. They act as if all their investment is in a single currency area. This gives the MNCs based in strong-currency countries a financial advantage in raising additional capital for expansion of their overseas activities. Assets denominated in strong currencies will carry a lower risk premium than assets denominated in weak currencies. Hence MNCs based in strong-currency countries can raise capital more cheaply to finance an expansion of their activities in weak-currency countries than locally based firms. Shareholders in locally based firms will require a higher risk premium to cover the risk of the currency depreciating. Specifically, Aliber applied his theory to US direct investment abroad in the 1950s and early 1960s. The dollar was a relatively hard currency for much of this period and many of the European currencies were relatively soft. Hence the currency premium on certain European currencies was greater than on dollar-denominated assets. This meant that the effective rate of interest on borrowings for a US subsidiary operating in Western Europe was lower than for locally based companies. Put another way, US MNCs capitalized the future earnings derived from the acquisition of a profitable concern located in Europe at a higher rate than European investors. This being so, US MNCs took advantage of the opportunity to buy certain European companies cheaply.

Since the late 1960s, however, the dollar has become a relatively weak currency. Hence the argument cannot any longer satisfactorily explain conglomerate expansion by US MNCs. However, it may be used to explain direct investment abroad by Japanese and German MNCs caused by the relative strength of the yen and West German mark. One of the problems with the theory is that it fails to account for the fact that much FDI in recent decades has been of the two-way kind. MNCs have increasingly invested in the home markets of their rivals. The result has been that FDI has increasingly assumed the form of cross-investment involving all the major industrialized countries. This contradicts the predictions of the Aliber model.

The assumption that investors are myopic has also been questioned. Do they really act as if all their investments are in a single currency area when buying the shares of a multinational company? Even if they have been in the past, is it not likely that they will alter their behaviour in the light of experience? However, the theory is useful in stressing that the motives for much international conglomerate expansion are financial rather than economic. Economic gains from conglomerate FDI are likely to be minimal. The combining of two or more quite separate, unrelated activities under single ownership and on an international basis is unlikely to yield any great efficiency gains. Indeed, there may well be offsetting efficiency losses arising from the difficulties of co-ordinating interests spread across a number of industries. Thus the motive for such conglomerate FDI is more likely to be the prospect of a financial gain.

MULTINATIONAL COMPANIES AND WORLD TRADE: THE ROLE OF INTRA-FIRM TRADE

The growth of direct investment abroad since the Second World War and the subsequent rise of the multinational corporation has greatly affected the character of much world trade. MNCs account for a large and growing proportion of trade, especially the trade of the industrialized countries. A significant proportion of such trade takes the form of what is variously called intra-firm, in-house, or intra-group trade. This may be defined as trade between an MNC and its affiliate or associate companies in another country. Much of this trade takes the form of trade in intermediate products between the different plants of multi-plant, vertically integrated MNCs. The increased importance of the MNC as a conduit of world trade — and the increased importance of intra-firm trade as a component of world trade in particular — is of interest for a variety of reasons. Two considerations are of central importance for the subject-matter of this book:

1. Where MNCs account for a large proportion of world trade, patterns of international trade will be determined by the decisions taken by MNCs concerning the geographical location of their different plants. How MNCs plan and divide up the production process globally becomes a major determining factor in the products which different countries export and import.
2. Where a substantial proportion of world trade is intra-firm trade, conventional models of trade which are based on the assumption of perfect competition and arm's-length trade between independent buyers and sellers are unhelpful. One aspect of this concerns the prices at which trade takes place between the parent company and affiliate of an MNC. These so-called transfer prices may diverge markedly from market prices which prevail in the case of arm's-length transactions.

The role which MNCs can play in determining the pattern of trade constitutes a constant theme of this book. I shall return to this consideration on a number of occasions in later chapters. The subject of transfer pricing is one which will be discussed in the final section of this chapter. However, before doing so, it will be necessary to survey the statistical evidence concerning the nature and importance of intra-firm trade and to establish exactly how much of world trade is accounted for by MNCs. Unfortunately, data concerning the nature and extent of intra-firm trade is available in a much less comprehensive form than for intra-industry trade discussed in the previous chapter. The main reason is that companies are extremely reluctant to divulge much information about their in-house transactions. Nevertheless, we do now have fairly comprehensive data for intra-firm trade for both the United States and the United Kingdom. Since these two countries are the two largest gross exporters of multinational capital, this enables us to paint a fairly good picture of the role of intra-firm trade in the world economy as a whole.

United States

The US Tariff Commission reported that in 1970, MNCs accounted for some $21.7 billion out of a total of $31.7 billion worth of US manufactured exports, or about 68 per cent of the total. Of this, $8.8 billion were exported to majority-owned foreign affiliates (MOFAs), the equivalent of 41 per cent of MNC exports from the United States and 28 per cent of total US exports. However, some of these exports were undertaken on behalf of other firms, such that the actual total of MNC exports to MOFAs stood at $7.7 billion, which is equivalent to 35 per cent of MNC exports from the United States and 24 per cent of total US exports. Thus an estimated 24 per cent of US exports represented intra-firm trade. This compared with a figure of 18 per cent in 1962. The level of intra-firm trade appears to be increasing in relative importance (Lall 1978).

The US Department of Commerce found that 35 per cent of US manufacturing exports accounted for by MNCs and 22 per cent of total US manufacturing exports in 1970 were sent to MOFAs. This estimate was just below that of the US Tariff Commission. However, both of these figures may be taken as minimal estimates of the importance of intra-firm trade. Some of the exports of MNCs to nominally independent buyers could be treated as intra-firm trade since the buyers were related by ownership and other ties (Helleiner 1979).

More recent surveys have found intra-firm trade to account for a larger proportion of US exports. Thus the US Department of Commerce estimated that in 1977 intra-firm trade accounted for 36 per cent of US exports. This figure includes not only exports by a US parent company to a majority-owned foreign affiliate, but also exports by a non-US affiliate based in the United States to their parent company abroad. Thus it is a somewhat broader definition of intra-firm trade. Table 4.9 sets out the results of this survey. Of the 36 per cent of total exports which represented intra-firm trade, 27 per cent were exports by US parent companies to their affiliates abroad and 9 per cent were exports by non-US affiliates based in the US to their parents abroad. As we saw earlier, in 1970 an estimated 22 per cent of exports were sent from US parent companies to their overseas affiliates. The fact that this had increased to 27 per cent by 1977 suggests a strongly rising trend in the relative importance of such trade.

Table 4.9: Arm's-length and intra-firm trade as components of total US foreign exports in 1977

Trading partners	Exports ($bn)	Share of TNC generated exports (%)	Share of total exports (%)
ARM'S LENGTH TRADE			
US parents and non-affiliates	61.1	48.5	50.4
Other US persons and US affiliates abroad	8.4	6.7	6.9
Foreign affiliates in US and non-affiliates abroad	12.7	10.1	10.5
Subtotal	82.2	65.3	67.8
INTRA-FIRM TRADE			
US parents and their affiliates	32.4	25.7	26.7
Foreign affiliates in US and their parents abroad	11.3	9.0	9.3
Subtotal	43.7	34.7	36.0
Total TNC-generated trade [a]	125.9	100.0	103.8
Total US exports [a]	121.2	–	100.0

Source: UNCTC (1983).
[a] Since the data were obtained and compiled using different methodologies, the individual figures are not strictly comparable. In particular, the estimate of total TNC-generated exports exceeds total recorded US exports.

As far as US imports are concerned, the Foreign Trade Division of the US Bureau of the Census estimated that for 1977 the level of intra-firm imports amounted to about 48 per cent of total US imports (Helleiner 1981). Intra-firm imports were identified as 'related-party' imports, defined as imports which enter the United States through importing firms related by ownership — 5 per cent of voting equity or more — to the exporting firms in which they originated. This figure may be regarded as an underestimate if allowance is made for the fact that some US imports originated on a subcontracting basis. Such trade involves a degree of dependence of the foreign firm on the US importing company. Usually, the foreign firm carries out some further processing or assembly of semi-finished goods, components, or parts supplied by the US company. The foreign firm may not be related by ownership to the US buyer but is often fully dependent on him for technology and marketing. Such trade may, therefore, be included within the ambit of intra-firm trade. However, the extent of such trade is not fully known. We might also choose to include imports covered by licensing agreements or other contracts between the US importing company and foreign exporting company. G. K. Helleiner has concluded the 'it seems roughly safe to say that US intra-firm transactions make up more than half of total US imports' (Helleiner 1979).

The US Department of Commerce has also sought to estimate the importance of intra-firm trade as a share of US imports. Their estimates are presented in Table 4.10. Total intra-firm imports were found to amount to 39 per cent of total US imports, of which 21 per cent represented the imports of US parent companies from their overseas affiliates and 18 per cent of non-US affiliates based in the United States from their parents abroad. The figure of 39 per cent is less than that obtained by the US Bureau of the Census quoted above because definitions differ. Intra-firm imports in the US Department of Commerce survey are not the same as related-party imports in the US Bureau of the Census survey.

Table 4.10: Arm's-length and intra-firm trade as components of total US imports in 1977

Trading partners	Imports ($b)	Share of TNC generated exports (%)	Share of total exports (%)
ARM'S-LENGTH TRADE			
US parents and non-affiliates	45.2	35.3	28.7
Other US persons and US affiliates abroad	8.9	6.9	5.6
Foreign affiliates in US and non-affiliates abroad	12.7	9.9	8.1
Subtotal	66.8	52.1	42.4
INTRA-FIRM TRADE			
US parents and their affiliates	32.6	25.5	20.7
Foreign affiliates in US and their parents abroad	28.7	22.4	18.2
Subtotal	61.3	47.9	38.9
Total TNC-generated trade	128.1	100.0	81.3
Total US imports	157.5		100.0

Source: UNCTC (1983).

United Kingdom

Figures have been estimated for intra-firm trade for United Kingdom exports but not imports. A study by the Department of Trade and Industry found that, in 1976, foreign-owned enterprises located in the United Kingdom accounted for 30 per cent of all exports. This compared with 21 per cent in 1966, 25 per cent in 1970, and 29 per cent in 1973. In addition, a further 52 per cent of UK exports in 1976 were accounted for by UK enterprises with overseas affiliates. This compared with 45 per cent in 1966, 47 per cent in 1970, and 52 per cent in 1973. These figures are shown in Table 4.11. Thus in 1976 82 per cent of all UK exports were accounted for by MNCs, both UK-based and foreign-based. This compares with 66 per cent in 1964, 72 per cent in 1970, and 81 per cent in 1973. Thus a high and rising proportion of UK exports is accounted for by both UK and foreign MNCs.

Table 4.11: Export of manufactures from the United Kingdom by enterprises with foreign ownership and UK firms with investment overseas (%)

	1966	1970	1973	1976
By UK enterprises with foreign ownership:				
All exports	21	25	29	30
Exports to related concerns	10	12	14	14
By UK firms with investments overseas:				
All exports	45	47	52	52
Exports to related concerns	12	12	15	15
By all UK enterprises with international connections:				
All exports	66	72	81	82
Exports to related concerns	22	24	29	29

Sources: Batchelor, Major, and Morgan (1980); Department of Trade and Industry (1979); Panic and Joyce (1980).

Table 4.11 also includes estimates showing the proportion of UK trade which constitutes intra-firm trade. In 1976 29 per cent of all US exports went to related concerns. This compares with 22 per cent in 1966, 24 per cent in 1970, and 29 per cent in 1973. Thus the level of UK intra-firm trade is also high and was rising over the period covered. It is interesting to note that intra-firm trade was relatively more important for foreign-owned MNCs operating in the UK than for UK MNCs. The former accounted for almost the same share of intra-firm exports as the latter, although UK MNCs accounted for over 50 per cent of UK exports compared with 30 per cent for foreign-owned MNCs.

Other Countries

Much less information is available for other countries. One useful indication of the importance of intra-firm trade in the exports of other countries is given by a survey carried out by Dunning and Pearce of some 329 of the world's largest industrial enterprises. The results are summarized in Table 4.12. This showed that, in 1977, an estimated 33 per cent of parent company exports consisted of intra-firm sales. US MNCs had the highest ratio. An estimated 45.5 per cent of the exports of US MNCs were intra-firm sales. Japanese MNCs had the lowest ratio. This reflects the fact that the level of direct investment abroad carried out by Japanese companies has been much less than in other industrialized countries (Dunning and Pearce 1981).

Table 4.12: Intra-firm trade in the home countries exports of large industrial corporations, 1977, by home country (%)

Home country	Share of intra-firm trade in parent companies' total exports
Canada	39.3
EEC	29.6
Europe (total)	29.7
France	32.2
West Germany	34.6
Japan	17.0
Other Western Europe	29.8
Sweden	36.1
United Kingdom	29.6
United States	45.5
Other countries	22.8
TOTAL	32.8

Source: Dunning and Pearce (1981) quoted in UNCTC (1983).

There is some evidence to support the view that intra-firm trade has been more important as a component of trade between industrialized countries. Helleiner and Lavergne found that, in 1977, 54 per cent of US imports from the industrialized OECD countries were related-party imports. However, only 28 per cent of imports from Third World countries and 8 per cent of imports from centrally planned economies were related-party imports (Helleiner and Lavergne 1980). These figures are contained in Table 4.13. One reason for this is that intra-firm trade is higher in trade in manufactured goods, which account for a higher proportion of trade with industrialized than less-developed countries. It can be seen from Table 4.13 that intra-firm trade is higher for manufactures than for semi-manufactures and higher for semi-manufactures than primary commodities if petroleum is excluded. Intra-firm trade is high in petroleum products as is to be expected given the high degree of vertical integration achieved by the oil companies.

One conclusion which follows is that intra-firm trade is likely to become an increasingly important component of trade as a country becomes more industrialized. In addition, the more welcoming the stance which a country adopts in relation to MNCs, the greater will be the importance of intra-firm trade in total trade. Thus Helleiner and Lavergne found that intra-firm trade was greatest as a component of total imports for developing countries which adopted a hospitable attitude towards MNCs. Thus 71 per cent of all manufacturing imports from Mexico and 59 per cent of all manufacturing imports from Ireland were related-party imports. On the other hand, only 5 per cent of imports from Yugoslavia were of this kind (Helleiner and Lavergne 1980).

Industry Variations

A number of studies have been carried out to analyse the structure of US intra-firm trade with reference to both US exports and imports. S. Lall examined the level of intra-firm trade as a component of US exports in 1970 (Lall 1978). Table 4.14 shows the industry breakdown. Two measures are used (i) the IFX ratio, which measures intra-firm exports as a percentage of total MNC exports, and (ii) the IPX ratio, which

Table 4.13: US related-party imports as percentages of total imports by product group and origin, 1977

	Petroleum	Primary Primary excl. petroleum	Total primary	Semi-Manufactures	Manufactures	Total Total	Total Total excl. petroleum
OECD	57.2	35.9	41.3	43.4	61.1	53.7	53.6
Centrally planned	0	3.2	2.8	8.9	8.1	7.7	7.8
Third World	59.6	13.6	49.1	17.0	37.0	43.4	28.1
Total	59.4	23.5	47.3	37.6	53.6	48.4	45.2

Source: Helleiner and Lavergne (1980).

measures intra-firm exports as a percentage of production by majority-owned foreign affiliates. Substantial variations between industries were apparent. Lall found that the factors which best explained these variations were as follows:

Table 4.14: Intra-firm export and production ratios of US MNCs by industry, 1970

Industry	IFX ratio (%)	IPX ratio (%)	Industry	IFX ratio (%)	IPX ratio (%)
Food products:	34	5	Non-electrical		
Grain mills	47	8	machinery:	44	15
Beverages	19	1	Farm machinery	49	20
Combinations	23	na	Industrial	27	12
Other	32	5	Office	75	17
Paper	25	7	Computing	75	17
Chemicals	36	7	Other	40	20
Drugs	38	5	Electrical machinery	23	8
Soap and cosmetics	54	3	Household	25	5
Industrial	15	9	Equipment	15	7
Plastics	88	12	Electronic	29	8
Combinations	100	na	Other	92	12
Other	29	8	Transport Equipment	41	17
Rubber	39	6	Textiles, apparel	40	6
Primary & fabricated			Lumber, wood		
materials	12	4	furnishings	11	10
Primary	5	6	Printing, publishing	25	6
Fabricated (excl.			Stone, clay, glass	32	6
aluminium, brass			Instruments	62	18
& copper)	24	4	Other		
Aluminium	9	2	manufacturing	23	3
Other	50	6			
			All manufacturing	35	10

na = no data available
Source: Lall (1978).

1. The technological intensity of an industry as measured by R & D expenditure relative to sales turnover. The greater the degree of technological intensity, the higher the level of intra-firm trade. This perhaps reflects the fact that the advantages of internalization are greatest where products embody high quotients of technology. Lall points to the specificity of products belonging to such industries. By this is meant their uniqueness, high quality, and suitability for demanding and variable requirements. Where

intermediate inputs possess specificity, firms may prefer to rely on internal rather than external supplies.

2. The divisibility of the production process, as measured by the number of separate activities which it can be broken down into and which can be located in different countries. The more easily can the production process be split up into a large number of separate activities, which can also be located in different countries, the higher the level of intra-firm trade. In particular, the amount of offshore processing taking place within an industry affects the level of intra-firm trade. The offshore assembly provisions built into US tariff schedules were important.

3. The degree to which an industry is internationally diversified, as measured by the ratio of foreign investment to domestic investment. The more internationally diversified an industry, the higher the level of intra-firm trade.

4. The need for after-sales service within an industry. The greater the need for after-sales service, the stronger the incentive to channel exports through affiliates, especially in the case of high-technology products.

Helleiner and Lavergne examined the nature of intra-firm trade as a component of United States imports (Helleiner and Lavergne 1980). They measured the percentage of US imports which were related-party imports at the two-digit level of aggregation. Their results are shown in Table 4.15. It is apparent that there are equally great differences in the level of intra-firm trade for US imports as for US exports. Helleiner and Lavergne distinguished between (1) imports of non-US firms located in the United States (i.e. foreign MNCs operating in the United States) and (2) related-party imports of US firms. In 1977 some 48 per cent of all intra-firm imports were accounted for by non-US firms located in the United States. In the case of intra-firm imports from Japan, all such imports were accounted for by non-US (presumably Japanese) firms operating in the US. In the case of intra-firm imports from the EEC, 78 per cent were accounted for by non-US firms located in the United States. On the other hand, only 15 per cent of intra-firm imports from less-developed countries were accounted for by non-US firms.

Table 4.15: US related-party imports as a percentage of total imports by category, 1977

Category	%	Category	%
Live animals	12	Dyeing, tanning & colouring materials	70
Beverages & tobacco	20	Medical & pharmaceutical products	47
Dairy products	13	Essential oils & perfumes	27
Fish & fish preparations	23	Fertilizers, manufactured	23
Cereals & cereal preparations	12	Explosives & pyrotechnic products	9
Fruit & vegetables	40	Plastic materials	55
Sugar, sugar preparations	3	Chemical materials & products, n.e.s.	49
Coffee, tea, cocoa, spices	9	Leather & leather manufactures	6
Feeding stuff for animals	16	Rubber manufactures, n.e.s.	73
Miscellaneous food	24	Wood & cork manufactures	15
Beverages	24	Paper, paperboard, etc.	21
Tobacco & manufactures	8	Textile yarn, fabrics, made-up articles	23
Hides & skins	1	Non-metallic mineral manufactures	16
Oil seeds, nuts, kernels	19	Iron & steel	62
Crude rubber (inc. synthetic)	38	Non-ferrous metals	34
Wood, lumber, cork	17	Manufactures of metal, n.e.s.	25
Pulp & waste paper	41	Machinery other than electrical	60
Textile fibres	17	Electrical machinery, apparatus, appliances	63
Crude fertilizers & minerals	38	Transport equipment	84
Metalliferous ores & metal scrap	52	Sanitary & other fixtures	16
Crude animal & vegetable materials	14	Furniture	26
Coal, coke & briquettes	14	Travel goods & handbags	13
Petroleum & petroleum products	57	Clothing	11
Gas, natural & manufactured	55	Footwear	7
Animal oils & fats	15	Professional & scientific instruments	51
Fixed vegetable oils & fats	9	Miscellaneous manufactures	28
Animal & veg. oils & fats, processed	5		
Chemical elements & compounds	43		
Mineral tar & chemicals from coal, petroleum & natural gas	34		

Source: Helleiner and Lavergne (1980).

Helleiner and Lavergne found that 75 per cent of intra-firm imports by non-US MNCs were finished products for resale or distribution. In other words, a high proportion of intra-firm imports of foreign-based MNCs with affiliates in the United States consisted of finished products for sale in the United States. Such companies (especially Japanese companies) were keen to sell their goods through their own sales networks. By way of contrast, intra-firm imports by US MNCs largely consisted of intermediate goods requiring further manufacture. These are products which constitute inputs into 'a vertically integrated multinational production structure', that is international production proper.

Helleiner and Lavergne sought to test the explanatory power of a number of variables in determining inter-industry differences in the levels of intra-firm trade measured as a component of US imports. They found the following to be the most important factors:

1. The skill intensity of an industry, as measured by the level of the average wage. For imports from developed countries, the higher the degree of skill intensity of an industry, the higher the level of intra-firm trade.
2. The importance of barriers to entry of new competition in an industry, as measured by the size of firms within an industry. For imports from developed countries, the higher the level of entry barriers to an industry, the greater the level of intra-firm trade.
3. The degree of technology- or research-intensity of an industry, as measured by the level of R & D expenditure as a percentage of sales. For imports from both developed and developing countries, the greater the degree of research-intensity of an industry, the higher the level of intra-firm trade. This variable performed particularly well in explaining differences in the level of intra-firm imports from developing countries and changes in the level of intra-firm imports.

These results are consistent with what was said earlier about the factors giving rise to vertical FDI and the vertically integrated MNC. In particular, it would appear that the degree of technological intensity within an industry is a powerful factor working towards internalization of markets, leading in turn to high levels of intra-firm trade. Thus Buckley and Casson have found that, of the largest 300 US-based MNCs, the most research-intensive had the highest intra-firm trade ratios (Buckley and Casson 1976). This point is further illustrated by Table 4.16, which shows the level of intra-firm exports for the world's 329 largest industrial enterprises. If aerospace is omitted from the highly research-intensive industries, it is apparent that the level of intra-firm trade is generally higher in these industries than others. The ratio for the medium research-intensive industries is higher but this is largely due to motor vehicles and industrial and farm equipment. Intra-firm trade ratios for all low research-intensive industries are significantly lower. The fact that the relationship between research intensity and the level of intra-firm trade is not perfect is to be expected. Many other factors are at work at the same time to influence the level of intra-firm trade.

Table 4.16: The share of intra-firm exports in the total exports from their home countries of 329 large industrial corporations by industry, 1977

Sector	Share
HIGH RESEARCH-INTENSIVE INDUSTRIES	
Aerospace	1.8
Office equipment (including computers)	91.3
Petroleum	51.0
Measurement, scientific & photographic equipment	58.2
Electronics & electrical appliances	36.5
Chemicals & pharmaceuticals	35.0
Subtotal	34.5
MEDIUM RESEARCH-INTENSIVE INDUSTRIES	
Industrial & farm equipment	52.6
Shipbuilding, railroad & transportation equipment	0.1
Rubber	–
Motor vehicles (including components)	62.4
Metal manufacturing and products	12.8
Subtotal	36.9
LOW RESEARCH-INTENSIVE INDUSTRIES	
Building materials	8.7
Tobacco	0.5
Beverages	20.3
Food	9.2
Paper & wood products	9.5
Textiles, apparel, leather goods	12.8
Publishing & printing	5.4
Other manufacturing	5.9
Subtotal	9.5
All sectors	32.8

Source: Dunning and Pearce (1981); UNCTC (1983).

Professor Casson has used the 1977 data concerning intra-firm exports and imports of US MNCs to examine the factors influencing the level of intra-firm trade (Casson 1986). He established that manufacturing industries account for over 70 per cent of US intra-firm exports, with motor vehicles and equipment accounting for no less than 46 per cent. Casson measured the amount of intra-firm sales by US companies to their overseas affiliates as a percentage of total US exports to affiliates to measure the dependence of foreign affiliates on the parent company for sources of supply. This was very high for the petroleum industry, manufacturing, and the wholesale and retail trades. Some of these products comprised capital equipment, especially in mining, petroleum, services, and agriculture. However, a much higher proportion of these goods was for resale without further processing. This ratio was especially high for printing and publishing and motor vehicles and equipment.

With regard to intra-firm imports, Casson found that the petroleum industry accounted for 44 per cent of all such imports and manufacturing for only 47 per cent, rather different from intra-firm exports. Within manufacturing, the levels of intra-firm imports were especially high in transport equipment and electronic components. High levels of two-way intra-firm trade are in evidence in these industries. Affiliates of US MNCs were found to have a high degree of dependence on parent companies for exports in manufacturing industry. Casson sought to identify those manufacturing industries which had both high degrees of export dependence of affiliates on parent company and high degrees of import dependence of affiliates on parent company. These may be regarded as the industries demonstrating the highest levels of intra-firm trade. The industries meeting these qualifications were electronic components, drugs, non-electrical machinery, and non-ferrous metals. However, he found that, in general, there was not much association between industries with high degrees of export dependence and high degrees of import dependence. This would suggest that different measures of intra-firm trade will give different pictures of the precise industries in which intra-firm trade is greatest (Casson 1986).

TRANSFER PRICING

Transfer prices are the prices used by multinational companies for intra-firm or in-house sales of goods and services. Transfer pricing refers to the manipulation of these prices by multinational companies such that prices diverge from so-called arm's-length prices which prevail for equivalent transactions between independent (i.e. unrelated) parties. Sometimes the term 'transfer prices' is confined to cases when such prices do diverge from arm's-length prices, and the term 'internal prices' is more loosely used whether or not transfer-price manipulation takes place (Plasschaert 1979). However, we shall draw no such distinction.

There are several problems with the concept of transfer pricing. First, there is the problem of the nature of the relationship between two companies. How closely related must two companies be for trade between them to be referred to as intra-firm trade and the prices used for such trade to be referred to as transfer prices? There is no problem where the affiliate is a wholly-owned or majority-owned subsidiary of the company in question. However, the multinational company may hold a minority, non-controlling interest in the overseas company. Even if it owns no equity stake in the overseas company, it may exercise some element of control (e.g. a licensing agreement, management contract, etc.). In such cases the prices used in trade may not be manipulated in quite the same way as when the overseas company is wholly or largely owned by the multinational. However, it may also be true that the prices used do not correspond to freely determined arm's-length prices. Thus the concept of transfer pricing may have a broader application than the case of trade between a parent company and overseas affiliate belonging to the same multinational company.

Second, the concept of transfer pricing need not be confined to trade transactions. It may equally well be applied to non-trade flows within a multinational company. A multinational company may divert funds from one unit to another through non-trade channels such as the payment of fees to the parent company for the provision of services, the payment of royalties for licences covering patents or other know-how, the payment of interest on loans from the parent company, and so on. Transfer pricing in non-trade transactions is often more difficult to identify. This is because the payments involved are typically for resources which are highly specific to the firm and which, therefore, have no equivalent free-market, arm's-length prices for comparison.

Motives for Transfer Pricing

Why might a multinational company fix a different price on the sale of goods to an overseas affiliate than the free market, arm's-length price for an equivalent transaction between two unrelated parties? There exist several possible motives for transfer pricing. The following are the most important ones:

1. Differences in rates of corporate taxation between countries

Whenever rates of corporate taxation differ markedly between one country and another, an incentive exists for multinational companies to manipulate transfer prices. This is because, by means of such transfer price manipulation, a multinational company can reduce its overall, global tax payments and thus increase after-tax profits. For example, if the rate of corporate taxation is higher in country A than in country B, a parent company based in country A and selling goods to an affiliate located in country B could underinvoice the sale of such goods. In this way, it can shift some recorded profits from country A to country B and reduce its total tax payments in the two countries taken together. Conversely, if the rate of corporate taxation is lower in country A than country B, it could overinvoice the sale of goods to the affiliate located in B. In this way, it could shift some recorded profits from B to A, again reducing its total tax payments.

Since rates of corporate taxation do differ between countries, it might be thought that transfer pricing along these lines is quite common. If so, the effect will be to deprive the tax authorities in the high tax country of important tax revenues. It is sometimes argued that such transfer-price manipulation undermines the ability of a developing country to extract a larger share of the profits earned by foreign companies by a policy of high taxation. It would also have a deleterious effect on their terms of trade and balance of payments by raising the unit price of imports. However, it does appear that nominal rates of corporate taxation are typically lower in developing countries (Plasschaert 1985). In addition, developing countries often assess taxable profits less severely and offer more generous tax incentives. The gap between developed and developing countries in the levels of corporate taxation is accordingly much greater if effective rates and not nominal rates of tax are compared. On the other hand, there are a few developing countries where above-average nominal rates are applied. In addition, many developing countries impose punitive withholding taxes on repatriated dividends, interest, and royalties.

One factor which may reduce the incentive for MNCs to manipulate transfer prices to reduce their global tax liability is the system operated by many industrialized countries for preventing the double taxation of profits. For example, in the United States, corporate taxes paid by an overseas affiliate to the host country on profits earned can be deducted from the tax payable in the United States when profits are remitted. Such taxes paid to host-country governments count as foreign tax credits against taxable profits in the United States. Withholding taxes paid on repatriated dividends, interest, and royalties may also qualify for such tax credits. The aim of these arrangements is to ensure that profits earned overseas do not get taxed twice over and thus prevent any discrimination against foreign as opposed to domestic investment. The effect is to reduce the benefit from any transfer price manipulation designed to avoid penal profits taxation in countries abroad.

In addition, the United States tax system contains a built-in incentive for MNCs to retain profits abroad. Any profits earned abroad but not repatriated are not subject to assessment for taxation in the United States. This is known as the 'deferral rule'. At the same time, any MNC which reinvests profits in the local subsidiary rather than repatriating those profits, avoids paying withholding tax. The effect of all these arrangements is to reduce the potential gain to be reaped from transfer-price manipulation should overseas profits tax rates be higher than the rates applicable in the home country.

However, there are also the cases of so-called 'tax havens', countries where zero or extremely low rates of corporate taxation exist. Many MNCs set up subsidiaries, typically non-producing subsidiaries, in such tax havens and seek to siphon profits to these companies by means of transfer-price manipulation. If a large proportion of profits earned is recorded in such countries, global tax liabilities may be reduced. However, the ability of MNCs to avoid tax in this way is more limited than it seems. Governments of most capital-exporting countries are now aware of these practices and have introduced legislation to clamp down on this type of abuse. However, it may be more difficult for developing countries to stop this kind of activity. From the point of view of a MNC its ability to avoid paying taxes in its home country by using subsidiaries especially set up for this purpose in such tax havens is probably limited. Eventually, profits recorded as occurring in the tax haven will have to be remitted to the parent company to pay dividends to shareholders.

2. **Differences in the levels of tariffs between countries** Another inducement to manipulate transfer prices may arise from different import tariff levels. When a multinational company is selling goods to an overseas affiliate and faces a high *ad valorem* tariff, the company can minimize the customs duty payable by underpricing the merchandise. An *ad valorem* tariff is set as a percentage of the unit value of the imported product and differs from a specific tariff which is set as a fixed amount per unit of the product imported. Transfer price manipulation will only be profitable where the tariff in question is an *ad valorem* tariff. Once again, it is argued that MNCs have engaged in this kind of practice when exporting goods to affiliates based in developing countries. Many developing countries impose high tariffs on imported intermediate goods in an effort to promote import substitution. High tariffs are one method of fostering the development of infant industries and reducing dependence on imported supplies of such goods. In addition, high import tariffs are also an important revenue-raising device in developing countries which lack a large tax base.

It is argued that such transfer price manipulation is harmful to developing countries because (i) it deprives the customs authorities of important revenue and (ii) undermines the protective effect of the high tariff. On the other hand, it is beneficial to the balance of payments of the country concerned and improves the importing country's terms of trade. However, the main problem with such a practice is that it is likely to conflict with other objectives of the MNC. Underinvoicing goods sold to the overseas affiliate will siphon profits abroad and enlarge the recorded profits of the overseas affiliate while reducing those of the parent company. If rates of corporate taxation are lower in the host country, there will be no conflict of objective. Where, however, such rates of taxation are higher in the host country, there will be a conflict with the wish to minimize global tax liability by shifting recorded profits to the country where taxation is lowest. Equally, underpricing goods exported to the overseas affiliate may expose the MNC to increased financial risk. There is always the danger that the currency of the host country will be devalued or depreciate suddenly, or that the host country government will suddenly impose tighter exchange controls preventing the company from repatriating profits. For these reasons, it may not be desirable to tie up too many profits in an overseas country, especially a weak or politically unstable one.

Much depends on the type of good imported. The tariff structure of developed and developing countries tend to escalate. This means that the more advanced the stage of production, the higher the rate of import tariff applied. Thus finished manufactures tend to be subject to higher tariffs than semi-finished manufactures. The latter are subject to higher tariffs than raw materials. Economists would say that the effective rate of protection is greater than the nominal rate of protection. It follows that if the affiliate imports from the parent company raw materials, components, or parts, the nominal rate of tariff will be quite low. If it imports finished consumer or capital goods for resale, the nominal rate of tariff will be quite high. However, it seems likely that affiliates based in developing countries will tend to import semi-finished goods from the parent company, while the parent company will tend to import largely finished goods from the overseas affiliate. The stage of production should advance as the good moves from the parent to the affiliate and back again to the parent. It follows that more underpricing of imports is likely to take place when the affiliate supplies the parent company with a finished manufacture. Developing countries ought not to lose out too seriously from this type of transfer price manipulation. On the other hand, it seems likely that the customs authorities of most developed countries will be quite effective in spotting blatant examples of these types of practices.

3. **Exchange risks** The existence of different currencies and the fact that exchange rates either fluctuate or are subject to periodic adjustments create risk for all companies involved in international trade. Hence all traders seek to reduce their exposure to losses caused by exchange rate changes. One way in which they seek to do so is through alteration or variation of the timing of their payments and receipts. These alterations or variations are sometimes called 'leads' and 'lags'. 'Leads' refer to the bringing forward of payments in weak currencies which are expected to depreciate. 'Lags' refer to the delay of payments in strong currencies which are likely to appreciate. Thus,

if the pound sterling looks likely to depreciate, UK importers with payments to make to overseas suppliers will be anxious to make such payments before the sterling cost of such imports rises. On the other hand, if the pound sterling looks likely to appreciate, UK importers with payments to make to overseas suppliers will wish to delay payments in order to take advantage of the coming reduction in the sterling cost of such imports.

Such leads and lags are considered to be an important source of exchange rate speculation. In fact, they contain a mixture of both speculation, with traders taking up definite positions in a particular currency with a view to making a gain, and hedging, with traders seeking to protect themselves against the risk of the exchange rate changing. Whatever the motive, the practice is adopted by all companies involved in international trade and not just multinational companies. However, MNCs are especially well placed to undertake such operations because of the substantial amount of intra-firm trade with which they are involved. By overpricing or underpricing the sale of goods from one unit of the company to another, they can bring forward or delay payments and reduce their exposure to currency loss. Consider the case of a UK-based MNC with an affiliate in the United States. The parent company supplies the affiliate with finished goods for resale. If sterling is expected to depreciate (the dollar appreciate), it will be best to postpone payments. If sterling is expected to appreciate (the dollar depreciate), it will be best to bring payments forward.

It is important to note that it is not transfer-price manipulation *per se* which reduces exchange rate risk. The overpricing or underpricing of goods sold by the parent company to an overseas affiliate merely shifts currency assets from one unit of the company to another. For example, if the parent company overprices goods sold to an overseas affiliate, the parent company acquires foreign currency from the affiliate. If the currency in question depreciates, the affiliate loses less than it would otherwise because it is not caught holding the depreciating currency. However, the parent company loses more than otherwise. Thus transfer-price manipulation *per se* cannot eliminate exchange rate risk. Rather, it is the combination of transfer-price manipulation with the leading and lagging of payments that enables an MNC to minimize exchange rate risk.

4. **Restriction on the repatriation of profits or capital** Limitations on the repatriation of profits from other countries in which

affiliates are located will create a strong inducement for MNCs to engage in transfer-price manipulation. This will take the form of the overpricing of goods sold by the parent company to the affiliate or the underpricing of goods sold by the affiliate to the parent company. In this way, a disguised repatriation of profits may be effected. Many developing countries seek to restrict the repatriation of profits by MNCs for both tax and balance of payments reasons. Such restrictions may take several different forms:

  (i) Legal stipulations covering the maximum dividend payable out of profits to the shareholders of the parent company.

 (ii) A system of multiple exchange rates under which foreign currency for the purpose of profits repatriation is only available at highly unfavourable exchange rates.

(iii) Severe and discriminatory taxation of profits which are remitted, often including payments of royalties on the use of know-how, management fees, and the interest on any loans from the parent company.

5. **Political and social pressures** A wide variety of different kinds of political and social pressure in either the home or host country may create an inducement for a MNC to engage in transfer-price manipulation. Two such cases may be cited:

  (i) Trade unions want a larger share of declared profits of the affiliate, so the parent seeks to disguise some of the profits made by the affiliate by overpricing goods sold to the affiliate.

 (ii) The government of the host country threatens nationalization on account of alleged excessive profits being made by the MNC, so the parent company seeks to disguise profits by overpricing goods which it sells to its overseas affiliate.

However, in any of these situations, an MNC must tread carefully. It must take care to act discreetly. Overt transfer-price manipulation will merely attract the attention of trade unions and government and increase the risk of trade-union or governmental pressure being exerted.

6. **Direct threats to profits** The profits of an MNC may be threatened in a variety of ways such that it is led to manipulate transfer prices. Four cases may be cited:

(i) The declaration of high profits by an MNC may cause the government of the host country to reduce or remove altogether any protection from imports which the MNC previously enjoyed. The level of the import tariff may be determined by reference to domestic costs of production plus some acceptable mark-up. If so, the MNC will have an incentive to overprice the cost of any raw materials, semi-finished goods, or intermediate goods sold to the overseas affiliate so as to secure a higher level of protection.

(ii) The declaration of high profits by an MNC may alternatively lead to the host country government imposing price controls. Often these controls establish prices by reference to the domestic costs of production plus some fair and acceptable mark-up for profits. This creates an incentive for the parent company to overprice the sale of raw materials, semi-finished goods, or intermediate goods to inflate domestic costs artificially and secure a more favourable controlled price. Such price controls are quite common in industries such as the pharmaceutical industry, where MNCs often enjoy patent protection and governments are fearful of excessive profits being made.

(iii) The declaration of high profits by an MNC may invite other MNCs or local firms to set up in competition so as to gain a share in the excess profits being earned. Transfer price manipulation may constitute a device for both disguising such profits from envious onlookers and deterring entry to the industry by potential rivals.

(iv) The declaration of high profits by an MNC may cause the host-country government to impose higher taxes or to insist on greater local shareholder participation to ensure more of the profits are retained locally. The MNC may see the latter as undermining its control as well as reducing the amount of profits going to shareholders in the home country. Transfer-price manipulation may be resorted to as a means of concealing such profits.

Constraints on Transfer Price Manipulation

Although there exists a variety of inducements for MNCs to engage in transfer price manipulation, these must be set against certain constraining factors. Constraints on transfer price manipulation are of two kinds:

1. **Internal limitations** The most important set of internal constraints on manipulation of transfer prices by an MNC are as follows:

(i) The existence of substantial local shareholder participation: Where a substantial proportion of the shares of the local subsidiary are owned by local investors, it may prove more difficult to siphon profits abroad through the parent company overpricing goods sold to the local subsidiary. Local shareholders will resist such a process because it reduces the amount of profit which goes to them. For this reason, local equity participation is one way in which a country can protect itself against transfer-price manipulation by foreign companies. On the other hand, it will not be effective if local shareholders are apathetic or lacking in sufficient technical and business acumen to check transfer prices. Furthermore, there is also the possibility that local shareholders may collude with their foreign partner. They may see their interest as bound up with those of the parent company and go along with any action which maximizes global profitability. However, it would seem more likely that the presence of local shareholders will act as a constraint on transfer pricing.

(ii) The case of a joint venture of a MNC and local company: Joint ventures will be more fully discussed in the next chapter. However, for the purposes of restraining transfer-price manipulation, joint ventures work in a similar fashion to local shareholder participation. Attempts to siphon profits abroad through overpricing goods sold to the local affiliate risk incurring the opposition of local partners in the joint venture. On the other hand, the incentive to shift profits abroad in this way may be greater in order to ensure that local partners get a smaller share of the profits from the enterprise.

(iii) The organizational structure of the company: Transfer-price manipulation presupposes a high degree of integration and centralization of control within the company. Each of the local subsidiaries is subordinate to the parent company. Each conforms to centrally directed profits targets. Each puts maximization of global profits before maximization of local profits. However, much modern organization theory is opposed to such a management structure on the grounds that it stifles local effort and initiative. Where local managers are deprived of control, morale will suffer and a sense of commitment will be lost. This creates a preference for a more devolved organizational structure involving the establishment of autonomous 'profit centres' and the granting of freedom to local managers to maximize profits. One way around this may be for the company to operate two sets of accounts, one showing the real profits and the other the taxable profits, in order to stimulate and encourage local managers. However, overcentralized control also makes for less efficient decision-making. It makes for slower response to changing circumstances and requires a very large amount of information transmission. The parent company must be fed with a very large amount of information which then has to be processed before any decision about prices can be made. The flow of information is continuous with each new set of information having to be fed into centralized computers and prices altered accordingly. Where a company is very large, it seems improbable that such a highly centralized control structure can operate. On the other hand, large firms may be better able to equip themselves with computers and other technology to facilitate the operation of such a policy. Small firms will also lack the experience both of world conditions and of dealing with host country governments to manipulate transfer prices efficiently and successfully.

2. **External limitations** External constraints on transfer pricing are those which arise from outside the firm. They arise from the intervention of governments, specifically the customs authorities and the tax authorities. Both sets of authority are likely to be concerned about transfer pricing. The customs authorities will be concerned about the loss of tariff revenue due to the underinvoicing of imports. The tax authorities will be concerned about the loss of tax revenue through the siphoning of profits abroad, especially to tax havens. This may be achieved through both the overpricing of imports or underpricing of exports and through non-trade channels, such as interest payments to the parent company, payments of royalties and fees for R & D, and so on.

The great problem involved in the control of transfer pricing is that of identifying and determining its extent. It requires the customs and tax authorities to establish some notion of what the arm's-length price would be on such a transaction. In some cases this will not be difficult. Where the product is traded on the market involving the coming together of independent buyers and sellers, the price in question is the arm's-length price. If prices diverge substantially from this, this is evidence for transfer-price manipulation. The authorities will require the company to make tax payments or pay customs duties as if such a comparable uncontrolled price is the operative one. In this case companies will be wary of drawing attention to themselves by markedly overpricing or underpricing their intra-firm sales of goods or services.

However, for many goods and services traded within companies, there exists no comparable uncontrolled price. The good or service in question may be highly specific to the firm, or there may exist no open market for such a good or service. In such cases the authorities may have to establish an arm's-length price by some other method. They may seek to impute a price by collecting information about costs and adding some reasonable mark-up. However, transfer prices often include some payments to the parent company for services such as R & D and other overheads. There is the problem of how these are to be apportioned. These problems are compounded where the prices in question relate to highly specific, intangible property, such as patents, technical expertise, management contracts, and so on. In brief, it is often quite difficult for the customs and tax authorities to control transfer pricing. Nevertheless, it remains the case that where companies engage in overt transfer price manipulation they risk attracting the attention of the authorities. This may act as a constraint on their doing so.

Empirical Evidence on Transfer Pricing

The empirical evidence on transfer pricing is still rather limited. Companies are unwilling to disclose information about their pricing policies except on a highly confidential basis. They are unlikely to admit to transfer price manipulation. Often we simply do not know the prices charged by MNCs on their intra-firm sales. Even when we do know these prices, we may lack adequate information about equivalent arm's-length trans-actions. As we have already seen, in many cases there simply does not exist any comparable uncontrolled price. Even if we had information about both MNC transfer prices and arm's-length prices, we would not know to what extent the company had been constrained from manipulating transfer prices by the fear of being discovered and investigated.

Despite these difficulties some empirical work has been carried out. Much of this would lead us to suppose that transfer pricing is an important phenomenon. For example, Vaitsos made a comparison of the transfer prices declared by multi-nationals in Colombia with the prices of the same products sold on the open market. He found that intermediate goods imported by Colombian subsidiaries of multinational com-panies were substantially overpriced — 40 per cent in the case of rubber, 25 per cent in the case of chemicals, and 155 per cent in the case of pharmaceuticals. Profit remittance was singled out as the main inducement with diversion of taxable profits to the tax haven of Panama as also important (Vaitsos 1974).

In another study covering multinationals operating in Colombia, Lall found similar evidence of transfer pricing. Lall examined fourteen foreign firms operating in Colombia over the period from 1966 to 1970. Lall found evidence of overpric-ing ranging between 33 per cent and 300 per cent in the case of pharmaceuticals and from 21 to 81 per cent in the rubber and electrical sectors (Lall 1973). Roumaliotis analysed the in-cidence and distribution of overpricing of imports to Greece. He found that, in one half of the eighty-four import cases analysed covering the metallurgical, chemicals, and pharmaceu-ticals sectors, substantial overpricing could be detected. Over-pricing ranged from 5 per cent to 230 per cent, with the highest percentages in the chemicals (including the pharmaceuticals) sector (Roumaliotis 1977). In another study covering the export of aluminium from a subsidiary in Greece to the parent com-pany, Roumaliotis found that export prices were substantially lower than the comparable world price. Underinvoicing ranged from 1 per cent to 19 per cent according to the type of aluminium exported (Roumaliotis 1977).

A study by Natke of import pricing in Brazil further supported the view that MNCs operating in developing countries typically overprice sales to their subsidiaries. Natke examined 141 manu-facturing firms operating in Brazil, some of which were foreign owned and others domestically owned. The year covered was 1979, and the product coverage was some 127 product groups spread over eighteen industries. He found that, in aggregate, MNCs paid higher prices for imports from their parent companies than that paid by Brazilian firms. The extent of the overpricing ranged from 21 per cent to 39 per cent. However, there was greater variety in prices of such goods between foreign-owned companies and domestic firms. This would suggest that both overpricing and underpricing of imports took place. MNCs would appear to manipulate transfer prices but not always in the same direction (Natke 1985).

Another study by Lecraw examined import and export pricing practices of some 111 MNCs operating some 153 subsidiaries in six light manufacturing industries in five countries of the ASEAN region (Thailand, Malaysia, Singapore, Indonesia, and the Phillipines). The year covered was 1978. He found support for the view that MNCs engage in widespread and systematic transfer pricing. The most important reasons were found to be (1) reduction of import duties (2) reduction of profits taxation (3) to move funds across national boundaries (4) to reduce risk (5) to circumvent government price and capital-profit remittance controls. Lecraw also found that Japanese MNCs operating in the ASEAN region were more inclined than US or European MNCs to use transfer pricing in intra-firm trade. Lecraw explains this in terms of the purported tendency for Japanese MNCs to adopt more centralized systems of management control (Lecraw 1985).

The Control of Transfer Pricing

One question which follows from what has been said about transfer pricing is: does it matter? Is transfer pricing harmful? Should it be controlled? If so, how can it be controlled? To examine this subject in depth would involve a digression from the principal themes of this book. The interested reader is encouraged to consult a more specialized text on the subject (e.g. see Rugman 1985). The issues involved in seeking properly to examine such an issue are complex. The following is little more than a comment pointing to some of the issues involved.

First, does transfer pricing matter? Is it harmful? One of the problems appears to be securing agreement on criteria for judging the effects of transfer pricing. There would appear to be two sets of economic criteria for evaluating the effects of transfer pricing:

1. Efficiency: Are transfer prices economically efficient? Efficiency is generally interpreted in the sense of Pareto efficiency. A state of Pareto efficiency is said to exist when it is not possible to make one person better off without making someone else worse off. Transfer prices can be said to be efficient if they bring prices closer to marginal costs of production than would otherwise by the case. In so doing, they would be maximizing global economic welfare.
2. Equity: Are transfer prices equitable? If, as is alleged, transfer prices are redistributing income from poorer developing countries to richer developed countries, a quite separate case can be made out for intervention to control or outlaw transfer pricing.

It is apparent that these are two rather different economic issues.

In addition, there may exist non-economic reasons for controlling transfer pricing. Specifically, it is argued that the ability of MNCs to manipulate transfer prices undermines national sovereignty. It limits the power of individual governments to pursue the economic policies they choose. Control of transfer pricing may be desired in order to give governments greater control over their own economies.

With regard to economic efficiency considerations it should be born in mind that one of the main reasons for the existence of MNCs is the failure of external markets to allocate resources or imperfections which distort the workings of such markets. MNCs represent an attempt by firms to internalize such markets. In so far as MNCs create markets which otherwise would not exist (e.g. for certain intangible assets such as knowledge) or successfully overcome imperfections in the workings of such markets, they may serve to increase economic efficiency, not reduce it. For example, one reason for transfer pricing is the existence of certain kinds of imperfections caused by government intervention, for example tariffs, taxes, capital controls, and so on. It can be shown that many of these interventions reduce efficiency (i.e. lower global economic welfare) by distorting the allocation of resources domestically and internationally. In so far as transfer pricing is an attempt to overcome such market imperfections, it may increase efficiency.

One of the great problems involved in evaluating the effects of transfer prices is to know what is the comparable uncontrolled price. How can we say whether transfer prices are harmful if we have no standard against which to make a comparison? In some cases equivalent arm's-length prices do exist, but these prices themselves may not be Pareto-efficient. Moreover, are they the appropriate prices to use for intra-firm trade where the firm is pursuing a strategy of global profit maximization rather than maximization of the profits of individual divisions or units of the company? Moreover, in many cases, no equivalent arm's-length price actually exists. For many assets which are highly specific to the firm, there exists no external market to use as a comparison. This also poses problems in controlling transfer prices should it be considered desirable. The authorities have to determine the price at which internal transactions should take place yet may lack any criteria for doing so. One may even choose to conclude that, in such cases, it is better for governments not to intervene as there is no assurance that government control will cause more efficient prices to be established.

A second set of considerations is concerned with the equity effects of transfer pricing. It is argued that transfer pricing by MNCs gives rise to undesirable income distribution effects. Specifically, it is argued that, through the manipulation of transfer prices, MNCs redistribute incomes and profits from poorer developing countries to richer developed ones. A number of economists have concluded that the temptation to practise transfer pricing by MNCs is probably greater in developing countries than developed countries (e.g. Plasschaert 1985) because the former impose more restrictions on MNCs than the latter. Hence transfer pricing may be more of a problem in developing countries than developed countries. We have seen that there exists a significant amount of empirical research to support the view that such transfer-price manipulation does take place in many developing countries. If governments were willing to surrender some national sovereignty by bringing their various kinds of intervention more closely into line (e.g. harmonization of taxes), some of the incentive to manipulate transfer prices would disappear. However, governments are unlikely to make much progress in this direction in the immediately forseeable future.

If control of transfer pricing is considered desirable, how is it achieved? The most direct way is for the tax and customs authorities of a country to determine what should be the prices used for a given intra-firm transaction. This constitutes a major regulatory task for the government of a large industrialized country. MNCs may account for a very large proportion of a country's total trade. However, it may be a more manageable task for smaller developing countries since the number of firms involved is much fewer. The authorities may either seek to enforce a predetermined price, or tax the company on the assumption that such a price is the operative price. Alternatively, an attempt may be made to allocate notional profits to a foreign-owned company based on the global profits of the company and the share of sales or assets which the local firm accounts for. These notional profits may be taken as the basis for applying profits tax rather than actual, declared profits of the MNC. Finally, the government of a host country may insist on substantial local equity participation or require the foreign company to undertake a joint venture with local companies. We saw earlier that the need to collaborate with local investors may make it more difficult for an MNC to manipulate transfer prices.

HOW DO MULTINATIONAL CORPORATIONS AFFECT THE PATTERN OF WORLD TRADE?

This chapter has examined how the growth of foreign direct investment over the last half-century has resulted in a growth in the importance of multinational corporations in world trade. A large and growing proportion of world trade is now accounted for by MNCs. A significant proportion of such trade takes the form of intra-firm trade. The question arises as to how this affects the pattern of world trade and specialization? Is the basis for trade in a world in which MNCs play such a prominent role fundamentally different to one in which trade takes place between independent, nationally based firms? How valid are the conventional theories of trade discussed in Chapter 1? Do we need a radical overhaul of existing trade theory to take account of the increased importance of MNCs, or can existing theory be modified in minor ways to take account of the new realities?

Perhaps the single most important weakness of the conventional Hecksher–Ohlin, factor-proportions theory of trade discussed in Chapter 1 is its assumption that all factors of production are internationally immobile. In the real world, capital is a highly mobile factor of production. One approach is to modify conventional theory to allow for such mobility of capital. One possible approach has been proposed by Max Corden. Corden has argued that it is possible to use existing trade theory to analyse the location decisions of MNCs and the effects which these decisions have on trade flows. In this way, patterns of trade can be predicted for a world in which MNCs are important using conventional trade theory. Major modifications are needed, but there is no need to dispense with the whole of existing theory (Corden 1974). Chapter 1 examined the product life-cycle theory expounded by Professor Raymond Vernon and other technology-based theories which give prominence to the role of the MNC in the transmission of knowledge across national boundaries (Vernon 1966). This represented an attempt to develop an alternative model of trade and investment incorporating technological innovation. Yet another approach has been proposed by Professor John Dunning involving the integration of trade theory and investment theory in an attempt to construct a new theory of international production (Dunning 1977; Norman and Dunning 1984). Dunning's 'eclectic approach' represents an attempt to break with the framework of conventional trade theory, although it incorporates aspects of trade theory. As such, it constitutes a rather different approach to that of Corden. Let us consider each of these two approaches:

The Corden Locational Approach

Max Corden has proposed a model based on orthodox trade theory which can explain the locational decisions of the MNC and how these affect patterns of trade. Orthodox trade theory is modified to take account of certain realities relevant to a world in which MNCs play an important role. Specifically, the model assumes that capital is mobile internationally. MNCs transfer capital across national boundaries by means of direct investment. The model incorporates knowledge as an additional internationally mobile factor of production. Conventional trade theory either analyses trade flows within a static framework where innovation is absent or assumes that any new knowledge is freely and instantly diffused internationally. This is clearly unsatisfactory for a world in which MNCs play a major role. One of the major roles of MNCs, as has been seen in earlier sections of this chapter, is the transfer of knowledge across national boundaries.

The Corden model analyses the location decisions of a MNC which produces a number of different products which it sells to various markets in the world. The model begins with the following assumptions:

1. Three factors of production are used in the production of all goods – capital, knowledge, and labour. Labour is assumed to be the only immobile factor. Capital and knowledge are mobile internationally. (Alternatively, one may envisage two types of mobile capital, conventional capital and human capital which embodies knowledge.)
2. Capital and knowledge are internationally mobile within the MNC.
3. The production functions and factor endowments facing the MNC do not change over time.
4. There are constant returns to scale in all production functions.
5. Government restrictions and taxes, such as tariffs and profits taxes, are absent, or at least do not affect the MNC's location decisions.
6. There are no transport costs.
7. Production functions for any given product in all locations are identical.
8. In each location, there is only one immobile factor, namely, labour, which is also identical between countries.

The above model closely resembles a conventional Hecksher–Ohlin theory. The major difference is that knowledge is included as a third factor of production and that capital and knowledge are assumed to be internationally mobile. The above assumptions will lead to an equalization of the returns to capital and knowledge throughout the empire of the MNC. Capital and knowledge will move between countries in such a way as to equalize factor prices. The marginal product of labour and therefore wage rates will be equalized in different countries also. Costs of production will be the same in all locations. The MNC will be indifferent as to where it locates production.

If, now, various of the above assumptions are gradually relaxed, the factors affecting the location decisions of an MNC can be identified. First, the assumption that labour is the only immobile factor may be removed. Suppose that there are two immobile factors — say, skilled and unskilled labour or labour and land. This leads to the prediction that countries well endowed with skilled labour will enjoy relatively cheap skilled labour and countries well endowed with unskilled labour will enjoy relatively cheap unskilled labour. The MNC will locate production of products intensive in skilled labour in the former and products intensive in unskilled labour in the latter. A pattern of trade and specialization emerges which is consistent with a conventional, Hecksher–Ohlin framework.

Second, the assumption that the production function for any given product is identical in all locations may be removed. Some countries may enjoy superior efficiency in the production of all commodities perhaps on account of better infrastructure, different political conditions, or immobility of certain types of knowledge. Such countries will tend to attract more of the mobile factors. As a result, they will tend to specialize in industries which are intensive in these mobile factors, that is capital-intensive and knowledge-intensive industries. Third, the assumption of no transport costs may be relaxed. High transport costs tend to discourage trade and encourage production near to markets. MNCs will locate their production near their largest markets. The location of these markets will be determined by the particular tastes of consumers in different countries. Differences in production costs due to different factor endowments might act as an offsetting factor. Fourth, the assumption of no government restrictions or taxes may be removed. The existence of tariffs and other import restrictions will encourage MNCs to produce locally rather than service overseas markets through exports. Differences in levels of taxation will also influence location decisions. Fifth, the assumption of constant returns to scale may be removed. If the MNC is subject to increasing returns to scale, this will favour locating the production of any one product in a single location. Centralization of production will be preferred. This will tend to increase trade and may help to offset the trade inhibiting effects of high transport costs and trade restrictions. In addition, there will be a tendency for production of particular products to be centralized in countries with large domestic markets. Such countries will enjoy a comparative advantage in goods which are costly to transport long distances and which are produced under conditions of increasing returns to scale. The model makes the prediction that large countries will tend to export the products of increasing-returns activities, especially when costs of transport are high.

Finally, we can relax the static assumptions of the model to take account of changes over time. We can relax the assumption that production functions and factor endowments are static over time. Investment in education will increase a country's stock of human capital and improve the country's production function. Such changes will alter the comparative costs of producing a product in different locations and cause a MNC to reallocate its resources. In a similar manner, we can relax the assumption that knowledge is perfectly mobile internationally. In Chapter 1 we saw that much knowledge is only diffused around the world after a time-lag. This gives the home country an initial advantage in the production of knowledge-intensive goods. Eventually, however, this comparative advantage shifts to other countries of the world. This incorporates Raymond Vernon's product life-cycle approach.

Corden has concluded that it is possible to use various bits of conventional trade theory to explain the location decisions of MNCs and thus to predict trade flows. The existence of MNCs does not necessitate an abandonment of conventional trade theory. The theory only needs to be reconstructed and developed in a way which takes account of new realities. Specifically, the assumption that all factors of production are immobile must be dropped. However, it does not follow that international trade is determined by precisely the same considerations as domestic trade. Trade theory should not be abandoned altogether as if the world market were a single market comparable to national markets. This is because not all factors are mobile internationally. Labour is still fairly immobile internationally. Certain kinds of human capital may also be relatively immobile internationally. Physical capital embodied in infrastructure should also be regarded as being immobile except over a very long period. Government restrictions and taxes differ between countries. Thus it is necessary to retain basic trade theory but to modify it to take account of the role played by MNCs.

The Dunning Eclectic Approach

One of the weaknesses of the Corden locational approach is that it remains within a neoclassical framework. It explains the locational decisions of MNCs but fails to explain why, in the first place, firms seek to internalize markets through direct investment abroad rather than selling goods through external markets. In other words, it fails to incorporate important conclusions of the theory of multinational companies. Professor Dunning's eclectic approach is rather different. It seeks to bring together both aspects of trade theory and the theory of multinational companies within an integrated framework incorporating all forms of international business involvement. It represents an attempt to develop a theory of international production which includes both trade and FDI within a single framework. In addition, by incorporating imperfections in markets and thus breaking with the restrictions of a neoclassical model, it becomes possible simultaneously to explain both intra-industry trade and FDI. This is because both intra-industry trade and FDI in part originate in the fact that markets are imperfectly competitive.

Let us examine the main elements of the Dunning approach. First, there is the need to appreciate that international business involvement can take a wide variety of different forms. Trade takes place in both products and assets. Trade in products includes both trade in final and intermediate products. Trade in assets includes both the export and import of capital and the purchase and sale of property rights (e.g. proprietary knowledge). The export and import of capital may take the form of either portfolio investment (the purchase and sale of financial assets) or direct investment abroad by MNCs. The sale of asset rights includes licensing agreements, management contracts, subcontracting, and so on. Many of these other kinds of international business involvement will be discussed in depth in the next chapter.

Second, there is the need to appreciate that all these different kinds of transactions take place in different kinds of markets. Markets range from perfectly competitive markets to markets which are subject to considerable imperfections. Such imperfections may be due to the structure of such markets (e.g. number of firms, degree of product differentiation, and barriers to entry) or due to various forms of government intervention (e.g. tariffs, subsidies, taxes, etc.). Some of these transactions take place between independent buyers and sellers on an arm's-length basis, others take place within the same multinational company. Some transactions lie between these two extremes, as when buyer and seller are independent yet related in some way. For example, where a buyer is subcontracted by a seller, trade cannot be adequately categorized as either arm's-length trade or intra-firm trade.

Third, it follows that any theory of international business needs to be able to explain all these different forms of transaction. However, different types of theory are needed in each case. The Hecksher–Ohlin theory of trade may be able satisfactorily to explain inter-industry trade in standardized goods which takes place on an arm's-length basis in perfectly competitive markets. It may be easily modified to take account of imperfections arising from time-lags in the international diffusion of knowledge by treating technology as an additional factor of production. The neoclassical approach may also be valid for explaining much portfolio investment between one country and another since portfolio investment is heavily influenced by differences between countries in the yields on different kinds of financial assets. However, the neoclassical approach is largely unsatisfactory when it comes to either the explanation of intra-industry trade or direct investment abroad. As we have seen, although some intra-industry trade is compatible with the Hecksher–Ohlin theory (especially if this theory is modified to take account of real-world conditions), the greater part of intra-industry trade requires the construction of new theories. In the same way, direct investment abroad cannot be adequately explained within a neoclassical framework. Without the possession of some firm-specific asset, foreign firms would be at a disadvantage in competing with local firms. In this case, exporting would be preferable to foreign production as a way of supplying a foreign market. In addition, there must exist some imperfection in the markets for either goods or assets to create a preference for internal over external markets and an environment for conducting such transactions. Thus intra-firm trade needs a different set of theories from those of the neoclassical school for its proper explanation.

Thus what, in essence, Dunning is proposing is the use of different theories to explain different forms of international business involvement. This does not involve an abandonment of the conventional theories of trade. These may still be used to explain certain types of international transaction which remain important. However, for other kinds of transactions — most notably, much intra-industry trade, direct investment abroad by multinational companies, and intra-firm trade — a different set of theories is required. It is not possible merely to 'patch up' the Hecksher–Ohlin theory to take account of the realities of the real world. However, a body of theory is gradually emerging which has the attraction that it can account for both the growth of intra-industry trade and direct investment abroad. As we have seen, both activities have largely arisen out of the growth of imperfect markets. This is the starting-point for the explanation of both kinds of transaction.

Professor Dunning's eclectic approach has played an important role in bringing together different strands of thinking from both trade theory and the theory of the multinational company and has thereby enhanced understanding of the nature and process of international production. However, it does not yet amount to a theory of international production. It constitutes a useful starting-point for further advances in the theory of how trade takes place in a world dominated by multinational companies. However, much work has still to be done before economists can satisfactorily explain and predict trade flows within a single model incorporating both trade and direct investment by multinational companies.

5

New Forms of International Economic Involvement

INTRODUCTION

The last chapter examined the growth of foreign direct investment since the Second World War and the emergence of the multinational corporation. It also discussed the impact which the multinational corporation has had on the nature of international trade, including the pricing of goods and services entering into trade. In this chapter, we shall continue to examine the role played by the MNC in the world trading system with an emphasis on some of the forms of foreign direct investment and other forms of international business involvement which have become important in recent years. We shall also discuss some other types of international trade which have become important in recent decades, some of which are related to the activities of multinational companies in the world economic system.

First, I will take a further look at the kind of foreign direct investment which is taking place between the western industrialized economies. Chapter 4 noted that much the most important type of FDI over the past half-century has been that which has been taking place between industrialized countries. Much of this has assumed the form of a two-way flow of FDI. In many cases this has taken place within the same industry. This kind of direct investment abroad has come to be called 'intra-industry foreign direct investment'. There is an analogy with intra-industry trade which was considered in Chapter 3.

Second, I will examine some of the changes which have been taking place in direct investment carried out by industrialized countries in some of the newly-industrializing developing countries. We shall see that a large share of this investment has taken the form of so-called 'export platform investments', in which MNCs based in the industrialized countries hive off certain labour-intensive final assembly stages of production to developing countries where a cheap and well-disciplined labour force is available. We shall see that one of the results of this process is the emergence of what has been called a 'new international division of labour' (NIDOL).

Third, I will discuss some of the alternatives to direct investment abroad which are available to companies seeking to expand overseas. There is some evidence that, in the last decade or two, multinational companies have been seeking alternative ways to that of direct investment to maximize the rent from their firm-specific assets. These include licensing agreements, joint ventures, management contracts, and international subcontracting. These forms of international business involvement appear to be becoming more important.

Finally, we shall discuss a seemingly unrelated phenomenon which has become an increasingly important and much talked-about element in world trade in recent decades, namely countertrade or international barter. This refers to a variety of arrangements which, to some degree, involve the elimination of money from international trade and the direct exchange of goods. Although countertrade still only accounts for a small fraction of world trade, it is important, and its importance may be increasing. There are signs that some developing countries are resorting to countertrade as a way of coping with the shortage of foreign exchange. Concern has been expressed by a number of international organizations such as the GATT and the OECD about the extent of countertrade and the challenge which it poses to the multinational trading system which has existed since the Second World War.

INTRA-INDUSTRY FOREIGN DIRECT INVESTMENT

Intra-industry FDI may be defined as follows: 'two-way FDI by multinational enterprises based in different countries, in each other's home markets, to produce goods and services that are close substitutes in either consumption or production, and thus can be classified in the same industry' (Erdilek 1985). One-way FDI may be referred to as inter-industry FDI. Intra-industry

FDI is really a sub-set of cross FDI. Cross FDI is two-way FDI involving any pair of countries. When such cross FDI takes place in the same industry it becomes intra-industry FDI. As with the concepts of inter- and intra-industry trade, there is a certain arbitrariness involved in the distinction between inter- and intra-industry FDI. Much depends on how broadly or narrowly industries are defined. Moreover, where products are grouped together statisticaly yet belong to essentially different industries, aggregation bias will result when measuring the extent of intra-industry FDI.

The Measurement of Intra-Industry FDI

Unfortunately, much less information is available concerning the extent of intra-industry FDI than intra-industry trade. Few countries publish information at a sufficiently disaggregated level for direct investment flows to enable intra-industry FDI to be accurately measured. Nevertheless, despite these difficulties, attempts have been made to obtain broad indicators as to its extent and importance. Professor John Dunning has provided some information about the level of intra-industry FDI in five industrialized countries — the United Kingdom, the United States, West Germany, Japan, and Sweden — for the years 1965, 1970, and 1975 (Dunning 1982). These data are shown in Table 5.1.

Intra-industry FDI is measured as the proportion of a country's total stock of FDI (inward plus outward) for any industrial sector which is matched or balanced (i.e. inward equals outward FDI). The formula is:

$$\text{Intra-Industry FDI for sector i} = \frac{(KX_i + KM_i) - |KX_i - KM_i|}{(KX_i + KM_i)}$$

where KX_i is the country's outward capital stake in sector i and KM_i is the country's inward capital stake in sector i. The closer the ratio to one, the greater the importance of intra-industry FDI. The closer the ratio to zero, the less the importance of intra-industry FDI. Table 5.1 shows that high levels of intra-industry FDI exist in all five countries. The level of intra-industry FDI was slightly lower in Japan and Sweden than in

Table 5.1: Intra-industry direct capital stake ratios, by country and industry, 1965, 1970, 1975

	United States			Japan			United Kingdom			Sweden			West Germany		
	1965	1970	1975	1965	1970	1975	1965	1970	1975	1965	1970	1975	1965	1970	1975
MORE TECHNOLOGY INTENSIVE															
Chemicals & allied products	0.77	0.75	0.79	0.14	0.28	0.51	0.91	0.99	0.99	0.66	0.53	0.57	0.86	0.77	0.79
Mechanical & instrument engineering	0.85	0.86	0.92	0.50	0.45	0.59	0.27	0.50	0.54	0.37	0.65	0.68	0.73	0.70	0.82
Electrical engineering	0.57	0.50	0.59	0.40	0.72	0.94	0.98	0.96	0.92	0.68	0.78	0.98	0.54	0.73	0.98
Transportation equipment	0.03	0.03	0.03	0.09	0.34	0.70	0.40	0.32	0.63	0.30	0.11	0.28	0.84	0.94	0.91
	0.65	0.65	0.71	0.27	0.42	0.63	0.65	0.77	0.81	0.53	0.63	0.70	0.76	0.78	0.85
LESS TECHNOLOGY INTENSIVE															
Food, drink and tobacco	0.74	0.71	0.75	0.48	0.59	0.44	0.50	0.62	0.64	0.12	0.19	0.10	0.57	0.64	0.73
Primary and fabricated metals	0.75	0.80	0.69	0.92	0.98	0.57	0.94	0.61	0.81	0.62	0.78	0.88	0.49	0.98	0.97
Textiles, leather, clothing & footwear	0.83	0.86	0.89	0.18	0.12	0.05	0.48	0.23	0.31	0.12	0.18	0.16	0.58	0.76	0.95
Paper, printing & publishing	0.99	0.93	0.99	0.21	0.15	0.21	0.49	0.62	0.90	0.68	0.42	0.53	0.96	0.86	0.78
Other manufacturing industries	0.79	0.98	0.98	0.78	0.75	0.78	0.89	0.75	0.94	0.54	0.36	0.76	0.86	0.67	0.66
	0.80	0.84	0.83	0.53	0.51	0.38	0.62	0.61	0.73	0.49	0.49	0.54	0.60	0.80	0.86
Total	0.71	0.72	0.76	0.39	0.46	0.53	0.64	0.70	0.78	0.52	0.59	0.65	0.71	0.79	0.86

Source: Dunning (1982).

West Germany, the United Kingdom, and the United States. It is also noticeable that all five countries experienced an increase in their intra-industry FDI ratios between 1965 and 1975. Japan and Sweden experienced the fastest proportionate increase.

There is no clearly discernible pattern for intra-industry FDI across industrial sectors. For the United States, the ratio was slightly higher for the less technology-intensive industries, whereas, for the United Kingdom and Sweden, the ratio was consistently higher for the more technology-intensive industries. However, with the single exception of West Germany, intra-industry FDI increased fastest in the more technology-intensive sectors. One weakness of Table 5.1 is that the product groups used are too wide. Hence aggregation bias gives a misleading picture of the true extent of intra-industry FDI. This has probably caused the level of intra-industry FDI to be exaggerated. In addition, comparisons between countries may have been distorted by large imbalances in an individual country's inward–outward capital stock balance. For countries with a large imbalance between the total outward and inward stock of FDI, the importance of intra-industry FDI may have been underestimated.

John Dunning and George Norman of Reading University have sought to produce improved estimates of intra-industry FDI which take account of the above drawbacks (Dunning and Norman 1984). Their results are set out in Table 5.2. They were obtained using data published by Vaupel and Curhan giving details of the number of subsidiaries of some 187 US MNCs and 226 non-US MNCs. The data for US MNCs were for 1 January 1968 and for the non-US MNCs for 1 January 1971 (Vaupel and Curhan 1974). Together these MNCs accounted for about 70% of all FDI in manufacturing. The formula used was the equivalent of the Aquino index used to calculate intra-industry trade:

$$\text{Intra-industry FDI for sector } i = \frac{(a_j O_{ij} + b_j I_{ij}) - |a_j O_{ij} - b_j I_{ij}|}{(a_j O_{ij} + b_j I_{ij})}$$

where O_{ij} = the number of subsidiaries in industry i formed overseas by firms based in country j and I_{ij} = the number of subsidiaries in industry i formed in country j by firms not based in country j and

$$a_j = \frac{\sum_i (O_{ij} + I_{ij})}{2\sum_i O_{ij}} \quad \text{and} \quad b_j = \frac{\sum_i (O_{ij} + I_{ij})}{2\sum_i I_{ij}}$$

which show the adjustment for any imbalance between inward and outward FDI. Note that inward and outward FDI are measured by the number of subsidiaries set up in country j by foreign companies and the number of overseas subsidiaries set up by companies based in country j. Thus it is the flow of direct investment into and out of country j and not the outward and inward stock of direct investment which is being measured.

Table 5.2 once again shows high levels of intra-industry FDI in all five countries, although the overall index is slightly lower than in Table 5.1. This is to be expected because of the more disaggregated nature of the data. Once again, Japan stands out as having a much lower ratio than other countries. No clear industrial pattern is apparent. However, fairly low intra-industry FDI ratios are recorded for food products, although not in the case of the United States and United Kingdom. Fairly high intra-industry FDI ratios are recorded for most forms of engineering, especially electrical goods.

Dunning and Norman also calculated intra-industry FDI ratios at a disaggregated level for selective manufacturing and service sectors of the West German economy. These calculations made use of data showing the inward and outward capital stock on a disaggregated basis. West Germany is one of the few countries which provides such information. The results are shown in Table 5.3. High levels of intra-industry FDI are apparent in both manufacturing and the services sectors. However, it is noticeable that intra-industry FDI fell in just as many sectors as it rose over the period from 1976 to 1981.

The Causes of Intra-industry FDI

What are the causes of intra-industry FDI? Is intra-industry FDI significantly different from one-way FDI? Do we need any separate theoretical explanation for intra-industry FDI distinct from those explanations given for one-way FDI? In many respects the causes of intra-industry FDI are identical to those giving rise to one-way FDI. For this reason, no separate theory of intra-industry FDI is needed. Nevertheless, it would seem

221

Table 5.2: Intra-industry foreign direct investment, 1968 and 1971

Industry	United States	United Kingdom	West Germany	France	Japan	Average
Ordnance	0.00	0.00	0.75	0.00	0.64	0.28
Meat products	0.00	0.92	0.00	0.00	0.00	0.18
Dairy products	0.70	0.68	0.00	0.00	0.64	0.40
Canned foods	0.77	0.97	0.00	0.00	0.00	0.35
Grain mill products	0.35	0.92	0.00	0.00	0.00	0.25
Bakery products	0.00	0.09	0.00	0.00	0.00	0.02
Confectionery products	0.29	0.93	0.00	0.55	0.38	0.43
Beverages	0.64	0.68	0.00	0.00	0.00	0.26
Other food products	0.66	0.32	0.96	0.17	0.92	0.61
Tobacco	0.65	0.00	0.00	0.00	0.00	0.13
Textiles	0.74	0.76	0.54	0.76	0.37	0.63
Apparel	0.00	0.93	0.00	0.72	0.19	0.37
Lumber & wood	0.66	0.90	0.00	0.00	0.52	0.42
Furniture	0.90	0.63	0.00	0.94	0.00	0.49
Paper products	0.74	0.69	0.91	0.39	0.88	0.72
Printed matter	0.30	0.71	0.72	0.52	0.64	0.58
Industrial chemicals	0.86	0.93	0.77	0.80	0.11	0.69
Plastics & synthetics	0.77	0.61	0.87	0.39	0.49	0.63
Drugs	0.73	0.46	0.63	0.79	0.35	0.59
Soap & cosmetics	0.72	0.53	0.49	0.00	0.00	0.35
Paints	0.76	0.56	0.51	0.00	0.17	0.40
Agricultural chemicals	0.56	0.84	0.43	0.49	0.00	0.46
Other chemicals	0.26	0.72	0.61	0.97	0.59	0.63
Refined petroleum	0.84	0.75	0.07	0.76	0.11	0.51
Other petroleum products	0.62	0.68	0.73	0.55	0.00	0.52
Tires	0.23	0.87	0.53	0.74	0.38	0.55
Other rubber products	0.49	0.48	0.61	0.95	0.91	0.69

Leather products & shoes	0.89	0.43	0.00	0.00	0.00	0.26
Glass products	0.69	0.20	0.23	0.13	0.27	0.30
Stone clay & concrete	0.24	0.71	0.63	0.52	0.74	0.57
Iron & steel products	0.45	0.94	0.39	0.97	0.11	0.57
Non-ferrous smelting	0.67	0.89	0.77	0.83	0.83	0.80
Non-ferrous products	0.93	0.56	0.29	0.45	0.00	0.45
Metal cans	0.82	0.24	0.00	0.00	0.00	0.21
Structural metal products	0.49	0.74	0.52	0.72	0.46	0.59
Fabricated wire products	0.40	0.53	0.89	0.36	0.00	0.44
Other fabricated metals	0.82	0.53	0.91	0.74	0.88	0.78
Engines & Turbines	0.70	0.35	0.83	0.25	0.44	0.51
Farm machinery	0.76	0.28	0.00	0.37	0.00	0.28
Construction machinery	0.23	0.39	0.53	0.00	0.83	0.40
Special industry machinery	0.89	0.44	0.33	0.44	0.77	0.57
General industry machinery	0.89	0.77	0.99	0.42	0.17	0.65
Office machinery and computers	0.76	0.21	0.31	0.00	0.27	0.31
Other non-electrical machinery	0.62	0.39	0.69	0.25	0.77	0.54
Electrical transmission equipment	0.87	0.96	0.31	0.42	0.74	0.66
Electrical lighting & wiring	0.68	0.81	0.41	0.61	0.52	0.71
Radio, TV, & appliances	0.75	0.95	0.65	0.95	0.45	0.75
Communications equipment	0.79	0.73	0.25	0.69	0.97	0.69
Electric components	0.24	0.45	0.91	0.88	0.97	0.70
Other electrical equipment	0.80	0.97	0.86	0.79	0.83	0.85
Motor vehicles & equipment	0.18	0.80	0.66	0.76	0.61	0.60
Other transportation	0.63	0.35	0.91	0.90	0.00	0.63
Precision goods	0.46	0.30	0.99	0.34	0.00	0.42
Miscellaneous products	0.97	0.43	0.34	0.32	0.00	0.41
Overall index of IIFDI	0.64	0.64	0.61	0.56	0.46	0.58

Source: Norman and Dunning (1984), based on the subsidiaries of 187 US MNEs (as of 1 January 1968) and 226 non-US MNEs (as of 1 January 1971).

Table 5.3: Intra-industry foreign capital stake in selected manufacturing and service sectors: West Germany, 1976 and 1981

Industry	Capital stake 1976	1981
MANUFACTURING		
Food	0.40	0.30
Tobacco	0.91	0.35
Textiles	0.65	0.69
Clothing	0.56	0.40
Wood-working	0.62	0.94
Paper, board, printing, etc.	0.50	0.61
Chemical industry	0.66	0.65
Plastics	0.66	0.54
Mineral oil processing	0.19	0.18
Rubber	0.36	0.43
Leather industry	0.40	0.50
Fine ceramics and glass	0.53	0.55
Earthen & stoneware	0.91	0.93
Iron & steel products	0.89	0.89
Foundries	0.47	0.31
Non-ferrous metals	0.99	0.51
Drawing, rolling & forming	0.52	0.64
Steel, light metal engineering	0.87	0.86
Iron tin-ware, metal goods	0.67	0.55
Mechanical engineering	0.97	0.92
Electrical engineering	0.88	0.69
Transport equipment	0.85	0.65
Instrument engineering	0.90	0.95
SERVICES		
Transport & communications	0.81	0.91
Building	0.66	0.37
Trade	0.51	0.47
Banking	0.90	0.88
Finance institutions	0.03	0.68
Insurance corporations	0.81	0.54

Source: Norman and Dunning (1984).

useful to identify intra-industry FDI as a specific phenomenon. First, the fact that much two-way FDI takes place between countries within the same industry or product grouping may tell us something about the factors which lie behind multinational investment activity. Second, the fact that intra-industry trade is now understood as being a form of trade quite different to inter-industry trade and having specific causes poses the question as to whether or not there exists any relationship between intra-industry trade and intra-industry FDI. We shall consider each of these issues in turn.

What of the causes of intra-industry FDI? It should be apparent that the phenomenon of intra-industry FDI is quite compatible with everything which has been said in Chapter 4 about the determinants of FDI. In discussing these determinants we drew a distinction between horizontal, vertical, and conglomerate FDI. With regard to horizontal FDI, emphasis was put on the transactional approach proposed by Caves (Caves 1982). This explains horizontal FDI in terms of three sets of factors. First, firms possess certain unique, firm-specific, intangible assets from which they seek to derive the highest possible rent (e.g. knowledge about how to produce a product more cheaply). Second, the market for such assets is often either non-existent or subject to a number of imperfections. For this reason firms will seek to internalize such markets through the creation of multi-plant and multinational enterprises. There is no reason why these realities should lead to one-way FDI only. Indeed, it would be more logical if the result were two-way FDI involving rival firms based in different countries yet operating in the same industry. Thus intra-industry FDI is entirely compatible with the transaction theory of FDI.

Rugman has illustrated this further with reference to the pharmaceuticals industry (Rugman 1985). A glance at Table 5.2 shows quite a high level of intra-industry FDI for drugs. The pharmaceuticals industry is a highly research-intensive industry. Drugs firms spend large amounts of money on discovering, developing, and marketing new products. The industry is characterized by a rapid rate of product innovation. A large number of new products are constantly coming on the market. Market lives of products are typically quite short. This means that firms are confronted with quite high risks and need to maximize the return on money spent on product innovation as quickly as possible. Patents give firms temporary protection from competition, but such patents are not always respected by all countries and can often be circumvented. For all these reasons, pharmaceutical firms have strong incentives to internalize markets in order to ensure full appropriability. Each pharmaceutical firm will seek to achieve this by setting up subsidiaries in a large number of different countries. High levels of intra-industry FDI are therefore to be expected.

Vertical FDI is unlikely to give rise to much intra-industry

FDI. Where MNCs seek to integrate forwards or backwards, the result is likely to be one-way FDI. On the other hand, conglomerate FDI is very likely to lead to intra-industry FDI. This will be the case to the extent to which conglomerate FDI arises from similar factors to horizontal FDI, namely the existence of a firm-specific advantage and the need to internalize the market for such assets. If the cause of conglomerate FDI is seen to lie in foreign-exchange-rate risk, as in the Aliber model, it is hard to see how this will give rise to intra-industry FDI. It can explain the switchover from US to European and Japanese FDI in the 1970s. This can be seen as being due to the weakening of the dollar in relation to the European currencies and the Japanese yen. The weakening of the dollar increased the currency premium paid to holders of dollar assets. However, European or Japanese MNCs investing in the United States had no need to pay their shareholders this currency premium and so could raise capital to finance an expansion of their activities in the United States more cheaply than US companies. This can explain the increase in such FDI by European and Japanese MNCs in the 1970s. Thus it can explain the increasingly two-way nature of United States FDI. However, as Rugman has convincingly argued, the cause of much conglomerate FDI may lie in similar factors to horizontal FDI, namely the existence of a firm-specific advantage such as knowledge and the need to internalize the market for such knowledge in order to ensure full appropriability (Rugman 1985). This constitutes a stronger explanation for intra-industry FDI.

However, although intra-industry FDI can be explained from the theories of FDI advanced in Chapter 4, these theories fail to give sufficient, explicit consideration to the role played by oligopoly in giving rise to intra-industry FDI. Indeed, it has been argued by some economists that the oligopolistic nature of many manufactured goods markets is the more important determinant of FDI whether of the one-way or two-way type. The markets for many manufactured goods are characterized by oligopoly, that is a small number of sellers each accounting for a relatively large share of the market. Such industries are characterized by a high degree of seller interdependence. The actions of any one seller (e.g. in cutting his price) have a big effect on other sellers. For this reason, each seller will be anxious not to allow rivals to gain any advantage that might jeopardize their own position in the market. Much FDI undertaken in these types of industries may be primarily motivated by the desire to reduce risk and to prevent competitors from gaining an advantage. For example, a backwards investment in the production of a key raw material may be designed to ensure that competitors do not cut off the supply of such a vital raw material. Another example might be the case of an oligopolist setting up an overseas subsidiary to ensure he is not barred from access to an important overseas market. In both cases, the motive behind the decision to invest is the desire to eliminate some specific risk. The oligopolistic character of many industrial goods markets is one of the main sources of such uncertainty.

One outcome of this type of process may be a bunching of foreign investment. That is to say, when one firm invests in a plant in a particular country, he is followed by rival sellers anxious not to be outdone. For example, if one seller of a certain product invests in the production of some raw material vital to the production of the finished product — presumably out of fear that access to raw material supplies might be prevented in some way — other sellers are likely to follow suite. It does not matter whether or not such an investment constitutes a good or bad one. If it proves to be a bad one, the higher cost can be passed on to buyers in the form of a higher price. Firms in oligopolistic industries are typically price-fixers able to exert some determination over market price. However, if they do not follow the firm which is making the initial investment, they face the risk of being pre-empted. The leader may succeed in gaining acness to some cheap source of raw material supply. Hence, the tendency will be for other firms to follow suite and set up plant in the same country.

The same tendency will be apparent when one seller sets up a plant in another country in order to establish a foothold in this market. Fearful of being pre-empted, rival sellers will follow suite. If they do not, there is a danger that the first entrant to the new market may persuade the host government to impose import restrictions which will deprive rivals of access for their product. Thus rivals will set up their own subsidiaries in the country in question regardless of whether or not their own calculations provide commercial support for such an investment. They will be more concerned with eliminating risk in the knowledge that any error in judging the profitability of the investment can be passed on to the consumer in a higher price.

Exponents of this view of FDI claim that many real world investment decisions fit the theory. Examples might be the wave of investment in semi-conductor production by foreign firms in South-East Asia. Knickerbocker has sought to lend empirical support to this follow-the-leader theory of FDI. He found that the degree of bunching of foreign investment by US MNCs was positively correlated with the degree of concentration. However, the degree of bunching was also strongly correlated to a range of other factors (Knickerbocker 1973). One obvious weakness of the theory is that it fails to explain why firms undertake direct investment abroad in the first place. The oligopolistic character of markets and the desire on the part of firms selling in such markets to eliminate risk may constitute an important cause of such investment. However, it does not fully explain why they invest where they do. As such the theory appears to be incomplete. Nevertheless, in drawing attention to the role played by market structure in causing firms to set up subsidiaries abroad, a new and important determinant of multi-national investment activity has been established. Moreover, the emphasis on oligopoly and risk avoidance fits well with the observation that much FDI has been of the intra-industry type.

Intra-industry FDI may be more explicitly accounted for by the so-called 'exchange of threats' hypothesis associated with Hymer and Rowthorn (Hymer and Rowthorn 1970). This asserts that, when threatened by a foreign company setting up a subsidiary in their home market, the leading firms in an industry tend to respond by setting up subsidiaries in the invader's market. Such cross-investment is designed as a counter to the aggression of the initial investor. It represents a kind of shot across the bows warning the aggressor that any attempt by him to compete energetically in the foreign market will be met by equivalent, retaliatory action in his own home market. Again, the underlying motive in such a sequence of investments is the desire to reduce risk. In this case, it is the risk generated by the intrusion of a powerful rival into the home markets of other sellers.

Raymond Vernon has emphasized the risk of lagging behind in technological innovation as another factor giving rise to intra-industry FDI (Vernon 1985). Oligopolists are afraid of falling behind their rivals in technological innovation. The tendency is for most MNCs to undertake the bulk of their research and development in their own home markets. In developing new products, they are accordingly strongly influenced by local conditions. For example, many innovations made by US firms involved labour-saving products or processes of production stimulated by the high cost of labour in the United States. This creates a potential threat for firms in oligopolistic, high-technology industries that a rival in one country will make some major technological discovery stimulated by local conditions. This discovery may give the firm in question an important technological lead which will eventually enable that firm to threaten producers in other markets. Vernon cites the example of the threat posed to US car manufacturers by Japanese superiority in small fuel-saving motor cars. Japanese car producers originally developed this superiority by seeking to meet the needs of the Japanese home market. Faced with such risks, MNCs may set up subsidiaries in the home markets of rival producers in order to keep abreast of changes taking place in other market environments and to avoid being outwitted by competitors in the process of technological change. Such subsidiaries may be regarded as being a kind of 'technological listening post' within the territory of international competitors (Vernon 1985).

The Link Between Intra-industry FDI and Intra-industry Trade

The question has been posed as to whether or not there is any link between the factors giving rise to intra-industry FDI and those giving rise to intra-industry trade. Professor John Dunning has argued that there is evidence for some such linkage (Dunning 1982). He compared levels of intra-industry FDI with those for intra-industry trade differentiating between countries and industrial sectors. He found that the structure of the ratios was broadly similar. The country with the lowest intra-industry FDI ratio, namely Japan, also had the lowest intra-industry trade ratio. All five countries experienced an increase in their intra-industry FDI ratios, and all five, with the single exception of Japan, experienced a rise in their intra-industry trade ratios. Intra-industry trade ratios were consistently higher than intra-industry FDI ratios except for West Germany. This led Dunning to argue that patterns of direct investment lag those of trade. Intra-industry FDI tends to follow intra-industry trade with a time-lag.

229

With regard to industrial sectors, Dunning found that intra-industry trade was always higher in the more technology-intensive industries, whereas intra-industry FDI was generally, but not always, higher in the more technology-intensive industries. An important exception was the United States, where intra-industry FDI was higher in the less technology-intensive industries. However, intra-industry trade and intra-industry FDI both rose fastest in the more technology-intensive industries. Significantly, in the case of Japan, both intra-industry trade and intra-industry FDI fell in the less technology-intensive industries.

Thus there exists some superficial evidence that intra-industry trade and intra-industry FDI are related. However, Dunning's data provide only weak support for such a hypothesis. Only five countries were considered. Furthermore, as we have already noted, the product groups used for calculating intra-industry FDI were too broad, although this would not have affected the comparison over time. Professor Alan Rugman has reworked Dunning's figures to test for any similarity between intra-industry trade and intra-industry FDI in terms of industrial ranking. His results are reproduced in Table 5.4. These show that for five of the nine industries, there is only a deviation of one in the ranking. For a further two industries there is a deviation of only two. The only industries where there exists a major deviation of ranking are paper, printing, and publishing, and transportation equipment (Rugman 1985).

If there exists a statistical relationship between intra-industry FDI and intra-industry trade, what is the theoretical foundation for this? Do there exist any theoretical grounds for supposing that the two phenomena are related? One linkage between intra-industry trade and intra-industry FDI arises from the fact that both phenomena have their origins in market imperfections. In the case of intra-industry trade, these imperfections give rise to product differentiation and increasing returns to scale. In the case of intra-industry FDI, imperfections in the markets for firm-specific, intangible assets give rise to an incentive to internalize markets. In this respect, intra-industry trade may be seen as the natural bedfellow of intra-industry FDI. It is therefore not surprising to find intra-industry trade and intra-industry FDI occurring in the same type of industries.

Moreover, both intra-industry trade and intra-industry FDI are undertaken by MNCs. However, they may not take place at the same time. Much depends on the kind of intra-industry

Table 5.4: Ranking of industries by percentage of intra-industry foreign direct investment

Intra-industry FDI ranking	Description	Intra-industry FDI percentage	Intra-industry trade percentage	Trade ranking
1	Other manufacturing	77	74	3
2	Primary & fabricated metals	74	85	1
3	Chemical & allied products	67	74	2
4	Paper, printing, & publishing	67	39	8
5	Electrical engineering	63	72	4
6	Mechanical & instrument engineering	54	71	5
7	Food, drink, & tobacco	48	39	9
8	Textiles, leather, clothing & footwear	44	53	7
9	Transportation equipment	33	62	6

Source: Rugman (1985).

FDI carried out. Dunning and Norman have drawn a useful distinction between (1) trade-inhibiting intra-industry FDI and (2) trade-enhancing intra-industry FDI (Dunning and Norman 1985). In the case of trade-inhibiting intra-industry FDI, direct investment is a substitute for exports. The two are alternative ways of entering a foreign market. The model proposed by Tamir Agmon and discussed in Chapter 2 provides a useful theoretical foundation for such investment (Agmon 1979). Agmon has argued that intra-industry trade has its origins in the oligopolistic character of product markets. However, intra-industry trade is only a stage in the international expansion of the firm. Very often, oligopolistic firms initially enter a foreign market through exports. Exporting involves no fixed costs as does foreign investment, although there are higher variable costs arising from transporting the product to the foreign market. Moreover, a firm contemplating entry to a foreign market confronts uncertainty. Exporting may constitute a means of 'buying' more information about market conditions overseas prior to foreign investment. Thus exports may be a necessary preliminary phase to direct investment abroad.

231

Intra-industry trade is thus one stage in a dynamic process of international expansion of firms operating in oligopolistic markets.

This would lead to the prediction that intra-industry FDI will tend to follow intra-industry trade but with a time-lag. This may help to explain why there would appear to be very little correlation between intra-industry and intra-firm trade (see Helleiner 1983). Intra-firm trade will tend to increase with the level of FDI, both one-way and intra-industry FDI. Thus, one might expect the level of intra-firm trade to increase as the level of intra-industry trade declines. We have also seen that there is some evidence that in several industries, intra-industry FDI has lagged behind intra-industry trade (Dunning and Norman 1985). High levels of intra-industry trade in certain years are followed by high levels of intra-industry FDI in subsequent years. However, one cannot always expect intra-industry FDI to follow intra-industry trade. Much will depend on the industry in question. In industries where economies of scale are important there may be a tendency for producers to concentrate their global production in a relatively small number of strategically placed locations. In such industries the level of intra-industry FDI may be lower and the level of intra-industry trade higher. There will be a preference for concentrating production at a few plants in just a few geographical locations. On the other hand, where the economies of plant specialization are minimal there will exist a greater tendency to replace trade with overseas production. This will also be true where there exist high 'transfer costs' between the home and the foreign market. These may take the form of high transport costs in relation to the unit value of the product and the existence of high tariffs and non-tariff barriers which bar access to the foreign market. In such cases, intra-industry FDI may tend to follow intra-industry trade after a time-lag.

The second type of intra-industry FDI has been called trade-enhancing FDI. In this case direct investment abroad increases trade rather than displacing it. Such FDI occurs when a company brings under common ownership a large number of plants separately producing a particular product in different geographical locations. For example, there may exist ten different firms each producing refrigerators, each of which is slightly different from the other, in ten different countries. Each firm exports a proportion of its output to the other nine countries.

Thus there exists a high level of intra-industry trade in a differentiated product. However, through intra-industry FDI these ten different firms are eventually brought under partial or complete common ownership. This may lead to a rationalization of production leading to greater specialization of each plant. This may take the form of each plant specializing in a particular process or stage of production. Rationalization of this kind has been common in the motor car industry. We shall consider this so-called 'rationalized product' investment in greater depth in the next section of this chapter. However, at this stage we note that such FDI will result in increased trade between countries. This will take the form of increased intra-firm rather than intra-industry trade, although, where parts and components are treated as belonging to the same industry as the finished product, it may also be classified as intra-industry trade.

VERTICAL DISINTEGRATION AND THE NEW INTERNATIONAL DIVISION OF LABOUR

Recent decades have witnessed another important development associated with direct investment abroad and the growth of the multinational company. This may be referred to as 'vertical disintegration' to distinguish it from the more familiar vertical integration discussed in the last chapter. The rapid pace of technological change of past decades has made it both possible and desirable to split up the process involved in the production of certain manufactured goods into a much larger number of separate activities. Each of these processes is capable of being performed in separate plants, possibly located in different countries. The choice of location will depend on the factor proportions required for each separate activity. The more labour-intensive stages of manufacture will then tend to be located where the appropriate labour is available and cheap. The more capital-intensive stages of manufacture will tend to be located where suitable capital can be obtained at relatively low cost.

This makes possible considerable cost savings. First, each separate activity can be located where it is most economic to carry out that activity. Thus the comparative advantage enjoyed by different countries by virtue of differences in relative factor endowments can be more fully exploited. Second, the higher degree of specialization achieved by each individual plant will permit major cost savings through the fuller exploitation of available economies of scale. One result of this process is the emergence of a much finer degree of international specialization between countries. Individual countries specialize in particular processes or sub-activities within more general activities. For this reason it has been called the 'new international division of labour' (NIDL).

MNCs have played a leading role in bringing this about. They have done so through direct investments abroad. Through such investments, they have brought under common ownership a large number of plants, which they have then reorganized to achieve greater product specialization. Ford pioneered this approach in the European motor car industry in the late 1960s. Individual plants were reorganized such that each specialized in various different processes or activities rather than each plant performing all the stages involved in car production. However, in other industries, MNCs have actually relocated certain processes or stages of production in other countries to take advantage of more favourable costs. Especially important in this respect has been the relocation of the more labour-intensive final-assembly stages of manufacture at sites located in certain newly-industrializing developing countries. In some cases this has been achieved by means of so-called 'export-platform' investments in cheap-labour countries. Components and parts are produced at capital-intensive plants based in the industrialized countries before being exported to final assembly or processing plants sited in developing countries. Once assembled or processed, the finished product is then re-exported for sale and distribution in other countries.

In some cases the same result may be achieved by firms based in industrialized countries subcontracting producers located in developing countries to carry out the more labour-intensive making-up or finishing processes. In this case no direct investment is involved. This would appear to be quite common in the textile industries where subcontractors located in developing countries carry out the more labour-intensive making-up stages using fabrics supplied by textile firms located in the industrialized countries. Whatever the case, one of the main results of this process has been a rapid growth in the number of intermediate products entering into international trade. Much of this trade takes place within the multinational company and therefore constitutes intra-firm trade. Thus the NIDL has been an important factor fostering the growth of intra-firm trade.

Those industries in which this kind of narrow international specialization has taken place are sometimes referred to as 'rationalized product' manufacturing industries. The textile and clothing industry has already been referred to as a case in point. West European textile firms have led the way in promoting this kind of specialization. Textile and clothing production involves a number of stages each of which is capable of being separated. The earlier fabric-making stages are relatively capital intensive and skill intensive. This favours location of these stages in the industrialized countries. On the other hand, the making-up operations are more labour intensive and more efficiently performed in developing countries where labour is cheaper. Textile firms have sought to relocate these later stages in developing countries by subcontracting local producers. The latter are provided with pre-set designs and already-cut fabrics for making-up. The made-up garment is then re-imported by textile firms in Western Europe for finishing and packaging. A survey of West German textile and garment companies found that, in 1977, for every 100 workers employed in Germany, there were more than ten foreign workers employed abroad. Over the period from 1966 to 1974–5, the foreign employment of the West German textile and garment industry more than doubled while domestic employment decreased by roughly one-quarter (Fröbel, Heinrichs, and Kreye 1980). This illustrates the extent to which the more labour-intensive stages of textile production were being shifted to sites outside West Germany. These included certain Mediterranean regions, such as Greece, Malta, and Tunisia, certain South-East Asian countries, such as South Korea, and East European countries, such as Yugoslavia and Hungary.

Another example of an industry in which this kind of rationalized process investment has taken place has been the consumer electronics industry. The production of most consumer electronics involves three stages: (1) the conception and development of new products, (2) the production of components, and (3) the testing of parts and components and their assembly into finished goods. The first stage is highly research intensive and is best located in advanced industrialized countries well endowed with supplies of highly skilled and qualified engineers and scientists. The second stage is capital intensive such that there are major economies of scale to be reaped from concentrated production and plant specialization. Thus the principal components tend to be produced at highly specialized plants located in the developed countries. However, the final assembly and testing stages are more labour intensive. They have become more labour intensive as technological advances have cut the cost of components. The number of different components used has also been reduced, which has helped simplify the final assembly process. The degree of skill required of assembly-line workers has accordingly fallen. All of these considerations have increasingly favoured relocating the final assembly stage in developing countries where labour is cheap and more willing to undertake simple and repetitive tasks and less inclined to disrupt production.

In the consumer electronics industry, Japanese firms played the pioneering role in developing the NIDL. They were the first to spot the opportunities for cost savings through such a global reorganization of production. Final assembly stages were relocated at sites in newly-industrializing countries such as South Korea, Singapore, and Taiwan. As a result, Japanese companies were able to maintain a lead in the industry at a time when rising wage costs at home were increasingly eroding Japan's former comparative advantage in the production of standardized light manufactures. This success of the Japanese consumer electronics industry forced US firms to follow suit. They, too, carried out a rationalization of their production processes and shifted labour-intensive final assembly stages or processes to sites based in developing countries, most notably Mexico and certain South-East Asian countries.

A similar trend has also been apparent in industrial electronics. In the last decade, semiconductor manufacturers throughout the world have begun to face increasingly fierce price competition. In response, firms have sought to achieve cost reductions by rationalizing production processes and relocating the most labour-intensive stages at offshore sites in developing countries. For example, one survey of thirty-seven leading United States, Japanese, and West European companies, which in 1979 accounted for more than 90 per cent of world semiconductor production, found that the number of their ventures in developing countries rose from forty-six in 1974 to seventy-two in 1976 and eighty-seven in 1979. The number of these ventures which were located in South-East Asian countries rose from twenty-one in 1971 to forty-three in 1974 to fifty-two in 1976 and sixty in 1979 (UNCTC 1983). The rest were located in Latin American countries such as Mexico.

Causes of the New International Division of Labour

What factors account for the emergence of the NIDL? Professor Mark Casson has sought to develop a theory of the NIDL which can explain why it has come into being in recent decades (Casson 1986). He has put forward the following explanations:

1. **Technology** Historically, every major advance in the division of labour has been the result of some major technological innovation. Thus the growth of the factory system in the eighteenth and nineteenth centuries resulted from the development of steam power and the invention of new types of machinery. Further revolutions in methods of transport and the organization of factory work led to the emergence of mass-production methods. Since the Second World War, further progress in achieving increased specialization within industries has followed major improvements in product design. In response to the needs of the division of labour, products have been designed in such a way as to permit a further subdivision of the production process. This has affected both the design of new products and the redesign of older, maturing products. The main features of this process would appear to be the designing of products as so-called multi-component goods. Products have been designed or redesigned to be assemblies of a large number of standardized components, each of which is capable of being produced separately and on a large-scale in such a way as to exploit available economies of scale fully. Products are capable of being assembled with different subsets of components to achieve a highly versatile product capable of having many different uses. This makes possible considerable product differentiation and therefore non-price competition through differentiation and design. The same changes have affected the design of components themselves. Components have been redesigned as multi-components goods, so that we have a hierarchy of components which are assembled at various stages before being used in the assembly of the final product. In this process of

modifying the design of products, Japanese firms seem to have played a pioneering role. They have shown a special adeptness at taking products innovated in other countries and redesigning such products to take fuller advantage of the division of labour.

2. **Improved transport systems** The period since the Second World War has seen major improvements in methods of transport. Most important has been the reduction of bulk through such changes as the use of containerization. The effect has been to reduce the costs of transportation of both the final product and components. This in turn has made possible the location of the various separate activities involved in the production process at different geographical locations. As has been seen, this has made possible cost savings from siting particular processes according to relative factor intensities and relative factor prices.

3. **Rural–urban migration in newly-industrializing developing countries** Migration of workers from the agricultural subsistence sector to the industrial sector in a number of developing countries has created a pool of relatively cheap labour. This has coincided with rising labour costs, due to increased trade-union organization and rising living standards, in the older industrialized countries. At the same time, improvements in education and health in certain developing countries have created a supply of labour much more suitable for industrial employment than in the past. Additionally, such workers are generally more willing to adopt high-productivity working practices. The latter may be more important than low wage-rates in attracting 'export-platform' investments from the industrialized countries. This is demonstrated by the fact that some newly-industrializing countries have remained competitive despite rising wages (e.g. Hong Kong and Singapore).

4. **Lower co-ordination costs** The splitting up of the production process into a large number of separate activities each undertaken at different sites often separated by long distances requires greater co-ordination. A number of changes in recent decades have worked to reduce such costs of co-ordination. First, the skill of modern management has been raised through better and increased management education. Second, improved communications have resulted from cheaper telecommunications and the increased convenience of air travel. As a result, the costs of co-ordinating a large number of plants each located in different countries have fallen relative to the costs of co-ordinating an equivalent number of such plants all located in the same country.

5. **Reduced barriers to trade** Barriers to trade have been reduced through the formation of customs unions and free trade areas, the introduction of tariff preferences for exports of developing countries, and the creation of tariff-free zones. These reduced barriers to trade have promoted trade in both final and intermediate products. On the other hand, there would appear to have been an increase in so-called non-tariff barriers, while unstable exchange rates and increased use of exchange controls may also have an offsetting effect on trade.

6. **The creation of new low-cost industrial sites in newly-industrializing countries** In a number of newly-industrializing countries, special low-cost industrial sites have been created close to ports and other public transport systems and highly attractive as locations for export-platform investments. These are usually referred to as 'export-processing zones' (EPZs). They offer special infrastructure such as port facilities and power supplies at low cost. Firms operating in such areas are usually exempt from certain taxes, import duties, minimum wage laws, and other legislation applicable in the rest of the country. In the mature industrialized countries, also, there have been several such industrial sites established away from congested urban areas offering low-cost locations for such investments. Competition to attract such investment has acted to reduce site rentals, while government subsidies and rate rebates offered as part of regional development policy have further reduced the cost of such locations.

7. **Higher incomes** More rapid technological change leading to a more advanced division of labour has raised the incomes of those employed in manufacturing industry. Higher incomes have increased the demand for manufactured goods. An enlarged market has made it possible both to split up the production process into a larger number of separate units and increase the scale of production of each unit.

Chapter 6 will examine the emergence of the newly-industrializing countries. In so doing, it will discuss further the nature and effects of the NIDL. In particular, it will examine in more depth the role played by EPZs, as well as by trading arrangements such as tariff preferences and the offshore assembly provisions contained in the tariff schedules of several of the large industrialized countries.

How important has been this kind of direct investment

abroad? According to Stopford and Dunning, at the end of 1980 about 20 per cent of the stock of foreign direct investment was what they called 'rationalized investment'. Although this represents quite a small proportion of the total stock of FDI, since 1970, along with investment in services, it has been the fastest-growing type of FDI. If it continues to grow at the same rate, its importance will increase in the future (Stopford and Dunning 1983).

ALTERNATIVE FORMS OF INTERNATIONAL BUSINESS INVOLVEMENT

One of the most important developments of recent years has been the appearance of a number of forms of international business involvement other than direct investment abroad. These have included the following:

1. Joint ventures, where domestic partners share in the ownership and possibly the management of the enterprise.
2. Licensing agreements, where MNCs enter into an agreement with a foreign company (or overseas subsidiary) to grant to the licensee use of industrial property rights and unpatented know-how in return for agreed royalties and fees.
3. Management contracts, where an MNC provides a foreign company usually based in a developing country with management and technical services for a specified period of time in return for the payment of an agreed fee.
4. Turnkey operations, under which one company signs a contract to provide a range of goods and services needed for the design, construction, and commissioning of industrial plant (e.g. a nuclear power station).
5. International subcontracting, under which an MNC subcontracts a foreign company to carry out some specific work or to supply a particular good.

Essentially, these all represent alternative ways of transferring resources from one country to another. In Chapter 4 we saw that FDI involves the transfer of a package of resources from one country to another. This package includes money capital, ownership, control, management, and technology. All of the above alternatives enable the host country to acquire just some elements of this package and to exclude others. With the single exception of joint ventures, none of the above involve the foreign MNC taking an equity share in the local company. In the case of a joint venture, the MNC shares ownership with a local company or local shareholders. The host country may regard such an arrangement as preferable because it ensures greater local control over the newly-established enterprise.

There now exists considerable evidence for supposing that these other forms of international participation are becoming of increasing importance. We have no way of accurately measuring the true extent of such other forms of international business involvement such as we have for FDI. However, some superficial evidence points in this direction. Two factors stand out as explanations for this trend. First, there now exists a greater degree of regulation of MNCs by host country governments, especially in developing countries, than in the past. Many more countries now insist on local shareholders holding a substantial if not majority stake in any foreign enterprise established in their territory. This is supposedly to ensure that more of the benefits from such an investment are endogenized within the local economy. The last chapter showed how joint ventures or the inclusion of local shareholders in the newly-established foreign enterprise may be a way of preventing harmful transfer-price manipulation. Some host countries prohibit foreign ownership altogether. In this case the only means of entry to the domestic market for a foreign company, other than by exporting, is through some form of contractual arrangement, such as a licensing agreement.

Second, there is a growing desire on the part of many host countries to 'unbundle' the FDI package – that is to say, to acquire the various elements separately. In the case of some developing countries, domestic savings may be sufficient to provide the resources needed to finance increased investment without the addition of foreign capital. On the other hand, the country may be keen to purchase either foreign technology or management expertise to achieve a more rapid pace of industrial development. In this case a licensing agreement or management contract may be preferred.

The rest of this section of the present chapter will examine two of the most important alternative forms of business involvement listed: joint ventures and licensing agreements.

Joint Ventures

One of the most important alternative forms of international business involvement is that of the joint venture. This involves the partnership of two or more firms, which may or may not be local firms but at least one of which is foreign owned, with each of the partners holding an equity stake in the subsidiary. The term in fact covers a variety of different types of arrangement. Three general categories may be identified:

1. A joint venture between a foreign-owned firm and a privately-owned local firm or group of local investors. This involves the setting up of a new company in which both the foreign multinational and the local firm or individual local investors hold an equity stake. The foreign multi-national may own a majority stake or minority stake in the company, or the company may be co-owned with each partner having an equal equity stake in the company. Local shareholders may or may not be involved in the management of the company.
2. A joint venture between a foreign-owned firm and a local state enterprise or the local government. The equity capital is partly held by the foreign multinational and partly by the local state enterprise or by the host government. Again, the foreign multinational may have a majority or minority stake in the concern or an equal stake with the local state enterprise or host government. Such arrangements are frequently found in the oil-processing industry.
3. A joint venture between a number of foreign-owned companies without any local participation. Each of the foreign firms holds an equity stake in the company. Such a company is often referred to as a consortium. They are quite common in the raw-materials or extractive industries.

There is nothing new about such joint ventures. Joint ventures existed even before the Second World War. However, their importance has been increasing and, moreover, has spread to manufacturing industry. In the past, joint ventures were largely confined to either trading companies or mining and other raw-material-extracting companies. Table 5.5 shows that from 1951 to 1975 over two-thirds of the joint-venture activity undertaken by US multinationals has been in manufacturing (Hladik 1985). The share accounted for by manufacturing rose from 58 per cent in the early 1950s to 66 per cent in 1975. The share accounted for by the extractive industries has fallen from 11 to 5 per cent over the same period. In the 1970s the share accounted for by the extractive industries rose again slightly on account of increased joint venture activity in the oil industry.

Table 5.5: Joint ventures by principal activity as a percentage of total joint ventures formed, 1951–75

Activity	1951–5	1956–60	1961–5	1975	Total
Manufacturing	58	72	70	66	68
Sales & service	14	13	14	18	15
Extraction	11	3	2	5	4
Other	6	5	6	9	8
Unknown	11	6	8	1	5

Source: Hladik (1985).

At the same time, the extent of joint-venture activity has been increasing, especially in developing countries. This is illustrated by Table 5.6, which shows joint-venture activity as a percentage of the total subsidiaries abroad formed by US multinationals. As a percentage of the FDI by US multinationals in less-developed countries, joint-venture activity rose from 24 per cent in the early 1950s to 45 per cent in 1975. In the advanced countries, the percentage was almost constant. Since 1975 there has been a further significant increase. The number of joint-venture activities involving US firms almost doubled between 1975 and 1982 (Hladik 1985). Although joint-venture activity has been increasing fastest in developing countries as a proportion of FDI, new joint-venture activity has been proportionately more important in advanced or high-income countries. In 1975 roughly 51 per cent of all newly-formed joint-ventures took place in developed countries and 49 per cent in less-developed countries. However, the share of the LDCs had risen from 41 per cent in the early 1950s (Hladik 1985).

Table 5.7 illustrates the principal forms which this new joint-venture activity has taken. In 1976, 64 per cent of the joint ventures involving US multinationals involved partnership with local privately-owned enterprises, 9 per cent involved

Table 5.6: Joint ventures by location as a percentage of total subsidiaries formed, 1951–75

	1951–5	1956–60	1961–5	1975	Total
LESS-DEVELOPED COUNTRIES					
Majority-owned	11	13	13	12	12
Co-owned	5	5	8	10	7
Minority-owned	8	11	13	23	13
Total (5 to 94%)	24	29	34	45	32
ADVANCED COUNTRIES					
Majority-owned	10	8	11	6	9
Co-owned	6	9	10	11	9
Minority-owned	8	7	9	11	8
Total (5 to 94%)	24	24	30	28	26

Source: Hladik (1985).

partnership with the host government or local state enterprises, and 17 per cent partnership with other foreign firms on a consortium-type basis. A further 10 per cent of the joint ventures involved partnership with 'widely dispersed' local investors, defined as situations where a subsidiary's stock was held by more than five independent partners none of which has a significant share of the equity. This shows that where joint ventures involve local equity participation, share ownership tends to be quite concentrated. Partnership between a multi-national and local private capital is especially common in manufacturing. However, the involvement of local state enterprise or host government equity is common in the extractive industries. Consortia of foreign firms are also common in the extractive industries. The latter two types of joint venture activity appear to be of increasing importance. One reason may be the increased scale of investment in raw-materials industries which necessitates different companies combining together to provide the capital needed for giant projects.

Table 5.7 also shows that minority-ownership and co-owner-ship tend to predominate over majority-ownership in joint-venture activity. This was true of all four categories of joint-venture activity. In the early years of the post-war period, however, it appears that US multinationals preferred majority ownership when setting up joint ventures, especially in developing countries. They may still do so. However, developing countries have increasingly insisted on a substantial, majority-ownership stake. At the same time, they have become increasingly able to raise the necessary resources to put up the required

Table 5.7: Joint ventures by principal outside owner as a percentage of total joint ventures by activity for subsidiaries active, 1 January 1976

Owner and ownership share	Activity Manufacturing	Sales	Extraction	Total
LOCAL PRIVATE				
Minority-owned	22	20	16	22
Co-owned	24	21	8	23
Majority-owned	16	11	15	16
Unknown	4	3	5	4
Total	67	55	44	64
LOCAL STATE				
Minority-owned	3	3	13	4
Co-owned	2	3	3	2
Majority-owned	2	1	5	2
Unknown	1	1	2	1
Total	8	8	23	9
FOREIGN PRIVATE				
Minority-owned	7	13	16	9
Co-owned	4	10	7	5
Majority-owned	2	4	3	2
Unknown	1	1	5	1
Total	14	28	31	17
WIDELY DISPERSED				
Majority-owned	5	1	—	4
Co-owned	1	2	—	1
Majority-owned	4	5	2	4
Unknown	1	1	—	1
Total	11	9	2	10

Source: Hladik (1985).

capital. US multinationals have also been traditionally wary of joint ventures with state enterprises or state capital. Increasingly, however, developing countries are insisting on state participation, especially in the oil-processing industries.

One important feature of early joint-venture activity in manufacturing was that joint ventures tended to be highly localized. That is to say, sales were largely for the home market. The level of export activity of joint ventures was quite low. One reason for this may have been that host-country governments were better able to insist on local-equity participation where output was largely for the domestic market. Because of the existence of high trade barriers, multinationals may have had to accept such conditions as a prerequisite for entry into the local market. Another reason may have been that the technology being transferred was simpler, more mature, and less exclusive so that the foreign firm was less concerned about dissemination of such knowledge. A further reason appears to have been a bias on the part of US multinationals against using joint ventures for exporting. This is because the degree of control which the parent company can exercise over the export strategy of a joint venture is much less than in the case of a wholly-owned subsidiary. The parent company will be concerned that the exports of the joint venture will compete in third markets with the exports of its other subsidiaries. It may simply prefer to limit the output of the joint venture to local sales. However, Hladik has shown that, in the period since 1975, about one-half of the joint ventures newly formed by US multinationals did plan some form of export activity (Hladik 1985). This represents an important change compared with the period before 1975.

It has also been demonstrated that much early joint-venture activity was confined to firms with low research intensity. At the same time, joint ventures had relatively low levels of R&D, suggesting a low level of technological collaboration. This may have had something to do with the observation that joint ventures are inappropriate where the firm wishes to retain strict control over the technology being transferred. It will wish to do so where the technology is advanced, exclusive, and firm-specific. In this case, a wholly-owned subsidiary will be the preferred method of investment. At the same time, the host country will be in a weaker bargaining position to insist on local-equity participation. However, again, Hladik has demonstrated that, since 1975, although R&D remains relatively unimportant in US joint ventures abroad, its importance has been increasing (Hladik 1985). Where joint ventures are undertaking R&D, a greater proportion of their output will comprise new products, which are less likely to compete directly with the exports of other subsidiaries of the foreign firm in third markets. It follows that the foreign parent company will be less inclined to impose controls on exports. This may help to explain the observation that, since 1975, the importance of export activity of joint ventures has been increasing.

What factors can account for the increased importance of joint-venture activity? Why is it that joint ventures appear to be becoming more important relative to direct investment in wholly-owned subsidiaries? Much of the new joint-venture activity has been taking place in developing countries. It is largely in developing countries that joint-venture activity has increased relative to direct investment in wholly-owned subsidiaries. One major reason for this has been growing insistence by host-country governments on local-equity participation as a condition for entry to the local market. In some cases, multinationals have been unable to set up production in a developing country unless they are willing to accept substantial local-equity participation. Where output is largely intended for the home market, the host country of a developing country is in a powerful bargaining position, given the existence of sizeable trade barriers. The bargaining power of the host government is further enhanced where the technology involved is relatively mature and less firm-specific. One factor that has increased the strength of developing countries when bargaining with foreign multinationals for the transfer of technology has been the diversification of sources of investment. The growth in the number and relative share of other non-US direct capital exporters has meant that a developing country can choose between rival suppliers of certain types of technology and hold out for the best possible deal. Where the technology involved is advanced and more exclusive, however, the foreign firm will be less willing to surrender control, at least without very strict controls relating to the use of the relevant know-how. If, too, the output involved is partly for export abroad, insistence on local control over the foreign enterprise may cause the multinational to set up plant in another country. Alternatively, it may raise costs of production, which jeopardizes success in export markets. It is noticeable that, in some of the newly-industrializing countries, wholly-owned subsidiaries have remained more important than joint ventures. For example, Singapore with her strong export orientation has placed greater reliance upon attracting multinational investment for exporting and accordingly the role of locally-owned firms in manufacturing appears to have declined in importance (UNCTC 1983). By way of contrast, in South Korea, the importance of majority foreign-owned firms appears to have declined in importance in favour of minority ownership. One reason for this appears to be that much of the direct investment which Korea sought to attract was either in industries supplying the domestic market or in industries embodying well-known technologies (UNCTC 1983).

Another factor favouring the growth of joint ventures in developing countries has been the increased ability of developing countries, primarily the newly-industrializing countries, to resource joint ventures. In contrast to a wholly-owned foreign subsidiary, a joint venture requires the host country to put up capital and provide other inputs, for example managerial skills. The poorest, least-developed countries are generally unable to do so. They need to obtain the full package of resources available through FDI. To seek to divert scarce resources into a joint venture with foreign capital, for the sake of increased control, is unlikely to be a worthwhile trade-off. Other more socially-valuable projects may, as a result, be starved of funds. However, many of the newly-industrializing countries are able to put up the necessary resources themselves. It may be worthwhile for them to 'unbundle' the package of resources obtainable through foreign direct investment. A joint venture is one way of achieving this. The advantages are that the host country retains greater control over the foreign investment. This may enable it to increase the value of the flow of FDI into the country concerned. For example, the host country may be able to ensure that, to some extent, inputs are purchased locally, benefiting local firms and industries, rather than being imported from abroad. Of course, this may entail higher production costs. As we have seen, this will not be appropriate where output is largely for export. Where, however, output is principally for the domestic market and imports are restricted, such a strategy may maximize the spillover effects to the local economy. Other ancillary firms and industries benefit. The size of the domestic income multiplier is increased. At the same time, more of the profits from the investment are likely to be retained within the local economy. In particular, the host government may be better able to protect the local economy from transfer-price manipulation leading to profits being siphoned off to the parent company. The presence of local shareholders and the involvement of a local firm in the running of the joint venture will make it difficult for the foreign firm to evade remittance controls, beat price controls, or undermine high *ad valorem* tariffs through the underinvoicing of imports.

However, it should be born in mind that the dilution of ownership through the participation of local equity capital in a foreign venture does not ensure a shift of control. Local investors may view their interests as bound up with those of the foreign firm. In addition, too strong an insistance on the inclusion of local firms and investors in a foreign investment project may make it difficult for a country to attract the required package of foreign capital and technology. We have seen also that joint ventures tend to be biased against exports. Foreign multinationals tend to prefer wholly-owned subsidiaries when output is primarily designed for exporting. This is because of the difficulties of controlling the exporting strategy of a joint venture and the risk of exports weakening sales of other subsidiaries to third markets. Too heavy a reliance on joint ventures may mean reduced exports for the host country.

For multinationals themselves, a joint venture with a local firm or group of investors is often a necessity if it is to gain access to a particular country. However, there are other positive advantages. Through a joint venture, a foreign firm may be able to get round controls or restrictions imposed by the host government, for example borrowing from local banks, selling to government enterprises. They may be better able to obtain access to local distribution channels or secure the source of supply for an important raw material or intermediate good. Political risk is also reduced. The government of the host country is less likely to view with hostility a company in which local firms and investors hold a substantial stake. The evidence would suggest that a joint venture is often a particularly appropriate course for smaller, less well-known, less experienced firms wanting to expand overseas. The industry leaders are likely to prefer the establishment of a wholly-owned subsidiary. This is especially true where it is costly to lose control over the technology used. This will be the case in the more technologically-advanced industries where the state of technology is changing rapidly. If, however, the terms of the joint venture enable the firm to retain control over the use of the technology, joint ventures may be more acceptable. For firms with little overseas experience and/or little bargaining power, a joint venture may be the better of the two alternatives. Such firms tend to lack the information, skills, or capital to launch wholly-owned subsidiaries. Firms which have little to offer a host country in terms of scarce resources (e.g. technology or access to foreign markets) may also incline more toward joint ventures.

Thus the growth of joint-venture activity, especially in the developing countries, may be seen as the result of various changes taking place in the world. On the one hand, the developing countries are seeking greater control over foreign investments in their countries to ensure greater benefits, while being increasingly able to provide the resources for joint ventures and to insist on local-equity involvement. On the other hand, multinational companies may regard joint ventures as a way of reducing both economic risk (especially in the highly capital-intensive raw materials and oil-processing industries) and political risk (from host governments introducing penal restrictions on foreign firms or even outright nationalization). It seems likely that these trends will continue in the future. We can expect the importance of joint-venture activity to increase further. Whereas for multinational companies this may result in reduced control over their operations in developing countries, for developing countries themselves it may prove an important way in which they can maximize the benefits from direct investment and the transfer of technology.

Licensing Agreements

Another form of international business linkage which has been increasing rapidly in recent decades has been that of licensing agreements. A licensing agreement is an agreement between the owner of some body of technological knowledge (e.g. a design for a new product, a new method for producing a product, a brand name or trademark or some other type of industrial property) and a potential user. The technology cannot be imitated or obtained in any other form. The potential user is therefore prepared to pay a price for access to the technology. Payment may take the form of a lump-sum or of a percentage of the sales or profits from applying the technology, which is paid in the form of royalties or fees. The potential user may be an independent firm in no way related to the company selling the technology or he may be a wholly- or partly-owned subsidiary of the latter. Parent companies often supply their overseas subsidiaries with technology under a licensing agreement by which the subsidiary is required to pay the parent company in the form of royalties or fees. In other cases, where the licensee is unrelated to the licensor, the licensor may wish to acquire an equity stake in the licensee. In this way, it may be able to ensure greater control over the use of the technology sold. Thus the sale of technology by means of a licensing agreement may be accompanied by a flow of capital to the recipient country. Generally, however, licensing agreements involve a transfer of technology without an accompanying investment of capital. As such, they constitute a non-equity form of international participation. Thus, to an even greater extent than joint ventures, which seek to achieve a transfer of capital without a transfer of control, licensing agreements are an attempt to 'unbundle' the FDI package. Specifically, they seek to separate the technology component from the investment of capital and transfer of managerial control. However, very often, licensing agreements will involve accompanying management services and technical information ancillary to the technology sold.

Usually, a licensing agreement will contain certain clauses designed to ensure that the proprietor retains some control over the use of the technology or, at least, that the costs of losing control are minimized. These will seek to ensure that the information acquired by the licensee is not passed on to another company, that the use of the technology is confined to a particular geographical territory (so that the licensor's sales in third markets is not affected), and that the product in question is produced in conformity with certain standards of quality. Other restrictions may also be stipulated. The need to ensure adequate quality standards is especially important where the licensee buys the use of the licensor's trademark. Such restrictions are often viewed as being harmful by developing countries. One reason is that they create a dependence of the licensee on the licensor. This is the case when the agreement requires the buyer of the information to purchase components or further technology from the licensor. Another reason is that such agreements may prohibit the buyer from using the technology in third markets because of the effect on the sales of the licensor and/or her subsidiaries operating in such third markets. As such they represent a restraint on competition and distort the global allocation of resources. For these reasons, host-country governments often intervene to outlaw agreements which contain such restrictions. For example, the Indian government lays down guidelines for the negotiation of such agreements. The guidelines are designed to ensure that the technology acquired is assimilated as fully as possible by the local economy.

From the point of view of the multinational company which is licensing the technology, the need is to retain some control over the technology being sold or to minimize the cost of losing control. Knowledge possesses many of the characteristics of a public good. In particular, once knowledge has been made available, it is very difficult to prevent that knowledge from being dissipated. Other users may be able to obtain the knowledge without having to pay for it. If so, the value of the knowledge is depreciated and the original knowledge-producer fails to get a full return on the amount spent on the generation of that knowledge. The disadvantage of licensing is that the proprietor firm may be unable to ensure full appropriability. One solution is to include in the agreement, clauses which place restrictions on the use of the technology by the buying firm. However, it may prove difficult to police to enforce such restrictions. Licensees may disregard contracts containing restrictive clauses, because the penalty for doing so is not very great. Having gained possession of the knowledge sought, the firm in question has little to lose by disregarding restrictions stipulated by the original supplier of the technology. Enforcing adequate standards of quality, reliability, and service to protect the reputation of the licensor, as when a trademark is sold, is notoriously difficult. Furthermore, host governments in many developing countries may introduce legislation to outlaw agreements which contain restrictive clauses. These considerations may favour investment in the setting up of a wholly-owned subsidiary as a mechanism for transferring the technology in question. From the point of view of the foreign firm, this will ensure the internalization of the knowledge and help overcome the problem of the knowledge being dissipated. This is likely to be preferred where the technology in question is still relatively new and where, consequently, the risks of dissipation are very great. It follows that licensing is likely to be somewhat less common for products in the early stages of their life-cycle. By way of contrast, where the knowledge is relatively mature and likely to become obsolete soon, the costs of losing control of the technology will be less and licensing may be preferred. Licensing may also be the preferred alternative for a highly diversified firm which lacks the resources to set up plant overseas in all its existing product lines. For such a firm, it may be better to sell its technology, if it wishes to gain access to an overseas market, by means of a licensing agreement. For similar reasons, smaller firms appear to have a greater propensity to enter into licensing agreements. They lack the resources or skills to engage in international production. Finally, where the government of the host country prohibits the setting up of a foreign subsidiary, a licensing agreement may be the only way that a company with a firm-specific advantage can gain entry into the overseas market. For decades this was the case in Japan. Inward investment by foreign firms was tightly controlled. Licensing agreements were the only way that US and European companies could gain direct access to the Japanese market. Even where inward investment is permitted, this route may be inappropriate for a foreign company wanting to make an initial entry into a particular market. Licensing, perhaps involving some element of equity participation, may be preferred.

The statistical evidence available shows that licensing agreements have been of increasing importance in recent decades. Table 5.8 compares the growth in receipts of royalties and fees from licensing agreements with the growth in the stock of FDI over the period from 1971 to 1980. Whereas the stock of FDI grew at a rate of 12.7 per cent per annum, income from licensing grew at a rate of 15.7 per cent per annum. In a few countries the stock of FDI grew faster than income from licensing. However, these included the two countries — Japan and West Germany — which experienced the fastest growth in outward FDI of all. Japan's income from licensing grew by 21.5 per cent, faster than any other country except France and Australia.

Table 5.9 shows the balance of trade in technology for 1971 and 1980. In 1971, only two countries – the United States and the United Kingdom – had a trade surplus in technology. In 1980 they were joined by France. The table illustrates how the United States dominates trade in technology, accounting, in 1980, for 50 per cent of all income from licensing and with an overwhelming trade surplus in technology. Table 5.10 shows the composition of US receipts of royalties and fees from licensing. Between 1970 and 1981, total receipts increased more than threefold, rising from $2,449 million to $7,253 million. The greater part of these receipts came from affiliates of US multinationals – approximately 77 per cent in 1970 and 81 per cent in 1981. Thus US companies demonstrated a preference

Table 5.8: Growth in the receipts of royalties and fees by the developed countries relative to the growth in their direct investment stock abroad, 1971–80

| | Annual average growth in: | | |
	(a) Receipts of royalties and fees, 1971–80 (%)	(b) Direct investment stock, 1971–80 (%)	(a)/(b) (%)
United States	12.5	11.2	1.12
United Kingdom	14.4	13.5	1.07
West Germany	16.2	20.0	0.81
France	28.6	11.8	2.42
Italy	6.1[a]	8.8[b]	0.69
Netherlands	16.6	12.5	1.33
Belgium and Luxembourg	4.1	12.5	0.33
Sweden	2.3	13.0	0.18
Japan	21.5	26.7	0.81
Australia	26.8	16.0	1.68
TOTAL	15.7[c]	12.7[c]	1.24

Source: Stopford and Dunning (1983).
[a] For 1971–7
[b] For 1971–8
[c] Excluding Italy

for selling their technology within the multinational enterprise rather than to independent overseas buyers. Presumably this was to enable them the more effectively to retain control over the technology. For UK companies, the share of income from licensing which is intra-firm is much less – 43 per cent in 1980 and 40 per cent in 1977. UK companies appear to have a lower propensity to sell technology in-house. However, the share of income from licensing which is intra-firm may be artificially swollen due to transfer-price manipulation. Multinational companies may inflate their income from licensing agreement with overseas affiliates as a device for siphoning funds from their affiliates back to parent companies to minimize tax liabilities or to evade controls imposed by the host government on remittance of profits. This is likely to be more important where the affiliate is based in a developing country where such controls are common. Table 5.10 shows that, in 1981, 81 per cent of all receipts came from enterprises located in other developed countries and only 22 per cent from enterprises in developing countries. Sales of technology to firms based in developed countries grew faster than to firms based in

Table 5.9: Receipts and payments of royalties and fees to and by selected developed market economies, 1971 and 1980 (US $ million)

Country	1971 Receipts	1971 Payments	1971 Balance	1980 Receipts	1980 Payments	1980 Balance
United States	2,375	241	+2,134	6,685	769	+6,096
France	397	465	−68	3,828	2,318	+1,510
United Kingdom	358	300	+58	1,203	925	+278
Germany	157	426	−269	606	1,444	−838
Netherlands	105	116	−11	418	643	−225
Japan	61	468	−407	351	1,328	−977
Belgium–Luxembourg	129	169	−40	185	454	−269
Italy	85	329	−244	—[a]	—	—
Sweden	75[b]	218[b]	−143[b]	92	220	−128
Austria	8	33	−25	36	152	−116
Australia	4	63	−59	34	130	−96

Source: Stopford and Dunning (1983).

[a] Denotes information not available
[b] Includes items other than technology payments

developing countries over the period covered. One reason for this may have been growing restrictions imposed by developing countries designed to control such payments for the technology of developed countries.

Table 5.10: Fees and royalty receipts by the United States: 1970–81 ($ millions)

	1970	1975	1980	1981
RECEIPTS FROM AFFILIATES				
Developed market economies	1,404	2,770	4,841	4,805
Eastern Europe	–	–	–	–
Developing countries	491	722	1,227	1,331
Unallocated	24	51	−288	−268
Subtotal	1,919	3,543	5,781	5,867
RECEIPTS FROM UNAFFILIATED FOREIGN ENTITIES				
Developed market economies	510	641	950	1,104
Eastern Europe	4	14	20	22
Developing countries	66	102	215	260
Subtotal	580	757	1,185	1,386
Grand total	2,449	4,300	6,966	7,253

Source: UNCTC (1983).

COUNTERTRADE

One of the most important developments of recent decades has been the growth in importance of what is variously called international barter, or countertrade. The strict meaning of the term 'barter' is the direct exchange of goods for goods without the mediation of money. In fact, such strict barter is comparatively rare in international trade. The term 'countertrade' is used to refer to a number of different types of trade which contain an element of barter but may still involve the use of money. The Economist Intelligence Unit (EIU) uses the term countertrade in a generic sense to refer to forms of trade involving an element of reciprocity. In return for A buying from B, B buys from A. Money may still be used. A's purchases from B may not exactly match B's purchases from A. They may also be separated in time. Nevertheless, they are to some degree reciprocal. As the EIU puts it, 'the important point about countertrade is that it aims to equalise or partially balance foreign exchange expenditures.' As we shall see, 'countertrade' is really an umbrella term which groups together a range of trading practices which contain elements of such reciprocity (EIU 1984).

Types of Countertrade

The following are some of the major types:
1. **Pure barter** involving the direct exchange of goods/services for other goods/services is unusual in international trade. Usually it takes place on a government-to-government basis. Money enters the transaction only as a unit of account. The main problem with barter is that it requires a double coincidence of wants. A must want what B has to sell and B must want what A has to sell. More than that, the two commodities must have an equal exchange value. Such deals are quite difficult to arrange at an international level. One example was the barter agreement signed between the United States and Jamaica in February 1982, involving the supply of Jamaican bauxite in exchange for various surplus dairy products. In the same year, a deal was struck between New Zealand and Iran involving the exchange of New Zealand lamb for Iranian oil.
2. **Counterpurchase** is probably the most common form of countertrade. It involves an exporter who secures a sales order undertaking to purchase in return certain goods and services from the importing country. The reciprocal purchase is a condition for the original sale. Sometimes this is called 'compensation trade'. It is quite common in much east–west trade. The seller is likely to be a western company and the buyer a state trading company. Usually, there will be two separate contracts. One will relate to the sale of goods/services by the western company for which it will be paid a specified amount of hard currency. The second contract will require the western company to spend some proportion of this revenue to buy goods from a shopping list provided by the importing country. The counterpurchase may vary in value between 10 per cent and 100 per cent of the original export order. The imports bought need not be related to the goods/services exported. Usually there will be a time period specified (normally three years) within which the counterpurchase must be made. Thus

exports do not actually help finance the purchase of imports; they merely help balance expenditures on imports at a later date. Therefore such a transaction will not be undertaken because of a lack of convertible currency or inability to obtain commercial credit. Hard currency is still needed. Rather, it is preferred by some eastern-bloc states because it helps to plan and control foreign trade. It has also been used by some developing countries. For example, in August 1982 Indonesia announced a counterpurchase agreement with some twelve companies for the supply of fertilizer worth a total of $154 million. Counterpurchases are now a very common type of countertrade. One survey covering some 110 American companies found that 55 per cent of all their countertrade transactions were counterpurchases or compensation trade.

3. **Buyback** is another type of countertrade involving the supplier of capital plant and equipment usually to a developing country buying back part of the resultant output as payment. For example, a western company supplying a chemicals plant to a developing country may be paid with part of the resultant output from the plant. Buyback deals are most common in trade between a western industrialized country and an eastern-bloc country. They are attractive to eastern-bloc countries because they avoid the need to use or obtain hard currency. Buyback deals are most common where there takes place the export of process plant, mining equipment, or similar order. The agreements are usually of longer terms (ten to fifteen years) than for counterpurchase or other types of countertrade. One problem of buyback deals for western companies is that the quality of the output from the plants constructed, particularly in East European countries, is uncertain. This may necessitate a clause giving the western company control over quality. China has made great use of buyback deals, mainly with Japan, West Germany, and the United States, involving the exchange of specialist equipment paid for with a variety of products. One example of a buyback deal occurred in 1973 when Occidental Petroleum sold the Soviet Union superphosphoric acid, assisted in building an ammonia plant and pipeline and undertook to buy potash and ammonia from the Soviet Union in payment. Another example was the building of a gas-gathering pipeline from Siberia, in which the Soviet Union purchased European technology in exchange for Soviet gas. Coproduction agreements are very similar to buyback. In this case, there is an

agreement whereby a western company produces certain components required for the production of a particular product, while the eastern-bloc country or developing country makes the other, less sophisticated parts. Reciprocal deliveries take place. The western company thereby gains access to a new market, while being able to take advantage of lower wages in the partner country. The local firms in the developing country or eastern-bloc country, in return, gain western technology needed in production plus a wider market for their product. For some developing countries, such deals may be preferable to allowing western firms to produce locally.

4. **Bilateral agreements and clearings** groups together a wide variety of agreements between two countries involving exchange of goods and services. There is agreement that over a specified period (often five years) trade flows should roughly balance. The agreement may rigidly define the products to be traded or it may amount to nothing more than a loose and broad statement about best intentions. A clearing mechanism is established. This involves each country opening up a special account with the other country's central bank. Each country is paid for its exports by a credit in a special account. Debits to this account may then be used to obtain imports from the other country. A clearing currency may be specified. This may be each partner's own currency or a suitable foreign currency (e.g. US dollars). The use of foreign exchange may therefore be avoided. Effectively, 'book money' is used in place of foreign currency. They are therefore helpful to countries which lack adequate foreign currency reserves and whose own currency is inconvertible and therefore not acceptable in settlement of debt. Such agreements are greatly used by eastern-bloc countries, especially in their trade with developing countries. One example was the trade protocol agreed between Bulgaria and Mexico for 1981 to 1985 which provided for a reciprocal increase in trade of 150 per cent. Bulgaria exchanged complete plants, soda ash, chemical fertilizers, and machine tools in return for Mexican exports of non-ferrous metal concentrates, cocoa, citrus juice concentrates, chemical products, and consumer goods.

5. **Switch trading** is the most complex type of countertrade. When two countries enter into a bilateral trading agreement there may arise long-term payments imbalances. One country may accumulate large credit surpluses with another country.

Switch trading involves the resale of unused credits to third parties in exchange for convertible currencies. Suppose, for example, Argentina develops large credits as a result of bilateral trading with Romania. Argentina may use these credits as payment for imports from some third country, say West Germany. West Germany receives exports from Romania as payment for West Germany's exports to Argentina. This is a relatively simple example. Very often more than three countries are involved such that they become extremely complex. Discounts may also be used in the switch process. There exists a number of switch specialists — that is to say, banks and trading houses with a specialist knowledge of switch trading – which assist in arranging such reselling of unused credits.

6. **Offset** is one of the fastest growing types of countertrade. It involves an agreement under which an exporter must incorporate into his final product certain components and parts obtained from the importing country. It is very common in the case of high-value exports, especially civil and military aircraft and other types of military equipment. Typically, the exporter is a western aircraft or armaments firm who agrees to use components produced within the country purchasing the aircraft or equipment, typically a developing country. The western exporter may also provide the developing country with the necessary technical assistance. The agreement may also contain clauses which require the western exporting firm to take out quite unrelated products from the developing country; for example, an aeroplane manufacturer may take out tropical products over a period of years. One example of an offset agreement was an agreement whereby Boeing, in seeking to win the battle to supply Britain's airborne early warning system, offered to increase the amount which it offset in Britain from 100 per cent to 130 per cent of the contract's value (*Economist*, 20 December 1986).

Research carried out in the United States, based upon a questionnaire sent out to some 450 US companies – 110 of which were received back – found that counterpurchase was the most common type of countertrade, accounting for some 55 per cent of countertrade transactions. Offset accounted for another 24 per cent, buy-back 9 per cent, switch trading 8 per cent, and barter 4 per cent (quoted in EIU 1984).

The Importance of Countertrade

International barter, or countertrade, is not entirely a new phenomenon. Most countries have resorted to barter at some time in the past. The inter-war period, especially the years of the Great Depression, witnessed a spread of bilateral trading agreements amongst the countries of Western Europe. Bilateralism went hand in glove with the general proliferation of trading restrictions and exchange controls. Nazi Germany attached a major importance to bilateral trading as part of its programme to cut unemployment. Barter trade remained widespread during and immediately after the Second World War. In the 1950s, however, there occurred a shift back towards multilateralism in both international trade and payments. This was encouraged by the setting up of multilateral organizations such as the IMF, GATT, the OEEC (which later became the OECD), the European Payments Union, and later, the EEC and EFTA. Bilateralism was frowned upon as being harmful to economic efficiency, economic welfare, and world trade. Every effort was made to restore trade and payments to a multilateral status as quickly as possible. This was largely achieved by the western developed nations. Bilateral trading remained common, however, among some of the developing countries (especially those of Latin America) and the socialist-bloc countries. Bilateral trading declined in Latin America in the late 1950s following the establishment of LAFTA (the Latin American Free Trade Area) but never disappeared. The Soviet Union, Eastern Europe, and China continued to rely on countertrading for most of their trade with the west, as well as for their trade with developing countries and their trade with each other. In the 1960s east–west trade became somewhat more multilateral in character. Nevertheless, countertrade continued to typify east–west trade. There is now sufficient evidence to support the view that, in recent decades, countertrading has increased in relative importance. No one knows the true extent of countertrade. Estimates seem to vary from between 5 per cent to 40 per cent of world trade. The Economist Intelligence Unit guessed that the true range was something between 15 per cent and 20 per cent (EIU 1984). The Group of Thirty, an international research group based in New York, estimated countertrade at between 8 per cent and 10 per cent of world trade (*Economist*, 20 December 1986). The US International

Trade Commission estimated countertrade at some 5.6 per cent of the exports of the United States' 500 largest companies, with armaments sales accounting for 80 per cent of the total (*Economist*, 20 December 1986). Countertrade is known to have been of special and growing importance in the trade of developing countries. In its study of barter-like trade in six developing countries, the OECD found that, for most of the six countries, barter-like trade increased in importance as a component of total trade over the 1960s and 1970s (OECD 1979). As a component of exports, barter-like trade varied from 7 per cent in the case of Tunisia up to 78 per cent in the case of Egypt. Compared with the 1960s, this percentage increased in all six countries except Tunisia and Nepal (for which there was no data for the 1960s). As a component of total imports, countertrade ranged from 7 per cent for Tunisia up to 53 per cent for Egypt. Compared with the 1960s, this percentage increased in two countries – Egypt and India – but fell slightly in three countries: Sri Lanka, Ghana, and Tunisia. This would suggest that barter-like trade was growing in importance over the period, although its impact was greater on the export than on the import side. This growth in countertrade in recent decades is in conformity with the observation that countertrade has always increased during periods of recession and general economic crisis. Thus there was a growth of bilateral trading in Western Europe in the 1930s. In particular, the economic problems facing many developing countries, associated with over-indebtedness, falling commodity prices, and slower growth of world trade appear to have contributed to a growth of the barter-like component in their total trade.

The Determinants of Countertrade

The reasons for a country engaging in countertrade vary according to the type of country under consideration. Broadly speaking, we may divide the countries which engage in counter trade into four categories:

1. **The eastern-bloc countries and China** are important participants in countertrade. They use countertrade in their trade with both the western industrialized countries and the Southern

developing countries. The reasons for using countertrade are partly political and partly economic. Countertrade is useful to these countries because they operate centrally planned economies, which involve state control of foreign trade. Countertrade aids the planning process. Another reason for the use of countertrade since the war has been lack of foreign exchange. Tight exchange controls are in existence rendering the currencies of these countries inconvertible. Exporters are generally unwilling to accept payment in inconvertible currencies. Countertrade becomes a way of paying for imports. This may take the form of a counterpurchase agreement under which a western exporter undertakes to buy goods from the eastern-bloc country within a three- to five-year period or bilateral trading agreement involving a clearing balance. Buyback agreements are also common. Usually they involve a western firm supplying the eastern-bloc country with capital equipment and technology on a turnkey basis and receiving in payment part of the output generated by the factory once in operation. Again, this has the attraction that it enables the eastern-bloc country to obtain necessary foreign capital and technology without any expenditure of hard currency. In addition, it obviates the eastern-bloc country from the necessity of seeking out markets in the west. Many of these countries suffer from lack of access to markets abroad and lack of experience in western marketing methods. This may be another reason for seeking a countertrade agreement with western suppliers. An alternative to buyback is a coproduction agreement, under which an eastern-bloc state enterprise and a western company jointly produce a particular product. Each produces components used in the manufacture of a jointly finished product. Payments take the form of reciprocal deliveries of components. Such an agreement gives the western firm access to a new market along with the advantages of lower wages in the eastern-bloc country. The eastern-bloc country is enabled to purchase the more sophisticated parts produced by the western company, while the marketability of the finished product is enhanced. Many eastern-bloc products are viewed suspiciously in the west in respect of quality. Buyback agreements and coproduction agreements make it easier for these countries to sell their products on the markets of the west. As the quality of eastern-bloc products has improved, this factor has become of less importance. Accordingly, east–west trade has become more flexible in recent decades. Nevertheless, an estimated 25 per cent of such trade takes the form of counter-trade (DTI 1985). At the same time, countertrade remains of even greater importance in trade between eastern-bloc countries and the developing countries.

2. **The developing countries** account for the main growth in countertrade in recent decades. Economic reasons predominate:

(a) Financial: Lack of foreign exchange is a major reason for countertrade, as with the eastern-bloc countries. An OECD study found that, for a sample of six developing countries, this was the primary motive for countertrade (OECD 1979). Many developing countries find themselves unable to finance imports through conventional methods. They have exhausted their foreign currency reserves and are unable to obtain credit because they are regarded by lenders as a bad risk. Countertrade becomes a method of trade finance. The recession of the 1970s and 1980s has caused many developing countries to experience severe foreign exchange shortages. Export earnings have been depressed by slower export growth, depressed commodity prices and deepening debt. Western banks have become increasingly reluctant to increase their exposure through lending any more to countries with already large, outstanding debts.

(b) Commercial: Countertrade may be a means of securing increased export sales. In the markets for many bulk commodities (e.g. minerals, coffee, cocoa, cotton, rubber, etc.), there is a great struggle to secure a share in the market in the face of static and often declining demand. By forcing trading partners to accept exports of such commodities as payment for other goods or services, a developing country may be able to increase its share of the world market.

(c) Developmental: Developing countries may use counter-trade both to obtain vital technological, capital-intensive imports needed for development and to obtain development assistance. In the first case, the developing country pays for the foreign technology and capital equipment with products, possibly on a buyback basis. In the second case, a developing country may agree to purchase goods from a developed country on condition that the latter provides it with some sort of development assistance.

There may be a requirement that the developed country source some of the components locally as under an offset agreement.

The greater part of the countertrade of developing countries takes place in bulk commodities – agricultural products and raw materials. However, some countertrade takes place in non-traditional value-added goods, such as semi-processed and processed agricultural products, metals, textiles, handicrafts, petrochemicals, and industrial goods. Many developing countries face problems in marketing such goods and so conventional methods of trading are not appropriate. Countertrading is a way round this problem, since a western company, possessing greater marketing knowledge and expertise, takes over the marketing function. However, there are many problems involved in countertrading such products. One major difficulty is amassing sufficient value for the transaction since these products are generally exported in only small quantities. Accordingly, such products appear to account for only a small proportion of countertrade (Economist Intelligence Unit 1984).

3. **The oil exporters** have used countertrade to purchase capital equipment and raw materials needed for development. These countries enjoyed large surplus revenues from oil in the 1970s and have sought to use these revenues to raise their level of economic development. Following the oil crisis of 1973–4, many western oil-importing countries were anxious to secure guaranteed, long-term sources of supply in the event of another oil shortage. They were willing to offer goods and services in exchange for oil on a counterpurchase basis. Nuclear power stations, military hardware, and other types of goods were offered in exchange for oil. Such deals were designed to ensure stable sources of supply of oil for oil-importing industrialized countries. In more recent years the tables have been turned. The oil market has softened. Oil-importing countries have, in some cases, been able to insist on countertrade as an offset for continuing to buy oil at high prices. In other words, the oil-importing country continues to pay the former high price in return for the oil-producing nation purchasing goods from the western buyer. The cost of oil is effectively reduced to the oil-importing country, but this takes the form of a purchase of goods. In some cases the oil-producing country may be forced to pay an inflated price for the manufactured goods as a way of

effectively deflating the oil price. Countertrade is attractive to the oil-producing country if it is a member of OPEC because it enables them ostensibly to maintain prices at the set minimum level without losing profits through reduced sales. The OPEC country appears to be selling at the official, cartel price but in fact is selling at a discount. Not surprisingly, countertrade involving oil-producing nations has increased rapidly during periods of oil glut. Oil is now one of the main commodities used in countertrade.

4. **The western industrialized countries** engage in countertrade to a much lesser extent than other countries. One important exception to this concerns trade in military goods, aircraft, and high-technology goods. Very often these deals involve some element of offset, as with the example of Boeing, which offered offset of up to 130 per cent in an effort to win the contract to supply Britain's airborne early-warning system. Often western industrialized countries are forced to use countertrade to secure sales to developing and eastern-bloc countries. Countertrade becomes an imperative for western companies. Unwillingness to countertrade may involve the loss of an export order. Countertrade becomes a way in which a company differentiates its product from that of competitors. Especially for companies which are not the undisputed leaders in a particular market, countertrade is essential to clinch a sale (Eisenbrand 1986). Some governments insist on countertrade as a condition for making a purchase. For example, sales to the important and expanding market of China generally require countertrade; that is, the western firm doing business must be prepared to buy Chinese goods as a condition for clinching any order. This can create problems for western companies. The marketability of Chinese goods may be in doubt. Nevertheless, the western exporter may have to take a risk on being able to sell Chinese goods in order to penetrate the Chinese market successfully. Because of the growing need to countertrade as a condition for exporting to certain countries, more and more western exporters are having to set up countertrade departments and to acquire knowledge and expertise in the marketing and distribution of goods received in payment for exports.

The rapid growth of countertrade in recent decades would appear to be closely linked with the world economic recession. Previous such downturns (e.g. the 1930s) saw a similar upsurge in countertrade. For many western companies, countertrade has become one method of coping with the problem of surplus capacity. They have used countertrade in an effort to expand their sales of manufactured goods to developing and eastern-bloc countries at a time when exports to other industrialized countries are hit by recession. Similarly, many developing countries have used countertrade to be able to market goods which might otherwise be unmarketable. Countertrade may be a way around trade barriers erected by developed countries against the exports of manufactures of developing countries. The sluggish nature of world commodity markets may also act as an incentive for commodity-exporting countries to use countertrade to gain access to markets. We have mentioned how the oil glut has served as a spur to countertrade for both oil-producing countries anxious to maintain sales and oil-importing countries keen to take advantage of the weakness in the oil price. Finally, there has been the effect of the recession on the developing countries. Export earnings have been hit by the fall in world commodity prices and the slower growth of the developed countries. Many of these countries have found themselves unable to service their foreign debt. Some have gone into default and been forced to reschedule their debt repayments. Faced with large losses, western banks have been reluctant to increase their exposure further by lending more to developing countries. Consequently, many developing countries have found themselves short of convertible currency to finance their import requirements. In such circumstances, countertrade may offer a solution.

The Effects of Countertrade

Bodies such as the GATT, IMF, and OECD have tended to express disapproval of the growth of countertrade. They have done so on the grounds that it represents a retrograde step. It entails a drift back towards the bilateralism of the 1930s, which contributed to the fall in world trade and aggravated the depression of that time. It is argued that a retreat into barter in international trade will, similarly today, lead to a decline in world trade and world economic efficiency. Unless controlled, it will snowball. These arguments are not shared by the developing countries which regard countertrade as necessary and desirable for their development, especially in the present

267

climate of recession and protectionism. Let us consider the arguments on either side.

The Economist Intelligence Unit lists six arguments **against** countertrade which are commonly put forward (EIU 1984):

1. Countertrade reduces world economic efficiency by distorting the global allocation of resources. Under a conventional, multilateral trading system, exporters sell their products to whichever buyer is prepared to pay the best price. This ensures that goods go to where there utility is greatest. Similarly, importers seek to obtain supplies from the cheapest possible source. So goods are bought from the source which can produce them most efficiently. Under countertrade, it is argued, this is less likely to happen. The geographical source of exports and imports will, in part, be determined by reciprocity considerations: that is, the need wholly or partly to match exports with imports.

2. Countertrade reduces transparency. Under a multilateral, open trading system, the prices and quantities sold and other terms of the transaction are widely known. Buyers know which is the cheapest source, exporters know who will offer them the best price. This openness facilitates the efficient working of the trading system. Under countertrading, deals struck are often not expressed in price terms. Certainly, this is true of pure barter and, to some extent, of counterpurchase. At the very least, the prices used are not known.

3. Countertrade may delay difficult economic decisions within developing countries. Developing countries may use countertrade to cope with a problem of mediocre export performance. The problem is their inability to sell goods of satisfactory quality and at a price which buyers are willing to pay. If so, more fundamental reforms are needed. Countertrading may cause the country to procrastinate in introducing these necessary reforms. For example, because of countertrading, a developing country may fail to pay sufficient attention to developing its own marketing capability. Instead, it relies on countertraders to do its own marketing.

4. Countertrade results in certain additional costs which do not arise under conventional trading methods. There are considerable transactions costs involved in drawing up and executing a countertrade agreement. Companies engaging in countertrading need to set up special departments to handle

goods purchased under countertrade and which need to be marketed. These functions may be better performed by other specialist institutions. Legal costs may be quite substantial. If these costs are borne by the western company, the developing country need not lose out (although the consumer will eventually pay in the form of a higher price). If, however, these costs are, in part, met by the developing country, it is difficult to see why countertrading is preferable to more conventional methods of trading.

5. Countertrade may lead to the dumping of goods on world markets causing injury to local suppliers and market disruption. Countertrading is frequently resorted to as a means of selling unwanted surpluses of bulk commodities which cannot be sold by conventional means. Accusations of dumping may be difficult to prove because the price at which trade takes place is concealed.

6. Countertrading may penalize small and medium-sized companies in western industrialized countries. This is because countertrading tends to be dominated by the larger firms which alone can afford to engage in countertrading. Countertrading is considered to be impractical below a transaction value of $1 million. Yet, as we have seen, unless a company is willing to engage in countertrading, it may lose potential overseas sales.

To these six disadvantages of countertrading, a seventh may be added:

7. Countertrading may lead to increased protectionism. Because of its disruptive effect on markets through the dumping of unwanted surpluses, countertrading may trigger off protectionist measures in the form of trade barriers and tariffs. Of course, countertrading is often resorted to as a means of getting round import quotas or other protectionist devices.

The developing countries reject these arguments and claim that great benefits are to be reaped by countertrading. As we have seen, countertrading involves additional costs in comparison with conventional methods of trading. This reduces the benefit to be reaped from trade, unless the developing country can force the western exporter to absorb these costs. This seems unlikely. Some share of the costs must be born by the developing country. However, if countertrading results in other benefits, it may still be worthwhile.

Developing countries have claimed the following arguments **in favour of** countertrading:

1. Countertrading accelerates the growth of world trade. Countertrading enables a country to sell goods which it might otherwise be unable to sell, or to purchase imports which it might otherwise be unable to afford. Since some element of countertrade is reciprocal, increased exports are, in part, matched by increased imports, so permitting a balanced expansion of world trade. Thus it is argued that in recent years countertrading has risen faster than multilateral trade. However, it should be born in mind that some of the increase in countertrade may have been at the expense of multilateral trade. Countertrading may lead to trade-diversion, not just trade-creation.

2. Countertrading enables a developing country to achieve a greater geographical diversification in its exports. Through countertrading, a developing country may be enabled to seek out new markets for its exports. In particular, it is argued that it may be enabled to reduce its dependence on formal colonial powers and/or other dominant, neighbouring countries. In particular, it is argued that developing countries have been able to expand their trade with the eastern-bloc countries, which tend to insist on countertrading. It has also permitted more trade between developing countries.

3. Countertrading enables a developing country to achieve faster expansion of individual export commodity sales. Not only can a developing country expand overall exports but, it is claimed, countertrading may enable it to expand its sales of individual export commodities. Once again, however, care must be taken to distinguish between trade-creation and trade-diversion. Commodity sales achieved through countertrading may lead to a loss of sales through multilateral trading. Goods sold to another country under a countertrading agreement may be re-exported to a third market, depressing sales to the third market previously achieved on a multilateral basis. Moreover, sales achieved through a countertrade agreement may involve selling commodities at a discount, reducing the benefit. In a study of six developing countries, the OECD found that, in most cases, countertrading led to trade-diversion. In certain

cases, countertrading did genuinely help to compensate for declining export sales to multilateral markets (OECD 1979).

4. Countertrading enables a developing country to enjoy more stable export earnings. A frequent concern of developing countries is the instability of their export earnings due to fluctuating commodity prices and their overdependence on one or a few basic commodities for exports. Countertrading, it is argued, may help to combat this. Under a countertrading arrangement, price and quantities sold are determined in advance. However, the OECD, in its study of six developing countries, found little evidence to support this claim. Barter-like trade was no more stable than multilateral trade (OECD 1979).

5. Countertrading enables a developing country more effectively to achieve balance-of-payments equilibrium. One of the alleged benefits of countertrading is that trade is reciprocal. For every expenditure on imports, there is a reciprocal benefit in the form of increased exports. This, it is argued, may make possible the more effective attainment of balance-of-payments equilibrium. This is one of the attractions of countertrading for the state-planned economies of Eastern Europe. However, that would only be true if all of a country's trading took place on a countertrading basis. Thus even countertrading does not always involve offsetting payments. Equally well, a country may accumulate a credit surplus on its clearing balance. Or it may only be over a period of several years that imports are paid for in the form of additional exports.

6. Countertrade enables a developing country to achieve more favourable terms of trade. This implies that either the country gets a better price for its exports or pays a lower price for its imports. This will be so if a developing country would otherwise be forced to cut the price of its export commodity in order to sell it, or if the product is of poor quality or otherwise unmarketable. The gain in higher export prices must be greater than the costs of countertrading for this argument to stand up. In practice, it is extremely difficult to make meaningful comparisons, because barter-like trade may take place without the use of prices, or the prices used may fail to reflect accurately the true worth of the transaction.

7. Countertrading enables a developing country to improve the commodity structure of its exports and imports. It is argued that countertrading enables a developing country to improve

the commodity composition of its exports. It may be enabled to sell more non-traditional, higher value-added goods (e.g. more processed and semi-processed goods). The demand for such goods is generally more income elastic than bulky commodities. At the same time, increased exports of such products enables a developing country to diversify the structure of its exports, reducing its dependency on a limited number of primary commodities. Developing countries may, due to lack of marketing knowledge and expertise, face difficulties in selling such products. Countertrading may overcome some of these problems. Having established a foothold in western markets, a developing country may then be able to expand such exports by conventional means. In fact, as we have seen, there may be problems involved in countertrading such products, specifically the smallness of the value of such goods to be transacted. Countertrading may also enable a developing country to obtain imports of goods vital to its development (agricultural products, raw materials, basic manufactures) which it could not do otherwise.

8. Countertrading may be a means whereby a developing country can reduce its external debts. This has become important in the past decade with the increased foreign indebtedness of many developing countries. Countertrading conserves foreign exchange. As such it enables a developing country faced with an acute debt-servicing and debt-repayment problem to devote more foreign currency acquired from exports to servicing and repaying the foreign debt without having to cut imports of vital food, raw materials, or intermediate goods. Many developing countries have found that a condition for a loan from the International Monetary Fund has been to cut its expenditure on imports. Countertrading may help such a country to satisfy import restrictions stipulated by the IMF and other international creditors if it leads to increased exports which can be used to finance debt repayments. In some cases, international banks faced with large outstanding loans to heavily indebted developing countries have begun to countertrade rather than increase their financial exposure by lending more. In this way, they have been able to minimize the risk of the debtor country defaulting and loans having to be wholly or partly written off. In short, the bank exchanges risky loans for risky goods, but this may be better than not getting paid!

9. Countertrading may enable a developing country to get

more development assistance. We saw earlier that development assistance may be given to a country which purchases capital goods and technology from the donor country. The importing country is granted interest-free or 'soft' credit or a straight-forward grant to enable it to buy the goods and services in question. In the case of the eastern-bloc countries, repayments of loans and interest is often financed through the delivery of goods.

The conclusions of most studies carried out on the effects of countertrading have been agnostic. Countertrading has been regarded as neither wholly bad or fully desirable. The Economist Intelligence Unit, for example, concluded that while countertrading may have many of the effects alleged by its critics, in some cases, it was beneficial to the country making use of it. It argued for countertrading to be judged on a case-by-case basis rather than a blanket disapproval. The OECD has maintained that countertrading can be advantageous to developing countries in achieving certain of their objectives. On the other hand, it may have caused some trade-diversion and neglect of multilateral trading opportunities by some developing countries (OECD 1979).

6

The Growth of Japan and the Emergence of the Newly-industrializing Countries

INTRODUCTION

In Chapter 2, when discussing the principal changes which have taken place in the geographical composition of world trade since the Second World War, attention was drawn to both the growth of Japan as a trading nation and, more recently, the sudden and rapid emergence of the so-called newly-industrializing countries. This chapter will examine each of these two important developments in the geographical structure of world trade over the post-war period. I have chosen to discuss these two separate phenomena within the framework of the same chapter because there is a strong resemblance between the rise of Japan and the more recent and equally explosive growth of the NICs. Indeed, it has been argued that Japan was the first NIC. At the beginning of the post-war period she had the structural hallmarks of a semi-industrialized economy still awaiting industrial take-off. This she successfully achieved in the course of the subsequent decades. Like the NICs, export growth played an important role in this process, although, contrary to popular mythology, it was not the main source of Japan's rapid growth. Only in recent decades has export expansion played the leading role in propelling the Japanese economy. In the case of most of the recent NICs, however, export growth has been central to their success.

Although there are many similarities between Japan's experience over the post-war decades and that of the NICs of today, there are also important differences. We must be careful not to push the comparison too far. For example, many of today's NICs have adopted an open-door approach to foreign

MNCs. They have actively sought to attract such foreign capital. The creation of export-processing zones, discussed in Chapter 5, has been one example of this. By way of contrast, for most of the post-war period Japan eschewed foreign investment. She preferred to gain access to western technology through reliance on licensing agreements. Such foreign investment as was permitted was allowed only within the framework of a joint venture. Other differences between Japan's success and that of today's NICs can be observed. As I proceed to analyse the experience of the two regions, I will try to identify some of these differences.

However, there exists another good reason for treating Japan and the NICs together as part of the same chapter. Both the rise of Japan and the emergence of the NICs have created problems for the advanced industrialized countries. Recent years have witnessed a growth of friction between both Japan and the NICs on the one hand, and the advanced industrialized countries on the other. The cause of these frictions has been the rapid expansion of manufacturing exports from both Japan and the NICs. In the case of Japan, such export growth has contributed to her large trade surplus. The western industrialized economies have been unable to achieve equivalent penetration of the Japanese domestic market. Overall, trade between the western industrialized countries and the NICs is more balanced. However, the speed and intensity with which certain NICs have been able to penetrate the markets for certain products in the western industrialized countries has caused severe adjustment problems. These have occurred at a time of much slower overall economic growth and rising unemployment.

These tensions have been the primary source of the so-called New Protectionism of recent years. We shall discuss this growth of protectionism in the next chapter. The primary concern of this chapter is with the causes and effects of the rise of Japan and the NICs. The first half of the chapter is devoted to discussing the causes of Japan's post-war growth as a trading nation. I discuss the effect which Japan's unbalanced trade has had on the rest of the industrialized world and the prospects for more balanced trade in the future. In the second half of the chapter, I turn to a discussion of the rise of the NICs. I discuss the causes of the rise of the NICs and the effect which their manufacturing exports have had on the western industrialized economies. Finally, we consider the prospects and possibilities for reduced trading frictions in the future.

JAPAN

The Post-war Growth of Japan

Japan began the post-war period as a semi-industrialized country which had been devastated by the war. In 1947 one-half of the employed population was employed in agriculture and forestry. Only 16 per cent were employed in manufacturing. In her trade with the rest of the world, she specialized largely in the export of simple, labour-intensive manufactures, such as textiles and clothing. The largest share of her exports went to other parts of Asia. For much of the early part of the post-war period, she suffered from a chronic balance-of-payments deficit. Her exports failed to grow fast enough to pay for the imports of food, raw materials, and energy which she needed. However, in the decades which followed, Japan succeeded in achieving a rapid turn-around. Between 1953 and 1973 she achieved an annual average rate of growth of 9.7 per cent, roughly twice the rate of the western industrialized economies. It compares with a growth rate of 5 per cent per annum for France, West Germany, and Italy, under 4 per cent for the United States, and 2.6 per cent for the United Kingdom (Allen 1981).

The Japanese economy was structurally transformed. The fastest rate of growth was recorded by manufacturing. Between 1953 and 1973 manufacturing output grew by a rate of 12.5 per cent per annum. This was achieved by switching resources out of agriculture and into manufacturing. By 1979 agriculture employed only 10 per cent of the occupied population, while manufacturing employed 24 per cent and services employed roughly one-half (Allen 1981). Because services and agriculture are relatively more labour intensive, these figures understate the size of the manufacturing sector. In terms of total production, in 1980 manufacturing accounted for 42 per cent of total production, services for 54 per cent, and the primary sector for 2 per cent (Kagami 1983). The importance of the services sector may be taken as a sign of the maturity of the Japanese economy, a large and rising services sector being a symptom of post-industrialization.

By 1982 Japan's GDP per capita had reached $8,974, higher than that of the United Kingdom and close to that of France ($9,962). As a trading nation, her strength was still greater. In 1950 she accounted for only 1.3 per cent of world exports. By

1981 her share has risen to 7.7 per cent. In terms of manufactures, her performance has been even more outstanding. In 1955 she accounted for about 7 per cent of world manufacturing exports. By 1983 her share had risen to over 18 per cent. In the following year she overtook West Germany to rank first in terms of her share of world manufacturing exports. What factors can account for the very fast growth of the Japanese economy over the post-war period? Why has her economy performed so much better than that of most other countries? Are there any special factors which help explain Japan's post-war economic success?

The following is a list of some of the most important causes of Japan's fast growth since the Second World War:

1. **Fast export growth** The Japanese economy experienced an extremely rapid rate of export growth over the post-war period. This is illustrated by Table 6.1. Over the decade from 1950 to 1960, only West Germany's exports grew faster than those of Japan. In the decade from 1960 to 1970 Japan's rate of export growth totally outstripped that of all other countries, including West Germany. Over the whole period from 1950 to 1970, her export growth was roughly two to three times faster than that of most other developed market economies. In the decade from 1970 to 1980, Japan's exports continued to grow faster than all other countries, but the gap between Japan and other developed countries narrowed. However, although fast export growth has been an important factor in the growth of the Japanese economy, it would be wrong to describe Japan's post-war growth as export-led. Throughout the 1950s and 1960s the external sector contributed only marginally to economic growth. The main generator of growth was domestic demand.

Table 6.1: Annual average growth rates of exports of selected developed market economies, 1950–81(%)

Country	1950–60	1960–70	1970–80
Japan	15.9	17.5	20.8
United States	5.1	7.8	18.2
United Kingdom	4.8	6.3	19.1
West Germany	16.6	11.4	19.1
France	6.4	9.8	19.8
Canada	5.3	11.8	14.9
All DMEs	7.1	10.0	18.9

Source: UNCTAD (1983).

This can be seen from an examination of Table 6.2. Over the entire decade from 1961 to 1970, net exports contributed only 0.2 percentage points towards the 10.7 per cent growth in real GNP. The largest contribution to growth came from private domestic demand (private consumption and fixed investment). Only in the two recession periods of 1974–6 and 1979–81 was it true that Japan's growth was export-led. In both these periods domestic demand was sluggish and net exports played an important role in taking up the slack. This ensured that domestic growth could be sustained. In both these periods the problem was the big deterioration in Japan's terms of trade due to the rise in world oil prices.

Table 6.2: The growth of Japan's gross national product and its components (%)

| Fiscal year | Real GNP, average annual rates | Contributions by: | | | | Annual percentage change in terms of trade |
| | | Total | Domestic demand | | Net exports | |
			Private domestic demand	Gov't demand		
1961–70	10.7	10.6	8.9	1.6	0.2	−1.0
1971–3	6.8	7.4	6.1	1.3	−0.6	−2.4
1974–6	2.8	0.9	0.3	0.6	1.9	−8.9
1977–8	5.2	5.6	3.6	1.9	−0.4	10.4
1979–81	4.4	2.5	2.2	0.3	2.0	−12.3
1982–4[a]	3.8	3.5	3.2	0.3	0.3	0.6

Source: Kagami (1983).
[a]Forecast

The reason why the contribution of net exports to economic growth was quite small for much of the post-war period was twofold. First, the size of the export sector was quite small in comparison with other countries. Throughout the 1950s and 1960s exports accounted for only 11–12 per cent of Japan's GNP compared with over 20 per cent in the United Kingdom and West Germany. Second, rapid export growth was offset by equally rapid import growth. For much of the post-war period, Japanese manufacturing industry remained relatively protected from foreign competition by high tariffs and import quotas. Similarly, Japanese agriculture has continued to enjoy relatively high levels of protection. On the other hand, Japan is exceptionally deficient in natural resources and energy and has to meet most of her requirements for these resources through imports. For much of the early part of the post-war period, the Japanese economy was balance-of-payments constrained. In years of very rapid domestic growth, imports increased rapidly and the balance of payments on current account deteriorated. It was not until 1959 that Japan's exports reached their pre-war levels, and not until 1963 that they regained their pre-war share of world trade. Only in 1964 did she succeed in achieving a surplus on her balance of trade. Even then, her large deficit on invisibles meant that her current account was frequently in deficit.

Nevertheless, export growth was an important contributory factor in Japan's economic growth. First, as we have seen, fast export growth helped pay for imports and cover Japan's traditional deficit on invisibles. Without rapid export growth, domestic economic growth would have been constrained. Thus Japan's success in exporting abroad helped remove the balance-of-payments constraint on growth. Domestic demand could be allowed to expand more rapidly. Second, the rapid growth of exports had a stimulatory effect on the rest of the economy, especially the manufacturing sector. It created a climate conducive to high levels of capital investment and enabled Japanese firms to reduce costs through large-scale production.

2. **High levels of domestic savings and investment** The Japanese economy was successful in achieving extremly high levels of capital investment in relation to national income. A much larger proportion of her GNP was devoted to capital investment than in other industrialized countries. For example, throughout the 1960s capital investment in Japan averaged over 30 per cent of GNP compared with a ratio for other industrialized countries which varied between 17 per cent in the United Kingdom and 25 per cent in West Germany. Such high levels of capital investment played an important role in stimulating Japan's capital goods industries, as well as widening and deepening Japan's capital stock. Capital widening raises economic growth by increasing a country's productive potential; capital deepening increases the productivity of a country's existing stock of capital. Japan experienced both capital widening and capital deepening.

Such high levels of capital investment were among the principal causes of Japan's rapid rate of productivity growth. High levels of investment meant that the average Japanese worker worked with both more capital and newer capital than his counterparts in the western industrialized countries. Accordingly, each worker produced more for every man-hour worked than in other western industrialized countries. Between 1955 and 1970, output per worker in Japan rose at an average rate of 10 per cent a year compared with between 4 per cent and 7 per cent in Western Europe. High levels of productivity in manufacturing industry enabled Japanese manufacturers to cut costs and increase the competitiveness of their industries. This then fed through into faster export growth and higher levels of capital investment. Japan enjoyed a virtuous cycle of growth.

Such high levels of capital investment were made possible by Japan's high levels of personal savings. Personal savings were extremely high by international standards. During the 1960s they were as much as 20 per cent of distributed national income. These savings were made available through banks and other financial institutions at relatively low interest rates. Alternatively, companies could finance their capital investment programmes out of undistributed profits. Throughout the post-war period, profits were high as improvements in productivity outstripped increases in wages.

The high level of personal savings in Japan served also to hold down consumption and free resources for investment. Many factors account for Japan's low propensity to consume and high propensity to save. However, institutional factors have been especially important. Her old-fashioned social-security system has meant that families have to put aside a high proportion of their incomes for sickness, unemployment, and old age. The inadequacy of the education system necessitates families saving more to meet the costs of education. Japan's wages system, whereby employees receive a higher proportion of their annual earnings in the form of biannual bonuses, may also have contributed to high levels of personal savings. The absence of owner-occupation of housing and the high price of residential housing due largely to the cost of land may also have contributed to a low level of consumption and high level of saving. Finally, Japan's tax system served to encourage saving at the expense of consumption. Incomes in the form of interest on savings have, in the past, been largely exempt from taxation.

3. **A high rate of technological innovation** Throughout the post-war period, Japanese firms have been successful in achieving high rates of technological innovation. Technological innovation can play an important role in economic growth both

through raising the productivity of labour and capital and increasing the competitiveness of a country's industries, thus leading to increased exports. However, the skills of Japanese inventors have largely resided in their ability to put to commercial use ideas developed in other countries. This has led to the charge that Japan's success in selling new products or developing improved methods of production was based upon imitation. Certainly, many of the new products launched by Japan were taken from other western industrialized countries. This largely took the form of purchasing western technology through licensing agreements. For much of the post-war period, Japan was largely closed to inward foreign direct investment. Japan purchased western know-how and used it to launch a large number of highly successful new products. As a result, she has developed a strong position in a number of the most technology-intensive industries, such as electronics.

However, the charge that she merely copied other countries is not fully justified. She demonstrated innate inventive and innovative skill through her ability to improve products and processes already in existence in other countries. She successfully turned many of these ideas into commercial propositions. One example of this was the video tape recorder. Japan now accounts for roughly 85 per cent of world production of VTRs. Yet the VTR was first launched commercially by an American company, Ampex, but was suitable for professional use only. Sony of Japan successfully turned the basic idea into a commercial product having a much wider application. The secret was to introduce a new technique which made it possible to cram a lot of viewing material on to a single small tape. Suddenly, a new product with a much wider potential market emerged. Expanded sales made possible further substantial cost savings. Numerous other examples of this kind exist.

Many reasons have been put forward for Japan's fast rate of technological discovery. Probably no single factor can provide a complete explanation. Some economists believe that Japan's policy of buying the technology which she needed through licensing agreements proved exceptionally successful. High levels of investment in the education and training of scientists and engineers may also have been another factor. Thus Japan trains ten times as many engineers as Britain. On average, more people are employed in research and development in Japanese industry than in other western industrialized countries. Her

281

total spending on R&D as a proportion of GNP is about as high as in other western industrialized countries and Japanese firms do not appear to devote a larger share of sales revenues to R&D than their overseas rivals. However, it would appear that they use their research effort more efficiently. It has been suggested that one reason has been that Japanese firms concentrate more on improving technologies developed elsewhere rather than on inventing totally new ideas.

4. **An abundant supply of labour** Rapid growth of manufacturing output was only possible because of the existence of a large agricultural subsistence sector with a reserve of underemployed labour. The redeployment of such labour was one of the factors which made possible big improvements in productivity. At the same time it worked to hold down wages and boost the profits of manufacturing industry. Moreover, much of the labour which was so successfully absorbed by the manufacturing sector after the war was relatively highly educated. Once, however, this pool of labour was exhausted, labour shortages began to develop. Wage rates began to rise. Japan's initial comparative advantage in labour-intensive manufactures began to disappear. However, Japan responded to this change by shifting resources out of the more traditional, labour-intensive branches of manufacturing and into the faster-growing, capital-intensive industries.

5. **A high degree of adaptability** Throughout the post-war period, the Japanese economy demonstrated a high degree of structural adaptability. Each new challenge posed by either internal or external changes in demand or supply conditions generated a response. Thus in the early 1950s and 1960s, as the pattern of world demand changed, Japan successfully switched resources out of the slower-growing, more traditional light-manufacturing industries and into the faster-growing, heavier industries, such as chemicals and machine-tools. Both the pace and manner of the transformation which took place contrasted with the experience of some of the older, more mature industrialized countries.

More recently Japan has demonstrated a similar adaptability in switching resources into the newer, fast-growing, knowledge-intensive branches of manufacturing, such as electronics. Beginning first with consumer electronics, Japanese firms then moved on to industrial electronics (e.g. integrated circuits). The development of a capability in micro-chips then enabled her to advance further into telecommunications, computers, robots, and so on. In general, she showed greater speed and foresight in anticipating the opportunities which were to develop in these industries and in switching resources into these industries once the opportunities had been foreseen.

Sometimes it is argued that the greater adaptability of the Japanese economy is due to the more interventionist role played by the government. In particular, attention is drawn to the role played by the Ministry of International Trade and Industry (MITI) in indicative planning. Certainly the Japanese economy has been unique in having a government department playing such a central role in industrial planning. However, it is important to be clear that MITI is not directly involved in industrial planning in the same way as in a centrally planned economy. No attempt is made to direct industry. The role played by MITI is largely one of identifying priorities and setting targets for each industry. These are set out in five-yearly plans for the economy. There are detailed objectives for each industry. The aim is to discuss these targets with industrialists and where appropriate to guide, exhort, and coax industry into acting on these targets by investing in particular sectors.

The government places reliance on its close links with industry at various levels. It may also make use of fiscal incentives and discrimination in the provision of loan finance to guide industry into investing in particular sectors. This is a long way short of direct planning. However important it has been in bringing about greater structural adaptation, the actual structural changes which have taken place have been dependent upon a willingness on the part of industrialists and workers to go along with such changes. The role played by the government has been largely one of drawing the attention of industry to the opportunities ahead, setting out priorities, and encouraging industry to take advantage of these changes.

The Problem of the Japanese Trade Surplus

The main problem posed for the western industrialized countries by the growth of Japan has been the increasingly unbalanced nature of Japan's trade in manufactured goods. In recent decades Japan has run extremely large trade surpluses with her two most important trading partners, the United States and

Western Europe. This has coincided with generalized conditions of depressed output and high unemployment in the western industrialized world. Japan has been attacked for adopting deliberately mercantilist trading policies. She has been accused of combining an unduly aggressive attitude towards exporting with a highly restrictive attitude towards allowing western goods entry to Japan. The attempts of Japan to respond to such criticism through measures of liberalization and export restraint have so far met with only limited success. Her western trading partners have begun to show signs of increasing impatience. Pressure has grown for protectionist measures against Japan.

The problem of Japan's trade surplus largely dates from the late 1960s and early 1970s. As we saw earlier, throughout the 1950s and early 1960s Japan was running a balance of trade deficit. Moreover, in the early part of the post-war period, roughly one-half of her exports went to other regions of Asia. Both North America and Europe were relatively unimportant. This is illustrated in Table 6.3. As Table 6.4 shows, 40 per cent of Japanese exports comprised textiles and clothing products. During the late 1950s and 1960s both the commodity composition and the geographical composition of Japanese exports changed. The importance of textiles and clothing declined, while the share of machinery and transport equipment, metals and metal manufacture, and chemicals all increased. In other words, there occurred a shift away from labour-intensive, light manufactures towards more capital-intensive, heavy goods. At the same time, the importance of the Asian market as a destination for Japanese exports diminished, while that of North America and Europe increased.

Table 6.3: The geographical composition of Japanese exports, 1954–79, percentage of total value

	1954	1960	1967	1979
Asia	48.9	36.0	34.0	38.6
Europe	9.0	13.2	16.0	19.2
North America	21.7	33.2	34.7	30.2
South America	9.7	4.4	2.7	3.5
Oceania	2.2	4.5	4.5	3.4
Africa	8.5	8.7	8.1	5.1

Source: Allen (1981), Table 31, p. 162.

Table 6.4: The structure of Japan's export trade, 1954–79, percentage of total value

	1954	1960	1967	1979
Food & drink	8.3	6.6	3.6	1.0
Textiles & clothing	40.3	30.2	16.3	5.1
Chemicals	4.8	4.2	6.5	5.9
Non-metallic mineral manufactures	4.3	3.6	2.8	1.5
Metals & metal manufactures	15.3	13.9	17.1	17.8
Machinery & transport equipment	12.4	23.0	42.1	61.3
Miscellaneous	14.6	18.5	11.6	7.4
Total	100.0	100.0	100.0	100.0

Source: Allen (1981), Table 29, p. 161.

The 1960s witnessed an especially rapid growth in Japanese exports to the United States. By 1970, 31 per cent of Japanese exports went to the United States compared with 23 per cent in 1955. Thus by 1970 the United States was Japan's most important market. However, this rapid expansion of Japanese exports to the United States was not matched by an equivalent rise in Japanese imports from the United States. By 1971 Japan had a trade surplus with the United States amounting to $3.6 billion. This more than fully accounted for the record trade deficit recorded by the United States for that year. Japan was held fully to blame for the deterioration in the United States' trading position. In August 1971 President Nixon introduced a temporary 10 per cent tariff surcharge on all imports and suspended convertibility of dollars into gold. The aim was to put pressure on surplus countries to revalue their currencies in terms of the dollar. The measures were temporarily successful. The Japanese yen was allowed to appreciate against the dollar on the foreign exchange markets. In December 1971 fixed exchange rates (but with wider bands) were temporarily restored. The dollar was substantially devalued in terms of all other currencies including the yen.

However, these exchange-rate adjustments brought only temporary relief. Japanese exporters responded to the dollar devaluation by stepping up their efforts in the West European market. Japan's exports to Western Europe accelerated. In the early 1960s only 16 per cent of Japan's exports went to Western Europe. By the late 1970s the share had risen to 20 per cent.

Between 1970 and 1980 Japanese exports to the European Community increased ten times. However, EC exports to Japan increased only five times (Wilkinson 1983). By 1980 Japan had a trade surplus with the EC of $11.1 billion. The problem was acutely depicted by trade in motor cars. In 1981 Japan imported from the EC only one car for every nine which she exported (Wilkinson 1983). At the same time, Japan's trade surplus with the United States also continued to grow. In 1971 dollar devaluation proved too little and, although the dollar depreciated further in subsequent years, it failed to correct the gross imbalance in trade between the two countries. By 1984 Japan had a trade surplus with the United States of $33.5 billion. This was the equivalent of one-quarter of the United States' total trade deficit for that year of $123 billion. At the same time, Japan enjoyed a trade surplus with the EC of $11.7 billion. In the event of the United States introducing trade restrictions against Japan, this would cause Japanese exporters to concentrate their efforts on the West European market, and Western Europe would experience an even larger trade deficit.

What are the reasons for this large trade imbalance between Japan and the western industrialized countries? Are the latter justified in charging Japan with adopting unfair trading policies? Would they be justified in introducing restrictions against Japanese goods in order to correct such an imbalance? Before considering some of the reasons for Japan's large and growing trade surplus, we need to acknowledge the fact that a situation where one country (especially an important trading country) persistently earns a large trade surplus at the expense of other trading partners does create genuine difficulties for the rest of the world. First, a liberal trading system, such as that embodied in GATT, can only function properly if countries abide by the principle of reciprocity. This means that each country offers equivalent concessions to other countries—in the form of ready access for the products of the latter to their domestic market— to the concessions which they receive from other countries, in the form of the removal or lowering of trade barriers of relevance to exporters from the country in question. In brief, no country can be allowed to be a 'free rider', enjoying all the benefits of easier access for its products to the markets of other countries but not offering equivalent access to its own home market for the products of trading partners. This principle of reciprocity constitutes an important principle of the GATT to which most countries, including Japan, now adhere. In exceptional cases it may be agreed that this principle should be 'waived'. Thus, in the mid-1960s it was decided to exempt developing countries from this principle. However, this must always be an exception. If one country seeks to 'free ride', this will create frictions between that country and the rest. Other countries will be tempted to abandon freer trade and to introduce restrictions against the products of the offending country. Once this process has started, it is likely to spread, leading to the collapse of freer trade.

Second, at the macroeconomic level a chronic surplus country makes it more difficult for deficit countries to achieve balance-of-payments adjustment. Any international monetary system must be based upon the principle of symmetry of adjustment. That is to say, payments imbalances between countries require corrective action by both surplus and deficit countries. If surplus countries fail to take action to correct their payments surpluses, all the burden of adjustment will fall on deficit countries. This will impart a deflationary bias to the adjustment process within the international monetary system. The result will be a lower level of output, employment, and economic growth than otherwise. On the other hand, if surplus countries reflate their economies at the same time as deficit countries deflate, there need be no deflationary bias. The need for this kind of symmetry of adjustment was, in part, acknowledged with the signing of the Bretton Woods Agreement in 1944. A 'scarce currency' clause was built into the agreement which authorised IMF members to introduce payments restrictions against a country whose currency was declared 'scarce' by the IMF. This clause has always been controversial and in practice has never been activated. Nevertheless, it demonstrates a long-standing recognition by countries that the pursuit of policies which lead a country to build up persistent surpluses at the expense of the rest of the world may justify retaliatory action.

Can these arguments be applied to the case of Japan? There may be a case for doing so, but before any such conclusion may be arrived at, the following must be considered:

1. Account should be taken of Japan's overall, multilateral balance of trade not her bilateral trading balance with any one other country or region. This means that it is not enough to identify the existence of a large and persistent imbalance in

trade between Japan and the United States of Japan and the EC. No liberal, multilateral trading system can function on the basis of balanced trade between every pair of countries. The only requirement must be that multilateral payments balance over a reasonable period of time. In the case of Japan, her trading surplus with the United States and Western Europe is, in part, offset by her trading deficit with the OPEC countries. For example, in 1984 Japan ran a trading surplus of $33.5 billion with the United States, but had a trade deficit of $27.5 billion with OPEC. This is a reflection of the fact that Japan is deficient in energy and natural resources and has to import these goods from abroad. To pay for these imports, she must earn a large surplus from her exports of manufactures. Nevertheless, the fact remains that, even allowing for Japan's large trade deficit with the OPEC countries, in 1984 she earned a substantial trade surplus of $32.5 billion.

2. Further account should also be taken of Japan's traditionally large deficit on invisibles. This can be seen from an examination of Table 6.5, which shows Japan's balance of payments over the period from 1972 to 1986. Throughout this period Japan ran a large deficit on invisibles. This meant that, in some years, the current balance was in deficit. This was the case between 1973 and 1975 and 1979 and 1980. On both occasions, rising oil prices reduced Japan's trade surplus such that it was insufficient to pay for her invisibles deficit. The deficit on invisibles is due to (i) payments of royalties and fees to overseas companies for imported technology, (ii) investment income payable to foreign companies operating in Japan, (iii) a deficit on tourism, and (iv) a deficit on transport and shipping. By way of contrast, the United States and some of the West European countries earn large surpluses on invisibles, as will be seen in Chapter 8. Such a pattern of trade is fairly typical of a 'catching-up' country such as Japan. Such a country is initially very dependent on the more advanced industrialized countries for capital and technology in order to catch up in industrial development. Imported capital and technology is paid for in the form of investment income to foreign companies and royalties and fees arising from licensing agreements. In the case of Japan, as we have seen, greater importance was attached to acquiring western technology by means of licensing agreements.

Table 6.5: Japan's balance of payments, 1972–86 ($m)

Year	Trade balance	Services & transfers (net)	Current balance	Long-term capital (net)	Short-term capital, errors, & omissions	Overall balance
1972	8,971	-2,347	6,624	-4,487	2,604	4,741
1973	3,688	-3,824	-136	-9,750	-188	-10,074
1974	1,436	-6,129	-4,693	-3,881	1,735	-6,839
1975	5,028	-5,710	-682	-272	-1,722	-2,676
1976	9,887	-6,207	3,680	-984	228	2,924
1977	17,311	-6,393	10,918	-3,184	9	7,743
1978	24,596	-8,062	16,534	-12,389	1,805	5,950
1979	1,845	-10,599	-8,754	-12,618	4,710	-16,662
1980	2,125	-12,871	-10,746	2,394	-44	-8,396
1981	19,967	-15,197	4,770	-6,449	-465	-2,144
1982	18,079	-11,229	6,850	-14,969	3,148	-4,971
1983	31,454	-10,655	20,799	-17,700	2,078	5,177
1984	44,351	-9,327	35,024	-49,832	-392	-15,200
1985	55,986	-6,817	49,169	-64,542	3,055	-12,318
1986[a]	40,160	-2,707	37,434	-47,872	1,783	-10,322

Sources: OECD Economic Surveys; Lloyds Bank Group Economic Report (1985).
[a] Not seasonally adjusted

In recent years, as can be seen from Table 6.5, Japan's invisibles deficit has begun to fall. Since 1981 it has fallen from just over $15 billion to just under $3 billion in 1986. There are two main reasons for this. First, Japan's investment income account has moved from deficit to surplus. In 1980 Japan earned a net $854 million from investments abroad, the first time she has been in such a position since the war. By 1984 this figure had quadrupled to $4.2 billion (*Economist*, 7 December 1985). This is the direct result of Japan becoming a net exporter of long-term capital. Over the period from 1973 to 1982 Japan was a net exporter of long-term capital to the tune of $62.2 billion (Kagami 1983). Japan has gradually accumulated a large stock of overseas assets from which she derives an annual flow of income. This trend looks likely to increase in the future. In particular, direct investment abroad by Japanese companies looks set to increase. The dearer yen and mounting trade restrictions overseas are forcing many Japanese firms to shift some of their production overseas.

Second, payments of royalties and fees for imported western technology appear to be falling relative to payments received by

Japanese companies for know-how sold abroad. Increasingly, Japanese companies are becoming inventors in their own right. Instead of purchasing new ideas from companies based in Western Europe or the United States, Japanese firms are beginning to generate a flow of innovations of their own. In the future, this can be expected to generate a flow of income to Japan, which may eventually exceed the payments being made for technology purchased from abroad. Both of these changes in Japan's invisibles account are symptoms of the maturity of the Japanese economy. Japan can no longer be described as a 'catching-up' economy. She has caught up. As this happens, the structure of her current balance will change. The invisible deficit will fall, the visible surplus will fall. Her current account will come to resemble that of the other advanced industrialized countries.

3. There is very little evidence that foreign access to the Japanese home market is any more restricted than access to the home markets of other industrialized countries. This is contrary to popular belief. However, the facts support this view. At the beginning of the post-war period it is true that Japan exercised quite tight control over her foreign trade. Imports were restricted by high tariffs and non-tariff barriers. Exports were often directly subsidized. However, in 1955 Japan joined GATT, somewhat later than most countries. This meant abandoning many of her trading practices and being willing to negotiate a lowering of her tariffs. However, Japan was slow in doing so. It took several decades for Japan to dismantle many of the restrictions previously in existence. Tariffs were gradually lowered in the various GATT rounds which have taken place since. Japan's average level of tariffs on industrial goods now stands at no more than 2.9 per cent, which is lower than any other major developed market economy. Full implementation of the Tokyo Round tariff cuts will leave the average US tariff level at 4.3 per cent, while the average rates of the EC member states range between 5.2 per cent and 6.9 per cent (Saxonhouse 1983). Any further reductions in Japan's tariffs would have only a negligible effect on her trade balance.

However, it is often argued that the main problem is not so much high tariffs but the various kinds of non-tariff barriers which foreign companies face when selling to Japan. These include (i) import quotas, (ii) customs valuation procedures, (iii) strict and discriminatory standards, (iv) lengthy testing procedures, (v) discriminatory government procurement policies, (vi) discriminatory buying policies by state trading monopolies, (vii) indirect subsidies, and (viii) export incentives. It is not possible in this book to discuss fully each of these types of restrictions. Suffice it to say that such non-tariff barriers are common in most countries. Considerable problems exist in knowing how to dismantle and control such interventions. One of the problems is that the reason for such interventions by governments is not primarily to restrict trade. Very often there are other social, health, safety, and environmental reasons for governments introducing such measures. Nevertheless, the effect of such measures is to interfere with trade. The Tokyo Round of GATT negotiations attempted to tackle the problem principally by securing agreement concerning a code for each type of distortion. There exists fairly widespread scepticism concerning the effectiveness of these agreements.

However, there exists very little substantiated evidence to support the view that Japanese NTBs are any more restrictive than those imposed by other countries. Japan has now abandoned most of her import quotas on industrial products. However, quite a large number of quotas do still exist on agricultural goods. Japan operates an estimated twenty-two quotas relating to agricultural products. This is substantially higher than most other major trading nations, with the single exception of France. Some of these quotas do relate to products of considerable interest to Japan's aggrieved trading partners. For example, the United States has long been irate concerning Japan's quotas on imported oranges and beef. With regard to subsidies, there is not much evidence that these are any higher in Japan. The OECD concluded that large subsidies were of no significance in any industrial sector within Japan (OECD 1985). Subsidies going towards R&D have also been found to be no higher than in other advanced industrialized countries.

Other kinds of NTBs are more difficult to quantify, for example the exclusion of foreign products because they do not satisfy Japanese standards or pass Japanese testing procedures. However, these barriers are not insuperable. Foreign suppliers can gain access if they are willing to alter their products and adapt to Japanese conditions. Moreover, the Japanese government has introduced a variety of liberalization measures in response to western criticism. These have made access to the Japanese market easier than in the past. Western firms have also complained about the Japanese distribution system, which is made up of a myriad of wholesalers and retailers and many more small shops than in other countries. It is argued that this is extremely difficult to penetrate. Once again, however, this problem can be overcome. Japan's system of industrial groups is also frequently cited as another culprit. Japanese firms are organized into about six large groups—each linking together groups of firms, banks, and trading houses — plus another ten groups, each linking together the suppliers and subsidiaries of a big firm or bank. These sixteen groups account for about one-quarter of Japanese sales. There exists considerable loyalty between firms within these groups in both the purchase and sale of goods and services. It is argued that this makes it very difficult for outsiders to break in. However, although these kinds of difficulty may be very real, it should not be beyond the capability of most western exporters to overcome these problems.

4. It is by no means clear that further measures of trade liberalization on the part of Japan would greatly help western manufacturing exporters. It has been demonstrated that the main effect of further measures of liberalization by Japan with a view to reducing her trade surplus with the United States would be to boost United States agriculture and cause a contraction of United States manufacturing industry (Saxonhouse 1986). In Japan, on the other hand, manufacturing industry would gain at the expense of agriculture. The reason for this somewhat surprising result lies in the fact that Japanese protection is strongest towards agriculture, while US protection is relatively more biased towards manufacturing. Both countries operate quite low tariffs on industrial products, but as we have seen, Japanese average tariffs are somewhat lower than those in the United States. On the other hand, non-tariff barriers in Japan are mainly designed to protect agriculture and are generally steeper than in the United States. Thus, if both countries removed all tariff and non-tariff barriers, United States agriculture and Japanese manufacturing would be the main beneficiaries.

If services were included, it can be shown that trade liberalization between the United States and Japan would favour US services. This is because Japan applies relatively greater protection to her services sector than the United States. We shall return to a discussion of this consideration in Chapter 8.

However, the most important point is that, in the absence of any change in macroeconomic relationships, the main beneficiary of any liberalization of trade between Japan and the United States will not be United States manufacturing. This is because, if Japanese imports increase as a result of liberalization, in the absence of any change in macroeconomic relationships, other imports must decrease and/or Japanese exports to the United States increase. In other words, it is the structure of Japan's trade which changes. This structural change will benefit US agriculture but not manufacturing. In other words, trade liberalization *per se* will not solve the problem of the imbalance in Japan's manufactured goods trade (Saxonhouse 1986).

This serves to illustrate that the problem of the Japanese trade surplus is more macroeconomic than one concerning trade policy. It is macroeconomic policies which need to be altered. There is little evidence that further measures to give greater access to the Japanese market for western exporters will itself resolve the problem. As we shall see, a country's macroeconomic policies have an effect on a country's exchange rate and the exchange rate affects the competitiveness of a country's exports and imports. If we are seeking an explanation for the problem of Japan's persistent trade surplus, we do better to focus on the exchange rate and the factors which have in the past kept the Japanese yen relatively cheap. We shall consider this in a moment.

5. Over the course of the post-war period, Japan has had a much lower level of intra-industry specialization than other western industrialized economies. In Chapter 3 we saw that Japan had a much lower index of intra-industry trade than other developed market economies. This was true even after adjustment was made for Japan's trade imbalance.

For example, in 1972 Japan's trade imbalance-adjusted, intra-industry trade ratio was only 55 per cent compared with ratios of over 70 per cent for the most advanced industrialized countries. This figure related to trade in manufactured goods only, so it was not distorted by the small proportion of manufactures in Japan's imports. To a greater extent than her western trading partners, Japan has gone in for inter-industry specialization.

This is further illustrated by Figure 6.1. This compares the pattern of export and import specialization in Japan with that of the United States and West Germany. Export specialization is measured by the share of a product group in a country's exports relative to the product group's share in total OECD exports. Import specialization is measured in the same manner. It is apparent that Japan has a much higher level of export specialization in a comparatively few product groups—electrical machinery, transport equipment, precision and other manufacturing products, and steel. This constitutes inter-industry specialization. Similarly, Japan's import specialization is concentrated in quite a few products—food and tobacco, oil refining and oil products, and non-ferrous metals. The result is that Japan's export and import specialization profile is very spikey. By way of contrast, both the United States and West Germany have much lower export and import specializations covering a wider range of product groups. This reflects a higher level of intra-industry specialization. Accordingly, their export–import specialization profile is smoother.

Intra-industry specialization makes for much more balanced trade between countries. As such, it is probably accompanied by fewer trading frictions. Where countries are undergoing intra-industry specialization, trade expansion results in a simultaneous expansion of manufacturing exports and manufacturing imports. This has been true for most of the developed market economies of the world over the post-war decades. This can be seen from an examination of Table 6.6. Japan's imports of manufactures as a percentage of nominal GNP have failed to increase over the period from 1962 to 1972. In all other countries, the ratio of imports of manufactures to nominal GNP rose markedly over the period as a whole. Given that the largest share of Japanese imports is made up of primary commodities, the demand for which is not very income-elastic, it is not surprising that the ratio of total imports to nominal GNP for Japan was also constant.

The expectation must be that this situation will change with time. Japan is no longer in a process of catching up with other industrialized countries. Almost certainly, this will lead to more intra-industry specialization in the future. In particular, the rise in the value of the yen will force Japanese exporters to move up-market into the higher-quality, higher-value-added ends of the product spectrum. They will be forced to compete more on a non-price basis. This seems likely to lead to a much lower level of inter-industry specialization and higher level of intra-industry specialization. If so, the ratio of manufacturing imports

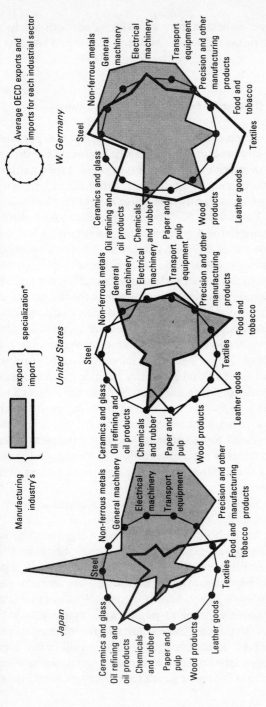

Figure 6.1 Patterns of export and import specialization in Japan, the United States and West Germany

Legend:
- Manufacturing industry's specialization* — export (shaded), import (line)
- Average OECD exports and imports for each industrial sector

Japan axes: Steel, Non-ferrous metals, General machinery, Electrical machinery, Transport equipment, Precision and other manufacturing products, Food and tobacco, Textiles, Leather goods, Wood products, Paper and pulp, Chemicals and rubber, Oil refining and oil products, Ceramics and glass

United States axes: Steel, Non-ferrous metals, General machinery, Electrical machinery, Transport equipment, Precision and other manufacturing products, Food and tobacco, Textiles, Leather goods, Wood products, Paper and pulp, Chemicals and rubber, Oil refining and oil products, Ceramics and glass

W. Germany axes: Non-ferrous metals, General machinery, Electrical machinery, Transport equipment, Precision and other manufacturing products, Food and tobacco, Textiles, Leather goods, Wood products, Paper and pulp, Chemicals and rubber, Oil refining and oil products, Ceramics and glass, Steel

* Export (import) specialization (i.e. relative share) = share of product group in country's exports (imports) relative to product group's share in total OECD exports (imports).

Source: A Survey of Japan: What Makes Yoshio run? *Economist*, 9 July 1983.

to GNP can be expected to rise. The result will be more balanced trade in manufactures between Japan and the rest of the world.

The Exchange Rate and Macroeconomic Adjustment

Earlier it was argued that where one country earns a persistent balance of payments surplus, this creates problems for the rest of the world. For much of the past fifteen years, Japan has been in this position, as can be seen from Table 6.5. Her current account has been consistently in surplus, except for the oil-crisis years of 1973–5 and 1979–80. These were years when most of the western industrialized countries were similarly afflicted by oil-induced balance-of-payments deficits. Whatever qualifications we may wish to make to this fact, it remains the case that Japan has acted in the manner of a chronic creditor nation. This has created genuine problems of adjustment for the rest of the western industrialized world. Moreover, Japan's large belance-of-payments surpluses are hardly of benefit to the Japanese, who have as a result foregone potential improvements in their standard of living. This is because a current-account surplus is an expression of the fact that a country has been underconsuming. She has been spending less than her income. This can be seen from Table 6.5. The counterpart of Japan's current-account surplus is her capital-account deficit. Japan has used her regular surpluses to accumulate long-term overseas assets. Although such assets will generate a flow of income to Japan in the future, they do nothing to raise the standard of living of the Japanese people.

The correct solution to such a problem is for countries either to (1) increase/decrease domestic expenditure, or (2) alter the exchange rate, or (3) both. In international economics the first approach is known as expenditure-changing policy and the second as expenditure-switching policy. In the case of Japan the solution to her current-account surplus lies in increasing domestic expenditure in relation to income. At the same time, on the assumption that Japan's export and import elasticities add up to more than one, the exchange rate must be raised. This makes foreign goods cheaper relative to domestic goods and so encourages Japanese consumers and foreigners to switch their spending from Japanese goods to foreign-produced goods.

Table 6.6: Japan's imports as a percentage of Japan's nominal GNP

(a) RATIO OF TOTAL IMPORTS TO NOMINAL GNP (%)

	1955	1973	1983
Japan	10.9	9.2	10.9
United States	2.9	5.3	8.2
West Germany	13.6	15.8	23.3
France	9.5	14.7	21.2

(b) RATIO OF IMPORTS OF MANUFACTURES TO NOMINAL GNP (%)

	1962	1973	1982
Japan	2.8	2.8	2.8
United States	1.3	3.4	4.7
West Germany	6.0	9.1	13.0
France	4.8	9.5	12.3
United Kingdom	4.7	12.0	13.4

Source: Saxonhouse (1986).

At the same time, deficit countries need to reduce their domestic expenditure relative to income and, on the assumption that their export and import elasticities add up to more than one, lower their exchange rate.

One of the weaknesses of the Bretton Woods fixed-exchange-rate system, which collapsed in 1971, was that there was no effective pressure on surplus countries to introduce such adjustment policies. They were generally unwilling to risk increasing inflation by increasing the level of domestic expenditure. Even if domestic expenditure was increased, there was no guarantee that this would be used to buy more foreign goods. Such expenditure-increasing measures needed to be supported with expenditure-switching policies which make foreign goods more attractive to buy. However, surplus countries were reluctant to reduce the profitability of their exporters by raising the exchange rate. Instead, surplus countries looked to deficit countries to put their houses in order first.

When the Bretton Woods system collapsed in 1971 the entire western industrialized world gradually moved over to various systems of floating exchange rates. At the time it was hoped that this would make adjustment easier. Now, there was no obligation on countries actually to alter their exchange rates.

Exchange rates would be determined by market forces. This would mean that the currencies of deficit countries would depreciate and those of surplus countries would appreciate. This would bring about balance-of-payments adjustment automatically through expenditure-switching. Governments would need do nothing except allow market forces to do their work.

The reality has been different. Exchange rates have been free to find their own levels on the foreign-exchange market. This has meant quite large movements in exchange rates from week to week and month to month. However, exchange rates have rarely moved in such a way as to achieve equilibria in countries' balance of payments. The result has been that for much of the period since 1971 the Japanese yen has remained grossly undervalued. Indeed, over the period from 1981 to 1985, the critical dollar–yen rate moved in entirely the opposite direction to that which was required to restore balance-of-payments equilibrium between the United States and Japan. The dollar appreciated and the yen depreciated. This aggravated the disequilibrium which already existed in the two countries payments balance with each other. The US trade deficit reached record levels. At the same time, as can be seen from Table 6.5, the Japanese current account surplus soared to new heights.

What were the reasons for this situation? The answer probably lies in two sets of factors:

1. **Inconsistent macroeconomic policies** Exchange rates will generally fail to achieve the necessary balance-of-payments adjustment if countries pursue entirely inconsistent macroeconomic policies. The existence of freely-floating exchange rates does not obviate countries from the need to co-ordinate their macroeconomic policies, even if it does give them a little more freedom to pursue the domestic policies of their own choosing. For much of the period in question, US and Japanese domestic economic policies were working in opposition to each other. The result was to bring about a perverse movement in the exchange rate which was aggravated by speculation. A country's current balance can be shown to be given by the difference between the country's private savings and investment $(S - I)$ and the public sector deficit $(G - T)$. Therefore the current balance $(X - M)$ may be defined as:

$$(X - M) = (S - I) - (G - T)$$

It follows from this that a current-account deficit is the result of either an excess of private investment over private savings or a deficit in the public sector or both.

The large current-account deficit experienced in recent years by the United States can be put down to both these sets of factors. First, the US economy has a traditionally low level of private savings relative to private investment. Second, in recent years, the public sector has recorded extremely large deficits. This can be seen from Table 6.7. This shows the financial flows (lending minus borrowing) of the different sectors of the economy. These are expressed as a percentage of the country's nominal GNP. It can be seen that the savings of the household sector in the US economy were more than sufficient to meet the investment needs of the corporate sector. In other words, the private savings–investment balance was positive. However, this was more than offset by the extremely large public sector deficit. This amounted in 1985 to some 5 per cent of GNP. It was not possible to finance all of this deficit from the excess savings of the private sector. Hence the need for an offsetting financial surplus for the foreign sector. This means that part of the public sector budget deficit had to be financed by an inflow of capital from abroad. This amounted to 1985 to some 2.9 per cent of US GNP. This inflow of capital from abroad (the US capital-account surplus) had its exact counterpart in the US current-account deficit. In other words, the US current-account deficit is fully accounted for by the large US public-sector deficit and the failure of private-sector savings fully to finance this. From Table 6.7 it can be seen that this financial imbalance only became pronounced in 1983. In 1981 and 1982 private-sector savings were just adequate to cover the public-sector deficit.

Similarly, the large Japanese current account surplus has arisen from reverse considerations. First, private-sector savings have vastly exceeded the private-sector borrowing requirements. As can be seen from Table 6.7, household savings have been so large that the household sector has regularly turned out a financial surplus of between 9 per cent and 11 per cent. This considerably exceeds the financial surplus of the household sector in the United States. The Japanese corporate sector has regularly run a financial deficit which is significantly higher than in the United States, but this is capable of being fully financed by the surplus of the household sector. Second, although the Japanese public sector has run large deficits in most years, this

299

Table 6.7: US and Japanese sectoral financial balances, 1981–5 (% of nominal GNP)

	1981	1982	1983	1984	1985
UNITED STATES					
Household	4.7	5.2	3.5	3.7	2.5
Corporate[a]	−2.1	−0.3	0.7	−1.6	−0.3
Financial institutions	0.3	0.2	0.5	0.3	0.4
Government[a]	−2.2	−4.7	−5.1	−4.2	−5.0
Foreign	−0.3	0.0	1.0	2.4	2.9
JAPAN					
Household	11.0	10.8	10.4	9.3	9.4
Corporate	−3.0	−3.8	−3.7	−2.1	−2.4
Financial institutions	−0.2	0.6	1.8	1.3	0.8
Government[b]	−7.3	−6.9	−6.8	−5.8	−4.1
Foreign	−0.4	−0.7	−1.8	−2.8	−3.6

Source: Masera (1986).
[a]Based on B.I.S. calculations
[b]Including public enterprise

is still small in relation to the financial surpluses of the private sector. (The Japanese public-sector deficit is not fully comparable with that of the United States because the former includes public enterprise.) Moreover, between 1981 and 1985 the public-sector deficit fell from 7.3 per cent of GNP to 4.1 per cent. This has left the private sector with a large surplus even after meeting the financial needs of the public sector. Accordingly, this has been invested abroad, giving rise to a large foreign-sector deficit. In 1985 this reached 3.6 per cent of Japan's GNP. Most of these excess savings found their way to the United States, being used to finance the United States' large budget deficit.

The mechanism through which these changes have taken place is as follows. In the United States the large public-sector deficit could not be fully financed out of private-sector savings. The demand for loanable funds exceeded the supply, forcing up interest rates. This expansionary fiscal policy was not matched by an equivalent, accommodating monetary policy, thus ensuring that interest rates remained high. In Japan the vast surplus of the private sector could not find sufficient outlets in the purchase of public-sector debt. The supply of loanable funds exceeded the demand, and interest rates fell. This caused a flow of capital from Japan to the United States. Japanese investors placed their excess savings abroad, where higher interest rates could be earned. This pushed up the value of the dollar and forced down the value of the yen. The strength of the dollar made the holding of US assets even more attractive to overseas investors so long as the dollar did not look likely to fall. At the same time, the strength of the dollar made US goods less price-competitive, while the weakness of the yen increased the price-competitiveness of Japanese goods. The US trade deficit widened, as did the Japanese trade surplus. Thus the counterpart of the large inflow of capital to the United States was the US current-account deficit. Similarly, the counterpart of the large outflow of capital from Japan was the Japanese current-account surplus.

Table 6.8 illustrates this divergence in both short-term (money market) and long-term interest rates in Japan and the United States respectively. Taking short-term rates first of all, nominal rates in the United States were consistently higher than in Japan. Real rates, adjusted for inflation, were slightly below those of Japan at the end of 1982 and end of 1985. This reflected the different stance of monetary policy at those times. However, for most years, real short-term rates were lower in Japan. The divergence in long-term (government bond) rates is even more pronounced. Nominal long-term rates were consistently higher in the United States throughout the period in question, and on some occasions they were nearly twice as high. The gap in real long-term rates was less but, even so, was apparent for every year covered. Only towards the middle of 1986 was there some evidence that real long-term rates were beginning to converge.

It follows that a solution to the problem of the Japanese current-account surplus and more specifically, the payments imbalance between the United States and Japan, requires an adjustment in macroeconomic policies in both countries. First, action needs to be taken in Japan to reduce the high level of savings of the private sector and to boost consumption. This might be achieved through a lowering of the general level of taxation in Japan and through taxing savings in the same way as consumption. However, as we shall see in a moment, Japan's high level of savings and low propensity to spend are partly rooted in Japanese institutions and require a different kind of reform of the Japanese economy. Second, the United States must act to reduce the size of its public-sector deficit whether by tax increases or public expenditure cuts. Third, action needs to

Table 6.8: Nominal and real interest rates in the United States and Japan, 1982–6

	1982 Dec.	1983 Dec.	1984 Dec.	1985 Dec.	1986 Jan.	Feb.	Mar.	Apr.	May	Jun.	Jul
MONEY MARKET RATES											
United States:											
N	8.9	9.5	8.4	8.3	8.1	7.9	7.5	7.0	6.8	6.9	6.6
R	4.9	5.5	4.3	4.3	4.1	4.5	5.1	5.3	5.2	5.1	4.9
Japan:											
N	6.9	6.4	6.4	8.0	6.8	5.8	5.5	4.7	4.2	4.4	4.6
R	5.0	4.6	3.7	6.1	5.4	3.9	4.4	3.8	3.0	3.8	4.5
LONG-TERM GOVERNMENT BOND RATES											
United States:											
N	10.6	12.0	11.6	9.7	9.6	9.1	8.1	7.5	7.8	7.7	7.3
R	6.5	7.9	7.4	5.7	5.5	5.7	5.7	5.8	6.2	5.8	5.6
Japan:											
N	7.5	6.9	6.3	5.8	5.8	5.2	4.7	4.7	5.1	5.0	5.1
R	5.6	5.1	3.6	4.0	4.3	3.3	3.6	3.7	4.0	4.4	5.0

Source: Masera (1986).
N = Nominal Rates
R = Real rates

be taken in the United States to reduce private consumption and encourage savings.

Only if such efforts to bring domestic economic policies into line in the two countries are pursued will it prove possible to achieve lasting adjustment in the two countries' current balances. Action to bring about a change in the exchange rate will be unlikely to succeed unless supported by such measures. In September 1985 the fact that exchange rates had moved grossly out of line was recognized by the Group of Five when they met at the Plaza Hotel in New York. Hence it was agreed to abandon the previous policy of not intervening on the foreign exchange markets and leaving currencies to find their own values. Instead, all five countries agreed to make a co-ordinated effort to bring about a substantial devaluation of the dollar in terms of the yen. There was a belief that if the authorities in all five countries acted with determination to bring about such a realignment of rates, this would be sufficient to affect the psychology of the markets. Neither the value of the dollar nor the yen bore any resemblance to the so-called trading 'fundamentals' which underlay them. Therefore all that was needed was action to alter the false convictions of the markets. The new approach of the Group of Five met with some success. In the following twelve months, the dollar plummeted and the yen rose sharply. The yen appreciated by approximately 40 per cent and the Plaza Accord was hailed as a major success.

It has demonstrated that, under certain circumstances, co-ordinated and determined intervention on the foreign exchange markets can achieve results. However, unless the problem of macroeconomic policy inconsistencies is tackled, the Japanese surplus will remain. At the time of writing, despite the sharp appreciation of the yen, the Japanese surplus remains high. Partly this is because of the so-called 'J-Curve' effect, whereby exchange-rate appreciation always causes a country's balance-of-payments surplus to increase before it decreases. This is because the rise in the yen increases the unit price of Japanese exports, while the volume of Japanese exports only falls in the longer-term as overseas buyers switch away from Japanese goods. However, the other reason why the Japanese surplus remains large despite the rise in the yen is the fact that domestic policies are still out of line. The US budget deficit remains large while Japanese consumption is too low. Unless this problem of policy imbalance is tackled, the problem of the Japanese trade surplus seems likely to remain.

2. **Illiberal financial institutions and markets** A second reason for the undervaluation of the yen over much of the post-war period has been the absence of competition in Japan's financial markets and the high degree of regulation exercised by the central authorities over Japan's financial institutions. Most important in this regard have been the controls exercised by the authorities over interest rates and regulations preventing competition between different kinds of financial institutions. This has had several effects. First, and most importantly, interest rates have not been free to rise in response to a change in market conditions. For example, until recently, government bonds were issued by the government at a rate fixed below the market rate. The bond issue was substantially underwritten by the city banks, so that the authorities never need be concerned about not selling all the debt issued. This arrangement was extremely convenient for the central authorities as it ensured that the government was able to finance its entire borrowing requirement at relatively low rates of interest. Other interest rates have also been tightly controlled by the authorities. In recent years substantial progress has been made towards liberalization of financial markets. Nevertheless, the interest rates which banks can charge are still controlled.

These controls have kept the price of capital relatively low in Japan. On the one hand, such low interest rates have failed to check Japan's high propensity to save. Household savings appear to be highly insensitive to changes in interest rates. On the other hand, low interest rates have acted as a definite stimulus to private investment spending. As we have just seen, the investment–savings imbalance is one of the causes of Japan's current-account surplus. At the same time, low interest rates have induced private investors to place their savings abroad where interest rates are higher. Under normal market conditions, this outflow of capital abroad could be expected to exert an upward pressure on interest rates. Higher interest rates would then act to increase the external value of the yen. However, because interest rates are prevented from responding to such market imbalances, the yen has remained undervalued.

Second, fewer financial instruments are available for both the Japanese investor and the foreigner wishing to hold yen-dominated assets than are to be found on other equivalent financial markets. For example, until recently there was only one type of government bond available to the investor, namely a seven-year coupon bond. Many of the various kinds of short-term financial instruments available to financial institutions and companies in the money markets of London or New York were non-existent in Tokyo (e.g. before 1979 there was no certificate-of-deposits market). The range of different savings instruments available to the ordinary household also remained very small. The greater part of personal savings was placed with postal savings banks which enjoyed special tax privileges. From the point of view of the exchange rate, the most important aspect of these regulations has been the effect which they have had on the international demand for yen assets. For example, until recently, there was no yen-denominated bankers' acceptance market. Such a market helps facilitate the use of commercial bills by enabling the issuers of such bills to get their bills 'accepted' by a reputable financial institution. The absence of such a market in the past has meant that yen-denominated bills of exchange cannot be traded. The effect has been to limit the use of the yen in trading settlements. For example, in 1982 only 37 per cent of Japan's exports were denominated in yen and only 2 per cent of imports, compared with the 80 per cent or more of German exports, which are priced in marks, and 40 per cent of imports (*Economist*, 19 November 1983).

Again, until recently the volume of Euro-yen lending was tightly controlled, while Japanese residents were restricted in issuing Euro-yen bonds. Euro-yens are yen deposited with banks in Europe which are then reloaned to borrowers inside or outside Japan. In other words, it is a market in yen assets outside Japan. These restrictions imposed by the Japanese authorities have impeded the development of a Euro-yen market equivalent to that which exists for dollars and other leading currencies. This has further reduced the attraction of the yen as an international currency.

Third, although progress is being made towards the removal of restrictions on foreign investment in Japan, capital inflows are still subject to certain restrictions. This further reduces the demand for yen and contributes to the undervaluation of the yen. In particular, there exist many restrictions on foreign banks and other financial institutions wishing to establish themselves in Japan. Until recently, foreign banks were not free to buy and sell Japanese government bonds. Admission of foreign securities firms to the Japanese stock exchange is still strictly limited, although the situation is changing slowly.

However, considerable progress has been made in recent years in the liberalization of Japan's financial markets. This is due to a variety of pressures. Domestically, the last few decades have seen a large increase in the Japanese government's borrowing requirement. There has taken place an enormous increase in the volume of government bonds outstanding. The old arrangements whereby banks underwrote the bond issue and bonds were issued at a rate fixed below the market rate have become too restrictive and too burdensome for the banks. The government has had to persuade non-bank investors to buy bonds in order to avoid the inflationary effects of large budget deficits. This has necessitated the development of a secondary market in bonds with rates determined by market forces. The authorities have also begun to offer a variety of different types of securities to attract different types of investors. Deregulation of the bond market has brought in its wake pressures to liberalize the markets for other short-term assets.

A further source of pressure for deregulation has been external. Japan has been under international pressure to widen the use of the yen as an international currency in order to reduce the risk of the yen being undervalued. At the same time, within Japan the rise of the yen following the implementation of the Plaza Accord in September 1985 has created pressures to encourage outflows of capital. This has led to the removal of certain restrictions on yen-lending to non-residents. Japanese companies are now raising more of their funds in the form of foreign currencies than in the past. Finally, Japan's financial markets are slowly being opened up to more foreign banks and securities firms. The UK government has been especially forthright in calling for rights of access such as are offered to Japanese financial institutions wishing to set up in London.

In one sense it could be argued that the root cause of the friction between Japan and the rest of the western industrialized world lies in the illiberal nature of Japanese institutions in general, not just financial institutions. This argument has been put forward by Gary Saxonhouse, who has emphasized the necessity of harmonization of microeconomic institutions as a prerequisite for maintaining the post-war liberal trading order (Saxonhouse 1983). It is no longer sufficient for international trading policy to be confined to ensuring that tariffs are non-discriminatory and that countries refrain from quantitative restrictions on imports. Trade may still be distorted by differences between countries in the liberalism of their microeconomic institutions. In Japan several of her institutions are subject to a much greater degree of regulation and government intervention than in other countries. Not only is the financial system highly regulated—as we have seen, government also plays an important role in industrial policy. We have also seen how the structure of the Japanese economy is highly concentrated in the hands of a comparatively few large trading companies. This may make it more difficult for foreign companies to penetrate the Japanese market. The Japanese government also plays quite a major regulatory role in the area of product standards, which may give rise to certain non-tariff barriers to trade.

To the extent that this is true, a solution to the problem of the Japanese trade surplus lies not so much in lowering trade barriers as in the harmonization of Japanese institutions. As Japan's microeconomic institutions are brought more closely into line with those of other western trading nations, some of the frictions between Japan and the rest of the world can be expected to disappear. In a sense this is part and parcel of the process which has been taking place since the Second World War—more precisely, following the admission of Japan to GATT in 1955—of integrating the Japanese economy into the western trading system. However, this process of incorporation must embrace the liberalization of microeconomic institutions and not just tariffs and commercial policy. However, in one important area of trade policy, trade restrictions do continue to contribute directly to Japan's large current-account surplus, namely agriculture. Although all other western industrialized countries operate highly protectionist policies towards agriculture, the degree of protection afforded to Japanese farmers is high even by European standards. Rice imports are prohibited and the price of rice is kept at some three times the cost of importing it. Wheat and barley are mainly imported, but the price is kept artificially high. Likewise, prices of beef, sugar, and dairy products are all kept high by government intervention buying. The result is that Japan is roughly 70 per cent self-sufficient in food (*Economist*, 7 December 1985). High food prices reduce the real incomes of consumers and thus contribute to low consumption. High levels of agricultural protection serve also to increase the price of land and thus the cost of residential sites. Earlier it was seen that this was one of the factors causing the cost of housing to remain high in Japan and contributing to

Japan's uniquely high savings ratio. Finally, high levels of agricultural protection directly contribute to Japan's current-account surplus by limiting food imports.

Future Prospects

Although there are many factors which have contributed to the problem of the Japanese trade surplus, in essence they can be reduced to a single causal factor—namely, the backwardness of the Japanese economy relative to her main trading partners for much of the post-war period and the fact that, for much of this time, she has been in a process of 'catching-up' with the rest of the industrialized world. Such relative backwardness has expressed itself in the character of many of her economic institutions and practices, which diverge from those in the more industrialized countries. Although, in terms of trade and income per head, Japan has caught up with the advanced industrialized countries of Western Europe, she has continued to lag behind in other respects. Perhaps this has been reinforced by the relative cheapness of the Japanese yen, which has discouraged investment abroad by Japanese companies and kept Japanese exporters shut into low-price, high-volume manufactures. This may account for the high level of her inter-industry specialization relative to other industrialized countries. However, the cheapness of the yen is, as we have seen, at least partially the result of institutional bias within the Japanese economy. For example, the high level of personal savings can be accounted for in terms of certain institutional defects in the Japanese economy.

From this it follows that the key to the solution of Japan's trade surplus lies in institutional reform. In recent years this has been taking place in response to a variety of external and domestic pressures. Unfortunately, progress has often been too slow for Japan's trading partners. Faced with rising trade deficits set against the background of persistently high levels of unemployment, the western industrialized countries have begun to drift towards imposing trade restrictions on Japanese goods. In the United States, in particular, considerable congressional pressure is building up for the federal administration to impose restrictions on Japanese goods, where equivalent access to the Japanese market is denied to US exporters. While such measures may serve to apply pressure on the Japanese government to speed up her programme of reform of the economy, they seem unlikely to resolve the main problem of the trade deficit. Such restrictions risk provoking counter-measures which will do more harm to US and West European exports. Moreover, they fail to tackle the main cause of the large Japanese current-account surplus. This, as we have seen, has its origins in inconsistencies between Japan's macroeconomic policies and those of her trading partners and the illiberal nature of Japanese institutions, especially in her financial markets. More important than any restrictions imposed on foreign manufactures is the high level of protection which Japan grants to her farmers. Low levels of farm protection and easier access for western agricultural products would do more to reduce the Japanese trade surplus than measures designed to restrict Japanese exports.

Although such changes require conscious action by the authorities in Japan as well as in other countries, we can expect to see some diminution of the tension between Japan and the western industrialized world in future decades with or without any such action. This is because of the growing maturity of the Japanese economy. Japan has now caught up with the rest of the industrialized world. This is bringing in its wake certain changes inside and outside Japan which will bring about changes in Japan's trading patterns and reduction in the size of her trade surplus. These are the changes which naturally accompany the progress of an economy from relative underdevelopment to maturity. They are changes which have already taken place in other industrialized countries and therefore can be expected to be repeated in the experience of Japan. The following are some of these changes:

1. **Slower export growth** Japan cannot expect to enjoy the same rates of export growth in the future as she has in past decades. One reason for this is the increase in the value of the yen. Already, at the time of writing, this process is in evidence. The days of the cheap yen would appear to be over. In addition to the cost of the yen, Japanese exports are already facing difficulties of access to many of her traditional western markets. A rising proportion of Japanese exports is now subject to voluntary export-restraint agreements or some other type of quantitative restriction. For all these reasons, Japan cannot rely

upon exports to achieve fast rates of growth in the future. A greater emphasis will have to be placed on domestic expansion if the Japanese economy is not to stagnate. For much of the post-war period, unemployment has been virtually unknown to Japanese workers, partly because of Japan's unique lifetime-employment system. Now, however, that is changing. This will necessitate government action to stimulate private-consumption demand which, if successful, will act to reduce Japan's investment–savings imbalance.

2. **A change in the composition of exports** The higher exchange rate is likely to bring about a change in the make-up of Japanese exports. In particular, it is likely to cause Japanese exporters to abandon some of the more traditional, low-price, high-volume lines and to move up-market into the higher-quality, high-value-added lines in which price competition is less important. As we have seen in earlier chapters, these are the kinds of products in which intra-industry specialization, as opposed to inter-industry specialization, prevails. Therefore this should result in a higher proportion of Japan's trade taking the form of intra-industry trade, bringing Japan more closely into line with the rest of the western industrialized world.

3. **A growth of Japanese direct investment abroad** Another effect of the higher exchange rate will be to increase direct investment abroad by Japanese companies. The growth of import restrictions aimed at Japanese goods in western markets will also serve as an incentive for Japanese companies to shift more of their production abroad. In Chapter 4 we saw that Japanese companies had a much lower degree of multinationality than their US and European rivals. They have preferred to service their North American and European markets through exports rather than overseas production. The cheapness of the yen has encouraged this. Already this situation is changing fast and looks certain to continue doing so in the future. This may have a further dampening effect on Japanese exports. On the other hand, the accumulation of more overseas assets will raise Japan's investment income from abroad, as was noted earlier. Japan's invisibles deficit will accordingly fall. This will serve to increase the value of the yen and reduce the visibles surplus.

4. **A reduction in Japan's high savings ratio** Although it is extremely difficult to predict the future course of the Japanese savings ratio, there are grounds for believing that this ratio will be lower in the future. Research has shown that the main cause

of Japan's high savings ratio has been the relatively low ratio of old people to the working-age population (Horioka 1986). Old people tend to dissave during their retirement while young people tend to save with a view to future retirement. Hence the greater the proportion of old people to young people, the lower the level of total savings. The ratio of aged people to working-age population is expected to rise in the future as a result of a declining birth rate and increasing life expectancy. Improved pensions and social-security benefits will also tend to reduce the need to save for retirement. Greater availability of house mortgages may also serve to reduce the high savings ratio. Any progress made in reducing high levels of agricultural protection would, by lowering the cost of residential sites, increase owner-occupation of housing and thus reduce the propensity to save.

5. **Liberalization of financial markets and institutions** Earlier we saw how the Japanese authorities have been compelled by domestic exigencies and external pressures to begin a process of deregulation of financial markets. This can be expected to continue in the future. This should lead to more flexible interest rates and greater competition in the financial markets. More market-based interest rates will serve to increase the attraction of yen-denominated assets and boost the value of the yen. The yen's importance as an international currency—both as a store of value and medium of exchange—will increase. This will act to reduce the extent of the private savings–investment imbalance in Japan, which is the counterpart of the current-account surplus. At the same time, easier access for foreign banks and other financial institutions to the Tokyo market will enable certain western industrialized countries to earn increased foreign currency from financial services, which should help offset their deficit on trade in visibles.

THE EMERGENCE OF THE NEWLY-INDUSTRIALIZING COUNTRIES

In hindsight Japan may be regarded as being the first of the post-war newly-industrializing countries. In the last ten or twenty years the Japanese experience has been partially repeated by a number of other developing countries. It is with reference to these countries that the expression 'newly-industrializing country' (NIC) has most commonly been used.

There exists no official definition or list of NICs, but the term has come to be loosely applied to a relatively small group of developing countries which have, in recent decades, become major exporters of manufactures. The OECD adopted a three-fold criteria for identifying a developing country as a newly-industrializing country:

1. Fast growth in both the absolute level of industrial employment and the share of industrial employment in total employment.
2. A rising share of world exports of manufactures.
3. Fast growth in real per capita GDP such that the country was successful in narrowing the gap with the advanced industrialized countries (OECD 1979).

Using these criteria, the OECD listed ten countries as NICs: Spain, Portugal, Greece, and Yugoslavia in Europe; Brazil and Mexico in Latin America; Hong Kong, Korea, Singapore, and Taiwan in South-East Asia. The choice of countries is necessarily arbitrary. Other countries, having large industrial bases, might also have been included, for example India or Argentina. Moreover, the list of countries to which the label NIC may be given will tend to change over time. Some countries will graduate from being NICs to becoming fully-fledged industrialized countries in their own right. Other developing countries may succeed in achieving take-off and will get added to the list.

All the ten countries listed above experienced an increase in the share of industrial employment in total employment over the period from 1963 to 1979. In addition, they all succeeded in significantly increasing their share of world exports of manufactures. In 1963 their share of world exports of manufactures stood at 2.6 per cent. By 1979 it had risen to 8.9 per cent. Finally, all ten countries enjoyed rapid growth in their real per capita GDP such that they began to catch up with the advanced industrialized countries. This is illustrated in Table 6.9, which shows the real per capita GDP of the ten NICs expressed as a percentage of United States' real per capita GDP. All ten countries were successful in increasing their real per capita GDP as a percentage of that of the United States.

Table 6.10 lists some nineteen upper-income developing countries, which to varying degrees display some of the characteristics of NICs, although not all of these countries would usually

Table 6.9: Real and nominal per capita GDP in selected countries, 1963–76

	Real per capita GDP at constant average international prices				Nominal GDP
	1963	1970	1974	1976	1976
ADVANCED INDUSTRIALIZED COUNTRIES					
United States	100	100	100	100	100
Canada	77	82	90	90	95.2
Denmark	65.4	73.4	73.1	73.4	94.4
Norway	62.5	68.4	72.7	76.4	94.0
Germany	67.4	74.5	75.7	76.0	93.5
Belgium	55.3	62.3	68.4	65.9	85.9
France	63.1	71.7	77.0	78.5	83.0
Netherlands	54	62.3	64.5	63.6	78.6
Japan	36.3	57.7	62.6	64.3	62.2
United Kingdom	63.9	62.5	61.4	60.1	51.0
NEWLY INDUSTRIALIZING COUNTRIES					
Spain	33	39.7	45.1	43.8	37.0
Singapore	23	31.7	40.2	42.4	34.2
Greece	28.7	38.7	42.2	44.9	32.8
Hong Kong	20.2	27.1	30.7	34.9	26.7
Portugal	20.7	27.1	33.8	31.5	21.4
Brazil	21.8	23.0	29.4	31.1	14.4
Mexico	23.8	26.0	26.5	25.4	13.8
Taiwan	14.4	18.6	22.1	23.7	13.6
Korea	9.3	13.2	17.0	19.9	8.5

Source: OECD (1979).

be listed as NICs. All the countries listed had a per capita GNP in excess of $1,000. Most enjoyed relatively fast growth over the period from 1965 to 1983. The fastest rates of growth were achieved by the South-East Asian NICs—Singapore, South Korea, and Hong Kong. Jordan also enjoyed a very fast rate of growth over the same period. At the other extreme, some of the South American countries experienced very little growth or even negative growth (Chile). Undoubtedly, this was due the debt crisis facing all of these countries and the fact that growth had to be sacrificed for these countries to meet debt repayments and service charges. Other countries experiencing somewhat slower growth included Israel and South Africa.

All nineteen countries had relatively high ratios of manufacturing to both GDP and total merchandise exports. The ten countries in the top half of the table, except for Mexico, had the

Table 6.10: Leading developing countries exporters of manufactures in 1983

Country	GNP per capita ($), 1983	Average annual growth rate 1965–83 (%)	Share of manufacturing in: GDP, 1983 (%)	Share of manufacturing in: Merchandise exports, 1983 (%)	Average annual growth rate of merchandise exports, 1973–83
Singapore	6,620	7.8	24	58	–
Hong Kong	6,000	6.2	22	92	10.3
Israel	5,370	2.9	–	80	9.0
Greece	3,920	4.0	18	51	9.7
Yugoslavia	2,570	4.7	32[a]	78	–
South Africa	2,490	1.6	–	74	5.6[b]
Portugal	2,230	3.7	35[a]	75	–
Mexico	2,240	3.2	22	12	14.4
Brazil	1,880	5.0	27	39	8.2
Korea	2,010	6.7	27	92	14.8
Uruguay	2,490	2.0	26[a]	32	9.2
Argentina	2,070	0.5	28	24	8.6
Chile	1,870	-0.1	20	10[a]	9.7
Malaysia	1,860	4.5	19	23	4.9
Jordan	1,640	6.9	15	50	17.8
Colombia	1,430	3.2	17	25	2.8
Tunisia	1,290	5.0	14	33[a]	-0.2
Turkey	1,240	3.0	24	43	6.3
Venezuela	3,840	1.5	17	–	-6.8

Source: World Development Report (1985).
Notes:
[a] 1981
[b] 1982

highest ratios of manufactured exports to total exports. In the case of Hong Kong and South Korea, manufactured goods accounted for over 90 per cent of total exports.

Finally, most of the countries listed experienced relatively fast rates of growth in the volume of their merchandise exports. Jordan, South Korea, Mexico, and Hong Kong all experienced the fastest annual growth rates. At the other extreme, Venezuela experienced negative growth (probably mainly due to declining oil exports), while Tunisia and Colombia experienced only slow growth.

It is apparent that there exist quite a few developing countries which possess some of the hallmarks of NICs. We may find it helpful to think of a number of different tiers of NICs. The countries listed in the top half of Table 6.10 may be regarded as 'first-tier' NICs, which display most of the characteristics common to NICs. Eventually, many of these countries can be expected to graduate to the status of fully industrialized countries. The countries listed in the bottom half of the table may be thought of as 'second-tier' NICs, which have yet to imitate fully the pattern and pace of industrialization of the first-tier NICs. Nevertheless, it seems probable that before very long some of these countries will gain promotion to the first division and become fully fledged NICs.

Whatever list of NICs is adopted, it is apparent that they comprise a wide variety of different countries. They differ considerably in terms of population, geographical size, culture, religion, political system, and economic policies. Some of these countries have adopted extremely *laissez-faire* economic policies, others have adopted more authoritarian, state-interventionist measures. However, one feature which is common to all NICs is the emphasis placed upon outward-looking, export-oriented economic policies. Such a strategy of development may be contrasted with one which is inward-looking, import-substitution in orientation. Many of the NICs began the post-war period with the latter approach to development in an effort to conserve foreign currency and to develop national industries sheltered from foreign competition. However, in the late 1960s and early 1970s some countries became increasingly disillusioned with such policies. The emphasis switched to policies which gave positive encouragement to the export of manufactured goods. The aim was to overcome the foreign currency constraint not so much by restricting imports but by fostering the development of a strong manufacturing export sector. This in turn would provide a stimulus to the domestic economy through the growth of ancillary industries and the increased demand for locally produced consumer goods and services brought about by the higher incomes earned by workers employed in the export industries.

Such policies met with a high degree of success in the 1970s and 1980s. At a time when world output and world trade was slowing down in the western industrialized countries, a number of developing countries were able to boost their exports of manufactured goods. Over the period from 1973 to 1983, the upper-income developing countries succeeded in increasing their exports at a rate of 4 per cent a year. This compares with a growth in the exports of developed market economies of only 3 per cent a year. Some individual NICs managed an even faster expansion of their exports. For example, the exports of South Korea grew by nearly 15 per cent a year, as can be seen from Table 6.10. Among the first-tier NICs, South Korea, Mexico, Hong Kong, and Greece all achieved over 10 per cent a year rate of expansion of their exports.

In the past, NICs have tended to specialize in the export of relatively simple, highly standardized, labour-intensive light manufactures. This is because their comparative advantage tends to lie in goods which require inputs of large amounts of relatively unskilled labour. However, in recent years a number of the NICs have successfully advanced up-market into a range of skill-intensive products in which they have become highly competitive. Table 6.11 illustrates the commodity composition of merchandise exports of various NICs. The relatively high share of total exports accounted for by textiles and clothing is apparent, especially for Hong Kong, South Korea, Portugal, and Greece. However, for certain countries, machinery and transport equipment also accounts for quite a high proportion of total exports. This was the case for Singapore, Yugoslavia, and South Korea. Other manufactures also accounts for a high proportion of the exports of certain NICs, notably South Africa, Israel, Yugoslavia, South Korea, and Hong Kong. For all NICs the share of total exports accounted for by non-oil primary commodities fell over the period from 1960 to 1981.

Some noteworthy differences do exist between different NICs. Thus the South-East Asian NICs appear to have developed

Table 6.11: The commodity composition of merchandise exports for selected NICs, 1960 and 1981 (% shares)

Country	Fuels, minerals, & metals		Other primary commodities		Textiles & clothing		Machinery & transport equipment		Other manufactures	
	1960	1981	1960	1981	1960	1981	1960	1981	1960	1981
Singapore	1	29	73	15	5	4	7	26	14	26
Hong Kong	5	1	15	2	45	42	4	18	31	37
Israel	4	2	35	17	8	6	2	19	51	56
Greece	9	18	81	28	1	20	1	5	8	29
Yugoslavia	18	6	45	15	4	11	15	29	18	39
South Africa	29	14	42	13	2	1	4	2	23	70
Portugal	8	9	37	20	18	27	3	13	34	31
Mexico	24	–	64	–	4	–	1	–	7	–
Brazil	8	14	89	45	0	4	(.)	18	3	19
Korea	30	2	56	8	8	30	(.)	22	6	38

Source: World Bank (1984)

a relatively stronger specialization in labour-intensive consumer goods, such as clothing products and footwear. On the other hand, some of the geographically larger NICs in Southern Europe (e.g. Spain and Yugoslavia) and South America (e.g. Argentina and Brazil) have a relatively strong specialization in capital-intensive, intermediate goods, such as steel and ship-building. One reason is that the latter group of countries was much slower to adopt outward-looking, export-oriented economic policies. For several decades they had sought to establish new capital-goods industries behind the protection of high tariffs and other import barriers. The relatively large home market which these countries enjoyed enabled such industries to grow to a size where they could fully exploit available economies of scale. This enabled these countries to become relatively competitive internationally in such products. By way of contrast, the South-East Asian NICs lacked any such market. They could not hope to establish strong, competitive capital-intensive industries by erecting high import barriers. At the same time, they lacked food and natural resources and had to export to pay for these necessities. Thus, from an early stage they were compelled to adopt outward-looking, export-oriented policies. Given these countries' abundant supplies of cheap labour, it was natural that their comparative advantage should develop in labour-intensive, highly standardized goods.

However, while that was the case to begin with, the situation is now changing fast. In many of the NICs, rising wage costs are eliminating their former comparative advantage in such labour-intensive, simple manufactures. This is forcing these countries to shift resources into the production of more skill-intensive goods, such as office machinery and electrical and electronic equipment. For example, in 1963 engineering products accounted for only 13 per cent of NIC exports. By 1976 they accounted for 29 per cent (Chenery and Keesing 1981). As the first-tier NICs move up-market, they vacate territory for second-tier NICs. Increasingly, the latter group of countries is occupying the position in world markets left vacant by the first-tier NICs. Whether or not this second generation of NICs will be able to repeat the experience of the first generation remains conjecture at this stage. However, before considering this question, it will be necessary to account for the rise of the first generation.

Explanations for the Growth of the Newly-industrializing Countries

What factors can account for the sudden and very rapid rise of the NICs in the late 1960s and 1970s? Was the process automatic in the sense of a gradual spread of industrialization from the more central regions of North America and Europe to peripheral regions such as Asia, South and Central America, and the south of Europe? Or were there specific factors at work during these two decades which fostered the growth of a group of developing countries as major exporters of manufactures? If it was an automatic process of industrialization spreading from central to peripheral regions, why did some developing countries succeed where others have failed? For example, there are virtually no NICs to be found in the continent of Africa. Even within Asia, some countries have been much more successful than others.

The following is an attempt to list and discuss some of the main factors at work both in the world economy and in the NICs themselves which explain their sudden emergence during this period.

1. **Global shifts in comparative advantage in manufacturing industry** Over the course of the post-war period, an important change was taking place in the geographical location of comparative advantage in certain sectors of manufacturing industry. At the beginning of the post-war period, the comparative advantage in most branches of manufacturing resided with the industrialized countries of North America and Europe. These countries had a unique advantage in the production of such goods. Their labour force was better educated and more skilled for employment in the production of manufactured goods. They enjoyed much higher levels of capital investment. Their home markets were larger enabling them to achieve the necessary economies of scale in capital-intensive industries. Above all, they possessed the technological know-how to produce most kinds of manufactured products.

However, over the course of the post-war period these countries managed to lose their competitive edge in certain branches of manufacturing. These were the more traditional, low-technology, labour-intensive industries, such as textiles and clothing, footwear and leather goods, certain kinds of simple

319

electrical goods, and a wide variety of miscellaneous consumer manufactures. To some extent they also included some of the older, capital-intensive, heavy-goods industries such as iron and steel and shipbuilding. One reason for this was the rise in labour costs in the advanced industrialized countries consequent upon the growth in the degree of trade unionism and the exhaustion of supplies of underemployed labour drawn in the past from the agricultural subsistence sector. By way of contrast, many developing countries could offer large supplies of such labour. Meanwhile, increased investment in education and training in certain developing countries meant that much of the available labour in such countries was suitable for industrial employment. Investment in physical capital also meant that many developing countries possessed an adequate infrastructure for the establishment of manufacturing industries capable of exporting part of their output abroad.

Especially important was the outworking of the product life-cycle in many branches of manufacturing. A number of products first discovered and produced in the advanced industrialized countries were coming of age. In the framework of the product life-cycle theory, such products had achieved maturity. This meant that to a large extent their production had become highly standardized. The technology required to produce such goods was relatively well known. In any event, countries could always acquire such technology either through attracting direct investment by multinational corporations or buying such know-how by means of a licensing agreement. The foreign-currency earnings from the resultant exports would help to pay foreign companies for the technology thus obtained. At the same time, developing countries enjoyed the advantage of low labour costs in the production of such goods. As such goods reach the stage of complete standardization, the demand for the product tends to become highly price-elastic. This places a premium on locating production where costs are lowest. Thus a number of developing countries were able to develop a strong comparative advantage in a range of highly standardized manufacturing products.

2. **The development of the new international division of labour**
An especially important role in this process has been played by the new international division of labour. This has been discussed in some depth in Chapter 5. In that chapter we saw that there were a number of factors which brought about the

development of the NIDL. One of those factors was techno-logical change. The post-war period led to a number of major advances in the design of products which made possible a more advanced division of labour. The production of many products was capable of being split up into a number of separate processes, each of which could be located at sites in different countries. Revolutionary improvements in methods of trans-port and communication and new developments in manage-ment co-ordination further facilitated such a division of labour. At the same time, the NIDL made for lower production costs because it made possible fuller exploitation of available econ-omies of scale at each separate stage of production and enabled each stage to be located where production costs were lowest.

This led multinational companies to relocate the more labour-intensive, final assembly, or processing stages of production at sites located in developing countries. This process of vertical disintegration of production played an important role in en-abling a number of developing countries to industrialize. They were able to attract foreign investment which led to the establishment of plants which assembled or processed semi-finished goods imported from developed countries. The finished good was then re-exported to markets in the industrialized countries for resale and distribution. In the case of the clothing and textile industries, the same effect was achieved through manufacturers in the industrialized countries subcontracting local firms to carry out the making-up stages of manufacture using fabrics specifically produced and supplied from abroad and according to predetermined designs. The result was that the manufacturing exports of such developing countries enjoyed an enormous boost.

3. **The role played in newly-industrializing countries by export-processing zones** In Chapter 5 it was noted that an important role has been played in the NIDL by specially established export-processing zones (EPZs). These have proved to be particularly attractive to companies based in industrialized countries who are contemplating an export-platform investment in a newly-industrializing country in order to take advantage of the NIDL. Such EPZs offer foreign companies possible sites for such investments with exemption from certain taxes, very low or zero levels of tariff, exemption from minimum-wage laws and certain other kinds of legislation, and cheap or subsidized infrastructure (e.g. port facilities, power supplies, etc.). Such

EPZs are a very common feature of all NICs. According to the United Nations, in 1980 there were fifty-three such EPZs in developing countries employing not quite one million people. The majority were located in NICs in Asia, Latin America, and the Caribbean (UNCTC 1983). Table 6.12 lists the main EPZs in existence in 1978 and shows where they were located. In EPZs 72 per cent of total employment was accounted for by seven NICs—South Korea, Singapore, Mexico, Hong Kong, Malaysia, the Phillipines, and Brazil. EPZs appear to be most common in electrical and electronic goods and textiles and clothing. In the electronics industry, United States, European, and Japanese companies have all set up processing plants in EPZs mainly located in South-East Asia and Latin America. In the case of the United States, Mexico has been highly important as a site for final assembly and processing of manufactured goods. This has been especially pronounced in the assembly and testing of semiconductors (micro-chips). In most cases, United States manufacturers have made use of EPZs in developing countries (UNCTC 1983). However, the importance of EPZs must not be exaggerated. They still account for only 4 per cent of the manufactured exports of South Korea, 12 per cent for the Phillipines, 26 per cent for Sri Lanka, and 41 per cent in Malaysia. However, we can expect the number of such zones to increase in the future.

4. **The offshore assembly provisions granted by certain industrialized countries** Another factor which has been important in facilitating the take-off of a large number of the NICs has been the offshore assembly provisions (OAPs) which industrialized countries have granted to certain manufactures imported from developing countries. Although the exact nature of these OAPs varies from one industrialized country to the next, they are generally confined to finished manufactures which have been assembled or processed overseas using components and parts imported from the country granting the OAP. The import tariff applied to such goods is imposed on the value-added in the exporting country, not the final selling price of the good. This means that the effective barrier to such imports is thereby reduced. For example, suppose the final selling price of a music centre assembled at an offshore site in a developing country is £500. Suppose that music centre embodies components and parts produced in the importing developed country before being exported for assembly at the offshore site overseas.

Table 6.12: Employment in export-processing zones in NICs

Country/territory	Employment
AFRICA	
Mauritius	17,500
Senegal	600
	18,100
ASIA	
Hong Kong	59,600
India	3,200
Malaysia	56,000
Phillipines	24,000
Republic of Korea	120,000
Singapore	105,000
Sri Lanka	5,200
Other Asia	77,400
	451,000
LATIN AMERICA & CARIBBEAN	
Brazil	27,300
Colombia	2,800
Dominican Republic	14,400
El Salvador	2,900
Haiti	40,000
Honduras	1,500
Jamaica	1,000
Mexico	70,000
Nicaragua	5,000
Panama	600
	165,000
MIDDLE EAST	
Egypt	10,000
Jordan	600
Syrian Arab Republic	600
	11,200
TOTAL	645,800

Source: UNCTC (1983), Table IV.6, p. 156

Suppose that the value of these components and parts was equal to £250, so that the value added in the developing country was £250. Suppose further that the developed country which imports the finished product operates a 10 per cent tariff on imported, fully assembled music centres. If the tariff is applied

323

to the final selling price, the effective tariff amounts to £50. If, however, the tariff is applied only to the value added abroad, the effective tariff amounts to only £25. Such provisions built into the tariff schedules of industrialized countries create an enormous incentive for multinational companies to hive off the final assembly or processing stages of manufacture of certain products and relocate these stages of production at offshore sites based in developing countries. Thus OAPs have played an important role in fostering the development of the NIDL and promoting the growth of NICs.

The United States includes such provisions in its tariff schedule. The relevant parts are (a) Item 806.30, covering metal articles manufactured in the United States but exported for processing and returned to the United States for further processing (mainly covering semiconductors) and (b) Item 807.00, applicable to any sort of article assembled in foreign countries with components manufactured in the United States regardless of whether the processing is carried out by a US firm or whether the good is subject to further processing in the US or whether foreign components have been combined with US components (although the import tariff falls on the value of the imported product less the value of US-fabricated components). Not all US OAP imports come from developing countries, but the share of developing countries in total OAP imports has been rising. By 1976 it amounted to nearly one-half. Of the share coming from developing countries, 97 per cent came from twelve developing countries. Mexico was the leading offshore processor and, along with Taiwan, Singapore, Hong Kong, and South Korea, provided 82 per cent of the total. In recent years, however, a number of new developing-country bases have begun to open up (Lall 1980). Of the OAP imports coming from developing countries, 81 per cent comprised metals and metal products, most of which were electronic products (e.g. semi-conductors, electronic memories, TV, and radio apparatus, etc.). A large part (58 per cent) of OAP imports coming from other developed countries consisted of motor vehicle imports (Lall 1980).

Other countries have also made use of OAPs in attempting to encourage offshore processing, but less data are available concerning the nature and extent of their OAP imports. In the case of West Germany, more of her OAP imports came from developed countries, mainly in Eastern Europe (most notably,

Yugoslavia). Some 59 per cent of her OAP imports came from Eastern Europe. However, many of these countries may be suitably classified as NICs. The majority of her OAP imports were textile products, in contrast to the United States, where electronic products predominated. Unlike the United States, German laws require that all overseas processing be conducted by German firms (Lall 1980). Similarly, most of the Netherlands' OAP imports came from East European NICs. Textiles again made up 41 per cent of the total, with machinery accounting for another 29 per cent (Lall 1980).

Such OAP imports appear to have grown rapidly in recent decades. Exports of manufactures by developing countries which are covered by OAPs in industrialized countries appear to have grown even faster than total developing country exports of manufactures. For example, between 1970 and 1976 total manufactured exports of developing countries rose by 305 per cent, while such exports subject to OAPs in the United States alone rose by 530 per cent (Lall 1980). If we compare the imports of non-OAP manufactures of developed countries with imports of OAP manufactures from developing countries, the rapid growth of OAP trade is even more apparent. For example, for the United States over the period 1966 to 1972, imports of non-OAP manufactures grew at an annual rate of 12 per cent per annum. Imports of OAP manufactures from developing countries grew at a rate of 60 per cent. The corresponding figures for West Germany were 11 per cent and 36 per cent and for the Netherlands 2 per cent and 39 per cent (Lall 1980).

For the advanced industrialized countries, such tariff provisions bring obvious benefits. They promote an increased division of labour between developed and developing countries, which may be mutually beneficial. Developed countries should experience a simultaneous expansion of both exports and imports. Hence their balance of payments need not suffer, while the total level of economic activity is likely to be raised. Faced with the alternative of losing large sections of manufacturing industry to developing countries, it may be preferable to encourage the hiving-off of the most labour-intensive processes in order to ensure some presence in the industry in the future. Moreover, in so far as offshore processing cuts production costs, it will increase the competitiveness of a given industry within the OAP-granting country relative to other non-OAP-granting competitors.

5. **The adoption of outward-looking, export-oriented policies by a number of developing countries** Earlier it was stated that one of the hallmarks of an NIC was the adoption at some stage in the country's development of an outward-looking, export-oriented development strategy. An important factor contributing to the sudden emergence of the NICs was the fact that such policies became fashionable in the late 1960s and early 1970s. The countries which switched over to such policies were invariably the countries which were the most successful. It may be helpful to compare an outward-looking, export-oriented economic policy with an inward-looking, import-substitution economic policy:

(a) Import substitution: Such policies were highly fashionable in developing countries for roughly the first two decades after the Second World War. Usually such policies involved two phases. In the first phase, an attempt was made to develop domestic production of consumer goods, usually initially of the non-durable type, such as food and beverages. This was achieved through imposing high tariffs or other restrictions on imports of the products in question. Multinational companies which previously exported these products to the country in question would now have an incentive to produce the goods locally. In the second phase, import barriers were similarly used to encourage the development of local intermediate-goods industries and the production of capital goods, as well as other consumer durable goods.

Alongside high import barriers, import-substitution policies often involved a variety of other measures similarly designed to restrict spending on imported goods such as multiple exchange rates. These involved charging residents a much lower exchange rate for foreign currency to acquire non-essential imports, than the rate applicable for necessities. However, in general an import-substitution policy aimed to achieve a high exchange rate so as to keep down the costs of imported raw materials and other intermediate goods needed for industrial development. The aim of all such measures is to protect domestic industry from foreign competition and encourage the development of local industry with or without the assistance of foreign capital.

Such a policy has many attractions for a developing country. First, in theory, it reduces the country's dependence on the advanced industrialized countries to the extent that it is successful in establishing local production of goods previously imported. Of course, the developing country may still be dependent on the advanced industrialized countries if the locally produced goods are manufactured by a multinational company. Second, such a policy will enable a developing country to conserve scarce foreign currency and ensure that it is used only for the purchase of essentials. All developong countries face such a foreign-exchange constraint to development because they lack the ability to earn sufficient foreign curency through exporting while the demand for imports tends to be great in the early stages of development.

Furthermore, a policy of high import barriers has strong theoretical support in the familiar infant-industry argument used to justify protection in developing countries. According to this argument, in industries where production is subject to increasing returns to scale, protection may be needed in the early years of the life of the industry so as to enable it to grow to a size where it can compete with the industries of developed countries. However, the record of such import-substitution policies in developing countries has been disappointing. Such policies have rarely worked in the manner intended for the following reasons:

(i) Fast growth of domestic demand for locally-produced light consumer goods in the first phase of such import-substitution policies enormously increased the demand for intermediate goods used as inputs by the consumer-goods sector. Since such goods could not be produced locally, they had to be imported. Thus such policies largely failed in achieving their primary objective of restricting imports.

(ii) Import-substitution policies tended to discriminate against industries that were more geared to exporting than to production for the home market. Export industries faced the double penalty of a high exchange rate and more costly intermediate goods because of the high tariffs applied to imports. Such policies had a home-market bias. By stifling the development of export industries, such policies increased the scarcity of foreign currency. At the same time since export industries often achieved higher levels of productivity than industries largely geared to the home market, economic growth was stunted.

(iii) Import-substitution policies often necessitated large

327

amounts of finance. The development of locally based industries required capital investment. Often, domestic savings were inadequate. Hence foreign capital had to be attracted. Especially in the second phase of import substitution, direct investment from abroad was needed since most developing countries lacked the necessary know-how to produce these goods themselves. This created a dependence on foreign capital, while necessitating a flow of investment income to foreign capital in the future.

(iv) Import-substitution policies also discriminated against agriculture. High levels of protection granted to consumer-goods industries—which, incidentally, were often retained even in the second phase of import substitution—raised the prices of consumer goods relative to agricultural goods. The domestic terms of trade were shifted in favour of manufacturing relative to agriculture. This proved to be detrimental to the long-term development of farming.

(v) High import barriers often served to increase the extent of monopoly and oligopoly power enjoyed by local producers in the affected industries. In many branches of manufacturing in developing countries, production is in the hands of a comparatively small number of producers. The presence of a large foreign multinational company may also act to prevent the emergence of indigenous local producers. The result may be high prices and high levels of inefficiency due to the lack of any import competition.

For these reasons, the import-substitution policies of the 1950s and early 1960s did not work as well as had been hoped. In the late 1960s and early 1970s, disillusionment began to set in with the results of such policies. It was against this background that a number of developing countries began to switch over to more outward-looking, export-oriented development strategies.

(b) Export promotion: Disillusionment with import-substitution policies was accentuated by a comparison of the difference in growth rates between developing countries adopting outward-looking strategies and those of countries still pursuing import-substitution policies. The South-East Asian developing countries—Hong Kong, South Korea, Taiwan, and Singapore—achieved exceptionally favourable rates of growth from adopting outward-looking strategies. As a result, their example was quickly followed by a number of other developing countries, notably those of Latin America.

What is an outward-looking, export-oriented economic policy? Although the balance of measures may vary from one country to the next, such a strategy usually involves a combination of the following:

(i) A more liberal trading policy, including lower tariffs, fewer import quotas, and fewer import prohibitions, although some of the Latin American NICs have continued to adopt quite high tariffs. However, exporters are accordingly subsidized to offset the cost of more expensive inputs.

(ii) A much lower exchange rate, making exports cheaper and imports more expensive. In this way, the discrimination against export industries is eliminated.

(iii) The introduction of a variety of direct and indirect incentives to encourage exporting, such as export subsidies, favourable tax treatment for exports, and the setting up of export-processing zones. For example, exporters may be granted exemption from indirect taxes.

(iv) The introduction of a relatively tight domestic monetary and fiscal policy in order both to keep down domestic costs and prices to ensure export competitiveness and to ensure that goods are not diverted from exporting to meet excess home demand.

(v) The elimination of many exchange controls, including multiple exchange-rate systems, but priority may still be given to exporters in the allocation of scarce foreign exchange.

The exact mix of these different policy measures may vary between countries. However, in all cases, the emphasis is switched from measures designed to promote growth through the restriction of imports, towards measures designed to promote growth through export expansion. Many advantages are claimed for such policies. The following are the main ones:

(i) Export-oriented policies give greater encouragement to the industries in which developing countries are likely to have a strong comparative advantage. These are the industries which require relatively large amounts of unskilled labour.

329

Import-substitution policies, by way of contrast, especially in the second phase of import substitution, tend to encourage the development of capital-intensive and skill-intensive industries, in which developing countries are unlikely, at least initially, to possess a comparative advantage. Because the industries promoted by export-oriented policies are generally more intensive in unskilled labour, such policies may also have a more egalitarian effect on income distribution.

(ii) Export-promotion policies provide local producers with greater scope for exploiting economies of scale. In many developing countries, the home market is too small for newly established, capital-intensive industries to achieve a size necessary for capturing all the advantages of large-scale production. However, under an export promotion policy, a developing country may be able to specialize on a limited number of products and thereby fully exhaust all available economies of scale.

(iii) Fast export growth can be expected to have a stimulating effect on the domestic economy through increased demand for the goods of ancillary industries and through increased demand for consumer goods as those employed in the export sector spend their higher incomes.

(iv) The removal of import barriers and the exposure of local producers to foreign competition may impose a much-needed discipline on firms, forcing them to hold down prices and increase efficiency.

(v) An export-oriented strategy makes it easier for a country to develop new industries in the future as the nature of the country's comparative advantage changes. For example, as a country industrializes and is successful in accumulating more capital and industrial skills, it will develop a comparative advantage in the more capital-intensive and skill-intensive branches of manufacturing. Resources will automatically shift out of the more labour-intensive and into the more capital-intensive and skill-intensive sectors as these changes take place. By way of contrast, there is a danger that an import-substitution strategy will shut resources into low-technology industries.

Other advantages have been claimed for outward-looking strategies. However, against all these advantages, we must set the one major problem which such a strategy poses: it is dependent on the willingness and ability of developed countries to go on absorbing large amounts of manufacturing exports from developing countries. Such outward-looking policies proved to be successful in the relatively liberal trading climate of the late 1960s and early 1970s. Increasingly, however, the western industrialized countries have become concerned at the threat posed by such exports to their ailing industrial sectors at a time of high unemployment and general recession. Should the advanced industrialized countries fall into permanent stagnation and/or introduce wide-ranging restrictions against developing-country manufacturing exports, the viability of such export-oriented strategies may be put into doubt. I will return to a discussion of this question towards the end of this chapter when discussing future prospects for NICs.

6. **The role played by trade policies in the western industrialized countries** Export-oriented policies worked in the environment of the late 1960s and early 1970s largely because the markets of the western industrialized countries were still growing and relatively open. One factor which may have helped the NICs to expand their exports of manufactures was the system of trading preferences for the exports of developing countries introduced by the western industrialized economies during this period. These preferences were known as the generalized system of preferences (GSP). These were introduced by the western industrialized countries in 1971 in response to pressure from the United Nations Conference on Trade and Development (UNCTAD). Ever since UNCTAD was first established in 1964, developing countries had been pressing for preferential treatment for their exports in the markets of the developed countries. This involved a fundamental alteration of the principles of non-discrimination embodied in the GATT and which had formed the basis of the liberal trading order of the post-war period. However, GATT rules did permit a 'waiving' of the non-discrimination principle should the member states agree to do so. In the case of exports from developing countries, it was seen as a way of assisting the growth and development of these countries. Preferential treatment of developing country exports was seen as a form of positive discrimination in favour of such countries.

These preferences were gradually introduced by all the main western industrialized economies, beginning with the EC in

1971, Canada in 1974, and the United States in 1976. They involved the application of a zero or very low tariff on imports of manufactures from developing countries. Superimposed on this system of preferences, the EC introduced its own additional preferences on imports from some forty-six African, Caribbean, and Pacific countries (the ACP countries) which in 1975 signed the Lomé Convention. The actual benefit accruing to developing countries from the granting of such preferences must not be exaggerated. Preferences are subject to a number of qualifications:

(a) Limited country coverage: Not all developing countries have benefited from these preferences because, for political or other reasons, they have been specifically excluded.
(b) Limited product coverage: Not all products are included, some of the more 'sensitive products' being specifically excluded (e.g. textiles, clothing, footwear, electronics products).
(c) Ceiling limitations: Preferential treatment is often restricted to only a certain quantity of imports, such that where imports exceed the stipulated ceiling limitation they are subject to the normal, non-preferential rate of duty.
(d) Stringent rules of origin: These require that the products be wholly or largely manufactured in the country of origin, this usually being stipulated in terms of some ratio of value-added in the country of origin to total costs of production.

The effect of the above qualifications is to reduce the amount of developing country exports which stand to gain from preferential treatment. Further account needs to be taken of the fact that some products were exempt from duty even before GSPs were introduced. Taking all these factors into account it has been estimated that GSPs affect only 12 per cent of the exports of developing countries (Stein 1985). A large number of countries appear to enjoy almost no benefit from the scheme. It has been argued that developing countries would stand to gain more from a general non-discriminatory reduction in tariffs on goods of special interest to them than from any extension of the existing GSPs. In many cases, developing-country exports are already competitive in price and quality and therefore benefit little from preferential treatment. Furthermore, a general non-discriminatory reduction in tariffs would not be subject to the quantity limitations mentioned above. There would also be no case of any developing country being excluded.

However, leaving aside these deficiencies of the GSP scheme as a means of assisting the developing countries, the facts remain that it did play some role in fostering the growth of the NICs. If not all developing countries benefited from the scheme, some countries clearly did. These were the countries best placed to take advantage of easier access to developed country markets. They showed great adeptness at expanding the exports of particular products not subject to rigid quantity limitations. Attempts to measure the effects of GSPs have found that some ten NICs accounted for all the imports of developed countries covered by GSPs in 1975. Five countries were identified in 1970 as being the exporters of 55 per cent of the goods exported by GSP benefactors—Taiwan, Mexico, Yugoslavia, South Korea, and Hong Kong (Stein 1985). In brief, trade liberalization through GSPs did play an important part in expanding manufacturing exports from a small group of NICs even if the benefits of the scheme were minimal for developing countries as a whole. Recent years, however, have seen a growth of protectionism in developed countries, which will make it more difficult for other developing countries to repeat the pattern of development of the first-generation NICs.

Effects of the Rise of the Newly-industrializing Countries

What has been the effect on the world economy of the sudden and rapid rise of the NICs? What problems have the NICs posed for the advanced industrialized countries? Are the fears and anxieties expressed by industrialists and trade unionists about import penetration by developing country manufactures well-grounded? It will not be possible to discuss fully all these issues until Chapter 7, when some of the theoretical aspects of trade adjustment will be discussed. The present chapter will merely consider the nature and extent of the alleged threat posed to the developed countries by developing-country manufacturing exports.

Table 6.13 shows the nature of trade in manufactured goods between the OECD countries (i.e. the major western industrialized countries) and the NICs. As we saw earlier, the OECD listed ten NICs—Spain, Portugal, Greece, Yugoslavia, Brazil,

Mexico, Hong Kong, South Korea, Singapore, and Taiwan. Table 6.13 shows OECD imports from NICs, and OECD exports to NICs. The trade balance shows the difference between exports and imports. Taking the trade balance to begin with, it can be seen that the OECD countries taken as a whole enjoyed a substantial trade surplus in manufactures. This rose from $3.97 billion in 1963 to $24.51 billion in 1979. Thus, in aggregate, the NICs were more important as markets for the manufactures of the western industrialized countries than as sources of manufacturing imports. However, two industrialized countries did face small deficits in their manufacturing trade with NICs. In 1979 the United States' trade balance in manufactures with NICs moved substantially into deficit. In 1973 and 1979 Canada also faced a small deficit in her trade in manufactures with NICs. However, all the other OECD countries listed had surpluses in their trade with the NICs. It is noteworthy that almost one-half of the OECD surplus in trade with NICs was accounted for by Japan. Germany was the only other OECD country to have a sizeable surplus on trade with NICs.

With regard to imports, column (B) shows the percentage share of total OECD imports coming from NICs. It can be seen that this share rose from 2.8 per cent in 1963 to 9 per cent in 1979. Although this represented quite a sharp rise, it remains the case that the NICs account for just under one-tenth of OECD imports. This is a relatively small share of the total. Moreover, since imports account for only a proportion of total consumption of manufactures in the advanced industrialized countries, the degree of overall market penetration achieved by NICs remains quite small. For certain individual OECD countries, the share of imports coming from NICs is somewhat higher. In particular, NICs accounted for 21 per cent of Japan's total imports of manufactures and 19 per cent of United States' imports. In the case of both Japan and the United States, this represents quite a big increase on the share shown for 1963. It is also noteworthy that, comparing 1979 with 1963, the NICs increased their share of total OECD imports in every one of the OECD countries listed (although for the United Kingdom the rise was quite small).

Column (A) shows the importance of the United States as a market for NICs manufactures. In 1979 over 40 per cent of NIC exports went to the United States, a slight increase on 1963, when 36 per cent of NIC exports went to the United States.

Table 6.13: Trade of OECD countries with NICs in manufactures, 1963–79

| | Imports (%) | | | | | | Exports (%) | | | | | | Trade balance ($bn) | | |
| | 1963 | | 1973 | | 1979 | | 1963 | | 1973 | | 1979 | | 1963 | 1973 | 1979 |
	(A)	(B)	(A)	(B)	(A)	(B)	(A)	(B)	(A)	(B)	(A)	(B)			
Canada	3.2	1.0	3.2	3.4	3.0	3.9	1.3	3.3	1.0	4.0	0.8	2.3	0.03	−0.20	−0.94
USA	36.3	5.9	42.2	17.1	41.4	19.4	26.2	9.5	22.5	16.4	24.5	16.5	0.92	0.06	−2.88
Japan	2.2	1.8	10.1	17.1	8.6	21.1	12.6	13.1	22.3	18.9	24.6	19.4	0.62	4.94	14.46
France	3.0	1.0	4.9	3.7	7.3	6.8	9.0	8.1	7.1	8.2	7.5	7.8	0.43	1.32	1.92
FRG	11.7	2.8	12.8	7.3	13.6	8.9	16.5	6.6	17.8	8.8	15.9	8.3	0.71	3.23	5.10
Italy	4.4	1.6	3.2	4.2	4.1	6.8	8.1	10.6	6.6	10.4	6.4	8.2	0.36	1.42	2.76
UK	22.6	7.3	9.1	8.2	8.1	7.9	11.2	6.3	6.9	9.1	6.3	7.7	0.32	0.64	0.58
OECD NICs	8.3	5.2	1.8	3.3	1.8	5.2	0.6	6.5	1.5	8.3	1.6	6.9	−0.06	0.15	0.25
Other OECD	8.3	0.8	12.6	3.0	12.0	3.8	14.5	5.2	14.2	6.5	12.4	6.0	0.64	2.48	3.25
OECD	100.0	2.8	100.0	7.2	100.0	9.0	100.0	7.6	100.0	10.6	100.0	10.1	3.97	14.04	24.51

Sources: OECD (1979); OECD (1981).
(A) = % share of country in OECD total
(B) = % share of NIC in country total

West Germany accounted for the next highest share of 13.6 per cent, slightly up on 11.7 per cent in 1963. By way of contrast, only 8.1 per cent of NIC exports to OECD countries went to the United Kingdom in 1979 compared with 22.6 per cent in 1963. With regard to exports, column (B) shows the share of OECD exports going to NICs. Thus, in 1979, 10.1 per cent of OECD exports went to NICs compared with 7.6 per cent in 1963. Once again there are important differences between individual countries. Thus over 19 per cent of Japanese exports went to NICs. Clearly a much higher proportion of Japanese trade takes place with NICs than for other developed countries. The largest share of such trade is with the South-East Asian NICs. It is noticeable that 16.5 per cent of United States exports also go to NICs, although these exports have not risen as fast as imports. Not all the countries listed in the table experienced an increase in the share of their exports going to NICs. Canada, France, and Italy all experienced a decline in the proportion of their exports going to NICs over the period from 1963 to 1979.

Column (A) shows the share of total OECD exports going to NICs which is accounted for by different OECD countries. It is striking that the United States and Japan together account for nearly one-half of total OECD exports to NICs. Japan's share increased from 13 per cent to 25 per cent over the period from 1963 to 1979. The increase in Japan's share of OECD exports to NICs was at the expense of all other OECD countries except the OECD NICs. The United Kingdom experienced an especially large drop in her share of OECD exports going to NICs. Her share was almost halved from 11.2 per cent in 1963 to 6.3 per cent in 1979.

Table 6.14 further examines the degree of import penetration achieved by NICs in the markets of the western industrialized countries. This shows manufacturing imports of western industrialized economies as a percentage of apparent consumption. Apparent consumption is domestic output less exports plus imports. In the top half of Table 6.14, such import penetration is measured by country of destination. Thus, in 1978–9 imports of manufactures from NICs accounted for only 0.37 per cent of apparent consumption. Total manufacturing imports accounted for 5.49 per cent of apparent consumption. This helps put the extent of the alleged threat caused by NIC imports into perspective. However, this did represent an increase from 0.25 per cent in 1974–5, at a time when the share of total manufacturing imports in apparent consumption increased only slightly from 5.21 per cent to 5.49 per cent. Moreover, the share of NIC imports in total apparent consumption was slightly higher in the three trading blocs shown—the EEC, United States–Canada, and Japan—than for all developed market economies. In particular, it is noticeable that the share of NIC imports in apparent consumption for the EEC (0.88 per cent) and the United States–Canada (0.83 per cent) was higher than that of Japan (0.73 per cent). However, these should be compared with the share of total manufacturing imports in apparent consumption in all three trading blocs. Japan's share of total imports in apparent consumption (5.96 per cent) is quite low. On the other hand, total manufacturing imports account for quite a large share of apparent consumption in the EEC (12.88 per cent). It follows that the degree of market penetration achieved by NICs in the North American market is quite high in comparison with that achieved in either the EEC or Japan. Furthermore, the share of NIC imports in apparent consumption increased fastest in North America, rising from 0.54 per cent to 0.83 per cent. In Japan this share fell from 0.82 per cent to 0.73 per cent between 1974–5 and 1978–9. However, this was also true of the share of total imports of manufactures in apparent consumption in Japan. In fact, the increase in the share of NIC imports in apparent consumption for the EEC was relatively great considering that total manufacturing imports as a share of apparent consumption increased much less than in the United States–Canada. Thus, although the degree of market penetration achieved by NICs appears to be relatively greater in the North American market, over the period from 1974–5 to 1978–9, it appears to have risen sightly faster in the EEC.

In Table 6.14 (b) the degree of market penetration achieved in different industries can be deciphered. Although the average level of market penetration is quite low, NIC imports do account for quite a large proportion of apparent consumption in certain industries. In particular, the share of imports in apparent consumption of clothing products was 6.59 per cent in 1978–9. High levels of market penetration were also achieved in textiles and machinery and other manufactured goods. It is in these industries that NICs have demonstrated their greatest competitiveness. These are the industries where the so-called NICs' 'threat' is most strongly felt. It can be seen that in all the product groups listed except chemicals, the NICs increased the

Table 6.14: Import of manufactures as a percentage of apparent consumption in the EEC, United States–Canada, and Japan, 1974–9

(a) BY DESTINATION

	EEC	United States–Canada	Japan	Total
Total manufacturing imports:				
1974–5	12.05	7.38	7.32	5.21
1976–7	12.50	6.73	4.89	4.84
1978–9	12.88	8.30	5.96	5.49
Imports of manufactures from NICs:				
1974–5	0.67	0.54	0.82	0.25
1976–7	0.84	0.65	0.58	0.30
1978–9	0.88	0.83	0.73	0.37

(b) BY PRODUCT GROUP

	1974–5	1976–7	1978–9
Textiles	0.74	0.83	0.99
Clothing	4.21	5.67	6.59
Wood products, paper, & printing	0.21	0.25	0.32
Rubber	0.12	0.22	0.32
Chemicals	0.21	0.17	0.21
Transport equipment	0.03	0.05	0.08
Machinery & other manufactured goods	0.53	0.71	0.86

Source: UNCTAD (1983).

level of their market penetration over the period covered. In clothing, textiles, and machinery, and other manufactured goods, the rise in the level of market penetration was quite fast. This illustrates that, not only is the NIC 'challenge' concentrated in a limited number of industries, in those industries it is characterized by a relatively rapid increase in the degree of market penetration compressed into a relatively short period of time. It is this suddenness with which NIC manufactures have captured certain western markets that appears to be the main reason why NICs have caused problems for the advanced industrialized countries. As we have seen, the overall level of market penetration is quite small.

Table 6.15 further illustrates this trend. This shows the share

Table 6.15: Shares of total OECD imports accounted for by NICs by commodity group, 1963–77 (%)

Commodity Group (SITC)	All NICs		OECD NICs		All NICs, of which: Brazil & Mexico		Far Eastern NICs	
	1963	1977	1963	1977	1963	1977	1963	1977
Clothing	17.3	38.5	1.2	4.6	0.0	0.3	15.3	29.9
Leather, footwear, & travel goods	7.2	31.3	2.3	7.9	0.5	3.9	3.3	17.7
Wood & cork manufactures	12.3	23.8	6.2	4.7	1.1	2.4	3.6	15.9
Electrical machinery	0.8	12.0	0.2	1.0	0.0	2.2	0.5	8.4
Miscellaneous finished manufactures	4.2	11.2	0.7	1.3	0.2	0.7	2.7	8.7
Textiles	5.7	10.8	2.4	3.4	0.7	1.7	2.1	5.8
Rubber manufactures	0.5	7.6	0.2	4.2	0.0	0.4	0.2	2.5
Manufactures of metals	1.5	7.4	0.5	2.0	0.7	0.7	0.6	4.3
Non-metallic mineral manufactures	2.7	4.9	0.8	1.5	0.8	0.9	0.8	2.3
Iron & steel	1.3	4.8	0.5	2.4	0.4	1.0	0.0	1.0
Transport equipment	1.0	2.8	0.5	1.7	0.0	0.4	0.1	0.5
Machinery other than electric	0.3	2.8	0.2	1.0	0.0	0.8	0.0	0.8
Chemicals	2.1	2.5	0.9	1.1	0.8	0.6	0.2	0.6
Paper	0.3	2.2	0.1	1.0	0.0	0.5	0.0	0.5

Source: OECD (1979).

of OECD imports accounted for by NICs by commodity group. It is apparent that, while the average level is quite low, NIC manufactures do account for quite a high proportion of imports for certain industries. In particular, in 1977 NICs accounted for 38.5 per cent of total imports of clothing, 31.3 per cent of leather, footwear, and travel goods, and 23.8 per cent of wood and cork manufactures. Quite high shares were also achieved for electrical machinery, miscellaneous finished manufactures, and textiles. What is also striking about the shares given in Table 6.15 is that NICs have considerably broadened their assault on western markets, such that, by 1977, they accounted for a high share of total imports in a much larger number of product groups than in 1973. In 1963 their share of total imports was high in clothing and wood and cork manufactures only. Thus today the NIC 'challenge' is being felt in a much larger number of product groups than two decades ago. Not only have the NICs been successful in achieving relatively high levels of market penetration in a fairly small number of product groups, but they have increasingly broadened the range of product groups where they have been successful. Table 6.15 also shows some of the differences between NICs in terms of the product groups in which each has been most competitive. The Far Eastern NICs have generally achieved the highest levels of market penetration, doing especially well in the more labour-intensive, light-manufacturing product groups, such as clothing, textiles, leather, footwear and travel goods, wood and cork manufactures, and other miscellaneous finished manufactures. The OECD NICs—Greece, Spain, Portugal, and Yugoslavia—achieved relatively greater import penetration in the more capital-intensive, heavy-goods sectors, such as rubber manufactures, iron and steel, transport equipment, and chemicals. Similarly, the Latin American NICs—Brazil and Mexico—appear to have done best in industries such as iron and steel, non-electrical machinery, and chemicals. In brief, where the Far Eastern NICs appear to have specialized in labour-intensive, light-manufacturing, consumer goods, the European and Latin American NICs have specialized much more in the more capital-intensive intermediate goods and capital goods.

However, even Table 6.15 conceals the high levels of market penetration achieved by NICs in particular products or narrowly-defined product groups. This is because the product groups used are quite broad. NIC export strategies have tended to emphasize 'a very marked selectivity both of products and markets' (OECD 1979). Many NICs have expanded their exports to western industrialized country markets by concentrating initially on a relatively few products aimed at a few selected markets. The resultant competition for the affected economies of the western industrialized world has been severe in the particular sectors involved. Eventually, however, a typical NIC will begin to branch out into other markets and other products. It will seek to diversify both the commodity composition of its exports and the geographical destination of its exports. The other major problem posed for the advanced industrialized countries arises from the fact that much of the competition which they face from NICs occurs in highly labour-intensive branches of manufacturing. Such imports have a very high employment-displacement effect. By way of contrast, the type of manufactures which the industrialized countries export to NICs are relatively capital intensive. They have a relatively low employment-creation effect within the industrialized countries. From this it follows that even if OECD exports to NICs expanded at the same rate as OECD imports from NICs, the net effect on employment in the industrialized countries would be negative. As we shall see in the next chapter, this need not cause an employment problem if the jobs losses from balanced trade with NICs are matched by new jobs created in other parts of the economy. However, this will depend on many factors. First, jobs created in other parts of the economy might require different skills from those possessed by workers made redundant in import-competing sectors. Second, whether or not new jobs are created elsewhere in the economy will depend on the level of money wages relative to the price of capital. If relative wages are inflexible in a downwards direction, the labour market may fail to clear and unemployment will result.

I will discuss the nature of the process whereby economies adjust to trade expansion—especially where the factor proportions of exports differ from those of imports—in Chapter 7. Suffice it to note that balanced trade between NICs and the western industrialized economies will tend to result in some initial employment displacement. However, as we have seen, the OECD countries enjoy a net surplus in their trade in manufactured products with NICs. Is the effect of such trade on the industrialized countries to cause a loss of employment or an increase in employment? Calculations by the OECD Secretariat found that the overall employment effect of trade between the western industrialized economies and the NICs over the period from 1973 to 1977 was positive. That is to say, the employment-creation effects of increased OECD exports to NICs more than offset the employment-displacement effects of NICs' exports to OECD countries (OECD 1979). There was some variation between countries. For some countries, the net effect on employment was large and for others quite small. However, it is striking that, even in the case of the United States, the employment effect was found to be positive, although it was less than for other OECD countries. Thus there is very little evidence to suggest that the NICs have caused any unemployment. If anything, trade with NICs has increased employment in the advanced industrialized countries. The decline in manufacturing employment which has taken place in the western industrialized countries over the past fifteen years cannot be adequately explained as due to the rise of the NICs.

How, then, do we account for the growth of protectionism in the western industrialized countries, much of it being aimed at imports from NICs? Was it a purely irrational response based on a presumed threat to employment posed by manufacturing imports from NICs? Or was there some rational basis for protection? Although the net effect on employment from NICs was positive, NIC manufactures may still cause unemployment in advanced industrialized countries. This is for the reasons already noted above. Workers must move out of the sectors where jobs are being displaced as a result of increased imports and into the sectors where jobs are being created due to increased exports. If this adjustment process fails to take place, structural unemployment may result. As we have already noted, the possibility may exist that workers in declining sectors lack the skills required in the expanding sectors. Or it may be that the expanding sectors are located in different geographical regions to the declining sectors and workers are unwilling to move. Other impediments may exist to the mobility of labour (e.g. the costs of housing). Leaving aside the problem of labour mobility, adjustment may fail to take place because of inflexibility in the price of labour. Unless there exists a suitable differential between wage-rates in expanding sectors and regions and declining sectors and regions, adjustment is unlikely to take place. Unless trade unions and employers allow such differentials to exist, structural unemployment will result.

The expansion of trade between any two countries necessitates such a process of adjustment. Unless an economy is centrally planned and resources are directed to where they are required, this adjustment must take place through changes in the relative prices of goods and factors of production. If final-goods markets and factor markets fail to work or work imperfectly, the result will be structural unemployment. However, the likelihood of such structural unemployment resulting is probably greater for trade between advanced industrialized countries and NICs because (1) much of this trade takes the form of inter-industry specialization and (2) the factor proportions used in NICs, exports differ greatly from those used in exports by industrialized countries to NICs. This will be discussed further in the next chapter. Suffice it to say that the risks of structural unemployment are probably greater with this type of trade. For this reason there tends to be greater resistance from within industrialized countries to imports coming from such countries. Added to that is the fact that exports from NICs have often been concentrated in narrow groups of products and concentrated on particular markets. The aim has been to achieve rapid market penetration in the shortest possible time. Adjustment is always more difficult to achieve in the short period than in the long period. The speed with which NIC exports have often reached western markets has added to the adjustment pressure. This is not to argue that protectionism represents a rational response on the part of the advanced industrialized economies. Although a case may be made out for temporary protectionism in order to create time during which the industrialized countries can adjust, permanent protectionism can only be harmful. As we have seen, the net effect on employment in the western industrialized economies from such an action would be negative. However, for workers and companies affected by sudden surges of imports from NICs, the beneficial effects of such trade even in the long run are not always apparent. Especially against a background of high levels of unemployment in all sectors and regions of the economy, it is not surprising if the response of those affected has been a call for increased import restrictions.

The Newly-industrializing Countries in the Future

One of the questions which arises from the discussion in the preceding sections with regard to the rise of the NICs is this: can the NICs continue to enjoy the rapid growth in their manufacturing exports which they have experienced in recent decades? Will NIC exports continue growing at the same rate in the future as in the past? Can the second-generation NICs, which are standing in the wings waiting to take the places vacated by first-generation NICs, hope to repeat the experience of their precursors? If so, what are the implications for the world trading system? Can we expect to see an increase in the level of friction between the advanced industrialized countries, on the one hand, and a growing band of highly competitive developing-country producers and exporters of low-cost manufactures on the other?

There are a number of grounds for believing that, in the next few decades, NIC exports of manufactures will grow more slowly than in the past. These are as follows:

1. NIC exports of manufactures cannot grow at the same rate as in the past because growth is taking place from a lower base than in the past. Some slowing down in the growth of NIC manufactured exports seems, therefore, to be almost inevitable, regardless of whether or not there exists a demand for these goods. The only two offsetting factors might be (a) the emergence of a new generation of NICs starting from the same low base as did today's generation of NICs some two decades ago and (b) the development of a new set of products within the NICs to take the place of the existing ones. As will be seen, there are grounds for supposing that neither of these two factors will be strong enough to maintain the former expansion of NIC exports.

2. There are comparatively few obvious candidates among second-tier NICs for filling the gap left by the first-tier NICs. If the exports of the latter are to grow more slowly in the future, which countries among existing developing countries can assume the mantle of fast-growing exporters of manufactures? Much depends on policies pursued from within the developing countries. In particular, it requires a willingness to abandon inward-looking, import-substitution policies and adopt outward-looking, export-oriented policies. This is essential if second-tier

NICs are to secure promotion to the first division. Chenery and Keesing, in assessing the prospects for developing-country exports, have questioned whether there are more than a few countries currently adopting such policies. The Phillipines and India are cited as the only two possible candidates (Chenery and Keesing 1981).

3. It is not clear which products NICs could develop to take the place of their existing ones. As we have seen, the tendency has been for the NICs to specialize in labour-intensive, light-manufactured consumer goods, such as clothing, textiles, footwear and travel goods, and so on, although some of the larger European and Latin American NICs have also been successful in the export of capital goods and intermediate goods. It may be that, in the future, a greater proportion of NIC exports will comprise capital and intermediate goods, as well as more technologically complex goods. However, it remains problematic as to whether NICs can achieve the same degree of export success in these sorts of products, the marketing of which requires skills which most NICs lack.

4. The development of new export industries able to grow as fast as the export industries of the past will require considerable investment of resources in production capacity, education and training of the workforce, and appropriate infrastructure. It is questionable whether many NICs will be able to obtain the finance needed for such a transformation of their economies. The last decade has seen a number of developing countries reach a situation of over-indebtedness. This means that, for many years to come, a number of such countries will be compelled to devote a large proportion of foreign-currency earnings to servicing and repaying foreign debt. At the same time, western banks will be less inclined to make further loans available.

5. Market access for NIC manufactures looks likely to become more restricted in the future. As we have noted earlier, pressure for protectionism in the advanced industrialized countries has intensified in recent years. The result has been a growing proliferation of trade barriers, many of which are aimed at NICs' exports. Much will depend on the success of the current Uruguay Round of tariff negotiations. This in turn will depend on the resolution of governments in the advanced industrialized countries to resist protectionist pressures.

Therefore, it seems certain that, in the immediately foreseeable future, NIC exports of manufactures will grow more slowly than in the past. At the very least, we can say that the NICs will find it more difficult than in earlier decades to achieve rapid export expansion. However, much will depend on the response of developing countries to the changed environment. Difficulties of increasing trade with the advanced industrialized countries are causing many developing countries to take a greater interest in the possibilities of expanding trade among themselves. For example, there is considerable evidence for a rapid expansion of intra-regional trade between the countries of the ASEAN region and between these countries and some of the North-East Asian NICs (Taiwan, South Korea, and Hong Kong) (Erzan and Laird 1984; Lorenz 1986). This may enable developing countries to maintain a fast rate of growth of their manufacturing exports at a time when developed country markets are slowing down and access is being restricted. However, it would seem doubtful that a rapid expansion of exports could result from increased integration among developing countries.

The fact that NIC exports cannot grow as in the past may serve to ease some of the pressures posed by such trade for the advanced industrialized countries. On the other hand, as we have seen, slower growth of NICs tends to mean slower growth of the exports of the advanced industrialized countries to developing countries. Adjustment pressures are reduced but at the expense of slower export growth and, therefore, overall economic growth. However, one relatively unexplored area which may open up opportunities for more trade between NICs and the advanced industrialized countries concerns the scope for increased intra-industry trade and specialization between the two blocs. More intra-industry trade between NICs and industrialized countries would mean more balanced trade and possibly fewer adjustment difficulties. This might enable NICs to expand their exports of manufactures to the advanced industrialized countries without creating pressures within the latter for import restrictions.

Is there much scope for such intra-industry trade between industrialized and developing countries? As we saw in Chapter 3, the degree of intra-industry specialization is a function of a country's stage of development. Countries which are at a low stage of development have a lower level of intra-industry trade.

They tend to produce and export mainly standardized, low-technology goods sold in markets characterized by conditions of classical price competition leading to inter-industry specialization. However, the potential for increased intra-industry trade between developed and developing countries in manufactured goods may be greater than is often thought (see UNCTAD 1980; Erzan and Laird 1984). This could take one of two forms. First, there may be scope for increased intra-industry specialization in differentiated products. Scope for intra-industry specialization in products such as clothing, textiles, footwear, and consumer electronics in which NICs specialize is greater than is often thought. It may be possible for developed countries to exchange the higher-quality, higher-value-added, up-market products for low-price, high-volume, standardized goods exported from NICs. In his three case studies of the impact of developing-country manufacturing imports on the United Kingdom, Vincent Cable cites certain examples of such specialization. Thus specialization by UK manufacturers in the cutlery industry in silverplated cutlery as an alternative to stainless steel; specialization by firms in the footwear industry in higher-priced leather goods, and the specialization by clothing firms in high-quality, high-fashion goods (Cable 1983). NICs continue to possess a comparative advantage in low-price standardized goods, but developed countries retain an advantage in goods requiring marketing skill.

Second, considerable scope exists for increased vertical specialization in what may be called the multi-process industries. That is to say, developed and developing countries may be able to specialize in different stages or processes involved in the manufacture of different products. Chapter 3 noted that such specialization, although it may show up statistically as intra-industry specialization, is in fact closer in kind to inter-industry specialization. This is because the basis for a country specializing in a particular process is cheaper supplies of the factors used in the greatest amounts in that particular process. However, whether or not such specialization is labelled as intra- or inter-industry specialization, it may make for more balanced trade between developed and developing countries. Trade frictions are likely to be less. As we saw earlier in this chapter, such specialization has been encouraged by the offshore assembly provisions which several industrialized countries have built into their tariff schedules. Thus the extension and liberalization of

347

such provisions would be one way in which developed countries could encourage this kind of specialization between themselves and NICs. Other modifications to tariff structures could also assist this process. In particular, by reducing the levels of protection of highly processed or finished goods, developed countries could encourage developing countries to invest in the later stages of the processing chain. The tariff structures of most industrialized countries tend to escalate such that the level of protection increases with the level of processing.

7

The Growth of the New Protectionism and the Adjustment Problem

Chapter 6 discussed the problems posed for the western industrialized economies by the rise of Japan and the sudden emergence of a second group of developing countries as major exporters of manufactured goods. The latter are what have been termed the newly-industrializing countries, or NICs. In the case of Japan, the problem has essentially been the unbalanced nature of her trade in manufactured goods. As we saw in Chapter 6, the root cause of the Japanese trade surplus lies in the savings-investment imbalance within the economy and the illiberal nature of many of her economic institutions, especially her financial institutions and markets. In the case of the newly-industrializing countries, the western industrialized countries taken as a whole enjoy a small trade surplus with the NICs. The problem is not so much one of unbalanced overall trade. Rather, it is the speed with which NICs have succeeded in penetrating certain markets in the western industrialized countries. Overall levels of market penetration remain quite low. However, in the markets for certain so-called 'sensitive' products (e.g. clothing, textiles, footwear, toys, etc), the NICs have achieved much higher levels of market penetration. The difficulties facing the western industrialized countries are essentially problems of adjustment. The difficulty is in bringing about the necessary shift of resources from sectors experiencing employment displacement, into sectors experiencing employment creation. This has proved especially difficult at a time when manufacturing employment has been falling and general unemployment rising.

In the last chapter it was noted that these difficulties have given rise to increasing protectionist tendencies in the western industrialized economies. Governments in these countries have come under increasing pressure from affected constituencies to introduce restrictions on troublesome imports. The result has been a proliferation of new import barriers, most of which have been designed to restrict imports coming from either Japan or one or more of the NICs. As we shall see later in this chapter, most of these new restrictions have taken the form of non-tariff limitations on trade. This is one reason why the protectionism of recent decades has been called the New Protectionism. This chapter will examine the nature and extent of this new protectionism and its implications for future patterns of trade.

The previous chapter noted that the problem posed for the western industrialized economies is essentially a problem of adjustment. In this chapter I will examine the nature of the so-called adjustment problem in greater depth. I will discuss the nature of the adjustment process and the so-called adjustment 'costs' which result from trade expansion. It will be seen that there are grounds for believing that developments within the mature industrialized economies over the post-war period have raised certain of these adjustment costs and made rapid adjustment more difficult to achieve. At the same time, the domestic and international pressures on countries to adjust have almost certainly increased over the past quarter-century. These factors may explain the rise of the New Protectionism as a response to increased competition resulting from the sudden emergence of the NICs. The fact that many western industrialized economies have adopted defensive adjustment policies which inhibit rather than promote trade adjustment (e.g. subsidizing high-cost, inefficient, declining industries) has further aggravated the situation. Such policies serve merely to pass on the costs of adjustment to other countries. As a result, pressure within these countries increases to adopt trade restrictions.

In earlier chapters of this book I have occasionally referred to the view that adjustment pressures are least when countries engage in intra-industry as opposed to inter-industry specialization. This may be one reason why trade between the western industrialized countries over the post-war period has been accompanied by relatively less friction than trade between the mature industrialized economies and the so-called 'catching-up' countries. The latter countries tend to have a much higher level of inter-industry specialization. Japan has a lower level of intra-industry specialization than other western industrialized economies. This looks likely to change in the future. At the same time, as we saw in Chapter 6, there may be scope for more intra-industry specialization between industrialized countries and NICs. In the present chapter I will examine the proposition that intra-industry specialization leads to lower adjustment costs. At the same time, it will be necessary to consider whether the welfare gains to countries from intra-industry specialization are as great as under inter-industry specialization. If the welfare gains are as great and the adjustment costs are lower, intra-industry specialization may be worth encouraging. If so, we shall need to consider how, if at all, countries can foster such specialization.

THE GROWTH OF THE NEW PROTECTIONISM

In Chapter 2 we saw that in 1973 the volume of world trade fell for the first time since the Second World War. Although growth was resumed in the following year, the rate of growth was slower than in preceding decades. Thus, over the period from 1970 to 1979, world exports grew at a rate of 5.5 per cent per annum, compared with 8.5 per cent per annum between 1960 and 1969. From 1980 to 1983 the rate of growth fell to a mere 0.5 per cent per annum. One factor which has contributed to this slowdown in world trade has been the growth of protectionism. The 1970s and 1980s have witnessed a significant increase in the level and extent of protectionism in the world trading system. As we have already stated, this has mainly taken the form of non-tariff interventions by governments. Tariff levels have gradually been reduced over the course of the post-war period. This has been the most important single achievement of the General Agreement on Tariffs and Trade (the GATT) set up in 1947. Over the course of seven rounds of multilateral tariff negotiations conducted through GATT, the average level of tariffs has been steadily lowered. Tariffs are no longer the main impediment to free trade. Thus, by the time the seventh Tokyo Round tariff reductions are fully operative, the United States' average tariff level will stand at 4.3 per cent, that of the EEC countries at 4.7 per cent, and that of Japan at 2.9 per cent (Cline 1983),

Although GATT does permit member states to raise tariffs in certain situations – such as those covered by article 19, the

351

famous 'escape clause' – countries often prefer other methods for restricting troublesome imports. As will be seen later, one reason for this is the GATT requirement that any tariff imposed on the products of another GATT member must be non-discriminatory. Thus, if the EEC imposes a higher tariff on imported footwear from Taiwan, it must also impose the same tariff on equivalent footwear imports coming from any other GATT member. This is the famous 'most-favoured nation clause', which constitutes one of the central pillars of the GATT system. At the same time, if one country invokes article 19 to justify the imposition of a higher tariff on a certain group of imports, it is required to offer compensation to all countries adversely affected. These conditions which accompany the use of higher tariffs to restrict imports, make tariffs an inferior weapon for countries wanting to act swiftly to control a flood of low-cost imports, possibly originating from just one supplier country. The need to make any tariff non-discriminatory risks incurring the displeasure of other supplier nations and makes the costs of any compensation excessive. For this reason, countries often find other means of limiting imports.

Attempts have been made to classify and measure the extent of the various kinds of non-tariff intervention which affect world trade. Sheila Page estimated that, by 1980, as much as 48 per cent of world trade was 'controlled' compared with 40 per cent in 1974 (Page 1981). Page defines 'controlled' or 'managed' trade broadly to refer to any trade which is subject to some form of non-tariff control whether by exporter, importer, or both. She has proposed the following system of classification:

1. International agreements, such as international cartels (e.g. OPEC, international commodity agreements, etc.) and market-sharing agreements (such as those common in textiles, steel, and shipbuilding).
2. National controls on trade, such as import quotas, anti-dumping duties, certificates of origin, and other administrative controls, price controls, voluntary export restraints, and government-imposed restrictions on the purchase of imports.
3. Other national controls whose major effect is on trade, such as safety, health, or technical product standards, domestic subsidies, customs clearance procedures, patent laws, or licences and price controls, but where the main motive may be domestic rather than any desire to restrict imports.

The level of such controlled or managed trade is much higher for non-manufactures. However, this has always been so. The disturbing finding is that the proportion of trade in manufactures which is controlled in any one of these ways is high and rising. Thus Page found that the proportion of trade in manufactures which is controlled or managed rose from 12.9 per cent to 23.6 per cent between 1974 to 1980 (Page 1981). The proportion of managed trade to total trade in manufactures was found to be highest on trade between the western industrialized countries and developing countries. In 1979 as much as 30 per cent of trade in manufactured products between industrialized and developing countries was managed, compared with 11 per cent for trade between industrialized economies. This would lend support to the view that the New Protectionism has been primarily aimed at manufactures exported by developing countries.

As we have just seen, the motive for certain kinds of non-tariff intervention is not always the restriction of imports. In many cases, domestic objectives are the overriding consideration. For example, safety, health, or technical product standards are generally imposed to protect the public from unsafe, unhealthy, high-pollution, or otherwise anti-social goods. However, the effect of these requirements may be to impose costs on foreign suppliers who must adapt their products to meet the national requirements. Similarly, an industry located in a regionally depressed area may receive some labour or capital subsidy in order to foster the development of the region, but the effect may be to discriminate against foreign producers. The growth of these kinds of interventions has more to do with the general growth in the level of government intervention in the economic systems of developed market economies which has been taking place over the course of the post-war period.

However, the motive for other kinds of non-tariff intervention which have become common in recent years is solely to restrain or control the flow of trade. One of the most important kinds of such non-tariff intervention, which is typical of the New Protectionism, is the voluntary export-restraint agreement (VER). A VER is very similar to an import quota except that the restriction is enforced by the exporting and not the importing country. Such agreements are generally bilaterally negotiated between an exporting and an importing nation. Very often such negotiations are accompanied by the threat of unilateral action by the importing country should the exporting nation not agree to limit its exports. Under the agreement the government of the exporting nation agrees to restrict its exports of the product in question to a certain quantity or share of the market over the course of a specified period of time. Usually it will do so by operating some kind of licensing system whereby exporting firms must obtain a licence to export the product to the country concerned and the licence will prescribe the maximum amount permitted. The details of such agreements are often kept secret.

Such VERs have become increasingly common in recent decades. In every sense they are the very essence of the New Protectionism. First, they involve a quantitative restraint on trade. Such quantitative limitations on trade are generally regarded by economists as having a more harmful effect on economic efficiency than tariffs, which deter imports by forcing up the price of such goods. Quantitative restrictions also raise the price which the consumer pays for the product, but do so indirectly by restricting supply. However, the problem with quantitative restrictions is that they freeze production patterns and increase inefficiency. Moreover, the degree of protection tends to increase over time, because any expansion of the domestic market is met from home production rather than imports, unless import quotas are raised. Second, VERs are discriminatory. Usually, they are aimed at the lowest-cost suppliers of a particular product. As such, they divert trade away from the world's most efficient producers of a particular product and thus have a more distorting effect on global resource allocation than a more straightforward non-discriminatory tariff. However, because they are not a unilaterally imposed restriction on trade (even if negotiation of the agreement is backed up by the threat of such action), they are not covered by GATT rules. No illegality is involved. This largely accounts for their growing attraction as a type of trade restraint in recent years. Third, both the negotiations accompanying the signing of such agreements and the exact details of the agreement reached are secretive. This makes it difficult to evaluate the impact of a specific agreement or to check to see whether or not the degree of restriction is diminishing over time.

The main industries affected by such restraints have been as follows:

1. Textiles and clothing: Restrictions on imports of textile and clothing products by western industrialized countries have a history dating back to before the Second World War. As early as the 1930s countries in both Western Europe and North America operated protectionist measures against 'cheap' Japanese textile exports. However, in 1962 the Long-Term Cotton Agreement was signed by the world's leading cotton-textile exporting and importing nations. This involved an agreement on quotas for the main types of cotton textile products. This lasted up until 1974, when it was replaced by the Multi-Fibre Arrangement (MFA). This extended the agreement to cover most kinds of textiles, including man-made fibres. MFA1 sought to limit the global rate of growth of textile exports to a ceiling of 6 per cent a year. Despite the claims of the industrialized importing countries that the MFA was designed to be a temporary restraint on trade – supposedly to give time for the industrialized countries to reorganize their textile industries and adjust – the MFA has become a more or less permanent feature of world trade in textiles. In 1977 MFA1 was replaced by MFA2. This gave way to MFA3 in 1981. An MFA4 was negotiated in 1986. Each new extension involved some tightening in the ceiling imposed on textile exports. Moreover, within the framework of these international agreements, bilateral restraints were separately negotiated. This meant that, under MFA2, textile imports were held below the agreed 6 per cent ceiling. Under MFA3, the United States allowed a rate of growth of only 0.5 per cent on two-thirds of textile and clothing imports. (Hamilton 1985). The number of separate bilateral agreements has tended to increase steadily from year to year. In 1974 there were only seven such agreements; by the end of 1977 there were thirty-three (Page 1981). At the same time, each new agreement has increased the number of products covered.

2. Steel: Restrictions on imports of steel date back to the late 1960s. The United States was the first industrialized country to impose a VER on imports of steel coming from Japan and the EEC. This lasted from 1968 to 1974, when it was allowed to lapse. In 1976 the United States negotiated a new agreement with Japan. This was based on a trigger-price system whereby any imports below an agreed reference price became subject to control. In 1982 a further VER was negotiated to regulate US imports of steel from Western Europe. Restrictions on imports of Japanese steel have enabled European steel-makers to expand

their share of the US market, leading to pressure from within the United States for controls on European steel imports. The EEC itself has also restricted imports of steel from developing countries but has done so through import controls. Thus the pressures of excess production caused in part by US protectionism have been passed on to producers in developing countries as their exports to Europe have accordingly been controlled. This illustrates how the failure of one major country to adjust causes added pressures in other countries and leads those countries to introduce trade restraints affecting the rest of the world.

3. Cars: In recent years there has been a growing use of VERs to regulate trade in motor cars. Indeed, since the mid-1970s the United Kingdom and France have operated 'voluntary' restraints on Japanese exports of motor cars. Italy and France have imposed similar restrictions on imports of motorcycles. In 1980 all imports of Japanese motor cars to the EEC were subject to 'voluntary' restraint. In 1981 the United States also negotiated a VER covering imported Japanese motor cars. Thus Japanese exports have been the main target of restriction in the motor car industry.

4. Electronics: Asian exports of certain kinds of consumer electronics to several developed countries are also subject to VERs. For example, in 1977 the United States negotiated an orderly marketing agreement (OMA) (more or less the same as a VER) with Japan which restricted imports of television sets. Subsequently, this was broadened to include Taiwan and South Korea. Imports of television sets to the United Kingdom from Taiwan, South Korea, and Singapore are also subject to a VER. In 1986 a novel type of market-sharing agreement was signed by the United States and Japan covering trade in semiconductors. This involved an agreement by which Japan undertook not to undercut US semiconductor manufacturers in pricing exports to the US market and to grant increased access to the Japanese market for US semiconductors.

5. Footwear: Controls on imports of shoes have been introduced by a number of developed countries in recent decades, including the United States and EEC. Although in some cases they have taken the form of import quotas, VERs have also been used. For example, in 1977 the United States negotiated an OMA with Taiwan, limiting imports of shoes. A similar agreement was signed with South Korea in 1977.

Although VERs/OMAs represent one of the major forms of the New Protectionism, it should not be thought that they are the only type of protectionism which countries have resorted to. For example, in recent decades there has been an increasing use of subsidies by governments which directly or indirectly interfere with trade. Direct subsidization of exports are less common except in agricultural trade because GATT specifically outlaws such interferences with trade. However, the same effect may be achieved by other means. Export credit subsidies are one important example. Government departments frequently offer exporters export credit at below-market rates of interest. In 1981, at a time of rising interest rates, governments effectively increased the element of subsidy by not raising the rates offered to exporters in line with market rates. This momentarily brought into prospect the danger of an export credit war, in which the governments of the United States, Western Europe, and Japan would each seek to increase the element of subsidy paid to its own exporters. However, export subsidies apart, increased domestic subsidies may also restrict and distort the pattern of world trade. The intention may not be to interfere with trade, as when governments subsidize firms which invest in depressed regions. However, in times of high unemployment, governments may use such subsidies in an effort to attract footloose multinational capital to their countries. The danger exists that the level of such subsidies will increase beyond that which is justified by the higher social costs of producing in depressed regions such that the pattern of trade is distorted. Direct subsidies paid to domestic producers work in a similar way to tariffs in reducing trade. Inefficient domestic producers are enabled to expand output at the expense of more efficient overseas suppliers. Such subsidies have become especially rife in industries such as steel, shipbuilding, motor cars, and mining, which in recent decades have been especially troubled by problems of excess capacity. Although the reason given for introducing such subsidies is usually the need to give temporary protection while the industry and workforce can adjust to more intense competition, the effect of such subsidization is invariably to forestall change. Old, inefficient plants are kept in existence such that the problems of global excess capacity persist.

The New Protectionism has also involved a variety of other non-tariff interventions by governments. Administrative and technical barriers have become more common. Governments may restrict imports by insisting on specific standards for products which effectively make certain goods non-tradable. For example, imported products may have to meet stringent health or safety requirements. Lengthy testing procedures may be insisted upon before a product can enter a particular country. Environmental regulations may be introduced which effectively discriminate against foreign goods. Thus legislation which requires motorists to drive cars with lead-free petrol will mean that overseas suppliers have to make costly mechanical adjustments to their product in order to continue exporting to that country. Customs valuation procedure has long been another important type of non-tariff barrier. By overstating the value of an imported product or applying an arbitrary system of value determination, an effective barrier may be erected against imports. Customs authorities may impose costs on importers by subjecting imports to unnecessary administrative delays. Governments may insist that imports pass through some specific customs post before they can enter the country, thus creating an unnecessary inconvenience for importers. Finally, governments may discriminate against foreign goods in their public procurement policies. Government agencies account for approximately 10 per cent to 20 per cent of all purchases of goods and services in most advanced industrialized countries. By not awarding a public contract to a foreign supplier even when the latter makes a lower bid or by making it difficult for foreign firms to make a bid for a public contract or by buying goods and services from domestic suppliers even when foreign sources are cheaper, governments discriminate against imports.

None of these various types of non-tariff intervention are new. Most have been in use for as long as countries have traded. Indeed, to a certain extent it is true that awareness of their importance has increased only as tariffs have been lowered. However, it seems equally probable that governments have increasingly resorted to such devices to restrict imports as their markets have become more open with the lowering of industrial tariffs and with the increase in the degree of interdependence of their economies. Increased international competition has caused governments to resort increasingly to such measures as a subtle means of restricting imports and protecting domestic producers. For this reason they have become the subject of growing interest in international trade negotiations.

Although tariff reductions may still be important in promoting the growth of world trade, these will be of limited value unless action is taken to contain the spread of non-tariff interferences with trade.

Some attempt was made in the seventh Tokyo Round of international trade negotiations to tackle the problem of non-tariff barriers. This was concluded in 1979. The approach adopted was to establish a series of separate codes of conduct covering some of the major areas of non-tariff intervention. These included:

1. Technical trade barriers – a code to prevent governments from devising product standards which favour home producers over foreign producers.
2. Customs valuation – a code to lessen the flexibility of customs inspectors to assign arbitrarily high values to imported goods subject to tariff duties (but developing countries dissented, wanting measures included to prevent MNCs from underpricing exports for customs purposes).
3. Government procurement – a code requiring governments to treat domestic producers and foreign producers equally in government purchases.
4. Subsidizing and countervailing duties – a code prohibiting direct export subsidies and containing guidelines for the use of domestic subsidies and a code for countervailing duties. (These are duties which countries impose on goods which have been dumped on the market of another country.) Under the new code, these could only be imposed when such dumping damaged or threatened to damage domestic producers and the duty must be no greater than the element of foreign subsidy involved.

At the time of the signing of the Tokyo Agreement, considerable doubt remained about the likely effectiveness of these codes. They do not themselves remove existing non-tariff barriers but merely create a basis for countries bringing before the GATT practices which infringe the codes. In other words, for their effectiveness these codes rely upon countries enforcing them. Furthermore, they only deal with certain types of non-tariff barriers. The forthcoming Uruguay Round (the eighth GATT Round) will provide an opportunity for countries to strengthen and extend these codes. However, as we have seen, arguably the most damaging form of non-tariff interference with trade in recent years has been the growing use of VERs and OMAs. These are much more difficult barriers over which to negotiate. Moreover, as we have seen, since they do not involve a restriction on the import side, they do not infringe GATT rules even if they contradict the GATT opposition to quantitative restrictions on trade. They clash with the spirit of the GATT but not with the letter of GATT. Perhaps the best hope lies in agreement not to introduce any further such restrictions on trade. Alternatively, one could reform the GATT escape clause (article 19) to allow countries to introduce selective tariffs against troublesome imports which are damaging or threatening to damage domestic producers. In other words, the non-discriminatory requirement could be dropped when emergency tariffs are introduced under article 19. This would make it easier for member states to use the safeguard clause and discourage resort to other methods of restriction. Such emergency tariffs would arguably be less harmful than quantitative restrictions such as VERs and would be easier to monitor as well as to dismantle when the damage or threat of damage had been removed. The case for such a reform of article 19 was put by the EEC countries in the course of the Tokyo Round but was opposed by the developing countries. The latter feared that such a reform of article 19 would open the way to even more damaging emergency tariff action, much of which would inevitably be aimed at their exports. Equally, it may be argued that such a concession would undermine the very principles on which the GATT is based and seeks to operate. The principle of non-discrimination constitutes a central pillar of the GATT trading system. Its removal could cause the collapse of the entire edifice. Nevertheless, the issue of a reformed safeguard clause looks certain to reappear on the agenda of the forthcoming Uruguay Round.

Reasons for the Growth of the New Protectionism

What factors account for this growth of protectionist activity in recent decades? We have already seen that much of the protectionism of this period has been aimed against imports coming from Japan and the newly-industrializing countries of South-East Asia, Latin America, and the south of Europe. Can we successfully identify any general forces at work within the world economic system which underlie the increasing resort to trade barriers to regulate trade with Japan and the NICs? It would seem that a variety of factors have been at work in contributing to the growth of such protectionist activity:

1. **A growth in import competition** In earlier chapters of this book I have discussed at length the nature of the competition posed for the western industrialized countries by the rise of Japan and the growth of the NICs. In the last chapter we saw how the exports of NICs to developed countries have increased extremely fast over a relatively short period of time. Quite high levels of market penetration were achieved in certain relatively narrow product groups and subgroups. Much of this competition took the form of classical price competition in relatively simple, low-technology, standardized consumer goods. NICs were able to penetrate western markets by taking advantage of low labour costs and charging low prices. In the industries affected within the industrialized countries, there was little margin for matching such low prices by cutting costs or squeezing profits any further. Moreover, many of the industries affected were labour intensive such that a given reduction in domestic production caused a relatively large drop in employment. Often the industries in question were highly concentrated in depressed regions with few expanding industries capable of absorbing the labour displaced.

2. **Difficulties within the western industrialized countries in adapting to the new import competition** In Chapter 6 we saw that the real problem posed for the advanced industrialized countries by the rise of the NICs lay more in adjusting to the new situation. The growth of the NICs enabled the advanced industrialized countries to increase their exports of manufactures to developing countries just as much as it brought about an increase in manufacturing imports from these countries. As we saw in Chapter 6, the net employment effect from such trade was positive. However, the problem was bringing about the necessary redeployment of resources from declining to expanding sectors. Workers displaced by such imports were often both unable and unwilling to move. Later in this chapter I will show that various processes at work within the western industrialized countries over the post-war period have made their economies less adjustable than in the past. It may be that the costs of

adjusting to trade expansion have increased, bringing in its wake a resistance to trade expansion. The benefits from increased trade and specialization considered in relation to the costs seem less than in former decades. Moreover, as we have noted on a number of occasions, the kind of specialization which resulted from trade between industrialized countries and NICs was inter-industry specialization. Trade between industrialized countries has a greater element of intra-industry specialization. If the adjustment problems are less under intra-industry specialization, this may explain the greater resistance to expanding trade with NICs than with other industrialized countries.

3. **A changed international economic environment** The rise of the NICs and the problems caused by the rapid expansion of Japanese exports coincided with a general economic slowdown in the advanced industrialized countries. As we saw in Chapter 2, although this was brought on by the sudden rise in world oil prices in 1973–4, there were signs that economic growth in the advanced industrialized economies was slackening even before the onslaught of the oil crisis. The brunt of this depression was felt by the manufacturing sector. Higher levels of unemployment combined with higher levels of unused capacity served to lower the 'pain threshold' that would be tolerated from increased import competition. At the same time, the slump in the advanced industrialized counties made adjustment more difficult because there were fewer new jobs becoming available to match jobs that were disappearing.

4. **The failure of the international monetary system to bring about the necessary adjustment in payments imbalances between countries** Chapter 6 indicated that the main reason for the large Japanese trade surplus has for years been the relative cheapness of the Japanese yen. This, in turn, has its origins in Japan's savings–investment imbalance and the highly regulated nature of Japan's financial markets. Only in recent years has the yen begun to appreciate in value to a level nearly sufficient to ensure balance-of-payments equilibrium. The reverse side to the undervalued yen has been the overvalued US dollar. Thus the system of floating exchange rates dating back to the collapse of the Bretton Woods system in the early 1970s has failed to bring about the necessary macroeconomic adjustments in trade flows and to perform its intended function of restoring payments equilibrium between countries. Persistent trade imbalances often aggravated by perverse currency movements have acted

to generate protectionist pressures within affected countries. Thus the United States' large trade deficit, made worse by the overvaluation of the dollar, has fuelled protectionist sentiments within Congress. The rise in the value of the yen may not entirely remove such tendencies. The new problem is the cheapness of the currencies of the so-called 'other Japans', that is, the South-East Asian NICs. The currencies of these countries have almost universally fallen in real, trade-weighted terms in recent decades. Since 1980 the Taiwan dollar, the South Korean won, the Hong Kong dollar, and the Singapore dollar have all fallen sharply. Such depreciations have served to increase the competitiveness of these economies, leading to larger trade surpluses. The trade surpluses of these countries have been reckoned to account for about one fifth of the US trade deficit.

The failure of exchange rates to alter in the right direction and by a sufficient amount to correct trade imbalances between countries has meant both large current-account imbalances between countries and these imbalances have tended to last for longer than in the past – hence the growing resort to trade protection to rectify these imbalances. The problem is made worse by the fact that even when exchange rates move in the right direction, they often fail to bring about the required adjustment. It has been suggested that the reason lies in the inflexibility of real wages in industrialized economies. This view maintains that relative prices fail to adjust in response to changes in the exchange rate in such a way as to correct any payments imbalance. Thus a fall in the exchange rate initially lowers domestic prices relative to foreign prices. However, workers resists cuts in real wages and demand increases in money wages which fully compensate for higher prices. Rather than resist such wage demands, employers concede the necessary wage increase and fully pass on the higher wage costs in higher prices charged to the consumer (Godley and May 1977). Clearly this argument is based upon a certain view about prices and markets in mature economies. However, to the extent that the theory fits the facts, exchange rates fail to perform fully the equilibrating role which they are supposed to. This leaves governments with the only alternatives for tackling a persistent balance-of-payments deficit of reducing relative prices through domestic deflation or import restrictions. It is argued that a higher tariff does not require a sacrifice of economic growth and risk of high unemployment. In brief, the tariff is transformed into a weapon of macroeconomic balance-of-payments adjustment. (See Pearce and Sutton, 1986, for a good discussion of this argument.)

Gatt rules have always permitted member states to impose import restrictions to safeguard their balance of payments providing that the restriction is temporary. This is article 12 of the GATT Charter. However, as we have seen, the hallmark of the New Protectionism has been the spread of industry-specific, selective import restrictions rather than general import controls. Whether or not an argument exists for the greater use of tariffs as a weapon of macroeconomic balance-of-payments adjustment, this kind of consideration would not appear to have caused the growth of the New Protectionism. However, if real wages are inflexible in a downward direction, this may help explain why exchange rates have failed to play their proper role in securing adjustment in payments imbalances between countries. The persistence of a trade deficit despite depreciation of the exchange rate can be expected to reinforce protectionist outcries in industries worst affected by import competition.

5. **The failure of GATT rules and mechanisms to cope with the new situation** We have already seen how the growing resort to VERs and OMAs has its origins in the requirements of the GATT escape clause (article 19). Article 19 was included in the GATT Charter in order to make the objective of freer trade acceptable to as many countries as possible. There had to be some provision for signatory states to opt out of freer trade in emergency situations as when imports caused serious injury or threatened to cause serious injury to domestic producers. The important requirement was to ensure that any restrictions introduced for this reason (a) were introduced in consultation with other GATT members affected by the restrictions (rather than being imposed unilaterally), (b) had as little distorting effect on the world allocation of resources as possible, (c) offered compensation to other GATT members adversely affected, and (d) provided for the eventual removal of the restrictions once the danger was removed. Furthermore, all such restrictions would be monitored by the GATT Secretariat and a proper dispute-settlements machinery established to resolve any differences between countries arising from the introduction of such restrictions.

As we have seen, the tendency has been for many countries to bypass article 19. VERs and OMAs involve restraints on trade but lie outside the GATT rules. This is because they involve a restraint on exports but not imports. Moreover, they are bilaterally negotiated and not unilaterally imposed. However, as we have seen, their effects are arguably worse than tariffs. They involve a quantitative restriction on trade – which GATT has always condemned in the strongest possible terms – and they are discriminatory, being very often directed against the world's most efficient, lowest-cost supplier of a product. Moreover, they are secretive such that their use is extremely difficult to monitor. The precise quantitative impact of such restraints on trade is very difficult to determine. There is very little assurance that the restraint will be ended when the cause of the restraint has been removed. Certainly there is no provision for the degree of trade restriction to diminish progressively as the situation improves. For all these reasons, VERs and OMAs are almost certainly worse than tariffs as forms of trade restriction. However, for countries making use of such restraints they have the attraction that they deal directly with the source of the problem without risking offending other suppliers of the product. This is because such restraints discriminate against the imports of the offending country. At the same time, they do not necessitate granting any compensation to suppliers of the product as would be required if article 19 were activated. Thus the use of such restraints has its origins in the failure of article 19 to achieve its objectives.

6. **The loss of a hegemonic power in international trade policy**
The liberal trading order set up after the Second World War had its origins in the US trade agreements policy of the pre-war period. This policy came into being with the passage through Congress of the Reciprocal Trade Agreements Act (1934). This Act reversed past US trade policy in a number of important ways. It provided for a negotiable and flexible US tariff, and it empowered the US president to enter into tariff-cutting trade agreements within a prescribed authority. The US president was empowered to cut tariffs by up to 50 per cent in return for equivalent concessions for US exports in overseas markets. This authority was granted for a period of three years but was subsequently renewed by means of fresh legislation. The basis for the establishment of the GATT after the Second World War was the US desire to cut its own import tariff in return for (a) non-discriminatory treatment of its exports (so-called 'most-favoured-nation' treatment) reciprocally granted to other

countries and (b) easier access for US exports to the domestic markets of other countries. The passage of new trade legislation through Congress enabled the US president to initiate and enter into multilateral negotiations with other countries to bring this about. Every major round of GATT negotiations since the war has tended to follow upon Congress granting the US president new authority to negotiate cuts in the US tariff. This is because no meaningful multilateral tariff negotiations could take place without the involvement of the United States as the world's leading trading nation. GATT trade negotiations involve countries making reciprocal cuts in their own import tariffs. However, any concession extended by one country to another is automatically extended to all other countries under the most-favoured-nation principle. Clearly no such negotiations could take place without the involvement of the United States.

Thus, over the post-war period the United States has played a vital leadership role. Progress towards freer trade has depended on the willingness of the United States to move in this direction. Although there were times during the post-war period when US zeal for more free trade appeared to wane, this never lasted for long. However, beginning in the early 1970s there were signs of a permanent change in attitudes within the United States. The passage of the 1974 Trade Act provided for further tariff negotiations, but in a number of respects involved a retreat from the liberal stance of earlier years. Congress granted the president new powers to cut tariffs but also introduced certain encumbrances on his authority. Congress was given greater power to override presidential actions. Domestic interests were given easier access to import relief when imports caused or threatened to cause damage. Greater power was granted to the International Trade Commission, a body independent of the president, to investigate grievances and recommend relief or redress. The judicial branch of government was given a larger role in trade policy (Cohen 1978).

Faced with a mounting trade deficit, attitudes within Congress have hardened further in recent years. Although the United States has played an important role in initiating an eighth round of GATT, the demand for protectionist action against certain imports continues to grow. In particular there has been growing support within the United States for so-called 'reciprocity' in trade policy. Nowadays this is interpreted to mean something rather different from that in the past. It is generally used to mean that, where a country does not grant comparable access to US exports, the United States should retaliate by imposing trade restrictions against the country in question. A large number of bills which have been put before Congress in recent years have called for the implementation of this principle. If adopted, however, such a policy would result in a radical break in the continuity of US trade policy since the war. It would involve the United States in introducing trade restrictions against any country deemed not to grant equal access to US products. It would therefore involve a break with the principle of non-discrimination which has been the hallmark of US trade policy for the past sixty years. Almost certainly, such action would invite foreign retaliation. This would risk an international trade war.

The gradual erosion of US authority and leadership in international trade policy may be seen as one of the factors fostering the growth of the New Protectionism. The United States is no longer willing or able to play the role which it played in the past. At the same time, there is no other country which is willing or able to do so. Yet the number of countries now involved in international trade negotiations has increased. The need for a hegemonic power is greater than ever before. The distinct lack of any country willing to play such a role has weakened the impetus towards freer trade through GATT negotiations and given a greater freedom to protectionist forces.

THE ADJUSTMENT PROBLEM

I now turn to an examination of the so-called adjustment problem. Our concern is primarily with trade-related adjustment, that is to say adjustment within countries necessitated by changes in trade flows. Specifically, I am concerned with the need for adjustment within countries arising from the expansion of trade. Such adjustments are required whenever trade between any pair of countries is liberalized. When trade barriers are reduced by each country, some high-cost production in each country will be displaced by lower-cost imports. Resources will have to move out of such high-cost industries and firms and shift into the lower-cost, expanding industries and firms. Even in the absence of trade liberalization, adjustment will be needed. As we saw in Chapter 2, comparative advantage is a dynamic process. Comparative advantage in the production of a particular good can move from one country to another over the course of time. Technological change may give one country a comparative advantage in a certain product which it did not have before. Countries themselves undergo important changes as their economies grow and develop. The nature of their comparative advantage begins to change. All these processes put pressures on countries to adjust. Producers of a certain product may suddenly face new, more fierce competition from abroad. Where imports are free to flow into a country without restriction such competition will compel firms to make a response. This may necessitate shifting resources out of the industry in question and moving into an entirely different line of production. Alternatively, it may be forced to rationalize the company to achieve cost savings or concentrate on certain particular product lines in which it can compete. If it is not able to do so, it may have to close down. Workers employed by the firm will have to seek employment either with another firm in the industry or with firms operating in different industries.

Thus adjustment is a process which is taking place all the time. Even in a closed economy unaffected by alternating trade flows, adjustment is needed. Over the course of time, the pattern of demand for different goods and services changes. Some industries expand, others decline. The process of competition within industries means that some firms expand while others contract, new firms appear while some old firms disappear. All these changes require movements of resources (physical and human) out of certain activities and into others. In a centrally-planned, state-owned economy, these adjustments take place through state direction of resources. Resources are allocated to particular industries in accordance with some centrally-determined national plan. In a free-market economy, resources are allocated through the price mechanism. Reallocation of resources between different activities takes place through changes in relative prices and costs. It is important to bear in mind that, at any given time, many adjustment pressures are at work within a country. Trade-related adjustment pressures are only one such pressure, although, especially in very open economies, a highly important one. The growth in the degree of economic interdependence of countries over the post-war period has made countries more vulnerable to such external adjustment pressures. At the same time, the dynamic nature of comparative advantage is more real than ever before. Partly because of the increased international mobility of capital, the location of a particular comparative advantage can change quickly. Because of the openness of most industrialized countries, the effects of such changes may be felt rapidly in the form of more intense import competition. Such pressures to adjust operate alongside adjustment pressures created by structural changes within the domestic economy.

The Nature of the Adjustment Problem

Let us begin with a consideration of the exact nature of the adjustment problem arising from increased trade. It can be shown that, if the markets for goods and factors of production were perfect, no adjustment problem would be involved. Increased trade would result in a decline of those industries in which the country was at a comparative disadvantage and an expansion of those industries in which the country enjoyed a comparative advantage. Resources would instantly shift out of the former and into the latter in response to changes in relative factor prices. Thus wage rates would rise in the former and decline in the latter, inducing workers to withdraw from low-paid employment and seek high-paid employment. No unemployment would result. If the expanding, exporting industries are more capital intensive than the declining, import-competing industries, it might be expected that unemployment will result. How can all the workers displaced by the latter be re-employed in the former? The answer is that excess supply of labour will bring about a fall in the price of labour relative to the price of capital. This will encourage firms in both sectors of the economy to substitute labour for capital. Cheaper labour will encourage firms to invest in more labour-intensive methods of production. This process will continue until such time as all labour and capital within the economy is fully employed. Under perfect competition, such a process of adjustment takes place instantly and without friction.

Adjustment problems arise because markets are not perfect. To illustrate the process of adjustment to trade expansion, let us consider the following simple model, illustrated by Figure 7.1. Such a model is sometimes referred to as a specific-factors model (see Neary 1985). This is because it makes the

Figure 7.1 **Adjustment to trade expansion in a specific-factors model**

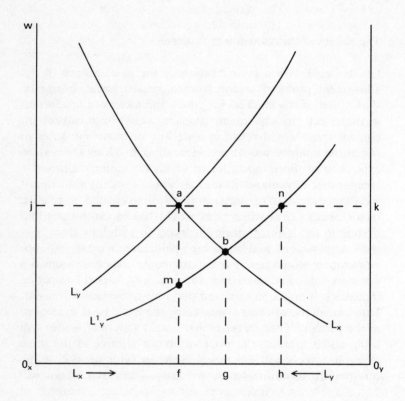

assumption that all factors of production except labour are specific to a particular sector. That is to say, these factors can only be used in either the export-expanding sector or the import-competing sector but cannot be transferred from one to the other. On the other hand, labour can switch from one sector to the other and will do so in response to changes in the price of labour in either of the two sectors. In Figure 7.1 the horizontal axis shows the demand for and supply of labour in the two sectors, x and y. The vertical axis shows the wage-rate w. The demand curve for labour in the two sectors is given by L_x and L_y respectively. The initial equilibrium wage-rate is j = k with $O_x f$ labour employed in sector x and $O_y f$ labour employed in sector y.

Now, let us suppose that a new, cheaper producer of the product of sector y emerges in some other part of the world. He begins to export his product to the country shown in Figure 7.1. The immediate effect is to cause a fall in the price of product y. The fall in the price of product y reduces the marginal revenue product (marginal product x price per unit) of workers employed in sector y. The demand curve for labour (which is the marginal revenue product curve) shifts downwards to the right from L_y to L^1_y. At wage-rate j = k, there now exists a disequilibrium in the labour market. Wage-rates are now too high to clear the market. At wage-rate k, the demand for labour is now n and not a. Unemployment of a n exists. However, if the labour market is a perfect market, wage-rates will fall. A new equilibrium will be re-established at b. This will involve more workers being employed in sector x and fewer workers in sector y. The market is cleared. No unemployment exists.

In reality, however, markets are not perfect. It is the existence of certain market imperfections which give rise to an adjustment problem. Two sorts of imperfection may be identified:

1. Segmentation of the labour market: The labour market in reality consists of a large number of separate segments or subsectors. This is due to the occupational and geographical immobility of labour. Workers are either unable or unwilling or both to move from one occupation to another or from one geographical region to another. For example, in the model above it may be that the skills required in sector x are different from those required in sector y. Alternatively, factories based in sector x may be located in a different region from those based

in sector y, and workers may not be willing to move from the one region to the other. The problem underlying both occupational and geographical immobility of labour is not so much that workers cannot move but that the costs involved in doing so (e.g. the costs of retraining or the costs of moving house) are unduly prohibitive. Whatever the case, it is not possible for all the transfer of fg workers from sector y to x shown in Figure 7.1 to take place. Effectively, the two markets for labour are segmented. This will give rise to a disparity in wage-rates between the two sectors. Wage-rates remain at fa in sector x but fall from fa to fm in sector y. At wage-rate fm, firms in sector y are willing to employ $O_y f$ workers, so the labour market clears. No unemployment results but workers employed in the import-competing, declining sector experience a large fall in wage-rates.

2. Downward stickiness of wage-rates: If, for the moment, we assume perfect mobility of labour, a second source of difficulty may arise if wage-rates are inflexible or sticky. That is to say, they do not move in response to changes in the demand for and/or supply of labour. One possible source of such stickiness may be the existence of trade unions able to resist any reduction in wage-rates. Suppose trade unions force employers to pay the wage-rate $j = k$. Wage-rates cannot fall to clear the market. The result will be unemployment equal to a n. Employment in sector x will be unchanged at $O_x f$, but employment in sector y will fall to $O_y h$.

At any given time, both sorts of imperfection will exist. Both are more of a problem in the short run than in the long run. In the long run one can expect some movement of workers from the declining import-competing sector into the expanding, export sector in response to the disparity in wages. In the real world, workers never move instantly from one sector to the other in response to differences in relative wages. Some frictional unemployment is therefore inevitable. In the long run, however, this will tend to fall. Similarly, the existence of high levels of unemployment in the declining, import-competing sector will, in the long run, undermine the ability of trade unions to enforce the same wage rate as in other parts of the economy. Some disparity in wage rates will open up. Accordingly, in the long run, unemployment will be less.

The Costs of Adjustment

It is apparent that, where markets operate imperfectly, the need to adjust involves certain costs for those involved. The following is a list of the major kinds of private and social costs caused by adjustment:

1. The loss from the transitional unemployment which results from rigidities in the labour market: This is the principal type of cost associated with adjustment. It is possible to measure this cost by taking the income foregone by workers made redundant during the period of their unemployment. In practice there are considerable difficulties involved in carrying out this exercise. For example, how does one determine the length of time during which a worker is unemployed? How does one determine the income foregone by a worker? Income earned in subsequent employment may be lower or higher than in a worker's previous employment. One may choose to include the costs of job search in such assessment of the private costs of adjustment. The latter, however, is hardly a cost to society as Banks and Tumlir have observed (Banks and Tumlir 1986). Every worker must allow for some minimum search time when seeking to move from one job to another. This cannot be avoided in a dynamic society. Moreover, it is actually in a worker's best interests to spend time seeking to find the job that will best satisfy him. This cannot be counted as a cost to society.

2. The cost of such transitional unemployment to the government: Part of the private loss of workers made redundant by imports are born by the state in the form of payment of unemployment benefits. This must be subtracted from the income which the worker is assessed as having foregone to get the net loss of income to the individual. Equally, the worker may receive some lump-sum redundancy payment from private employers, in which case part of the income foregone is born by the firm.

3. The decline in the wealth of individuals caused by the drop in the value of assets used in the declining industry: The value of capital employed in the contracting industry and held by individuals will fall, inflicting a wealth loss on the owners of such assets. However, care must be taken in deciding whether or not to include such losses in the costs of adjustment. First, if the capital in question (e.g. machinery) had no alternative use, is

373

there any loss involved? Cost in economics is opportunity costs, that is, the cost of alternatives foregone. Second, such losses in wealth experienced by certain asset owners will be offset by the gains in wealth of other asset owners. The latter will consist of those who own assets in the expanding export sector where increased demand for certain specific assets raises their value. Thus these losses are essentially losses to certain individuals but not costs to society as a whole. Indeed, if we take the view that such assets have no alternative use, we cannot count them as private costs either. On the other hand, although this may have analytical appeal, it is unhelpful from a practical point of view. Businessmen clearly do regard such declines in capital values as 'avoidable' costs. They are therefore an additional factor contributing towards domestic resistance to trade expansion.

4. The lower wages received by workers employed in the declining industry: The fall in the wages of workers employed in the declining, import-competing sector constitutes a private loss analogous to the decline in wealth experienced by the owners of assets held in the same sector. This may be viewed as being a reflection of the decline in the value of human capital tied up in a particular skill specific to the industry in decline. However, it is clearly not a cost to society, since other skills are now in greater demand, being reflected in the higher real wages received by workers possessing such skills.

The existence of such adjustment costs has sometimes been used as a basis to justify trade restrictions, as in the case of protection in the clothing and textiles sector. However, the argument would only hold if it could be shown that such short-run adjustment costs were greater than the welfare gain from free trade. Even then it would be necessary to ensure that trade restrictions were progressively lowered as adjustment took place within the importing country. The existence of short-run adjustment costs provides no justification for permanent protection. If trade restrictions are justifiable on such grounds, their aim must be to slow down the rate of adjustment, not prevent it from taking place altogether. In practice, as is demonstrated by the example of trade in clothing and textiles, what may begin as temporary protection on the grounds of minimizing short-run adjustment costs, becomes permanent. The Multi-Fibre Agreement, which has its origins in the Long-Term Cotton Textile Agreement of 1962 and which was justified on the grounds of the need to slow down the rate of adjustment in the industrialized countries, has increasingly become a permanent feature of trade policy.

In fact there is little empirical support for the view that short-run adjustment costs outweigh the gains from trade. It is true that there exist very considerable difficulties in accurately measuring both the gains from trade and the adjustment costs. However, such attempts as have been made lend very little support to the view that short-run adjustment costs are of sufficient magnitude to justify temporary trade restrictions. For example, one attempt to simulate the effects of protection and trade liberalization on the UK economy incorporating both the static and dynamic gains from trade and certain adjustment costs found little support on welfare grounds for trade restrictions on clothing and textile products. Both high import tariffs and the restriction of imports by means of a VER were found to have a negative effect on UK personal disposable income. GDP was also reduced in the case of a tariff, but not in the case of a VER. Significantly, however, in the case of motor vehicles, trade restrictions were found to have a beneficial effect on personal disposable income and GDP. However, the author was anxious to stress that the assumptions used were extremely generous towards the protectionist case (Cable 1983).

Even if it can be shown that the need to adjust does impose substantial costs on society, it is not evident that the solution is to restrict trade. A better solution is to tackle the market imperfections which give rise to such adjustment costs. As Banks and Tumlir have convincingly argued, the so-called costs of adjustment are not so much the result of the need to adjust as of market imperfections which are correctible (Banks and Tumlir 1986). If this is so, the role for any trade adjustment policy must be the elimination of such imperfections, not defensive measures which avoid the need to adjust. If these imperfections cannot be corrected, how can we talk of such adjustment costs as costs at all, because 'cost' in economics exists only where there is an opportunity foregone? If no alternative exists, no opportunity has been foregone and therefore no cost has been incurred by society (Banks and Tumlir 1986).

Factors Impeding the Adjustment Process

What are these factors which impede adjustment? What forms of market imperfection prevent adjustment from taking place instantly and without friction in the manner described in Figure 7.1? Following Banks and Tumlir, we may identify the following kinds of impediments:

1. Restrictive practices of trade unions: Three sorts of trade-union practices may impede adjustment, leading to structural unemployment or lower economic growth or both:

   (a) Monopoly pricing of labour: Monopoly wage-fixing will encourage firms to substitute capital for labour and lead to higher unemployment than otherwise.
   (b) Fixed wage relativities: Wage demands which maintain fixed wage relativities between skills and industries cause structural unemployment, because they prevent labour from moving from slow-growing or declining industries to fast-growing ones. This is largely due to nation-wide fixing of wages.
   (c) Resistance to the introduction of new technology: Trade unions may block the introduction of new technology or impose conditions upon its use.

2. Minimum-wage legislation: Minimum-wage laws prevent wages from falling for certain kinds of unskilled labour or in certain declining industries and thus contribute towards high unemployment among such low-skilled labour. In addition, they discriminate against both those industries which use high proportions of low-skilled labour (e.g. the textile and clothing industries) and declining regions which need to attract new investment through lower labour costs.

3. Employment protection legislation: Various kinds of employment legislation (relating to the hiring and firing of workers) may serve to raise the costs of employing workers. By so doing, their effect is to encourage firms to substitute capital for labour and so increase unemployment. Although some such legislation may be considered desirable to protect workers from arbitrary dismissal, legislation which gives to workers lifetime job security is likely to be counter-productive. The result is that fewer jobs are available for those without work.

4. High levels of social security benefit and high marginal rates of income taxation: The combined effects of high levels of unemployment benefit (especially for large families) plus payment of income tax at relatively low levels of income is to create a 'poverty trap'. Low-paid workers have little incentive to seek alternative employment because the net income from work is little more than what they receive in social security benefits.

5. Imperfections in capital markets: Capital markets play an important role in the adjustment process by making investable funds available to the new, expanding activities, at the same time as capital is scrapped or not replaced as it wears out in the older, declining sectors. In the short run, of course, capital is much less mobile than labour (as in the specific-factors model considered above). Much of the capital stock is specific to a particular sector and cannot be re-employed in another sector. However, in the long run, capital mobility can and does take place through the scrapping of part of the capital stock — or its non-replacement as it wears out — and net additions to other parts of the capital stock. Various kinds of government intervention may impede this adjustment process. For example, the system of corporate taxation may subsidize various kinds of investment (through the granting of tax allowances) and discriminate against others. By discriminating against the small firm, the tax system may impede adjustment in so far as small firms are more flexible and adaptable than large firms. Government regulations of the financial markets may impede adjustment. For example, controls on interest rates may prevent the faster-growing, high-productivity, more dynamic sectors of the economy from obtaining sufficient additional capital. Inflation may also have a distorting effect both on the absolute amount of new investment taking place within an economy and the form of that investment.

6. Monopoly power and monopolistic practices in product markets: Monopolies interfere with adjustment by fixing prices above marginal costs and by restricting supply. Resources are prevented from entering an industry in response to the opportunity to earn excess profits. Monopolization and oligopolization of markets has resulted in prices becoming more 'sticky' and less responsive to changes in demand and supply conditions.

7. Impediments to the mobility of labour: Even when the pricing system sends off the right kind of signals with regard to relative scarcities, various impediments may prevent labour

from moving in response to these signals. Barriers impeding the occupational mobility of labour include the costs of retraining when these are not born by firms or by government, and the existence of non-transferable occupational pension schemes which add to the costs of changing jobs. Barriers impeding the geographical mobility of labour include the costs of moving house, the costs of finding a new house, the costs of buying and selling houses. Large differences in house prices between different regions of a country are an important impediment to the geographical mobility of labour. The provision of low-cost council housing may also create an impediment to the mobility of labour as when council housing is allocated on a waiting-list basis.

There are grounds for believing that, as countries grow to maturity, the impediments to adjustment, and hence their inability to adjust, increase. Growing state intervention in factor and product markets, alongside the growth of both monopoly power in product markets and monopolistic trade unions in the labour market all serve to increase the impediments to adjust. As such, they raise the so-called costs of adjustment. Such tendencies have been taking place in most of the mature, western industrialized economies in recent decades. This has taken place at a time when the pressure to adjust has almost certainly increased. In particular, the rise of the NICs, posing increasingly intense competition in certain highly 'sensitive' sectors of the economy of western industrialized countries, has served to increase such pressure considerably. Many of the industries affected employ a disproportionately large number of relatively underprivileged, economically weak groups of workers. Typically these are relatively low-skilled workers, often either female workers or belonging to an ethnic minority group. Many of the firms operating in such industries are relatively small-scale and least able to cope with the adjustment pressures involved. In addition, many of these industries are highly concentrated in particular regions, often depressed regions with few alternative sources of employment and unattractive as locations for new investment.

Adjustment Policy

In the face of such pressure to adjust, many of the advanced industrialized countries have taken what appears to be the road of least resistance and imposed restrictions on imports of sensitive products. Hence the New Protectionism may be regarded as a defensive reaction to an increase in (1) the pressure to adjust and (2) the costs of adjustment within the advanced industrialized economies. An alternative to trade restrictions is for governments to introduce measures which facilitate the adjustment process. This is what is commonly known as adjustment policy. Earlier it was argued that the only legitimate adjustment policy is one which acts to remove the principal impediments to adjust. Thus a policy of import restrictions lies outside the ambit of adjustment policy because such a policy seeks to remove the need to adjust. Much the same is true of a policy which subsidizes declining activities or firms. By making it remunerative for resources to stay in declining sectors in the face of pressure to shift out of such sectors and into new, expanding ones, such a policy obviates the need to adjust.

In practice, many of the measures introduced by government in the advanced industrialized countries in recent decades have been of the latter type. They have been designed to compensate particular groups of individuals for the effects of increased import competition. Such 'adjustment assistance' is justified on the grounds that it is offsetting the social costs of adjustment and thus serving to reduce resistance to freer trade. As such, it is an alternative to trade restrictions and helps promote freer trade. As we have seen, there are social costs of adjustment, although some economists have raised doubts concerning whether all of these so-called costs really do constitute costs in the economic meaning of the term (Banks and Tumlir 1986). The expansion of trade may also impose considerable private costs on certain individuals. It may be felt desirable on equity grounds to compensate individuals adversely affected by trade through the payment of such adjustment assistance financed out of taxation imposed on income groups which gain from trade expansion. Furthermore, it may be considered politically expedient to pay adjustment assistance to individuals harmed by trade expansion to 'buy off' their opposition.

However, the following points need to be born in mind:

1. If, on grounds of equity, governments decide to compensate all individuals adversely affected by the expansion of trade, on the same criteria they should also compensate every other social

379

group affected by change whether such change originates from abroad (as in this case) or from at home. Such a policy would not only be extremely costly and necessitate quite high levels of taxation, but would be extremely difficult to operate. Even if it is felt appropriate for governments to insulate individuals from the worst consequences of economic change, the question must be asked: how far should such a policy be carried? How much protection can governments give without stifling progress itself? If governments perfectly compensated every individual for the income reduction caused by change, individuals would have no incentive to initiate change or to adapt in response to change. Moreover, the danger exists that government will reduce equity, not increase it, as it would have to make arbitrary decisions about which groups are entitled to compensation and which are not.

2. It is by no means certain that the offer of adjustment assistance to those adversely affected by trade expansion will be successful in 'buying-off' their resistance. To begin with, it is by no means clear that the proper function of democratic government is to placate sectional interests when this involves sacrificing the general interests of society as a whole. However, even if such a course of action were felt to be justifiable in order to gain the assent of a minority group to the wishes of the majority, it is not apparent that such a policy will succeed. Might not the granting of such 'bribes' to one vested-interest group provoke other groups to demand equivalent such 'bribes'? Moreover, how does one determine the amount of such a 'bribe' and what form should it take? There exist no satisfactory criteria for answering these questions.

It is questionable whether compensatory policies which are designed to redistribute income or 'buy off' social groupings harmed by trade expansion, constitute adjustment policy. A legitimate adjustment policy is one which seeks to facilitate (not thwart) adjustment by either (1) removing impediments to the workings of the market or (2) augmenting the workings of the market (Greenaway 1983). The former involves any measure which brings about more rapid adjustment — whether in response to external trade pressures or domestic pressures (e.g. changes in the pattern of demand, technological change, etc.) — by freeing the market from factors impeding its proper operation. With reference to the various impediments discussed above, we may cite the following example of such measures:

1. Trade union reform to reduce the power of trade unions to fix wages.
2. An effective anti-trust law for trade unions confining their organization to the level of the individual firm.
3. Legislation to give enterprises in certain industries greater freedom to employ workers at low wages.
4. Tax and social-security reforms designed to lower the high, punitive marginal rates of taxation operative at very low levels of income.
5. Measures to deregulate financial markets and free interest rates to move in response to market conditions.
6. Tougher competition and anti-trust legislation to reduce barriers to entry and make product prices more responsive to market conditions.
7. Measures to increase the occupational mobility of labour, such as increased spending on education and vocational training, support for retraining programmes, and so on.
8. Measures designed to increase the geographical mobility of labour, such as a reform of housing policies.

Policies which seek to augment the workings of the market are not so much concerned with removing impediments to the workings of the market as with assisting the market to work quicker and with less friction than it might otherwise. As we saw earlier, the adjustment problem is essentially a short-run problem. Adjustment takes place, but not instantly and without friction. The existence of both frictional and structural unemployment is the reflection of this. Such policies will include grants or tax relief to assist with the scrapping of capital or closure of plant in declining industries, grants paid to firms in declining industries to meet the costs of redundancies, grants towards the retraining of workers whose skills have become redundant, and so forth. All such measures are designed to accelerate change. Such policies may also play an important role in reducing the social costs of adjustment since such costs are greater the longer the adjustment process takes place.

Adjustment policies of one kind or another are now a common feature of industrial policy in all the advanced industrialized countries. However, not all such policies promote adjustment. An increasing tendency throughout the 1970s was for governments to dress up essentially protectionist measures in the guise of adjustment. Thus the payment of subsidies to ailing firms or industries were often justified on the grounds that they were adjustment policies when in practice the effect was to forestall adjustment. Such defensive, compensation policies acted in precisely the same way as trade restrictions to distort trade. Indeed, the effect of such measures was to increase the adjustment burden for other countries. If domestic firms in one industrialized country received state assistance to enable them to continue in business in the face of competition from lower-cost imports, overseas suppliers switched their offensive to other foreign markets. The adjustment pressures on these countries were thereby increased, tempting governments to yield to sectional interests and grant 'damage compensation'. In brief, policies of this kind tended to proliferate. Far from reducing adjustment pressures, the global effect was to intensify such pressures.

Concern about such policies led the Council of the OECD to publish in June 1978 a document calling for countries to adopt so-called 'positive adjustment policies' in place of purely defensive, compensatory policies, which served merely to impede adjustment and to keep resources shut into declining sectors (OECD 1978). The OECD Council proposed a five-year programme designed to bring about a modification of adjustment policies to make them 'more positive'. Policies were to be designed so as to improve the capacity of economies to adjust, not to impede their ability to do so. Purely compensatory policies were to be reduced to a minimum. It advocated a shift away from sector-specific adjustment policies — policies designed to help a particular firm or industry which is in difficulty — towards more general, indirect adjustment policies (e.g. improved functioning of the labour market, improved access for industry to capital markets, etc.). If assistance were to be given because the short-run adjustment costs were felt to be too high, such policies should be degressive. That is to say, the scale of assistance should fall over time and eventually be terminated once adjustment was deemed to be complete. In addition, any such assistance should be designed to give the greatest incentives to the best, most efficient firms. Greater reliance should be placed on the tax system to correct the so-called inequities caused by adjustment and to achieve any desired redistribution of income. A greater proportion of public funds should go towards the support of long-term research and development, research and investment in other areas which limit growth (such as energy, pollution, etc.), and towards providing small and medium-size firms with greater access to venture capital. Such policies promote economic growth. Faster growth, it was argued, ensures higher levels of employment and make adjustment easier to achieve.

While the publication of the OECD's 'Positive Adjustment' document served to draw attention to the fact that many adjustment policies operated to prevent adjustment and reduce economic growth, the impact of the document has been minimal. At best, it has required governments to provide greater justification for some of the policies which have been introduced under the umbrella of adjustment policies. Nevertheless, it would seem doubtful that it has done much to bring about an actual modification of such policies. Guidelines published by the OECD are not mandatory. Member states are not obliged to adapt their policies to fit these guidelines, let alone to submit them to any external inspection or supervision. Moreover, most governments have no difficulty in justifying their particular policies in terms of the criteria of 'positive adjustment'. Certainly, no government has felt obliged to abandon the granting of selective assistance to industries or firms adversely affected by change.

STRUCTURAL ADJUSTMENT UNDER INTRA-INDUSTRY AND INTRA-FIRM TRADE

So far in this chapter, we have seen how both the pressures to adjust and the costs of adjustment have tended to increase over recent decades as far as the western industrialized countries are concerned. This has contributed towards the growth of the New Protectionism. At the same time, so-called adjustment policy has increasingly come to assume the form of defensive, compensatory measures designed to assist individuals and social groups affected by the process of economic change. Such measures prevent adjustment from taking place and push the burden of adjustment on to other countries. However, two developments over the post-war period may have made adjustment easier. First, the growth of the multinational company, discussed in Chapter 3, has meant that a significant proportion of trade is now in-house, or intra-firm, trade. This means that quite a lot of the actual process of adjustment takes place within the firm rather than through the market. We shall see that this may make for easier, less costly adjustment. Second, as we saw in Chapter 2 a large proportion of trade, especially trade between the advanced industrialized countries, consists of intra-industry trade. At the time, I drew attention to the possibility that intra-industry specialization may give rise to fewer adjustment problems than inter-industry specialization. If the proportion of intra-industry trade to total trade increases in subsequent decades, this may mean easier structural adjustment for the industrialized countries. Let us consider each of these aspects of adjustment.

Intra-firm Trade Adjustment

In Chapter 3 we saw that as much as one-third of the trade of the western industrialized economies now takes the form of intra-firm trade between the parent company and affiliates of the same multinational company. What is the relevance of this for the adjustment process? It is important to appreciate that adjustment to trade expansion involves decisions by firms to cease or reduce production of a certain good and to increase or invest in the production of another good. It is easy to forget the role of individual firms in this process when viewing it from a macroeconomic point of view. Much discussion of the adjustment problem tends to be couched in somewhat abstract macroeconomic language, conveying the impression that firms are impassive objects which merely respond predictably to changes in the market situation. Such a view of the adjustment process is both false and misleading. To begin with, most firms are both multi-product and multinational. They operate in several different industries and in more than one national market. The adjustment process takes place through their decisions about what to produce, how much to produce, and where to produce. Precisely how they respond to new competition from abroad determines the ease with which adjustment takes place and the costs of such adjustment both for society as a whole and for the individuals involved.

Faced with more intense import competition from abroad, a

firm can choose between a variety of responses. At one extreme, it may be unable to adjust and go out of business altogether. There are grounds for believing that small, single-product firms are those which are most likely to close down in response to fierce competition from abroad. Multi-product firms are better able to switch resources out of one line of production and into another. Furthermore, small firms often lack the financial resources and managerial resources to move out of one line of production and into another. In this case, substantial adjustment costs may be involved unless the workers made redundant are able to secure new employment with other firms within a reasonably short period of time. Where a region has a large number of such small firms most of which are concentrated in a single declining activity, the result will be high levels of regional unemployment. Such has been the case with many of the clothing and textile-producing regions of countries such as the United Kingdom.

Larger, more diversified firms are arguably less likely to close down altogether. Smaller firms are generally more flexible than larger firms. They may therefore be quicker to respond to the challenge posed by more intense import competition. However, for the reasons given, larger firms are likely to have more options to choose from in determining their response to increased imports. This may still involve the closure of certain high-cost, inefficient, outmoded plants as part of a programme of company-wide rationalization. Alternatively, it may involve measures to cut costs and raise productivity through reductions in the size of the workforce employed at particular plants. In both cases, some unemployment will result. Adjustment costs will accordingly be involved. However, there is a greater possibility that some new jobs will be found for some workers at other plants within the same firm. If so, redundant workers will be instantly re-employed. It also seems probable that more of the costs of adjustment will be born by the firm itself rather than by the workforce. If some of the workforce need retraining, this may be undertaken by the company itself with no extra cost for the workers involved. If the rest of the workforce lose their jobs altogether, they may be paid by the company a lump-sum redundancy benefit. This may be required by law or by some statutory agreement entered into with trade unions. Clearly this serves merely to shift the adjustment burden from workers to the company, but large, multi-product, diversified firms may be financially better able to meet such costs. At the very least, such payments may serve to reduce the degree of trade-union resistance to adjustment. Trade unions may be more inclined to accept redundancies, a programme of rationalization, or the introduction of new labour-saving technology if adequate compensation is paid by the company to the workers thus affected.

However, large multi-product firms may find other methods of adjusting to new import competition. They may be able to switch out of product lines with poor prospects and concentrate on product lines with better prospects. This may involve diversification into other industries or concentration on other product lines within the same industry. Once again, larger firms will generally be better able to make such adaptation. They will have the financial resources to do so and are more likely to possess or be able to obtain access to the necessary technological and marketing skills required for such adjustment. Larger firms may also be better able to develop new product lines to replace the declining ones, since they will generally be able to spend large amounts on R&D. To a large extent, such adjustment may be possible without the need to close many plants or make redundant large numbers of workers. Existing plants may be adapted to produce other products and/or workers moved from existing plants to new ones and equipped with any new skills required.

There are various grounds for believing that multinational companies are even better placed to bring about such adjustment than purely nationally-based multi-product firms. First, multinational companies may be better informed about market trends and changes in international comparative costs than purely national firms. This means that they may be better able to anticipate the emergence of some new low-cost source of supply for a particular product and to plan accordingly. Adjustment will still be necessary, but the adjustment process is likely to be better managed when the need for adjustment is properly anticipated. This may necessitate shifting the production of a particular product from a developed country to a new low-cost location overseas. However, such a decision can be planned for and implemented gradually. Moreover, it need not involve the closure of all plants in the developed country. It may be possible to adapt these plants to enable them to specialize in some particular stage of the production process while only certain stages or processes are located at the new low-cost site overseas. As we saw in Chapter 4, this is what is involved in offshore processing. It need not result in less production and reduced employment in the developed country. On the contrary, by reducing overall production costs, it may serve to enhance the competitiveness of the company in question, enabling it to expand or maintain its sales of the finished product.

Alternatively, the plant in the developed country may be adapted to produce some other product. This will be the case where the multinational company is also a multi-product firm. Declining production of one product can be offset by expanding production of another such that the size of the labour force need not be drastically reduced and the need for plant closures is lessened. Of course, it may still be necessary to streamline and rationalize a company's operations in a particular country or region of the world, and this may entail some plant closures and redundancies. However, a large multinational company may be better able to 'manage' such adjustments so that the costs of adjustment are kept to a minimum. In addition, it seems probable that more of the costs of adjustment will be borne within the firm. Multinational companies would seem better able to internalize such adjustment costs because of their greater efficiency and superior financial resources.

Finally, since multinational companies invariably enjoy a degree of oligopolistic market power, they are better able to cope with increased competition from another country. They are not so affected by sudden new challenges posed by the emergence of some new low-cost producer of a product. Although they will eventually need to address themselves to the new challenge to their dominance just like any nationally based firm, they will not need to act with such haste. As we saw in Chapter 3, their ability to manipulate transfer prices may mean that funds can be redirected to some beleagured plant in one country to enable it to cope temporarily with a sudden surge of fierce competition. Thus a multinational company will not have to make such abrupt changes in the face of more intense import competition as a purely nationally based firm. It will be able to dampen the effects of market forces. Again, it is apparent that this does not remove the necessity to adjust. However, it does mean that adjustment can take place more smoothly and with less social disruption than otherwise. Accordingly, adjustment costs may be lower and resistance to trade expansion reduced.

387

Thus there are grounds for believing that the spread of multinational companies over the course of the post-war period has been one factor easing the adjustment strain on the western industrialized countries, at a time when the pressures to adjust have increased. This is because, in the large multi-product, multinational firm, adjustment takes place within the firm rather than through the market. In brief, the adjustment process is internalized. As such, the need to adjust is more readily anticipated and planned for. *Ex ante* co-ordination of the adjustment process essentially takes the place of the *ex post* co-ordination of the market-place. However although there exist a priori reasons for supposing that internalized adjustment will be easier and thus less costly, greater factual evidence is needed before such a view can be declared the rule. Franko and Stephenson have attempted to examine the role played by multinational firms in the adjustment process in a few sectors of manufacturing industry which have been most subject to competition from NICs, namely steel, synthetic fibres, consumer electronics, and petrochemicals (Franko and Stephenson 1982). They found evidence in support of the view that a high degree of multinationality makes for easier adjustment in an industry. However, this is really only true where multinational companies have significant operations in the NICs themselves. Many European multinationals adopted a much more 'stand-offish' approach to foreign investment in NICs, preferring to invest only where necessary to gain access to local markets. By way of contrast, Japanese multinationals invested in NICs to establish bases for exporting to the rest of the world. As a result, many European companies were as vociferous as any national firm in calling for protection from low-cost imports from NICs. Such companies would appear to have faced considerable pressures in adjusting to import competition from NICs.

Intra-industry Trade Adjustment

In Chapter 3 we saw that there are grounds for supposing that the adjustment problem will be less where the expansion of trade takes the form of intra-industry specialization rather than inter-industry specialization. One of the features of trade between the advanced industrialized countries and the NICs has been that a high proportion of such trade has taken the form of inter-industry specialization. By way of contrast, much of the increased trade between advanced industrialized countries over the post-war period has taken the form of intra-industry specialization. One exception to this has been trade with Japan, which has been characterized by a much higher level of conventional inter-industry specialization. As we saw in Chapter 6 one reason for this may have been that, during this period, Japan was in a process of catching up with the rest of the western, industrialized world. If the adjustment problem is less under intra-industry specialization, these considerations may explain why trade between the western industrialized countries and the NICs has been accompanied by more friction than trade between the industrialized countries themselves. After all, over much of the post-war period, trade between industrialized countries has been increasingly liberalized. This appears to have taken place with little friction and minimal resistance from vested interest groups. The one single exception has been trade with Japan. The reasons for this were discussed in Chapter 6. By way of contrast, trade with NICs, despite the fact that this runs in favour of the western industrialized countries as a whole, has met with very considerable resistance from adversely affected vested interest groups.

There are three reasons why intra-industry specialization may involve easier trade adjustment than inter-industry specialization:

1. **Greater similarity of factor intensities between sectors** In the case of intra-industry specialization, the export expanding sector and the import-competing declining sector are merely two sectors of the same industry. They are two subgroups belonging to the same one product group. By definition, the products belonging to the two subgroups will have broadly similar factor intensities. This being so, it should be easier for workers to move from one sector to another. In many cases this adjustment will take place from within the firm. Most medium- and large-size firms are multi-product firms. They will simply switch workers from one line of production to another. If the factor intensities are similar, there need be no net loss of employment. In practice, factor intensities do vary within industries, although much less than between industries. Hence we cannot rule out the disappearance of some jobs. However, these should be fewer than with inter-industry specialization and may anyway be absorbed within the firm. Of course, it is also possible that

the skills required in the production of one product may differ from those required to produce another. However, where such adjustment takes place within the firm, the firm will retrain workers as necessary.

2. **Less need for flexibility of factor prices** Earlier we saw how inter-industry specialization requires relative factor prices to respond flexibly to market forces for adjustment to take place with minimal friction and in the shortest possible time. First, wage-rates must move sufficiently to ensure that an appropriate wage differential opens up between the export-expanding and import-competing sectors. Second, where the declining sector is more labour intensive than the expanding sector, the price of labour in the economy as a whole may need to fall relative to the price of capital. The need for both these changes is reduced in the case of intra-industry specialization. First, much intra-industry specialization takes place within the firm. This may also be true of some inter-industry specialization, but it is easier for firms to change product lines within given industries than to move into and out of entirely different industries. Where adjustment occurs within the firm, the market is bypassed. Accordingly, relative prices are not needed as signals indicating the changes which must take place. Second, since the factor intensities of the expanding and declining sectors are similar, there is no need for the relative price of labour in terms of capital to rise or fall to ensure 'full employment'. Since, in practice, wage-rates are inflexible, adjustment to intra-industry specialization should be easier to achieve. Furthermore, the risks of industrial conflict are likely to be less.

3. **Reduced necessity for geographical mobility of labour** As we have seen, much intra-industry specialization takes place within the firm. It involves switching workers and plant from the production of one subgroup of products to the production of another subgroup. In this case, no geographical mobility of labour is involved. However, even when some displacement of workers is involved, it should be possible for them to be re-employed by firms located in the same area or industry. Industries are often geographically concentrated so that expanding firms and contracting firms will be located in roughly the same geographical area. Given that the geographical mobility of labour is often low in the short run, intra-industry specialization may be easier to achieve than inter-industry specialization.

Care must be taken not to push any of these arguments to extremes. As we have seen, factor intensities may differ considerably within industries. This will especially be the case with industries characterized by vertical product differentiation. High-quality products may embody larger proportions of capital relative to labour than low-quality products (Greenaway and Milner 1986). Furthermore, intra-industry specialization tends to be greatest in the most technologically advanced manufacturing industries. These industries require large inputs of highly skilled labour. This may mean that each worker is equipped with a fairly narrow range of quite specific skills not readily usable in other lines of production. Such a worker may need to undergo considerable retraining before he can be re-employed in some other activity, even within the same industry. To the extent that this is true, intra-industry adjustment may not always be as instantaneous and friction-free as has been suggested.

Nevertheless, there would appear to be considerable support for the view that adjustment problems will be less under intra-industry specialization. This being so, one possible solution to current tensions between the NICs and the industrialized countries may be to encourage more intra-industry specialization as and when scope exists for doing so. This may have certain implications for both trade policy and industrial policy in the western industrialized countries. However, before we consider some of these implications, we need to consider whether intra-industry specialization is likely to yield the same benefits as inter-industry specialization. A policy of promoting more intra-industry specialization would have little appeal if such specialization brought only limited benefits to the countries involved.

The Benefits from Trade Expansion under Intra-industry Specialization

Chapter 1 discussed the welfare gains to countries from inter-industry specialization. A country is able to obtain a greater bundle of both commodities than it could produce with its own productive resources under autarky. In Figure 1.3 (p. 7) it was seen how Britain was able to move from point A on her transformation curve to point F, beyond her transformation curve. Theoretically, this welfare gain can be divided into (1) a production gain and (2) a consumption gain. The production gain arises from the fact that the country is using her domestic resources more efficiently. More of her resources are now employed in the industry in which their efficiency is greatest. The consumption gain arises from the fact that consumers are able to buy the imported product at a lower price than under autarky. As a result, they are able to consume more of the imported product.

These are the so-called static gains from inter-industry specialization and trade. Such a model of trade is based on conventional Hecksher–Ohlin assumptions. The product in question is homogeneous. Conditions of classical price competition prevail. Factor and product markets operate under conditions of perfect competition. Factors of production are immobile internationally. Average costs rise with output. Under these assumptions, the benefits from international specialization are easy to identify. As was seen in Chapter 1, both countries will gain, although the terms of trade will determine how these gains are distributed between countries. However, while the country as a whole will always be better off, it does not follow that all groups within the country will gain. In Chapter 1 I referred to the Factor Price Equalization Theorem according to which trade will give rise to a tendency for factor prices to be equalized in the two countries. From this it follows that the owners of a country's scarce factor of production will lose out from trade. Consider the case of America in Figures 1.2 (p. 6) and 1.4 (p. 9). Labour is the scarce factor and capital the abundant factor. Therefore, before trade, labour is relatively expensive and capital relatively cheap. However, after trade, America specializes in steel production, which is more capital intensive than cloth production. This increases the demand for capital relative to labour. The price of labour falls relative to the price of capital. Workers experience a drop in their money wages. However, real wages may still increase if the price of cloth falls by more than money wages. Nevertheless, it is possible to demonstrate that, under certain assumptions, trade will reduce the real incomes of the owners of a country's scarce factor of production. Theoretically, this can be resolved by the better-off income groups compensating the worse-off income groups, leaving the country as a whole better-off than before. In practice, however, this may not happen. For this reason, the owners of a country's scarce factor may resist the lowering of trade barriers and the expansion of trade.

In addition to these static effects, trade expansion may bring other indirect benefits. These are sometimes referred to as the 'dynamic' gains from trade. The most important types of dynamic gain are as follows:

1. Gains from economies of scale — export expansion creates opportunities for reducing costs per unit of output through (a) larger plant size, (b) longer production runs, and (c) so-called 'learning-by-doing' effects.
2. Efficiency gains resulting from increased competition — especially reductions in so-called 'X-inefficiency' (managerial slack leading to waste) and the elimination of high-cost excess capacity.
3. Stimulus to capital investment — expansion of exports will stimulate firms to undertake more capital investment, leading to both capital-widening and capital-deepening.
4. Stimulus to technical innovation — wider and faster-growing markets in the country's export industries, plus an environment of more competition at home, will stimulate greater innovation (both in the form of new lower-cost methods of production and new products).
5. Output expansion from reduced inflation — by lowering prices and exposing domestic monopolists and oligopolists to more competition, trade serves to reduce inflation, leading to faster long-run economic growth.

Attempts to measure the static gains from trade have generally found these gains to be quite small. However, we have very little information concerning the magnitude of the various dynamic gains listed above. However, there are grounds for believing that the dynamic benefits from trade are quite considerable (especially for trade in manufactured goods) and may well be quantitatively more important than the static gains which have generally received more attention in the past (see Owen 1983).

Let us now consider the case of intra-industry specialization. As we saw in Chapter 3, intra-industry specialization does not arise from differences in comparative costs. It involves countries specializing in essentially similar yet differentiated goods. On first impression this leads to an expectation that the gains from such specialization will be less than those resulting from inter-industry specialization. There are no production gains from countries employing more of their resources in those industries in which efficiency is greatest. Nor do consumers gain from being able to purchase certain goods at lower prices. The static benefits from such trade would appear to be non-existent. In fact, consumers do benefit, but the benefits take the form of increased variety and choice of goods rather than lower prices. There are no grounds for believing that these gains will be less than those resulting from inter-industry specialization (Greenaway 1982).

David Greenaway has proposed a model for analysing the gains from intra-industry specialization. This is illustrated by Figure 7.2. On the horizontal axis the two main attributes, x and y, which are possessed by a certain good, are shown. Different possible varieties of the good are obtainable. Each variety involves different combinations of these two attributes. These are known as 'variety specifications'. V_1 is one such variety. We assume that consumer preferences are uniformly distributed over all possible varieties such that a potential demand exists for all possible varieties. On the other hand, because certain fixed costs are associated with the production of a particular variety (the costs of product development and production start-up), we assume that unit costs of production fall with output. This means that it is not profitable for producers to produce all possible varieties. Thus some consumers are not able to purchase their preferred variety. The gain from intra-industry trade arises from some consumers being able to purchase varieties of a given product which are closer to their preferred variety.

In Figure 7.2 it is assumed that country 1 produces only one variety, V_1. Consumer preferences are assumed to be uniformly distributed across the plane between points S and T. The welfare gain derived by each consumer from the purchase of a particular variety can be measured by the size of his/her consumer surplus. The closer is a particular variety to the consumer's preferred variety, the greater the size of consumer surplus. In Figure 7.2 the total consumer surplus which consumers derive from the purchase of variety V_1 is shown by the shaded area SCTP. For consumers whose preferred variety lies at one of the extremes S or T, the size of consumer surplus is negligible. For consumers whose preferred variety is V_1, a very large amount of consumer surplus is obtained.

Figure 7.2 The gains from trade under intra-industry special-ization: before specialization

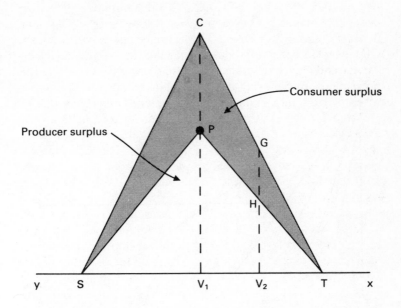

To derive the welfare gain to society, account must also be taken of the producer surplus which producers derive from producing V_1. This is the difference between the market price of the producer and each producer's supply price (i.e. the price at which he would be prepared to supply the product). Producer surplus is shown by the unshaded area SPT. Consumers whose preferred variety lies at the extremes S or T will buy very little of variety V_1. Hence their purchases will result in very little producer surplus. Consumers whose preferred variety is V_1 will buy a large amount of V_1 resulting in much producer surplus. Thus the total triangle SCT shows the welfare derived by society as a whole (comprising both consumer and producer surplus) from the production of variety V_1.

To see how area SCT is obtained, consider Figure 7.3. Let us assume there is only one, monopoly producer of variety V_1 in country 1. The market demand curve for the product is DD_1. This is the summation of all the individual consumer demand curves, such as d_1 d_2 and d_3. MR is the marginal revenue curve.

Figure 7.3 Obtaining area SCT (welfare gained by society as a whole)

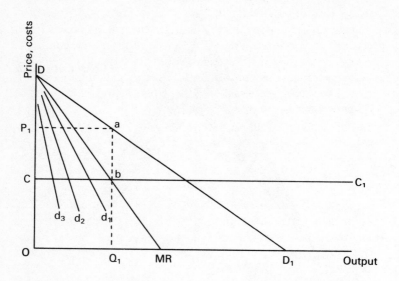

Let us further assume that average costs are constant over the relevant range of output. CC_1 is the average cost curve. With average costs constant, marginal costs equal average costs. OQ_1 is the monopolist's equilibrium level of output where marginal costs equal marginal revenue. OP_1 is the market price. Then, DaP_1 is total consumer surplus, which is equal to SCTP in Figure 7.2. CP_1ab is the monopolist's supernormal profits or total producer surplus, which is equal to SPT in Figure 7.2. How is this consumer and producer surplus distributed among consumers? Consumers whose preferred variety lies close to V_1 will demand a large amount of the product at any given price. Hence their individual demand curve will be far to the right, such as d_1. Other consumers whose preferred variety lies closer to V_2 in Figure 7.2 will demand much less at any given price. Hence their individual demand curve will be further to the left, such as d_2 or even d_3. It can be seen that total consumer surplus and total producer surplus is less when the demand curve is d_3 than when the demand curve is d_2 or d_1. Hence, for the consumers with a demand curve further to the left, the height of SCT is less. In this way, we get the pyramid shape of SCT.

Now, what happens when trade takes place? Suppose country 1 enters into trade with another country, country 2, whose consumers have slightly different preferences. This situation may be illustrated by Figure 7.4. Before trade, producers in country 1 produce variety V_1 and producers in country 2 produce variety V_2. If these two countries now engage in intra-industry trade, consumers in both countries can obtain a variety closer to their preferred variety. Specifically, consumers in country 1 whose preferences lie in the range vt can now buy variety V_2 and consumers in country 2 whose preferences lie in the range sv can now buy variety V_1. As a result, total welfare will be higher. First, consider consumers in country 2 whose preferred variety lies in the range sv and who switch from buying V_2 to buying V_1. Their consumer surplus will rise by areas $(d - b)$. At the same time, producer surplus will rise by areas $(a + b + c)$ less area a, representing lost producer surplus as some consumers in country 1 switch to buying variety V_2. So the total gain in economic welfare derived from consumers in country 2 switching to variety V_1 is:

$$(d - b) + (b + c) = (d + c)$$

Similarly, a welfare gain will result from consumers in country 1 switching from buying variety V_1 to buying variety V_2. Consumer surplus will increase by areas $(f - e)$. At the same time, producer surplus will rise by areas $(h + e + g)$ less area h, representing lost producer surplus as some consumers in country 2 switch to buying variety V_1.

The total gains may be summarized as follows:

	Gains to country 1	Gains to country 2
Consumer surplus	$(f - e)$	$(d - b)$
Producer surplus	$(b + c)$	$(g + e)$

The assumptions used in this model ensure that the distribution of these gains between the two countries will be proportionate.

Thus, under intra-industry specialization the gains accruing to countries from trade take the form of improvements in

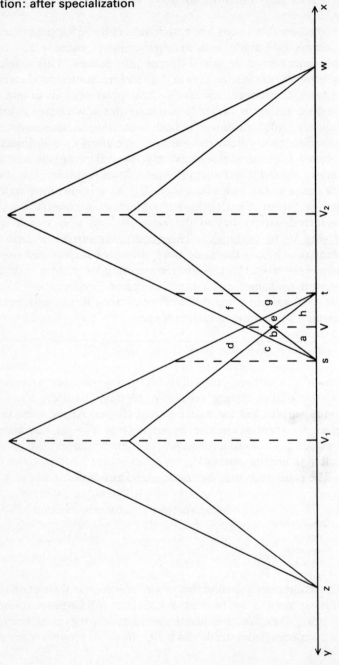

Figure 7.4 The gains from trade under intra-industry specialization: after specialization

welfare resulting from consumers being able to choose from a greater variety of consumer goods. The size of these gains will be greater, the greater the degree of taste overlap between countries. Consumers may also benefit from lower prices as under inter-industry specialization but there is an expectation that the price effect will be less under intra-industry specialization. This is because, in industries characterized by a high degree of product differentiation, competition tends to take the form of non-price rather than price competition. However, to the extent that price competition also ensues, consumers will enjoy additional benefits from lower prices. In addition, intra-industry trade should result in the same dynamic gains as may accrue from inter-industry specialization. Indeed, there are grounds for believing that intra-industry specialization results in greater dynamic benefits than inter-industry specialization. One reason is that intra-industry specialization yields scope for cost savings from longer production runs. The production line can be kept working for longer with less waste from the need to stop production and switch over to the production of another product.

A second reason is the stimulus which the opening up of intra-industry trade generates for product innovation. Firms are stimulated both to introduce new varieties of existing products (horizontal differentiation) and introduce alternatives to existing products (technological differentiation). First let us consider variety innovation. Intra-industry trade will stimulate each producer to introduce new varieties which are closer to the preferred variety of some consumers in the foreign market (the aggressive motive) and to introduce new varieties in order to erect barriers to entry for potential new entrants into the home market (the defensive motive). Although such competition may equally well take place in the absence of trade where there exists more than one producer of the product, the opening up of trade is likely to give an impetus to such non-price competition. Moreover, the potential market for a new variety is now greater because the new variety can be sold in both the home and foreign market. This may justify investment in the development of new product varieties. On the other hand, producers must beware of introducing too many new varieties since each new variety will reduce the market for existing varieties. Where, however, new varieties are introduced, consumers will enjoy a welfare gain from the availability of varieties closer to their preferred variety. In social terms, the gain will be the difference between this increased consumer welfare and the costs of developing such new varieties.

Let us now look at product innovation. Intra-industry specialization may increase the pace of product innovation, bringing further welfare gains to society. Firms will seek to introduce new products for the reasons already given for variety innovation. However, intra-industry specialization may also reduce the risks associated with innovation. In industries such as the pharmaceutical industry, where firms must innovate to maintain their share of the market, firms must devote a high proportion of their earnings to R & D. Large sums of money must be spent on the discovery and development of a product long before the product can be produced and sold. In the pharmaceuticals industry, products also have to undergo lengthy testing procedures before they can be marketed. In addition, once a product has been put onto the market, its probable market life is quite short. The rapid rate of product innovation within the industry renders products obsolete within quite short periods of time. These considerations mean that firms must seek to maximize their earnings from the sale of a new product in the early years of its product life. As Dr Meyer has argued, intra-industry specialization provides an important escape route for such firms (Meyer 1978). Intra-industry specialization enables each firm to concentrate on a limited range of products and to sell these in a large market for the highest price which the market will bear. This will permit more rapid recuperation of fixed R & D costs as well as enabling firms to spread these costs over as large a market as possible.

It follows that there are no grounds for supposing that the gains from intra-industry specialization will be any less than those resulting from inter-industry specialization. In some industries the gains may be greater. In addition, as we have seen, the adjustment problems associated with intra-industry specialization may be less. Lower adjustment costs will further serve to maximize the social gain from intra-industry specialization. Moreover, the income distribution effect resulting from intra-industry specialization should be much less acute than that resulting from inter-industry specialization. As we have seen, factor intensities are quite similar within industries. Hence intra-industry specialization will have little, if any, effect on relative factor prices. The owners of scarce factors of production should not experience any drop in their money earnings and their real earnings seem likely to improve. Professor Paul Krugman has constructed a formal model to show that intra-industry trade poses no serious income distribution problems (Krugman 1981). Where two countries are similarly endowed with the different factors of production, both factors gain from trade. Intra-industry trade results in which each country exchanges similar yet differentiated goods. The factor intensities of these goods are broadly the same, so no change in factor prices results. The welfare gains from specialization are enjoyed to varying degrees by all income groups. It follows that intra-industry specialization is less likely to meet with resistance from the owners of scarce factors who stand to lose from trade.

Trade Adjustment Policy under Intra-industry and Intra-firm Trade Adjustment

Given that intra-industry specialization is likely to generate just as large a welfare gain to countries as inter-industry specialization — given also that the income distribution effect is likely to be less serious and the adjustment problem more manageable — it may seem preferable for countries to encourage more intra-industry specialization. Certainly intra-industry specialization will meet with less domestic resistance than inter-industry specialization. This was the experience of the western industrialized countries over much of the post-war period. It was for this reason that GATT was relatively successful in lowering trade barriers on manufactures in the first twenty-five years after the war. Most trade took the form of trade in manufactures and this took place between mature industrialized economies possessing similar factor endowments. Intra-industry specialization was the predominant type of international specialization. It was only in later decades that frictions began to develop, first with the admission of Japan to GATT and, later, with the growth of developing-country exports of manufactures. The NICs possessed relatively different factor endowments to the advanced industrialized countries and so their trade with the latter tended to take the form of inter-industry specialization. The result has been considerable friction between the NICs and the advanced industrialized countries.

The same has been true of much of Japan's trade, as we saw

in Chapter 6. The cheapness of the yen served to encourage inter-industry specialization on the part of Japan even when in material terms Japan had caught up with the rest of the industrialized world. Lack of proper macroeconomic adjustment was a further cause of the tension between Japan and her trading partners in the industrialized world. As the Japanese economy matures, Japan's trade looks likely to become more balanced. Tensions should accordingly diminish. An important role in this respect will be played by the exchange rate. If the yen should once again become cheap, Japan may revert back to inter-industry specialization. A dearer yen puts pressure on Japanese exporters to move up-market into higher-quality, higher-value-added products, leading to more intra-industry specialization. At the same time the rising cost of labour within Japan will rapidly eliminate any comparative cost advantage based on factor proportions.

To some extent the same will be true for many of the NICs. As their economies mature, more of their trade will take the form of intra-industry specialization. Rising wages costs have already begun to reduce these countries' traditional comparative cost advantage in labour-intensive manufactures. However, it will benefit the western industrialized economies if they adopt policies that encourage more intra-industry specialization. This view has been put forward by the UNCTAD Secretariat (UNCTAD 1980). The UNCTAD Secretariat has expressed the view that the scope for more intra-industry trade between the western industrialized countries and the NICs may be much greater than is often supposed. As was seen in Chapter 6, this may take the form of more vertical specialization in which developing and developed countries specialize in different stages or processes involved in the production of a specific product. This involves promoting the development of the NIDL. Because factor proportions invariably differ at different stages of the production process, this kind of specialization resembles inter-industry specialization even if it is classified as intra-industry specialization. As such, it may encounter similar adjustment problems and income distribution effects as inter-industry specialization proper. On the other hand, it makes for more balanced trade between industrialized countries and NICs. Moreover, it may enable developed countries to retain a presence within what would otherwise be condemned sectors. Scope for horizontal intra-industry specialization may also be greater than is often thought. This involves developed and developing countries exchanging similar yet differentiated consumer and capital goods.

Chapter 6 suggested how industrialized countries could adapt their trade policies to encourage more such intra-industry specialization with NICs. For example, greater use of the offshore assembly provisions might help promote more vertical intra-industry specialization. Imposing lower tariffs on finished or processed goods would help to encourage NICs to invest in final assembly or processing stages of certain kinds of manufacturing. In addition, industrialized countries might be advised to lower non-tariff barriers on simple, labour-intensive, low-price manufactures coming from NICs. Very often the only effect of such restrictions is to encourage NICs to move up-market and seek out higher-quality products which they can export to the industrialized countries free of such restrictions. Yet it is in such high-quality, high-value-added products that the industrialized countries are most able to compete.

What of adjustment policy? One possibility is that governments could make an effort to seek out those niches within individual industries subject to intense import competition in which their firms can compete. The aim would then be to introduce policies to help coax resources out of declining segments of the industry and into potentially profitable ones. This would be consistent with a switch away from purely defensive, compensatory adjustment policies towards positive adjustment policies. It would not involve the total abandonment of a government's commitment to an industry faced with chronic import competition. Rather the aim of such an adjustment policy would be to help seek out niches within a troubled industry where it may be able to compete. In so far as it was felt necessary to grant a troubled industry temporary protection so as to reduce adjustment costs, such protection should be concentrated on those segments of the industry where the potential for future expansion is greatest.

It may be argued that industry itself is a much better judge of the areas within an industry in which prospects for the future are brightest. However, a case can still be made out for an active industrial policy which seeks to point industry in specified directions, if only in the sense of establishing the priorities of government policy. Such an approach has typified the work of the Ministry of International Trade and Industry (MITI) in

Japan over the post-war period. As was mentioned in Chapter 6, MITI has sought to establish future priorities and then to encourage, exhort, and persuade industry to invest in such areas. It is often thought that this role of the MITI has been a factor contributing towards the much greater adaptability and speed of adjustment of the Japanese economy over the post-war period. It is sometimes helpful for industry to know what view the government is taking of the future and which priorities are likely to guide government in its policy-making in the medium- and long-term future. This is important for the problem of structural adjustment. Adjustment costs can be reduced where the need to adjust is properly anticipated. One reason why intra-firm trade adjustment is subject to less friction is that multinational companies have more information than is available through the market and can accordingly anticipate the need to adjust. Governments may be able to play a useful role in overcoming some of the uncertainties of the market and thus enabling firms to make forward adjustments. However, in a world characterized by intra-industry specialization, the proper focus of any such industrial policy must be non-sectoral. That is to say, policy must shift away from the traditional emphasis on 'declining' and 'expanding' sectors or 'winners' and 'losers' (White 1984). Instead, the aim must be to encourage shifts within sectors.

Clearly, in attempting to promote more intra-industry specialization, western industrialized countries need to attach a special importance to R&D. This is likely to play an especially important role in promoting increased horizontal intra-industry specialization in industries subject to intense competition from NICs. R&D expenditure is the key to the development of new products and processes in which the advanced industrialized countries can hold their own in the face of fierce price competition in the more traditional product lines. Governments may be able to play an important role both in creating a general climate conducive to innovation and in generating resources to support R&D programmes in industries where the pressures of adjustment are great. In a world of intra-industry specialization, the aim of such programmes has to be to seek out narrow segments rather than an across-the-board approach.

8

Trade In Services

INTRODUCTION

In Chapter 2 attention was drawn to the increased importance of the services sector in the gross domestic product of the developed countries. The post-war period witnessed a major growth in the importance of services. By 1978, 55 per cent of the GDP of developed market economies was accounted for by services. Manufacturing accounted for only 26 per cent. This represented a major transformation in the structure of economic activity in the developed countries. The relative decline of manufacturing and rise of services has been referred to as 'de-industrialization'. Although a large proportion of services is non-tradable, trade in services accounts for a large and probably growing proportion of world trade. Exports of services constitute an important source of export earnings for a number of developed countries. For this reason, any book dealing with new patterns of world trade must concern itself with trade in services. In addition, as we shall see during the course of this chapter, different factors may affect trade in services than those governing trade in goods.

In particular, throughout the post-war period, trade in services has been unaffected by the process of liberalization taking place in merchandise trade. Trade in services is not directly governed by the GATT. Until recently, no attempt was made to tackle the issue of barriers to trade in services. No internationally agreed rules govern trade in services. This is now seen by certain developed countries, principally the United States, as a major weakness of the GATT Charter. GATT is viewed as being one-sided since members are required to ensure liberal access for the goods of other members but no equivalent provisions exist for exports of services. It is argued that such an arrangement discriminates against countries which heavily depend on trade in services for vital export earnings. In response to such arguments, GATT members have agreed to include the issue of trade in services on the agenda of the forthcoming eighth GATT round. It remains to be seen what progress will be made.

In this chapter I will examine the nature and importance of trade in services and discuss the prospects for negotiating more liberal trade in services. I begin with an attempt to define services and to evaluate their importance in the national economies of various countries. Next, I will examine the importance of trade in services in total world trade. Finally, I will consider the major issues involved in liberalizing world trade in services. The emphasis throughout this chapter is on trade in services. However, as we saw in Chapter 4, multinational investment activity has been of some considerable importance in service industries. As Table 4.7 (p. 162) shows, services accounted for over one-quarter of direct investment abroad in all major developed market economies. Thus, much of what has been said about the multinational company in earlier parts of this book is especially relevant to the services sector. Moreover, as we shall see, trade and investment issues are peculiarly inter-related in services in a way which they are not in goods. This is especially apparent when the issue of liberalizing trade in services is discussed. It becomes impossible to separate issues of freer trade from issues concerning the right of foreign service firms to set up in other countries.

THE IMPORTANCE OF THE SERVICES SECTOR IN THE NORMAL ECONOMY

Defining Services

What are services? There exists no exact universally agreed definition of a service activity. However, in using the term 'service activity' in contrast with the production of a good, people have in mind some general notion of what constitutes a service. T.P. Hill has defined a good as 'a physical object which is appropriable and therefore transferable between units'. By way of contrast, he has defined a service as 'a change in the condition of a person, or of a good belonging to an economic unit, brought about by the activity of another economic unit with the former's consent' (Hill, 1977). Some services affect persons, for example education, medical care, hairdressing, entertainment, and so on. Other services affect goods, for example construction, advertising, wholesaling, insurance, and so on. Some services affect both persons and goods, for example banking and other financial services.

Stern and Hoekman have further suggested three criteria for distinguishing between goods and services (Stern and Hoekman 1987):

1. The production and consumption of services have to take place simultaneously whereas they need not for goods.
2. Services cannot be stored whereas goods can.
3. Services are intangible whereas goods are tangible.

In practice it is often extremely difficult to distinguish between a good and a service. First, goods and services are frequently supplied together. For example, a meal at a restaurant involves both the sale of a tangible output and the provision of a service. Second, many services are provided by firms for themselves. Many large firms employ their own lawyers and accountants. Where this happens, the provision of a service is subsumed within the output of the firm. On the other hand, where firms employ outside lawyers or accountants, a service is deemed to have been supplied. For statistical purposes, intra-firm transactions of this kind are often extremely difficult to measure. Even if such transactions can be identified, it is often impossible to assign a value for such services because no market exists. Third, in some cases a good may constitute a vehicle through which a service is provided. For example, a doctor may treat a patient through the prescription of certain drugs. Fourth, whether we classify a particular output as a good or a service may depend on the form in which it is made available. For example, electricity purchased through the Electricity Board is an intangible output and treated as a service. Electricity purchased in the form of a storage battery is tangible output and therefore is treated as a good.

All of these considerations make it extremely difficult to measure accurately the true extent of service activity within

407

national economies. Furthermore, they qualify the usefulness of any distinction drawn by economists between the
goods sector and the services sector of the economy. Is it
meaningful to draw such a distinction? The relevance of this
question is all the more apparent when we consider the wide
diversity of activities which are included under the umbrella
of the services sector. Services include some highly skilled
activities such as financial services, management consultancy,
and so on, and some very unskilled services such as window-
cleaning, launderettes, and retailing. Some services are provided locally (e.g. hairdressers, doctors, dentists), other
services are provided nationally and even globally (e.g. banking
and finance, shipping). Perhaps we need some other method of
classification.

Whatever the case, the term 'services' and the notion of
the services sector remains one which continues to be used.
This being so, how can we classify the different kinds of
services provided within the economy? For practical purposes,
the best approach would seem to be to use the method of
classification contained in the national accounts. Services may
be classified under four headings (Bank of England 1985):

1. Consumer services—for example restaurants, hotels,
   household services, private transport.
2. Social services—for example education, health care, and
   welfare, generally provided free or subsidized by the state.
3. Producer or intermediate services—for example consultancy, banking, and contracting, which are used in the
   production of final goods and services.
4. Distributive services—for example freight transport, whole-
   saling, and retailing.

It will be apparent that only a small proportion of these services
is tradable. Scope for trade in services is quite limited because
many services are 'consumed' at the point where they are
supplied. As we have seen, production and consumption cannot
be separated. Nevertheless, an important group of services is
tradable, and this will be our primary focus of attention in this
chapter. However, before discussing the nature of trade in
services, we need to establish the size of the service sector
within the national economy.

The Size of the Services Sector

How important is the services sector in the economies of developed and developing countries? Much depends on the method of measurement used. One approach is to take the contribution of the services sector to domestic employment. Table 8.1 shows the contribution of the services sector to total domestic employment in the United Kingdom and the United States over the post-war period (Bank of England 1985). This shows that the share of services in domestic employment in the United Kingdom rose from 42.8 per cent in 1950 to 59.3 per cent in 1980. Over the same period, it rose from 51.7 per cent to 65.7 per cent in the United States. Thus, by 1980 the services sector had become more important than manufacturing in total employment. As can be seen from Table 8.1, the largest category of services in terms of employment was social services. This reflects the post-war growth of state welfare provision as well as demographic trends. However, the fastest growth has occurred in producer services. In both countries the share of producer services in total employment more than doubled over the period from 1950 to 1980. As will be seen later, part of this may be attributed to the practice of contracting out services previously performed within firms. Services such as advertising, accountancy, or consultancy may be performed by outside specialists rather than undertaken by departments within the firm. On the other hand, the number of service-type jobs performed within the firm has also increased. Mechanization has reduced the number of manual jobs. The share of distributive services in total employment remained fairly constant in the United Kingdom but fell in the United States. The share of consumer services in employment was also fairly constant in the United Kingdom until 1970 but rose thereafter; in the United States the share fell throughout the period.

The share of services in total employment may give a misleading picture because service activities tend to be quite labour intensive. Their contribution to employment may therefore exaggerate their importance in the national economy. Furthermore, labour productivity tends to grow more slowly in the services sector than in manufacturing. As a result, figures showing the share of services in total employment may exaggerate the growth in the size of the services sector over time. Therefore it may be preferable to take the share of services in

409

Table 8.1: Distribution of the labour force by industrial sector in the United Kingdom and the United States (% of total labour force)

		1950	1960	1970	1980
NON-SERVICE INDUSTRIES					
Agriculture, fishing,					
mining, & quarrying	UK	8.0	6.1	3.5	3.2
	US	14.4	8.1	4.5	4.1
Manufacturing, utilities,					
& construction	UK	49.2	47.5	46.6	37.5
	US	33.9	35.7	33.8	29.6
SERVICE INDUSTRIES					
Consumer	UK	8.3	8.9	8.1	11.3
	US	12.1	11.4	10.1	9.9
Social	UK	12.4	13.2	17.0	21.2
	US	12.4	16.4	21.7	24.7
Producer	UK	3.3	3.8	6.0	7.7
	US	4.8	8.1	9.1	11.3
Distributive	UK	18.8	20.0	18.8	19.1
	US	22.4	20.5	20.9	19.8
Total services	UK	42.8	45.9	49.9	59.3
	US	51.7	56.4	61.8	65.7

Source: Bank of England 1985.

total output. Table 8.2 shows the share of services in GDP in six industrialized countries. In five of the six countries the share of services in total employment is higher than in GDP volume. The share of services in GDP value rose in all six countries. In the case of France, the share dipped somewhat after 1972. The share of services in GDP volume was noticeably flatter. In the case of Japan, it actually fell from 51.7 per cent in 1964 to 48.8 per cent in 1982. One possible explanation for the faster growth in the GDP value share may have been a tendency for the prices of services to rise faster than the prices of goods. However, although this was true for the United Kingdom, it may not have been true for all other countries (Bank of England 1985).

The growth in the size of the services sector in the advanced industrialized countries is often cited as evidence that these economies are being transformed from 'industrialized' economies into largely 'service' economies. This is seen as evidence that these countries have entered a new phase of 'post-industrialization'. However, the above trends in the size of the services sector within the national economy need to be qualified. First, a

Table 8.2: Output shares of services in GDP and employment (%)

	GDP value	GDP volume	Employment
UNITED KINGDOM			
1954	44.5	47.9	42.5
1963	46.2	47.6	48.7
1973	47.8	46.9	54.3
1983	50.5	50.3	63.8
UNITED STATES			
1953	44.5	50.4	49.5
1963	47.5	51.4	54.5
1973	51.5	51.9	61.8
1983	54.1	54.6	66.7
JAPAN			
1964	43	51.7	
1972	50	50.3	44.2
1982	53.9	48.8	52.7
GERMANY			
1964	39.6	45.2	37.4
1972	44.4	45.9	42.4
1981	50.3	49.7	48.1
FRANCE			
1964	47.2	51.6	
1972	49.9	49.7	52.5
1981	46.7	53.7	58.0
ITALY			
1964	45.5	48.2	36.1
1972	49.7	48.6	42.6
1982	51.4	49.6	50.0

Source: Bank of England 1985.

large proportion of service activities are directly related to the production of goods, for example transport, wholesaling, retaining, and financial services. Second, as we observed earlier, the growth in the importance of many producer services is due to a tendency for firms to contract out specialist activities, for example data-processing, advertising, and accountancy, which were previously performed within the firm. To the extent that this is true, some of the growth in services is merely the result of a reclassification of jobs which were previously counted as part of the goods sector. Third, as we observed earlier, in practice, it is not always very meaningful to draw a distinction between goods and services.

One of the fastest-growing spheres of services is that of the 'information' sector. This is the direct result of the technological revolution which has taken place in data-processing and telecommunications. It has created an explosion of communication and information services as well as other intermediate services (e.g. financial services). In the United Kingdom this sector has created more new jobs than any other sector of the economy in recent years. However, this growth in service employment is directly related to the production of new data-processing and telecommunications equipment. It may be argued that this is hardly a sign of deindustrialization. Rather, we may prefer to talk of a 'softening' of the industrial structure of such countries. The software elements of all economic activities are coming to be valued more highly than before relative to the hardware content of actual goods and materials (Kagami 1983).

On the other hand, there may be a tendency for official statistics to underestimate the actual importance of the services sector. This is because a large number of personal services go unrecorded as they are part of the so-called 'black economy'. High levels of personal taxation have resulted in many services being performed without being declared. Increased leisure time has also resulted in people doing many more services for themselves. Such services are not included in the official statistics. In addition, while some manufacturing firms have begun to contract-out services previously supplied in-house, other firms have diversified by purchasing service firms. This may lead to some service jobs disappearing into the manufacturing goods sector.

One reason for the growth in the relative importance of services is the high income elasticity of demand for services. As per capita incomes rise, people choose to spend a larger proportion of their income on services rather than goods. This could account for the growth in the service economy in the advanced industrialized economies over the post-war period. In addition, rising per capita incomes may give rise to an increased demand for goods which have high service inputs. For example, many consumer-durable goods require considerable after-sales service (e.g. motor cars) as well as large inputs of 'software' (e.g. video-cassette recorders, televisions, hi-fi systems). However, as we have seen, consumer services have not been the fastest growing area of service employment in either the United Kingdom or the United States (see Table 8.1). In the United Kingdom, consumer expenditure on services appears to have risen over recent decades at about the same rate as expenditure on goods (Bank of England 1985). One reason for this may have been a tendency for the prices of services to rise relative to the prices of goods. This may have caused households to buy less consumer services relative to consumer goods. Another explanation is a tendency for wants previously satisfied by unmeasured services performed within households (self-services) to be met by marketed goods and services in the form of new consumer durables, for example washing-machines, washing-up machines, and hoovers (Bank of England 1985).

One of the most surprising results of cross-country comparisons is the absence of any systematic relationship between the share of services in total output or employment and a country's level of per capita income. Chapter 2 noted that the size of the services sector is quite large in developing countries. Table 2.3 (p. 47) shows that, in 1978, services accounted for 45.2 per cent of GDP compared with 55.3 per cent in developed market economies. Moreover, between 1960 and 1980 the share of the services sector in GDP in developing countries rose from 42.9 per cent to 45.2 per cent. Only in the high-income developing countries did the share fall as one would expect in countries undergoing industrialization. As we saw in Chapter 2, there exist a number of explanations for these figures. First, there may be a tendency for many white-collar workers employed in services in developing countries to earn considerably higher wages than manual workers. To the extent that the contribution of services to GDP is measured by factor costs, the importance of the services sector in developing countries will be over-estimated. Second, more workers in developing countries are employed in 'porterage, petty trade, and personal services' due to high rates of population growth and rural-to-urban migration (Ballance and Sinclair 1983).

THE IMPORTANCE OF SERVICES IN INTERNATIONAL TRADE

Defining Trade in Services

As we observed earlier, only a small proportion of service activity enters into international trade. By their very nature, services are much less tradable than goods. Services have to be consumed at the point where they are produced. This means that either the supplier of a service must move to where the consumer is located, or the consumer of the service must move to where the producer is located. Only a small proportion of services are capable of being traded like goods with neither the producer nor the consumer being required to move. To illustrate this point, we can make use of a fourfold categorization of service activities proposed by Stern and Hoekman (Stern and Hoekman 1987):

1. 'Separated' services requiring no movement of the provider or demander of the service between countries: Transport services such as civil aviation or shipping fit this category. A civil airline can provide the citizens of another country with a service without the need for the civil airline to be located in the overseas country or for the consumer to go to the country where the airline in question is located.

2. Demander-located services requiring the movement of the provider of the service only: in this case the provider of the service needs to be in close geographical proximity to the demander of the service. Banking and insurance both fit this category. A British bank which wishes to gain a share of the Japanese market for retail banking will need to establish a presence in Japan. This will require foreign direct investment involving a movement of both capital and labour.

3. Provider-located services requiring the movement of the demander of the service only: the provider of the service supplies the service in his own contry but the service is purchased by a citizen or firm based in another country. Examples of these kinds of services are tourism, education, and medical services.

4. Footloose, non-separated services, which require both movement of consumers and producers: the provider of the service carries out foreign direct investment in another country and utilizes the subsidiary thus established to supply a service to the citizen of or firm based in some third country. Thus a British bank with a subsidiary in Japan may, through its Japanese subsidiary, make a bank loan to a firm based in the United States. This category is included for the sake of completeness.

This fourfold categorization of services illustrates the important point that a trade in services takes place whenever 'domestic factors receive income from non-residents in exchange for their services' (Stern and Hoekman 1987). Very often we are inclined to think of trade in services in the same way as we regard trade in goods. This confines trade in services to trade in 'separated' services, the first category listed above. However, this would seem to be too narrow a definition of services.

The above categorization serves also to demonstrate how trade in services may also be bound up with a movement of capital and labour across national borders. Both the second and fourth categories require both foreign direct investment and/or a movement of labour from one country to another. In this case the income derived by domestic factors of production (capital and labour) from their overseas activities should be included in the country's earnings from the export of services. They are just as much a part of the country's service exports as the foreign-currency earnings from domestically-owned civil airlines or shipping companies. In practice, as will be seen later, it is often difficult to obtain accurate data concerning these service exports. It is also important to note in passing that the issue of freer trade in such demander-located services is intimately bound up with the issue of the right of establishment for firms and individuals supplying such services.

Herbert Grubel has proposed a rather different taxonomy of ways in which trade in services takes place (Grubel 1987). He has distinguished between just two types of service trade:

1. Disembodied services, requiring the movement of people, capital, or firms across borders, or the movement of goods across borders for transformation: Thus tourism involves a movement of people across countries to 'absorb' services supplied by another country. Education and medical care similarly presuppose a movement of people from one country to another. The wages remitted by migrant workers or guest workers are similarly generally treated as service income. The income derived by banks from their foreign subsidiaries is an example of a service requiring a movement of capital across borders. Finally, the income derived by a country from packaging, warehousing, and whole-saling of goods for re-export (so-called entrepôt trade) is an example of trade in services which requires a movement of goods across borders.

415

2. Splintered, or separated, services, so called because the services involved have been splintered or separated from their original production in the sense that they are now embodied in goods for separate sale: Obvious examples of such services are films, books, scientific documents, patents, and electronic discs containing data or computer programmes. In all these cases citizens or firms from the exporting country derive an income from the sale of a service embodied in a good. Thus film producers receive royalties from the showing abroad of a film which they have produced, and authors also receive royalties from the sale of books which they have written. Trade in such services requires no movement of people, capital, or firms across borders. Instead, goods embodying services are transported across borders. Thus trade in these kinds of services more closely resembles trade in goods. What distinguishes such trade from merchandise trade is the proportion of value-added accounted for by service as opposed to manufacturing industries.

The concept of splintered, or separated, services is a useful one for understanding some of the growth in services trade in recent decades. It is apparent that part of this growth is attributable to an increase in the relative importance of service inputs in manufacturing industry. Many goods embody large amounts of service inputs. In many cases this is a reflection of greater investments of human capital in the production process. As production becomes more capital and knowledge intensive, so the level of service input increases. What was previously treated as trade in goods now becomes categorized as trade in embodied services. As Grubel observes, it is in many ways meaningless to treat such trade in services in a different way from trade in goods. To some degree all goods embody splintered services. What separates such trade from trade in services is merely the relative importance of services input (Grubel 1987).

Measuring Trade in Services

The most important data base for measuring the extent of trade in services is the balance-of-payments statistics of a country.

A country's total invisible earnings may be taken as a measure of her exports of services, and total invisible payments as a measure of her imports of services. In the United Kingdom, invisibles are broken down into three categories: (1) services, (2) interest, profits, and dividends from investment abroad, and (3) transfers. Services are subdivided by type: shipping, civil aviation, travel, banking and financial services, consultancy, films and television, and other miscellaneous services. Much less detail is available for global trade in services. However, balance-of-payments data are inadequate as a true measure of the extent of trade in services. First, a large but unknown proportion of trade in services goes unrecorded. This problem is even greater than for trade in goods. By their very nature, because services are intangible, it is extremely difficult for the authorities to measure every such transaction. In particular, much intra-firm trade in services is extremely difficult to measure.

Second, some trade in so-called splintered or separated services goes unrecorded. This is because it is subsumed under the heading of trade in goods. As we have already seen, the distinction between trade in goods and trade in embodied services is somewhat arbitrary. All goods embody splintered services to some degree. However, only where service inputs account for a high proportion of value-added is such trade treated as trade in services. It follows that some trade in such services will be treated as trade in goods and not services. Apparently, it is reckoned that US balance-of-payments data under-record the extent of trade in separated services by between 45 and 100 per cent (Stern and Hoekman 1986).

Third, some trade in what Stern and Hoekman have termed provider-located services is not included in the balance-of-payments data. Tourism is really the only such service which is counted. Education and medical care, however, are two examples of provider-located services which are generally not counted. Very little accurate data are available in any country recording the extent of such trade. Fourth, trade in so-called demander-located services involves foreign direct investment. The interest, profits, and dividends earned on such investments may be taken as the measure of trade in such services. Although this is recorded as an invisible item in the balance of payments, no distinction is made between investment income derived from goods-related investment and service-related investment. Even if such a distinction were drawn, it would fail to record accurately the income derived by a country from such services. This is because some investment income may be re-invested abroad and not repatriated to the capital-exporting country. Furthermore, the flow of such income from a foreign subsidiary to the parent company is often subject to transfer-price manipulation. In some countries it is possible to use other data published by governments concerning foreign investment into and out of the country to draw a distinction between service-related and goods-related investment income.

It follows that official statistics showing trade in services fail to measure accurately the actual amount of such trade. Table 8.3 shows the level of such world trade for 1984 in comparison with trade in goods. Trade in 'pure' services amounted to $357 billion, or roughly 19 per cent of total trade in goods and services. If investment income and workers' remittances are included, trade in services amounted to $625 billion, or about 33 per cent of total trade in goods and services. Between 1970 and 1980, service exports grew at a rate of 18.7 per cent faster than world GDP growth but a little slower than trade in goods. To a certain extent, this runs counter to the popular impression that trade in services has been a more dynamic component of world trade than trade in goods in recent decades. However, the above figures show only the growth in the value of such trade. We have no information about the real rate of growth of such trade. If the prices of goods have risen faster than the prices of services entering into international trade, the volume of trade in services may still have grown faster than trade in goods. Moreover, if investment income is included, the rate of growth of such trade is broadly the same as for merchandise. If it is true that balance-of-payments data underestimate the actual value of trade in services, it may well be the case that trade in services is growing faster than trade in goods.

Table 8.4 shows the share of trade in services and the rate of growth of such trade over the period from 1973 to 1984 for a number of different countries. Services include investment income as well as 'pure' services. It is interesting to note some of the differences between countries. In a number of countries, exports of services grew at a faster rate than exports of goods. These included the United States, Japan, Belgium–Luxembourg, France, West Germany, Austria, Hong Kong, and South Korea. In terms of imports of services, fourteen out of the eighteen

Table 8.3: Total world exports of services and merchandise, investment income, workers' remittances, and GDP

	Value in 1984 ($ bn)	Average annual growth 1970–80 (%)
Service exports	357	18.7
Merchandise exports	1,545	20.4
Investment income	244	22.4
Workers' remittances	24	na
GDP	11,891	14.2

Source: Stern and Hoekman 1986.

countries listed experienced a faster growth of service imports than merchandise imports. It is noticeable that the six NICs listed in the bottom section of the table all experienced exceptionally rapid increases in both their imports and exports of services. However, the rate of growth of their imports of services was generally faster than their exports of services.

The Geographical Distribution of Trade in Services

Table 8.4 also illustrates the differences between countries in the importance of service trade in relation to GDP. In some countries, exports of services account for quite a large proportion of GDP. Singapore and Belgium–Luxembourg stand out in this respect. However, in these countries, exports of goods also account for quite a high proportion of GDP. In order to determine the relative importance of services in total trade, we need to compare the share of goods exports in GDP relative to the share of service exports in GDP. This exercise is performed in Table 8.5. A low ratio in column (1) indicates that service exports occupy a relatively important place in total trade. This was the case in Austria, Belgium–Luxembourg, the United States, Spain, France, Singapore, the United Kingdom, and Switzerland. In column (2) the same exercise has been performed for imports of goods and services. In column (3) the export ratio has been expressed as a percentage of the import ratio. A low percentage may be taken as evidence for a strong export specialization in services. The countries which appear to have such an export specialization are Switzerland, the United

Table 8.4: GDP and trade in goods and services[a] in 1973 and 1984 (shares and average annual rate of growth in %)

	SHARE IN GDP								GROWTH BETWEEN 1973 AND 1984				
	Exports of:				Imports of:				GDP	Exports of:		Imports of:	
	Goods		Services		Goods		Services			Goods	Services	Goods	Services
	1973	1984	1973	1984	1973	1984	1973	1984					
United States	5.4	6.1	2.9	3.9	5.4	9.1	2.2	3.4	9.7	10.8	12.5	15.0	14.3
Canada	20.9	26.4	3.4	3.7	18.7	21.5	6.1	8.3	9.4	11.7	10.1	10.8	12.5
Japan	8.7	13.7	2.0	3.4	7.9	10.1	2.9	4.1	10.4	15.0	15.7	12.9	13.8
Belgium–Luxembourg	36.7	51.0	13.1	34.4	35.3	52.0	11.5	32.3	5.9	9.1	15.6	9.7	16.4
France	14.3	18.8	4.9	11.4	14.0	19.7	4.7	9.9	6.3	9.0	14.7	9.6	13.9
West Germany	18.8	26.7	4.8	7.6	14.5	23.0	6.1	8.5	5.4	8.8	9.9	9.9	8.5
Italy	14.3	20.9	6.4	7.6	16.7	22.7	5.1	6.9	7.7	11.5	9.3	10.7	10.7
Netherlands	36.3	49.0	14.5	19.4	34.6	44.5	12.0	19.1	6.7	9.6	9.6	9.2	11.3
Spain	7.4	14.3	7.3	8.7	12.2	16.8	3.5	5.4	7.7	14.3	9.4	10.9	12.1
United Kingdom	16.2	22.0	10.9	11.4	19.7	23.3	8.3	9.1	8.1	11.2	8.5	9.8	9.1
Austria	18.7	24.1	11.9	17.3	24.8	29.6	6.8	12.9	7.9	10.4	11.7	9.6	14.3
Switzerland	23.4	39.5	12.2	20.4	27.7	42.3	5.6	12.2	7.5	12.7	12.6	11.7	15.4
Brazil	7.7	12.9	1.2	1.5	7.9	6.6	3.9	7.8	9.3	14.5	11.8	7.6	16.4
Hong Kong	56.7	55.3	8.5	17.6	65.7	56.1	6.1	11.9	15.2	15.0	23.8	13.6	22.4
South Korea	24.3	31.7	6.3	8.8	27.9	32.9	5.7	9.8	17.9	20.8	21.6	19.7	23.8
Mexico	3.8	13.7	4.9	4.7	6.7	6.4	5.1	10.0	11.1	24.8	10.7	10.7	18.5
Singapore	42.8	86.3	38.1	51.6	92.8	(120)	20.2	31.9	14.3	22.0	17.5	17.2	19.1
Taiwan	42.1	52.5	6.3	7.8	34.6	36.9	7.9	11.1	16.5	18.9	18.9	17.2	20.3

Source: GATT (1986).
[a] In nominal terms; services include income receipts and payments

States, Spain, Hong Kong, Austria, the United Kingdom, France, Belgium–Luxembourg, and Italy. In all these countries, exports of services relative to imports of services occupied an important position in relation to the GDP of the country when compared with exports of goods. These countries are those which might be expected to gain considerably from a liberalization of trade in services, depending on the type of service trade involved.

Table 8.5: The relative importance of service trade in the total trade of different countries, 1984

	Ratio of the share of merchandise exports in GDP to the share of service exports in GDP		
	(1) Exports	(2) Imports	(3) (1) ÷ (2) X 100
United States	1.56	2.68	58.21
Canada	7.10	2.59	274.13
Japan	4.03	2.46	163.82
Belgium–Luxembourg	1.48	1.61	91.93
France	1.65	1.99	82.91
West Germany	3.50	2.71	129.15
Italy	2.75	3.29	83.59
Netherlands	2.53	2.33	108.58
Spain	1.64	3.11	52.73
United Kingdom	1.93	2.56	75.39
Austria	1.39	2.29	60.70
Switzerland	1.94	3.47	55.91
Brazil	8.60	0.85	1,011.76
Hong Kong	3.14	4.71	66.67
South Korea	3.60	3.36	107.14
Mexico	2.91	0.64	454.69
Singapore	1.67	–	–
Taiwan	6.73	3.32	202.71

Table 8.6 shows the absolute value of trade in services which is accounted for by different countries as well as its distribution by type of service and country. It can be seen that four countries — the United States, the United Kingdom, West Germany, and France — account for 44 per cent of world exports of services. It can also be seen that three types of service trade — travel and tourism, shipping, and other transport and passenger services — accounted for roughly two-thirds of all recorded trade in services. Japan accounted for the highest proportion of trade in

Table 8.6: The geographical distribution of world exports of services, 1980

	Shipment	Other transport and passenger services	Travel and tourism	Other private services	Total %	Total Value ($ bn)
		Percentage distribution				
United States	9.9	34.5	26.8	28.8	100.0	37.5
Canada	11.0	10.1	41.1	37.8	100.0	7.0
Japan	38.2	31.4	3.3	27.1	100.0	19.4
United Kingdom	15.5	30.1	18.6	35.8	100.0	37.1
France	4.0	32.3	25.0	38.7	100.0	33.0
West Germany	15.6	19.3	19.4	45.7	100.0	33.8
Italy	14.2	14.6	38.0	33.2	100.0	23.5
Netherlands	19.6	38.6	9.0	32.8	100.0	18.6
Belgium	16.1	15.3	12.2	56.4	100.0	14.9
Switzerland	4.8	na	48.5	46.7	100.0	8.4
Sweden	22.2	23.3	12.0	42.4	100.0	8.0
Norway	54.1	22.8	8.2	14.9	100.0	9.2
25 largest exporters	14.5	25.4	25.8	34.4	100.0	
		Percentage shares				
United States	7.9	15.9	12.2	9.8	11.7	37.5
Canada	1.6	0.9	3.5	2.4	2.2	7.0
Japan	16.0	7.5	0.8	4.7	6.1	19.4
United Kingdom	12.4	13.8	8.4	12.1	11.6	37.1
France	2.8	13.2	10.0	11.6	10.3	33.0
West Germany	11.3	8.0	8.0	14.1	10.6	33.8
Italy	7.2	4.2	10.8	7.1	7.3	23.5
Netherlands	7.8	8.8	2.0	5.6	5.8	18.6
Belgium	5.2	2.8	2.2	7.7	4.7	14.9
Switzerland	0.9	na	5.0	3.6	2.6	8.4
Sweden	3.8	2.3	1.2	3.1	2.5	8.0
Norway	10.7	2.6	0.9	1.2	2.9	9.2
25 largest exporters	100.0	100.0	100.0	100.0	100.0	
Total (bn)	46.5	81.2	82.4	109.9		320.0

Source: Stern and Hoekman (1987).

shipping, followed by the United Kingdom, West Germany, and Norway. Over 50 per cent of Norway's exports of services took this form while 38 per cent of Japan's service exports were of this kind. The United States, followed by the United

Kingdom, and France, accounted for the highest proportion of other transport and passenger service exports. The United States, followed by Italy and France, also accounted for the highest share of travel and tourism exports. However, it is noticeable that nearly 50 per cent of Switzerland's and 40 per cent of Canada's exports of services took this form.

It would be wrong to assume that trade in services is only important for industrialized countries. Service exports account for a large proportion of total exports of goods and services in a number of developing countries. This is illustrated by Table 8.7. Of the countries for whom exports of services account for more than one-half of total exports of goods and services, all, with the single exception of Greece, would be classed as developing countries. Austria is the only other developed country with a share of more than 40 per cent of total export earnings coming from services. In the United States the share of services in total exports is 35 per cent, and in the United Kingdom the share is 34 per cent. Thus export earnings from services are important for a number of developing countries. However, it is also true that, taken as a whole, developing countries are net importers of services from developed countries. For example, in 1980 industrialized-country exports of services to developing countries amounted to $72 billion, while developing-country exports of services to industrialized countries stood at $30 billion. Industrialized countries enjoyed a net surplus from trade in services with developing countries of $42 billion (Sapir 1986).

Much trade in services is either capital intensive (e.g. shipping) or knowledge intensive (e.g. banking and financial services). Not surprisingly, there exists empirical support for the hypothesis that countries well endowed with physical and human capital will enjoy a comparative advantage in the export of services (Sapir and Lutz 1981). This may explain why the industrialized countries appear to enjoy a comparative advantage in the export of services. However, as we have seen in earlier chapters of this book, certain developing countries have been highly successful in accumulating human and physical capital. These are the NICs. As a result, some of these countries have developed a comparative advantage in the export of certain kinds of services. This is apparent from Table 8.5. Both Hong Kong and South Korea appear to have quite low ratios of goods exports to GDP relative to service exports to GDP. It follows that certain developing countries, mainly

Table 8.7: Share of services in total exports of goods and services (% shares in 1980)

Less than 10%	10-15%	15-20%	20-5%	25-30%	30-40%	40-50%	More than 50%
Algeria 6	Bahrain 13	Australia 17	Cameroon 21	Argentina 28	Belgium-Lux. 38	Antigua & Barbuda 44	Bahamas 83
Chad 0	Bolivia 11	Costa Rica 18	Germany, Fed. Rep. 24	Bangladesh 26	Colombia 32	Austria 45	Barbados 68
Ghana 9	Brazil 13	El Salvador 15	Iceland 21	Botswana 27	Denmark 31	Egypt 41	Cyprus 56
Guyana 5	Burma 13	Finland 19	Ireland 24	Burkina Faso 29	Dominica 39	Fiji 43	Greece 51
Indonesia 2	Canada 13	Guatemala 17	Korea 24	Central Afr. Rep. 28	France 37	Israel 41	Grenada 58
Liberia 2	China 15	Hong Kong 18	Kuwait 22	Chile 25	Haiti 30	Paraguay 42	Jordan 66
Libya 6	Congo 11	Ivory Coast 17	Mali 22	Dominican Rep. 27	India 33	Senegal 46	Lesotho 83
Nigeria 7	Ecuador 14	Japan 20	Pakistan 23	Ethiopia 28	Jamaica 32	St Lucia 48	Maldives 80
Oman 3	Gabon 13	Madagascar 16	Sao Tomé & Princ. 21	Gambia 27	Kenya 39	St Vincent 47	Malta 57
Papua NG 9	Honduras 12	Nether. Antilles 17	Sierra Leone 22	Italy 27	Mexico 35	Western Samoa 41	Nepal 62
Romania 9	Hungary 13	New Zealand 19	Sri Lanka 21	Mauritania 27	Norway 34		Panama 71
Uganda 3	Nicaragua 12	Peru 19	Sweden 22	Mauritius 25	Portugal 33		Seychelles 94
Zaire 7	Niger 10	Suriname 19	Thailand 21	Morocco 26	Somalia 35		Tonga 57
Zambia 9	Malaysia 13	Swaziland 17	Trinidad & Tobago 24	Netherlands 30	Spain 39		Yemen Arab Rep. 96
	Philippines 13	Syrian Arab. Rep. 18	Turkey 21	Rwanda 27	Sudan 33		Yemen, People's Dem. Rep. of 66
	Solomon Isl. 14	Togo 17		St Christopher 30	Switzerland 30		
	South Africa 12	Zimbabwe 16		Singapore 27	Tunisia 40		
	Saudi Arabia 10			Tanzania 29	United Kingdom 34		
	Taiwan 14				United States 35		
	Venezuela 14				Uruguay 34		
					Yugoslavia 34		

Source: GATT (1986).

NICs, could benefit from any progress made to liberalize world trade in services.

LIBERALIZING TRADE IN SERVICES

The Case for Freer Trade in Services

As was noted at the start of this chapter, in recent years there has been a growing interest expressed in bringing trade in services within the ambit of the GATT. The United States has been the chief advocate for such a policy. This is a reflection of the growing importance of service trade to the United States balance of payments and the US economy in general. By 1980 the services sector accounted for two-thirds of all employment in the United States. In the same year the United States earned $37.5 billion from the export of services equal to 11.7 per cent of world exports of services (see Table 8.6.). US exports of services amounted to 3.9 per cent of her GDP in 1984 compared with 6.1 per cent for goods. In other words, roughly 40 per cent of the United States' total exports of goods and services came from the services sector. Between 1973 to 1984 her exports of services grew at an annual rate of 12.5 per cent compared with 10.8 per cent for goods (see Table 8.4). At a time when the United States has been facing a growing deficit on her trade in goods, her traditional surplus from trade in services has been of vital importance. The United States has become increasingly reluctant to lower barriers on imports of goods when US service firms are denied access to foreign markets. Thus the United States has called for similar rules to be applied to trade in services as apply to trade in goods. In brief, the GATT should be extended to embrace trade in services as well as trade in goods. The United States has enjoyed the support of certain other industrialized countries, such as the United Kingdom, which equally depend on the export of services for export earnings.

Other GATT members have not always been as zealous as the United States for opening up the market for services in the same way as has happened for trade in goods. In particular, a number of developing countries have strongly resisted the inclusion of services within the current eighth round of GATT

425

trade negotiations (the Uruguay Round). India and Brazil have been the leading opponents of extending the GATT to services. Other developing countries with a keen interest in expanding trade in services have been in favour. For example, both Hong Kong and Singapore derive a significant proportion of their foreign currency earnings from the export of services. In 1984 exports of services accounted for 17.6 per cent of Hong Kong's GDP and 51.6 per cent of Singapore's (see Table 8.4). Both countries enjoyed a net surplus from trade in services. Between 1973 and 1984 Hong Kong's export of services grew at a rate of 23.8 per cent and those of Singapore at a rate of 17.5 per cent (see Table 8.4). For Hong Kong that was considerably faster than her exports of merchandise and faster than the growth in service exports of any other country. Thus certain developing countries stand to gain from the liberalization of trade in services. However, a large number of other developing countries remain fearful of any extension of GATT to services. First, they see such a measure as largely benefiting the advanced industrialized countries, such as the United States. These countries had hoped that any fresh round of trade negotiations would have been primarily concerned with improving access for developing country exports to the developed country markets. Second, it is felt that many of the native service industries of developing countries would be unable to withstand direct competition from the large, more efficient service industries of the industrialized countries. Third, there is a fear of a loss of national sovereignty if important service industries (e.g. banking, transport, telecommunications) were to fall under foreign control. Strong non-economic arguments are involved in any discussion concerning the merits of liberalizing trade in services.

Although it is true that the United States and certain other industrialized countries would benefit significantly from a general freeing of service trade, this consideration should not be allowed to obscure any argument about the desirability or otherwise of freeing trade in services. As was seen earlier in this chapter, services do constitute a large and probably growing element of world trade. Roughly one-third of world trade is now trade in services as opposed to goods. Although to some extent such trade is already subject to GATT rules — as when such trade takes the form of embodied services or when it is covered by existing codes such as the code relating to government procurement policies — a large proportion of trade in services is subject to no universally agreed rules. The sheer magnitude of such trade constitutes an argument for seeking to lower existing barriers governing such trade. A number of countries — developed and developing — enjoy a comparative advantage in the export of certain types of services. Such countries should enjoy the same rights of access to foreign markets for their service industries as other countries enjoy for their exports of goods. This will enable these countries to exploit more fully their existing comparative advantage to the benefit of the world as a whole. Global economic welfare will be increased in the same way as with increased specialization in goods industries. Trade barriers which prevent such countries from fully exploiting their comparative advantage serve only to lower the level of global economic welfare. Barriers to trade in services may be even greater than the barriers to trade in goods. This is because service industries are usually subject to greater government interference than goods industries. For a variety of reasons — often largely non-economic — governments regulate and intervene in service industries to a much greater degree than in goods industries.

Developing countries need not be afraid of such a process. It is true, as we have seen, that, taken as a whole, developing countries face a net deficit on their trade in services with developed countries. A lowering of trade barriers seems likely to lead to some deterioration in developing countries' services trade balance. This is because many service industries require large inputs of knowledge and skilled labour. This favours countries with relatively large endowments of physical and human capital, that is the industrialized countries. It may be that developing countries enjoy a comparative advantage in certain highly labour-intensive service industries, but the kind of labour typically required is skilled labour (Sapir and Lutz 1981). Some NICs which have been successful in accumulating capital do possess a comparative advantage in certain service industries; other developing countries can expect to develop a comparative advantage in the future as they move to a higher stage of development. In general, however, freer trade in services *per se* will benefit industrialized countries. However, this need not be harmful to the developing nations if, in return, they can secure a reduction in the barriers restricting their goods exports to developed country markets. In this case, developed countries would increase their specialization in

427

services which they would exchange for more goods produced by developing countries. A new pattern of international division of labour could emerge. This would enable developing countries to increase the proportion of their exports which constitute manufactured goods while developed countries would specialize in the export of more services. Not only would such a pattern of specialization be beneficial to developing countries, it would also permit an expansion of trade between developed and developing countries which need not create excessive friction within the developed countries. The employment content of service exports would appear to be roughly equivalent to that of manufactured goods exported by developing countries, so that a balanced expansion of trade of this kind need not have a negative effect on employment levels in developed countries (Sapir 1985).

Thus, freer trade in services, if accompanied by a lowering of trade barriers on the part of the developed nations, could provide an escape from some of the frictions which have bedevilled trading relations between the North and the South in recent decades. If developing countries are willing to open up their markets to the service industries of the industrialized countries, they may be able to increase their exports of manufactures to the industrialized countries. In addition, they may be able to obtain more cheaply certain services vital to their economic development. Many of the services in which developed countries enjoy a comparative advantage (e.g. banking, communications, transport) are vital to the infrastructure of developing countries. Developing countries face a choice between seeking to establish such infrastructure by their own efforts at relatively high cost or importing such services at lower cost from developed countries. Not only is it often cheaper to import these services but, by so doing, developing countries are enabled to acquire western technology crucial to the development process. Against this must be set the loss of national control over certain important service industries and greater dependence on developed countries for the supply of strategic services. It is these non-economic considerations which are often paramount. For this reason, developing countries are reluctant to permit a totally free market in services. However, this is not an argument against seeking progress in freeing trade in services. Any agreement reached could provide for reasonable exceptions to the agreed code. The existing GATT Charter covering trade in goods is not a charter for free trade, only for freer trade. Article 19, the famous escape clause, allows countries to impose tariffs if domestic interests are harmed or threatened by a sudden surge of imports. A similar safeguard could be included in any agreement on trade in services. Exceptions to the rules would be allowed. Indeed, the inclusion of such exceptions and safeguards would be an essential requirement for any agreement to gain world-wide acceptance. However, the need is to establish clearly what these exceptions are and what type of restrictions are permissible in these cases. Only in an environment of certainty of this kind can trade in services flourish.

It would be wrong to allow the issue of trade in services to become the basis for a North–South polarization. As we have already seen, many developing countries will directly gain from the opening up of markets for services. However, the main expansion of trade in services in the future can be expected to take place between the developed countries rather than between developed and developing countries. For countries with a comparative advantage in service industries, the greatest scope to expand their exports of services will be from the markets of other industrialized countries. Such an expansion of trade can only be beneficial when viewed from a global viewpoint. At a time when the volume of trade in goods is growing more slowly than in the past, the liberalization of trade in services could constitute an important counteracting influence. The growth in the relative importance of the services sector in the economies of the industrialized countries means that the buoyancy of the service industries is going to be important for growth in the developed market economies in coming decades. Even in the absence of any agreement to lower barriers to trade in services, such trade looks certain to outpace the growth of trade in goods. Technological change will cause a big expansion of service exports in coming decades. This will be especially true of the so-called 'information-based' services. Increased opportunities for economies of scale in services such as banking and financial services — due largely to the increased use of computers and other new technologies — will lead to an increase of trade in such services.

Furthermore, failure to open up markets in the service trades could have adverse effects on trade in goods. Countries such as the United States will become less willing to maintain open markets to foreign manufactures unless their service firms are granted equivalent access to foreign markets. At the time of writing this issue has assumed considerable importance in the dispute between Japan and her western trading partners. Countries such as the United States and United Kingdom have expressed a growing unwillingness to allow fair treatment for Japanese goods if Japan continues to block access to the foreign service firms of these countries. Japan has been strongly criticized for restricting access to western companies in banking and financial services and in telecommunications. Increased exports of services would enable the United States and West European economies to offset some of the effects of their large trade deficit with Japan in goods. If, on the other hand, exports of services remain subject to 'unfair' restrictions, this will increase the pressure on governments in affected countries to impose restrictions on imports of goods. Finally, action is needed on services to prevent any increase in the level of regulation and restriction of trade in services. As we have seen, government regulation and intervention is probably greater in the service industries than the goods industries. Unless controlled, such restrictions look likely to increase. If only to prevent an increase in the degree of protectionism affecting trade in services, services need to be brought within the ambit of the GATT.

Lowering the Barriers to Trade in Services

What sort of barriers restrict trade in services? What action is needed to reduce or eliminate such restrictions? Can the same approach as has been adopted to liberalizing trade in goods be applied to trade in services? What problems are involved in bringing about freer trade in services? From the outset it must be stated that we are dealing with issues which are still largely unexplored. There has been little or no attempt made in the past to tackle the problem of barriers to trade in services. It is not yet clear what is exactly the right course of action to adopt. Therefore I can only tentatively consider some of the major issues involved.

A wide variety of different types of impediments exist in services trade. These vary a great deal from one industry to the next as well as from one country to the next. In general, however, it can be said that they are closer in kind to non-tariff barriers affecting trade in goods. As with such NTBs, their precise quantitative impact is very difficult to determine. For this reason, countries cannot bargain over such restrictions in the same way as is possible with tariffs. It follows that any GATT negotiations concerning barriers to trade in services will tend to follow the approach adopted for tackling NTBs in the Tokyo Round. This involved establishing a series of codes relating to specific types of practice setting out the kinds which were or were not permissible. It is evident that such negotiations will be lengthy and highly complex. For this reason, any agreement on services is likely to be achieved only over quite a long period of time. Although agreement could be reached on certain general principles, the application of these principles to different services sectors must inevitably involve a gradualist approach.

As we saw earlier, trade in services has been subdivided into two broad types: (1) disembodied services, which require the movement of people, capital, or firms across borders and (2) splintered or separated services, which are embodied in goods for separate sale (Grubel 1987). As we have seen, trade in embodied services is analogous to trade in goods. Therefore it should not be too difficult to extend the GATT to trade in these kinds of services. All goods embody services to some degree. What separates embodied services from goods is the proportion of the value-added which is attributable to service as opposed to manufacturing industries. Thus the extension of the GATT to such services should pose no major conceptual problem. Trade in disembodied services, however, is rather different. Trade in such services requires the movement of people, capital, or firms across national borders. The liberalization of trade in such services requires the removal of all restrictions on the rights of firms and individuals to produce and sell their services in other countries. This is known as the right of establishment abroad. In many countries this right is denied to foreigners. Even where it is granted, foreign firms and individuals may face other forms of discrimination which place them at a disadvantage relative to nationals. They may have to satisfy demanding licensing and certification requirements. Limitations may be placed on the range of services which they can offer. Restrictions may be imposed on the nationality of employees or the amount of foreign equity which may be issued by the company. They may be discriminated against in the award of government contracts (Diebold and Stalson 1983).

Agreement to tackle these kinds of restriction constitutes the more controversial area of trade liberalization in services. Sometimes it is argued that since freeing trade in services involves guarantees of the right of establishment for foreign firms, the issues involved are an investment and not a trade issue. Should not such issues be settled in a different forum from that of the GATT since GATT's concerns are limited to matters of trade? On the other hand, to exclude the issue of the right of establishment from GATT negotiations would be to omit a major area of service trade from the liberalization process. It would be difficult to achieve meaningful liberalization of trade in services without an attempt to tackle the issue of the right of establishment. It would also mean that the impact of any agreement reached would be uneven as between countries. In seeking to liberalize trade in services, it is simply not possible to separate trade and investment issues. However, it is the case that any attempt to tackle the issue of the right of establishment is certain to meet with considerable national opposition. Countries are extremely reluctant to abandon laws controlling the right of establishment. Powerful interest groups exist within all countries which can be certain to resist any attempt to allow unrestricted competition from foreign firms. For this reason, progress in this area is likely to be quite slow.

Two alternative approaches exist in any negotiations to bring about freer trade in services:

1. **The principle of national treatment** One approach would be to secure agreement on the principle of national treatment. This guarantees to foreign firms and individuals producing and supplying services in a particular country the same treatment as national firms and individuals. Foreign firms are allowed to do no more and no less than comparable domestic firms. In most cases the adoption of this principle would involve improving the treatment of foreign service firms by affording them the same treatment as nationals. However, in some exceptional cases it could mean treating foreign firms less leniently than before. Adoption of the principle of national treatment would involve a radical break with the existing situation. However, it is unlikely to be acceptable in all service industries without certain qualifications. In particular, governments would want to retain certain

existing regulations in banking and financial services which are designed to provide the general public with prudential protection. Any agreement would need to provide for such exceptions if agreement to the general principle is to be reached. The main problem with such an approach is that it would leave certain countries at a distinct disadvantage in specific service industries. The service industries of some countries would be unable to withstand the competition implied by the adoption of such a principle. For this reason, agreement may be difficult to achieve.

2. **The principle of reciprocity** An alternative approach is for each country to grant reciprocal treatment to the service industries of other countries. This is based on the idea that 'I will treat our service firms in the same way as you treat mine.' Service firms belonging to country Y and operating in country X are granted the same treatment as country Y gives to firms belonging to country X. It has the attraction that it endorses the principle that trade between any two countries must bring reciprocal gains if the two countries are to be willing to lower trade barriers or enter into any kind of trade agreement. No set of trading rules will command universal support unless all countries enjoy some element of reciprocal benefit. On the other hand, the adoption of such an approach would involve a movement away from a multilateral settlement towards a bilateral solution. It would thus involve a departure from the GATT principle of non-discrimination which operates for trade in goods. In fact, it amounts to a kind of conditional most-favoured-nation (MFN) policy rather than the unconditional MFN policy on which the post-war liberal trading system has been based. The danger would exist that, if such a principle were conceded for trade in services, it could spread to trade in goods. In addition, it would be administratively very costly to operate. Foreign service firms would each be treated differently according to what treatment their own governments afforded the service firms of the host country. A myriad of different regulations would be required. It would also risk the danger of retaliation. A basis would exist for countries imposing new restrictions on the service firms of another country where the latter fails to give national treatment to the service firms of the former. For all these reasons, the principle of reciprocity is less desirable than that of national treatment. However, it seems more likely that there will have to be some trade-off between these two principles.

Other approaches in international negotiations might include the extension of GATT rules to those services which are directly linked to trade — for example transport, distribution, advertising, and so on — on the grounds that freer trade in these services is a prerequisite of freer trade in goods. Thus the extension of the GATT to trade in such services would be a logical step in extending the liberalization process achieved in previous GATT rounds. A further alternative would be to secure agreement to the general principle that trade in services should be governed by the same principles as trade in goods. Reasonable exceptions could be worked out and specified. The main disadvantage with this approach is that it fails to tackle the more investment-like issues which are not covered by the GATT but are important for services. These are the issues concerned with the right of establishment. One further alternative might be to secure agreement to a standstill on any fresh imposition of barriers to trade in services. This would be a major achievement if agreed upon. The United States has included such a proposal in its plan for freeing trade in services. Such a step is seen as a first stage in any programme for negotiating a new framework for trade in services. However, it is unlikely that it would be acceptable to all countries. At the very least, exceptions would have to be allowed to ensure protection of vital national interests. Diebold and Stalson have suggested that some short-cuts such as have been discussed may be needed if international negotiations are to make progress (Diebold and Stalson 1983).

At the time of writing, negotiations under the eighth Uruguay Round are in progress. Despite the opposition of certain developing countries, agreement has been reached to include services on the agenda. It remains to be seen how much progress will be made. Enough has been said in this chapter to show that negotiations will be complex and agreement difficult to secure. Almost certainly, it will take more than one GATT round to make meaningful progress. Whatever the case, trade in services is certain to become of increasing importance in coming decades. Failure to tackle the matter of barriers to trade in services will not augur well for maintaining liberal trade in manufactured goods.

References

Adler, M. (1970) 'Specialisation in the European Coal and Steel Community', Journal of Common Market Studies 8.

Agmon, T. (1979) 'Direct investment and intra-industry trade, substitutes or complements?', in H. Giersch (ed.) *On the Economics of Intra-Industry Trade*, Tübingen: J.C.B. Mohr.

Aliber, R.Z. (1970) 'A theory of direct foreign investment', in C.P. Kindleberger (ed.) *The International Corporation*, Cambridge, Mass.: MIT Press.

Allen, G.C. (1981) *The Japanese Economy*, London: Weidenfeld and Nicolson.

Aquino, A. (1978) 'Intra-industry trade and inter-industry specialisation as concurrent sources of international trade in manufactures', Weltwirtschaftliches Archiv 14(2).

Balassa, B. (1974) *Trade-creation and trade-diversion in the European Common Market*, Manchester School, June, no. 2.

—— (ed.) (1975) *European Economic Integration*, Amsterdam: North Holland.

—— (1979) 'Intra-industry trade and integration of developing countries in world trade', in H. Giersch (ed.) *On the Economics of Intra-Industry Trade*, Tübingen: J.C.B. Mohr.

—— (1981) *The Newly-Industrialising Countries in the World Economy*, Oxford: Pergamon Press.

—— (1986) 'Determinants of intra-industry specialisation in United States trade, Oxford Economic Papers, no. 38.

Ballance, A. and Sinclair, S. (1983) *Collapse and Survival: Industry Strategies in a Changing World*, London: Allen & Unwin.

Bank of England (1985) 'Services in the UK Economy', Quarterly Bulletin, September.

Banks, G. (1983) 'Economics and politics of countertrade', World Economy, June.

Banks, G. and Tumlir, J. (1986), 'Economic policy and the adjustment problem', Thames Essay, no. 45, Trade Policy Research Centre.

Batchelor, R.A., Major, R.L. and Morgan, A. (1980) *Industrialisation and the Basis for Trade*, Cambridge: Cambridge University Press.

Bergstrand, J.H. (1983) 'Measurement and determinants of intra-industry international trade', in P.K.M. Tharakan (ed.) *Intra-Industry Trade*, Amsterdam: North Holland.

Brander, J. and Krugman, P. (1983) 'A reciprocal dumping model of international trade', Journal of International Economics 13: 313–21.

Buckley, P. J. and Casson, M. (1976) *The Future of the Multinational Enterprise*, London: Macmillan.

Cable, V. (1981) *Protectionism and Industrial Decline*, London: ODI/ Hodder & Stoughton.

REFERENCES

Casson, M. (1986) *Multinationals and World Trade*, London: Allen & Unwin.

Caves, R.E. (1981) 'Intra-industry trade and market structure in the industrial countries', Oxford Economic Papers, July.

—— (1982) *Multinational Enterprise and Economic Analysis*, Cambridge: Cambridge University Press.

Chenery, H. and Keesing, S. (1981) 'The changing composition of developing country exports of manufactures', in S. Grassman and E. Lundberg (eds.) *The World Economic Order: Past and Prospects*, London: Macmillan.

Cline, W.R. (ed.) (1983) *Trade Policy in the 1980s*, Cambridge, Mass.: Institute for International Economics and MIT Press.

Cohen, S. (1978) 'Coping with the New Protectionism', National Westminster Bank Review, November.

Corden, W.M. (1974) 'The theory of international trade', in J.H. Dunning (ed.) *International Investment: Selected Readings*, Harmondsworth: Penguin.

—— (1985) *Protection, Growth and Trade*, Oxford: Blackwell.

Culem, C. and Lundberg, L. (1986) 'The product pattern of intra-industry trade: stability among countries and over time', Weltwirtschaftliches Archiv, 122.

Department of Trade and Industry (1979) *Analysis of Foreign Enterprises in the United Kingdom: Census of Production 1975*, Trade and Industry, 27 July.

—— (1985) *Countertrade: Some Guidance for Exporters (July)*, London: DTI.

Diebold, W. Jnr and Stalson, H. (1983) 'Negotiating issues in international services transactions', in W.R. Cline (ed.) *Trade Policy in the 1980s*, Cambridge, Mass.: Institute for International Economics and MIT Press.

Dunning, J.H. (ed.) (1974a) *International Investment: Selected Readings*, Harmondsworth: Penguin.

—— (ed.) (1974b) *Economic Analysis and the Multinational Enterprise*, London: Allen & Unwin.

—— (1977) 'Trade, location and economic activity of the multinational enterprise: a search for an eclectic approach', in B. Ohlin (ed.) *The International Allocation of Economic Activity*, London: Macmillan.

—— (1982) 'A note on intra-industry foreign direct investment', Banca Nazionale del Lavoro (Rome), March.

Dunning, J.H. and Norman, G. (1985) 'Intra-industry production as a form of international economic involvement', in A. Erdilek (ed.) *Multinationals as Mutual Invaders*, Beckenham: Croom Helm.

Dunning, J.H. and Pearce, I.F. (1981) *The World's Largest Enterprises*, Aldershot: Gower.

Economist Intelligence Unit (1984) 'North–South countertrade', Special Report, no. 174.

Erdilek, A. (ed.) (1985) *Multinationals as Mutual Invaders: Intra-Industry Foreign Direct Investment*, Beckenham: Croom Helm.

Erzan, R. and Laird, S. (1984) *Intra-Industry Trade of Developing Countries and Some Policy Issues*, Institute for International Economic Studies, University of Stockholm, Seminar Paper No. 289, August.

Falvey, R.E. (1981) 'Commercial policy and intra-industry trade', Journal of International Economics 2.

Franko, L.G. and Stephenson, S. (1982) 'The micro picture: corporate and sectoral developments', in L. Turner and N. McMullen (eds) *The Newly-Industrialising Countries: Trade and Adjustment*, London: Allen & Unwin.

Fröbel, F., Heinrichs, J., and Kreye, O. (1980) *The New International Division of Labour*, Cambridge: Cambridge University Press.

GATT (1983) *International Trade*, Geneva: GATT.

—— (1986) *International Trade*, Geneva: GATT.

Giersch, H. (ed). (1979) *On the Economics of Intra-Industry Trade*, Tübingen: J.C.B. Mohr.

—— (1986) 'Perspectives on the world economy', Weltwirtschaftliches Archiv 121.

Glejser, H. (1983) 'Intra-industry trade and inter-industry trade specialisation: trends and cycles in the EEC', in P.K.M. Tharakan (ed.) *Intra-Industry Trade*, Amsterdam: North Holland.

Godley, W. and May, R.M. (1977) 'The macroeconomic implications of devaluation and import restriction', Cambridge Economic Policy Review 3.

Graham, L.M. (1985) 'Intra-industry structure, firm rivalry and performance', in A. Erdilek (ed.) *Multinationals as Mutual Invaders*, Beckenham: Croom Helm.

Grassman, S. and Lundberg, E. (eds.) (1981) *The World Economic Order: Past and Prospects*, London: Macmillan.

Gray, H.P. (1979) 'Intra-industry trade: the effects of different levels of data aggregation', in H. Giersch (ed.) *On the Economics of Intra-Industry Trade*, Tübingen: J.C.B. Mohr.

Greenaway, D. (1982) 'Identifying the gains from pure intra-industry exchange', Journal of Economic Studies 9(3).

—— (1983a) *International Trade Policy: From Tariffs to the New Protectionism*, London: Macmillan.

—— (1983b) 'Patterns of intra-industry trade in the UK', in P.M.K. Tharakan (ed.) *Intra-Industry Trade*, Amsterdam: North Holland.

—— (ed.) (1985) *Current Issues in International Trade: Theory and Policy*, London: Macmillan.

Greenaway, D. and Milner, C.R. (1983) 'On the measurement of intra-industry trade', The Economic Journal 93.

—— (1986) *The Economics of Intra-Industry Trade*, Oxford: Blackwell.

Grubel, H.G. (1987) 'Traded services are embodied in materials or people', World Economy, September.

Grubel, H.G. and Lloyd, P.J. (1975) *Intra-Industry Trade: The Theory and Measurement of International Trade in Differentiated Products*, London: Macmillan.

Hamilton, C. (1985) 'Economic aspects of voluntary export restraints', in D. Greenaway (ed.) *Current Issues in International Trade*, London: Macmillan.

Havrylyshyn, O. and Civan, E. (1983) 'Intra-industry trade and the stage of development', in P.M.K. Tharakan (ed.) *Intra-Industry Trade*, Amsterdam: North Holland.

Helleiner, G.K. (1981) *Intra-Firm Trade and the Developing Countries*, London: Macmillan.

—— (1979) 'Transnational corporations and trade structure: the role of intra-firm trade', in H. Giersch (ed.) *On the Economics of Intra-Industry Trade*, Tübingen: J.C.B. Mohr.

Helleiner, G.K. and Lavergne, R. (1980) 'Intra-firm trade and industrial exports to the United States', Oxford Bulletin of Economics and Statistics, November.

Hill, T.P. (1977) 'On goods and services', Review of Income and Wealth, series 23, no. 4, December.

Hladik, J. (1985) *International Joint Ventures*, Lexington, Mass.: Lexington Books.

Hood, N. and Young, S. (1979) *Economics of the Multinational Enterprise*, London: Longman.

Horioka, C.Y. (1986) 'Why is Japan's private savings rate so high?' Finance and Development, December.

Hufbauer, G.C. (1966) *Synthetic Materials and the Theory of International Trade*, London: Duckworth.

—— (1970) 'The impact of national characteristics and technology on the commodity composition of trade in manufactured goods', in Vernon, R. *The Technology Factor in International Trade*, New York: Columbia University Press.

Hymer, S. and Rowthorn, R. (1970) 'Multinational corporations and international oligopoly: the non-American challenge', in C.P. Kindleberger (ed.) *The International Corporation*, Cambridge, Mass.: MIT Press.

Jacquemine, A. (ed.) (1984) *European Industry: Public Policy and Corporate Strategy*, Oxford: Clarendon Press.

Johnson, H.G. (1970) 'Efficiency and welfare implications of the international corporation', in C.P. Kindleberger (ed.) *The International Corporation*, Cambridge, Mass.: MIT Press.

Kagami, N. (1983) 'Maturing of the Japanese economy in the 1980s', National Westminster Bank Review, November.

Kierzkowski, H. (1985), 'Models of international trade in differentiated goods', in D. Greenaway (ed.) *Current Issues in International Trade*, London: Macmillan.

Kindleberger, C.P. (ed.) (1970) *The International Corporation*, Cambridge, Mass.: MIT Press.

—— (1982) 'The world economic slowdown since the 1970s', Seminar Paper No. 229, Institute for International Economic Studies, Stockholm University, November.

Knickerbocker, F.T. (1973) *Oligopolistic Reaction and the Multinational Enterprise*, Boston: Harvard University Press.

Kojima, K. (1978) *Direct Foreign Investment: A Japanese Model of Multinational Business Operations*, Beckenham: Croom Helm.

438

Kreinin, M. (1979) 'Effect of European integration on trade flows in manufactures', Seminar Paper No. 125, Institute for International Economic Studies, Stockholm University, August.

Krugman, P. (1981) 'Intra-industry specialisation and the gains from trade', Journal of Political Economy 89.

Lall, S. (1973) 'Transfer pricing by multinational manufacturing firms', Oxford Bulletin of Economics and Statistics, August.

—— (1978) 'The pattern of intra-firm exports by United States multinationals', Oxford Bulletin of Economics and Statistics, August.

—— (ed.) (1980) *The Multinational Corporation*, London: Macmillan.

—— (1981) *Developing Countries in the International Economy*, London: Macmillan.

Lassudrie-Duchêne, B. and Muchieli, J.L. (1979) 'Les échanges comparés dans le commerce international', Revue Economique, May.

Lecraw, D. (1985) 'Some evidence on transfer pricing by MNCs', in A. Rugman and L. Eden (eds) *Multinationals and Transfer Pricing*, Beckenham: Croom Helm.

Lewis, A. (1981) 'Growth of world trade', in S. Grassman and E. Lundberg (eds) *The World Economic Order*, London: Macmillan.

Linder, S.B. (1961) *An Essay on Trade and Transformation*, New York: J. Wiley.

Lloyds Bank (1985) *Japan 1985*, Lloyds Bank Group Economic Report.

Lorenz, D. (1986) 'New situations facing NICs in East Asia', Inter-economics, November–December.

Masera, R. (1986) 'Europe's economic problems in an international perspective', Banca Naçionale del Lavoro, Quarterly Review 159, December.

McAleese, D. (1977) 'Do tariffs matter?' Oxford Economic Papers, March.

—— (1979) 'Intra-industry trade, level of development and market size', in H. Giersch (ed.) *On the Economics of Intra-Industry Trade*, Tübingen: J.C.B. Mohr.

Meyer, F.V. (1978) *International Trade Policy*, Beckenham: Croom Helm.

Moore, L.B. (1985) *Growth and Structure of International Trade since World War 2*, Brighton: Wheatsheaf Books.

Murray, R. (ed.) (1981) *Multinationals Beyond the Market: Intra-Firm Trade and the Control of Transfer Pricing*, New York: J. Wiley.

Natke, P. (1985) 'A comparison of import pricing by foreign and domestic firms in Brazil', in A. Rugman and L. Eden (eds) *Multinationals and Transfer Pricing*, Beckenham: Croom Helm.

Neary, P. (1985) 'Theory and Policy of Adjustment in an Open Economy', in D. Greenaway (ed.) *Current Issues in International Trade*, London: Macmillan.

Norman, G. and Dunning, J.H. (1984) 'Intra-industry foreign direct investment: its rationale and trade effects', a paper presented to the

International Economics Study Group, 9th Annual Conference, September.

OECD (1979a) *The Impact of the Newly-Industrialising Countries*, Paris: OECD.

—— (1979b) *The Impact of Barter in Developing Countries*, Paris: OECD.

—— (1979c) *Transfer Pricing and the Multinational Enterprises*, Paris: OECD.

—— (1981) *The Impact of the Newly-Industrialising Countries*: An Update, Paris: OECD.

—— (1985) *Annual Economic Surveys*: Japan, Paris: OECD.

Ohlin, B. (1935) *Inter-regional and International Trade*, Cambridge, Mass.: Harvard University Press.

—— (ed.) (1977) *The International Allocation of Economic Activity*, London: Macmillan.

Owen, N. (1983) *Economies of Scale, Competitiveness and Trade Patterns within the European Community*, Oxford: Oxford University Press.

Ozawa, (1979) *Multinationalism, Japanese Style*, Princeton, NJ: Princeton University Press.

Panic, M. and Joyce, P.L. (1980), 'UK manufacturing industry, international integration and trade performance', Bank of England Quarterly Bulletin, March.

Pearce, J. and Sutton, J. (1986) *Protectionism and Industrial Policy in Europe*, London: Routledge & Kegan Paul.

Plasschaert, S.R.F. (1979) *Transfer Pricing and Multinational Corporations: An Overview of Concepts, Mechanisms and Regulations*, New York: Praeger.

—— (1985) 'Transfer pricing problems in developing countries', in A. Rugman and L. Eden (eds.) *Multinationals and Transfer Pricing*, Beckenham: Croom Helm.

Posner, M. (1961) 'International trade and technical change', Oxford Economic Papers 13.

Roumaliotis, P. (1977) 'Underinvoicing aluminium from Greece', in R. Murray (ed.) *Multinationals Beyond the Market*, New York: J. Wiley.

Rugman, A. (1985) 'Determinants of intra-industry direct foreign investment', in A. Erdilek (ed.) *Multinationals as Mutual Invaders*, Beckenham: Croom Helm.

Rugman, A. and Eden, L. (eds) (1985) *Multinationals and Transfer Pricing*, Beckenham: Croom Helm.

Samuelson, P. (1948) 'International trade and the equalisation of factor prices', Economic Journal 59.

Sapir, A. (1985) 'North–South issues in trade in services', The World Economy 8.

Sapir, A. and Lutz, E. (1981), 'Trade in services: economic determinants and development-related issues', World Bank Staff Working Paper No. 410.

Saxonhouse, G. (1983) 'The micro- and macro-economics of foreign

sales to Japan', in W.R. Cline (ed.) *Trade Policy in the 1980s*, Cambridge, Mass.: Institute for International Economics and MIT Press.
—— (1986) 'Japan's intractable trade surpluses in a new era', The World Economy, September.
Schumacher, D. (1983) 'Intra-industry trade between the FDR of Germany and developing countries', in P.K.M. Tharakan (ed.) *Intra-Industry Trade*, Amsterdam: North Holland.
Stein, L. (1985) *Trade and Structural Change*, Beckenham: Croom Helm.
Stern, R. and Hoekman, B. (1987) 'Negotiation on services', The World Economy 10(1), March.
Stewart, M. (1983) *Controlling the Economic Future*, Brighton: Wheatsheaf Books.
Stolper, W.F. and Samuelson, P. (1941) 'Protection and real wages', Review of Economic Studies 9.
Stopford, J.M. (1982) *The World Director of Multinational Enterprises, 1982–83*, London: Macmillan.
Stopford, J.M. and Dunning, J.H. (1983) *Multinationals: Company Performance and Global Trends*, London: Macmillan.
Tharakan, P.K.M. (ed.) (1983) *Intra-Industry Trade*, Amsterdam: North Holland.
Tschoegl, E.A. (1985) 'Modern barter', Lloyds Bank Review, October.
Tugendhat, C. (1971) *The Multinationals*, Harmondsworth: Pelican.
Turner, L. and McMullen N. (1986) *The Newly-Industrialising Countries: Trade and Adjustment*, London: Allen & Unwin.
United Nations Centre on Transnational Corporations (1983) *Transnational Corporations in World Development*, Third Survey, New York: United Nations.
United Nations Conference on Trade and Development (1980) *A Case Study Approach to Trade-Related Structural Adjustment*, September, Secretariat Report.
—— (1983) *Handbook of International Trade*, Geneva: UNCTAD.
United Nations Industrial Development Organisation (1982) *Handbook of Industrial Statistics*, New York: United Nations.
Vaitsos, C. (1974) *Intercountry Income Distribution and Transnational Enterprises*, Oxford: Clarendon Press.
Vaupel, J.W. and Curhan, J. (1974) *The World's Multinational Enterprises: A Sourcebook of Tables*, Cambridge, Mass.: Harvard Business School.
Vernon, R. (1966) 'International investment and international trade in the product cycle', Quarterly Journal of Economics 80, May.
—— (1970) *The Technology Factor in International Trade*, New York: Columbia University Press.
—— (ed.) (1981) *Economics of International Business*, 3rd edn, London: Prentice-Hall.
—— (1985) *Exploring the Global Economy*, Cambridge, Mass.: Harvard University and University Press of America.
White, G. (1984) 'Intra-industry adjustment: European industrial

441

policies', in A. Jacquemine (ed.) *European Industry: Public Policy and Corporate Strategy*, Oxford: Clarendon Press.

Wilkinson, E. (1983) *Japan versus Europe*, Harmondsworth: Pelican.

Wolf, M. (1983) 'Managed Trade in Practice: Implications of the Textile Arrangements', in W.R. Cline (ed.) *Trade Policy in the 1980s*, Cambridge, Mass.: Institute of International Economics and MIT Press.

World Bank (1984) *World Development Report*, Washington, DC: World Bank.

—— (1985) *World Development Report*, Washington, DC: World Bank.

Glossary

Adjustment
This is the process whereby resources shift out of one industry or sector into another industry or sector in response to either changes in the pattern of demand or changes in relative costs of production or changes in international comparative advantage.

Barter trade
This refers to any trade which involves some element of reciprocity between countries; that is, in return for A buying from B, B buys from A. Another name for such trade is countertrade. Pure barter involves the direct exchange of goods for goods without the mediation of money.

Bilateralism
This is the name given to any situation in which any two countries consciously seek to balance their trade with one another rather than seeking to balance their overall trade with the world as a whole. Such a trade policy is a common feature of trade in eastern bloc countries.

Conglomerates
This is the name given to companies which produce a wide range of different and largely unrelated products. Such highly diversified companies have often become conglomerates by buying-up other companies involved in different activities.

Countertrade
Countertrade is another name for barter trade (q.v.) in which some element of reciprocity exists between the two countries engaged in trade. Thus, one country agrees to buy x amount of a certain product from another country if the latter buys y amount of exports from the first country.

Deindustrialization
This is a term generally used to describe the absolute and relative decline of manufacturing industry and the growth of the services sector which has taken place in many developed market economies in the last fifteen years.

Dumping

This is defined by the GATT as a situation when the products of one country are sold to another country at a price which is less than the price at which they are sold in the exporting country. The exporting firm may be subsidized by the government of its own country or may temporarily incur losses in an attempt to gain a foothold in the foreign market.

Expenditure-changing policies

This is the name given to macroeconomic policy measures introduced by a government which seek to correct a balance-of-payments disequilibrium by changing the level of domestic expenditure. In the case of a deficit country, the government will act to reduce domestic expenditure; in the case of a surplus country, it will act to increase domestic expenditure.

Export-platform investment

This is the name given to foreign investment by a multinational company which involves the establishment of a factory in a foreign country for the sole purpose of exporting finished goods. The finished good is usually processed or assembled in the foreign country using components and parts imported from the parent company or one of its other foreign subsidiaries.

Export-processing zones

This refers to special regions within a particular country where foreign companies can invest and pay low taxes, pay zero or very low tariffs, and enjoy exemption from minimum-wage laws and other kinds of legislation which are applied to domestic firms. Cheap or subsidized infrastructure such as low-cost port facilities and cheap power supplies are also provided. Such regions are designed to attract export-platform investments.

Factor intensities/proportions

These refer to the proportions in which different factors of production — land, unskilled and skilled labour, human capital and physical capital, natural resources, technology, and so on — are combined in the production of a particular product or group of products.

Foreign direct investment

This refers to foreign investment by a multinational company involving either the establishment of a wholly-owned foreign subsidiary or the acquisition of a controlling interest — usually taken to be a minimum 10 per cent of equity capital — in a foreign company.

Generalized system of preferences
The name given to the system of trading preferences — which involved the granting of preferential treatment to the exports of developing countries — introduced by most western industrialized countries after 1971. Those exports of developing countries which are subject to GSP may enter the market of developed countries at low or zero tariff.

Horizontal investment
The name given to foreign investment by a multinational company which involves either the setting up of a new overseas subsidiary or the acquisition of a controlling interest in a foreign company which produces the same or a similar range of goods.

Inter-industry trade
This is the name given to trade between countries which involves the exchange of products which belong to different industries. For example, one country exports cloth to another country in exchange for steel.

Internalization
This is the name given to the process whereby, through the multinational expansion of companies, certain transactions — whether in goods or asset rights — are administered internally rather than through the use of external markets.

Intra-firm trade
This is the name given to trade between a multinational company and its overseas affiliate or associate companies in another country. Sometimes, such trade is called in-house or intra-group trade.

Intra-industry foreign direct investment
This is the name given to two-way direct investment between any two countries which takes place within the same industry. Thus when United States chemical manufacturers invest in Western Europe and West European chemical manufacturers invest in the United States, such direct investment is called intra-industry direct investment abroad.

Intra-industry trade
This is the name given to trade between countries which involves the exchange of products which belong to the same industry. For example, Germany exports Volkswagens to Italy and Italy exports Fiats to Germany.

Invisibles
This is the term given to a wide variety of intangible items which appear in the current account of a country's balance of payments. They include receipts from, less payments to, other countries for trade in services (e.g. tourism, banking and insurance, transport, etc.); interest, profits, and dividends earned on overseas investments (less payments abroad); and transfers. Invisibles are distinct from visibles, which are trade in tangible goods.

Joint ventures
This is the name given to an enterprise which involves a partnership between one or more foreign companies and a locally based firm, which may be privately or state owned.

Licensing agreement
This is an agreement between a multinational company and a foreign company — which could be a subsidiary of the multinational — which involves the licensor granting the licensee the use of industrial property rights (e.g. a trade mark, knowledge about how to produce a particular product, etc.) in return for agreed royalties and fees.

Most-favoured nation principle
This principle states that a country agrees to refrain from discriminating against countries to which it has granted this status in the formulation and enforcement of its trade policy. It will treat equally all countries to which it extends this privilege. For example, any tariff imposed on imports from such a country will be no higher than equivalent tariffs imposed on imports from other countries but could be lower. This principle represents a central pillar of the GATT agreement.

Multilateralism
This is the name given to a situation where countries seek to balance their overall transactions with the world as a whole

rather than seeking to balance their bilateral payments with every single trading partner.

Multinational companies/enterprises

The name given to any company/enterprise which owns, controls, and manages production establishments in at least two countries.

New international division of labour

The name given to the process whereby different stages in the process of producing certain products are hived off and relocated in different countries so as to take advantage of differences between countries in factor costs and to exploit the economies of scale obtainable from greater plant specialization.

Newly-industrializing countries

This is a rather inexact name given to a group of developing countries which have, in recent decades, achieved fast growth and rapid industrialization through expanding their exports of manufactured goods — often labour-intensive, light manufacturing consumer goods — to the markets of the developed countries. Supreme examples of such countries are the South-East Asian group of countries — Taiwan, Hong Kong, South Korea, and Singapore.

New Protectionism

This is another rather loose term used by economists to refer to the protectionist tide which has occurred in recent decades and which has mainly taken the form of increased resort to non-tariff interferences in trade. The resort to non-tariff devices for restricting imports is what distinguishes the current wave of protectionism from past periods of protection, which have mainly involved higher tariffs.

Non-tariff barriers

This is a generic term for a wide variety of devices which intentionally or unintentionally interfere with the free flow of goods between countries. They include quantitative restrictions on trade, domestic subsidies, export subsidies, discriminatory public procurement policies, technical and health standards, customs procedures and delays, and so on.

Offshore assembly processing
This is the name given to the process whereby the final assembly of a finished good takes place at an offshore site in an overseas country so as to take advantage of lower labour costs. Such a process has been encouraged by special tariff provisions whereby developed countries apply tariffs on the value-added rather than the final price of goods which have been assembled or processed in this way.

Orderly-marketing agreements
The name given to an agreement between an importing country and one or more exporting countries under which the exporting country or countries agree to limit the quantity of a certain product which they sell to the importing country over a stipulated period.

Portfolio investment
This is the name given to the purchase by an individual, company, or financial institution of interest-bearing overseas securities — either government securities or company stocks and shares — but not involving the investor in acquiring control of the concern in which it is investing.

Positive adjustment
This is a term first used by the OECD to distinguish government policies which positively promote adjustment in the face of innreased import competition as opposed to policies which are purely defensive and compensatory and which reduce the ability of countries to adjust. For example, a blanket subsidy given to a firm or an industry unable to compete with low-cost imports from abroad forestalls adjustment. Government assistance to enable workers to retrain promotes adjustment.

Rationalized product industries
A term sometimes used to refer to industries which have reached the stage of maturity in their development but which have undergone a new phase of reorganization based on the redesign of the product, fragmentation of the production process, and greater plant specialization.

Rationalized product investments
This is the name frequently used to refer to direct investments abroad by multinational companies which aim to concentrate

certain stages or processes of production in particular countries. Such investments tend to be trade-enhancing as opposed to investments which jump trade barriers and are therefore trade-inhibiting.

Real exchange rates
These are nominal exchange rates adjusted for inflation. For example, if a country experienced a 10 per cent rate of inflation, a nominal depreciation of its currency of 10 per cent would leave the real exchange-rate unchanged.

Reciprocity
The principle of reciprocity applies to trade policy and means that, in international tariff negotiations, countries must offer tariff concessions in return for receiving concessions and not free ride. It is also sometimes used to mean that a country should apply the same treatment to imports of goods or services from another country as the latter applies to the exports of the former country.

Right of establishment
This refers to the right of individuals or firms of one country to produce and sell services (e.g. banking or insurance) in another country in the same way as local persons or firms. Since such trade in services involves foreign investment abroad, the right of establishment is a key principle in ensuring free trade in services.

Services
These may be defined as any activity which changes either a person (e.g. education, hairdressing, entertainment) or a good (e.g. advertising, retailing) or both (e.g. banking and finance). Unlike manufacturing, the output of the services sector is an intangible output.

Subcontracting
Applied at an international level, this refers to an arrangement whereby a company — possibly a multinational company — subcontracts a company in another country to carry out some specific process or type of work or to supply a particular good rather than do the work itself.

Terms of trade
This can be defined as the ratio of a country's average export prices to average import prices. If average export prices rise

faster than average import prices, the terms of trade of the country in question are said to have improved.

Transfer pricing
This is the term used for the pricing policies used by multinational companies for selling goods or services from one unit of the company to another. Such prices may diverge from the prices used in equivalent arm's-length transactions.

Turnkey operations
This refers to an agreement between a company in one country — usually an advanced industrialized country — and a company in another country under which the former designs, constructs, and commissions a plant and is paid partly with the future output generated by the new plant.

Vertical disintegration
This is a term used for the growing tendency whereby multinational companies are separating off various processes or stages in the production of a particular good and relocating these processes or stages at plants in other countries.

Vertical investment
This is the name given to direct investment abroad which involves setting up a new subsidiary or acquiring a controlling interest in a foreign company involved at a different stage of the production process, for example a raw material supplier or a distribution outlet.

Voluntary export-restraints
These are agreements between an exporting and an importing nation under which the former agrees to restrain its exports of a certain product either to some fixed quantity or some share of the market.

Index

451